Advances in Geoeconomics

While geopolitics has captured global attention, geoeconomics is often the hidden force that governs relationships between countries. Geoeconomics refers to the intersection of economic factors, relationships and conditions on global events. It is the economic psyche that shapes the new world order. A country's political and business alignments have an impact on individuals, companies and on future economic stability.

This book assembles leading scholars and experts from around the world to advance current thinking on geoeconomics. It is a thorough and authoritative reference work on world economics that aims to shape strategy formulation in business and government for years to come by expanding understanding on the topic of geoeconomics, analysing the implications of international geoeconomic events, and providing the reader with theoretical and practical approaches on the management of geoeconomics.

Geoeconomic concepts in this book will prove timely and highly insightful to students, academics, executives, entrepreneurs, government officials, consultants and policymakers.

J. Mark Munoz is a Professor of International Business at Millikin University in Illinois, and a former Visiting Fellow at the Kennedy School of Government at Harvard University, USA. He is a recipient of several awards including four Best Research Paper Awards, a literary award, an international book award and the ACBSP Teaching Excellence Award. Aside from publications in major journals, he has authored, edited or co-edited 12 books: *Land of My Birth*, *Winning Across Borders*, *In Transition*, *A Salesman in Asia*, *Handbook of Business Plan Creation*, *International Social Entrepreneurship*, *Contemporary Microenterprises: Concepts and Cases*, *Handbook on the Geopolitics of Business*, *Hispanic-Latino Entrepreneurship*, *Managerial Forensics* and *Strategies for University Management* (Volumes I and II). As Chairman/CEO of international management consulting firm Munoz and Associates International, he directs consulting projects worldwide in the areas of strategy formulation, business development and international finance.

Europa Economic Perspectives

Providing in-depth analysis with a global reach, this series from Europa examines a wide range of contemporary economic issues from areas around the world. Intended to complement the *Europa Regional Surveys of the World* series, *Europa Economic Perspectives* will be a valuable resource for academics, students, researchers, policymakers, business people and anyone with an interest in current world economic affairs.

While the *Europa World Year Book* and its associated *Regional Surveys* inform on and analyse contemporary economic, political and social developments, the Editors considered the need for more in-depth volumes written and/or edited by specialists in their field, in order to delve into a country's or a region's particular economic situation, or to examine economic theories in the context of current global economic affairs. Volumes in the series are not constrained by any particular template, but may explore any aspect of a country's recent economic issues in order to increase knowledge.

International Monetary Reform
A Specific Set of Proposals
John Williamson

Small States and the European Union
Economic Perspectives
Edited by Lino Briguglio

Advances in Geoeconomics
Edited by J. Mark Munoz

Advances in Geoeconomics

Edited by
J. Mark Munoz

LONDON AND NEW YORK

First published 2017 by Routledge

2 Park Square, Milton Park, Abingdon, Oxfordshire OX14 4RN
52 Vanderbilt Avenue, New York, NY 10017

Routledge is an imprint of the Taylor & Francis Group, an informa business

First issued in paperback 2019

Europa Commissioning Editor: Cathy Hartley
Editorial Assistant: Eleanor Simmons

British Library Cataloguing in Publication Data
A catalogue record for this book is available from the British Library

Library of Congress Cataloging in Publication Data
Names: Munoz, J. Mark, editor.
Title: Advances in geoeconomics / edited by J. Mark Munoz.
Description: 1 Edition. | New York : Routledge, 2017. | Series: Europa economic perspectives | Includes bibliographical references and index.
Identifiers: LCCN 2016054592| ISBN 9781857438307 (hardback) | ISBN 9781315312132 (ebk)
Subjects: LCSH: Economic geography. | International business enterprises. | International cooperation. | International organization.
Classification: LCC HF1025 .A38 2017 | DDC 330.9–dc23
LC record available at https://lccn.loc.gov/2016054592

ISBN: 978-1-85743-830-7 (hbk)
ISBN: 978-0-367-87663-0 (pbk)

Typeset in Times New Roman
by Taylor & Francis Books

Contents

List of illustrations

Figures

Tables

Contributors

J. Mark Munoz is a tenured full Professor of Management and International Business at Millikin University in Illinois, USA, and a former Visiting Fellow at the Kennedy School of Government at Harvard University. He is a recipient of several awards including four Best Research Paper Awards, a literary award, an International Book Award, and the ACBSP Teaching Excellence Award, among others. Aside from top-tier journal publications, he has authored/edited/co-edited 12 books: *Land of My Birth*, *Winning Across Borders*, *In Transition*, *A Salesman in Asia*, *Handbook of Business Plan Creation*, *International Social Entrepreneurship*, *Contemporary Micro-enterprises: Concepts and Cases*, *Handbook on the Geopolitics of Business*, *Hispanic-Latino Entrepreneurship*, *Managerial Forensics* and *Strategies for University Management* (Volumes I and II). As Chairman/CEO of international management consulting firm Munoz and Associates International, he directs consulting projects worldwide in the areas of strategy formulation, business development and international finance.

Richard Aidoo is an Associate Professor of Politics and Global Studies Advisor at the Department of Politics, Coastal Carolina University, USA. His research focuses on the economic and diplomatic engagements between countries in sub-Saharan Africa and Asia. He has made diverse contributions in scholarly journals, books and on different media platforms. He is the co-author of *Charting the Roots of Anti-Chinese Populism in Africa.*

Alina Amirzadova is a Product Control Analyst at Sberbank CIB, Russia. She obtained her Master's degree in Financial Risk Management from University College London. Her professional interests are in the areas of investment management, foreign direct investment (FDI) in emerging markets economies, risk management and stress testing.

Najiba Benabess serves as the Dean of the Tabor School of Business in Millikin University, USA. Dr Benabess holds a PhD in Economics from the University of Wisconsin–Milwaukee and a Master's degree in Economics from Western Illinois University. Her areas of expertise include industrial organization and international economics.

Viara Bojkova is a Head of Geoeconomics at the Global Policy Institute, London, UK, and her research focus is on cutting-edge global economic policy issues. Before she moved to the UK, she was a Monbusho scholar in Japan, where she explored the role of the Japanese industrial policy and keiretsu organization in the process of creating and sustaining companies' competitive advantages. She holds an MSc in Economics and Philosophy from the London School of Economics and Political Science (LSE) and was recipient of the prestigious LSE Graduate School Merit Award.

Hubert Bonin is Emeritus Professor in Modern Economic History at Sciences Po Bordeaux and at the Gretha Research Centre at Bordeaux University, France. He is a specialist in the history of service companies (Suez Canal Company, colonial and overseas trading houses and their maritime affiliates), and of French, Europeanized and overseas banking history (regional banks, Paris deposit, corporate and investment banks). He has authored several monographs and a few handbooks. As a specialist in business history, he is involved in programs pertaining to banking and business history with French, European or Asian perspectives, especially in the areas of investment banking, merchant and trade banking, economic patriotism, entrepreneurship and European business.

Işın Çetin is a Research Assistant of Econometrics at Uludag University, Turkey, and is in the Doctorate programme there. She has published several papers on applied econometrics in various academic journals. Her interests are in the area of macro-econometrics, spatial econometrics, financial crisis, non-linear econometric analysis, forecasting, qualitative and quantitative econometric techniques, the Organisation for Economic Co-operation and Development (OECD) and European financial studies.

Subhajit Chakrabarty, Associate Professor at the Narsee Monjee Institute of Management Studies (NMIMS), Mumbai, India, holds a PhD in International Business from the Indian Institute of Foreign Trade, New Delhi and is an alumnus of INSEAD. His working experience spans over 23 years in multiple domains, including trade policy liaison in India. His research interests are international business, research methodology computing, economic modelling, digital marketing and marketing research, among others.

Masud Chand is an Associate Professor of International Business and a Tilford Fellow at the W. Frank Barton School of Business at Wichita State University, USA. His research interests include the role of diasporas in facilitating international trade and investment, immigrant entrepreneurship, biculturalism, and the effects of ageing on global business. His work has been published in scholarly journals such as the *Academy of Management Perspectives*, *Asia Pacific Journal of Management*, *Journal of Business Ethics*, *International Business Review*, *Asia Pacific Business Review* and *Thunderbird International Business Review*.

Jonathon Cini is an employee at the World Economic Forum. Previously he worked as a diplomat and at the Peace and Security Institute, and was a contributor for Wikistrat on geopolitical issues in the Asia-Pacific and European regions. In addition, he has articles and academic papers published in *Thomson Reuters*, the *Geneva Centre for Security Policy*, the *International Security Observer* and by the *World Economic Forum*.

Arusha Cooray is a Professor of Economics at Nottingham University Business School, Malaysia. She is a Research Associate at the Centre for Applied Macroeconomic Analysis, Australian National University, and an External Associate at the Brooks World Poverty Institute, University of Manchester, UK. Her research interests include applied macroeconomics, macro-finance, development macroeconomics and open economy macroeconomics.

David Criekemans is Assistant Professor in International Politics at the University of Antwerp, Belgium, Assistant Professor in International Relations at University College Roosevelt in Middelburg, the Netherlands, and Lecturer in Geopolitics at the Geneva Institute of Geopolitical Studies (GIGS), Switzerland.

Gyula Csurgai holds university degrees in Political Science from Concordia University, Canada and the University of Toulouse, France. He obtained two Master's degrees and a Doctorate from the University of Geneva, Switzerland. He worked as scientific collaborator at the Geneva International Peace Research Institute (GIPRI), and has taught International Relations, Geopolitics and Geoeconomics in both undergraduate, Master's and Doctorate programmes at different universities. Dr Csurgai is currently Academic Director of the SIT World Learning University programme 'Multilateral Diplomacy and International Studies' in Switzerland, and has published several books and articles in the field of geopolitics and geoeconomics.

Louise Curran is Senior Lecturer in International Business at Toulouse Business School (TBS) in France. She obtained her PhD in 1995 from Manchester Metropolitan University, UK. She has published widely on European Union (EU) trade policy and its impacts on trade with its international partners.

André M. Everett is Professor of International Management at the University of Otago, New Zealand. He holds a PhD in artificial intelligence (University of Nebraska–Lincoln, USA), with three decades of experience in international, strategic and operations management. Professor Everett's research is focused on knowledge management, internationalization of management philosophies, and cultural influences in international business (with particular interest in China), where clusters are key components of the entrepreneurial ecosystem.

Zoltan Gal is a full Professor in Financial and Regional Economics at Kaposvar University, Hungary and researcher at the Centre for Economic and Regional Research of the Hungarian Academy of Sciences. His research fields include regional economics, regional finance, international finance, financial and economic geography, and regional innovation in transition countries as well as an EU and global context. He has been a visiting scholar at a number of prestigious universities including the University of Oxford, UK and Trinity College Dublin, Ireland. He holds a dual MA from the Central European University, Budapest, Hungary, and New York State University, Albany, USA, and a PhD in Financial Geography. He is a member of the editorial boards of the *Journal of Innovation & Entrepreneurship*, *Review of Economic Perspectives*, *Journal of Economic Development*, *Environment and People* and *Space & Society*.

Jayati Ghosh is a Professor of International Business in the School of Business Administration at Widener University, USA. Her research interests include trade, the role of small and medium-sized enterprises (SMEs), emerging markets, economic development, and health issues in Africa, particularly in Malawi and South Africa. She has presented her research at national and international conferences and published extensively.

Ezekiel Kalipeni is a Professor in the Department of Geography and Geographic Information Science at the University of Illinois at Urbana Champaign, USA. He has carried out extensive research on the population dynamics of Malawi and Africa in general, concentrating on fertility, mortality, migration and health care issues.

Hilal Yıldırır Keser is a Lecturer at Uludag University, Vocational School of Social Sciences, Turkey. She received her PhD from the Uludag University. She has had several studies and papers published in various academic journals. Her particular interests are in economic development, regional development, national competitiveness, economic geography, transport economics, international trade and trade logistics.

Wiboon Kittilaksanawong is Professor of Strategy and International Business in the Graduate School of Humanities and Social Sciences, Faculty of Economics, Saitama University, Japan. His research interests include global business and strategy, business strategies in emerging markets, and international entrepreneurship. He received a PhD in Management from National Taiwan University.

Robert E. Looney is a Distinguished Professor at the Naval Postgraduate School, USA. His interests include energy security, and the political economies of Latin America, Africa and the Middle East. He is the author of 22 books and over 250 articles in the professional journals.

Imelda K. Moise is an Assistant Professor in the Department of Geography and Regional Studies at the University of Miami in Florida, USA. She is a mixed-methods researcher of issues affecting vulnerable populations. Her research focuses on the two-way links between health disparities research and linking research to practice or policy. Her scholarly work has focused on program evaluation and addressing health disparities as it relates to: minority populations, health care/utilization; geographical targeting, food environments; maternal and child health in Sub-Saharan Africa, Southeastern United States and Illinois.

Joash Ntenga Moitui is a seasoned analyst and researcher on issues of human rights, conflict, public policy and international development at the Centre for Human Rights and Policy Studies (CHRIPS), Kenya. He served as a Conflict and Refugee Crisis Research Associate at the Organization for World Peace (OWP). He is a certified project in development professional (PMD Pro) with APMG International, USA, and also a Research Fellow at the Pan-African University's Institute of Governance and Humanities and Social Sciences (IGHSS) in Yaoundé, Cameroon. He has published in several international journals and Academia Commons, Columbia University.

Lakshmi Mudunuru is founder and chief mentor of Maateacher—a global network of professionals, teachers and learners who provide life skills training and mentoring services. With a PhD from Andhra University in India, she worked as a Professor of Geopolitics and International Business and Academic Chairperson of the School of Law at the Gandhi Institute of Technology and Management (GITAM University), from which she received the 2015 Best Teacher Award. She contributed a chapter to the pioneering *Handbook on the Geopolitics of Business.*

Richard B. Nyuur is a Senior Lecturer in Strategic Management and International Business at Newcastle Business School, Faculty of Business and Law, Northumbria University, UK. He obtained his PhD from University of Wales Swansea. He researches in the broad areas of ethics and corporate social responsibility, international business strategy, FDI in emerging economies, and SMEs' adaptiveness and management. His research has been presented at leading international conferences, and published both in peer-reviewed academic journals and books.

Michael J. Pisani (PhD, University of Texas–Pan American, USA) is Professor of International Business at Central Michigan University. Dr Pisani's research interests include the intersection of international business and development, informality, cross-border business and economic phenomena, sustainability, entrepreneurship, and microenterprise development primarily within Central America, the Caribbean and the US–Mexico borderlands. Professor Pisani is the author of 86 journal articles and book chapters, and two books, including *The Informal and Underground Economy of the South Texas Border* (University of Texas Press, 2012).

J. Uma Rao, Assistant Professor, School of Law, GITAM University, India, is a graduate in commerce from Calcutta University. She pursued her legal studies at Andhra University, Visakhapatnam, India, securing a gold medal in LL.B in taxation laws. She secured a first class in LL.M, leading to a doctorate for her thesis, 'Inter-linking of Rivers in India—Legal Perspectives & Social Dimensions'. She has international and national publications to her credit and has presented papers in many seminars. Her areas of interest include jurisprudence, family law, criminal law and frontier areas of research on globalization.

Philippe Régnier has been a Senior Lecturer and then a full Professor in International Development and Global Studies in Canada and Switzerland since the early 1990s. His field of specialization has focused on the private sector and development, especially in Asian emerging economies. Since 2014–15, he has also been associated as a Research Professor to the Schools of Management in Geneva and Freiburg under the University of Applied Sciences (UAS), western Switzerland. He chairs a new UAS applied research programme (2016–20) in entrepreneurship, innovation and appropriate technologies for international development, which is sponsored by the Swiss federal government.

Andrea Schmidt is an Assistant Professor at University of Pécs, Department of Political Science and International Studies, Hungary, and former Visiting Lecturer at the Josai Institute for Central European Studies, Josai International University, Tokyo, Japan, Polish University Abroad, London, UK, and Visiting Lecturer at Ivan Franko National University in Lviv, Ukraine. She is a member of the advisory board of *Politeja*, the scientific journal of the Faculty of International and Political Studies of the Jagiellonian University, Cracow, Poland. She specializes in international political economy and comparative political studies of the Central and Eastern European region. She is the author of several articles and book chapters related to the Central and Eastern European and post-Soviet regions.

Francis Schortgen is an Associate Professor and Chair of the Department of Political Science and International Studies at the University of Mount Union, USA. His research focuses on Chinese business internationalization, Chinese political economy, and China–US and China–North Korea relations, and he is presently working on a book-length research project on the evolution of China–North Korea relations since 1949. Prior to earning his PhD in Political Science from Miami University, Ohio, he worked as a business consultant in Seoul, South Korea, from late 2001 to mid-2004. He also holds an MBA from the National University of Singapore, an MA in Asia-Pacific Studies from the University of San Francisco, and a BA in Political Science and History from Miami University, Ohio.

Satyendra Singh is a Professor of Marketing and International Business, and Editor-in-Chief of the *International Journal of Business and Emerging Markets* at the University of Winnipeg, Canada. Dr Singh has published widely in reputed international journals such as *Thunderbird International*

Business Review, *Industrial Marketing Management*, *Journal of Services Marketing*, *Services Industries Journal*, *Management Decision*, *Marketing Intelligence and Planning*, *Marketing Management Journal*, *Journal of Global Marketing*, among others, and presented papers at international conferences such as the American Marketing Association, Academy of Marketing Science, British Academy of Management and European Marketing Academy, among others.

Artur Tamazian is an Associate Professor of Economics and Finance at the University of Santiago de Compostela (USC), Spain. Having pursued his PhD from USC in Quantitative Finance, he completed his studies at Harvard University, USA. He has collaborated with Denver University (USA), Aarhus School of Business (Denmark), Western Sydney University (Australia), Dhruva School of Business (India) and University of Coimbra (Portugal), among others. He has also acted as a consultant to the World Bank. Dr Tamazian has published in internationally recognized journals such as *Energy Economics*, *Energy Policy*, *Journal of Common Market Studies*, *Economic Modelling* and *Applied Economics*, among others. He is a board member of the editorial committee of the peer-reviewed *Indian Journal of Management*.

Krishna Chaitanya Vadlamannati has a PhD in Economics (Heidelberg University, Germany, 2012), and works as an Assistant Professor at the School of Politics and International Relations, University College Dublin (UCD), Ireland. His research interests include international political economy, development politics and political economy of development in India. He has been published in prominent economics and political science journals including *International Studies Quarterly*, *Journal of Development Economics*, *Oxford Economic Letters*, *World Development*, *Journal of Peace Research*, *Journal of Comparative Economics*, among others. He is an editorial board member of the *Journal of Peace Research* and *International Area Studies Review*.

Alexandre J. Vautravers is the Coordinator of the MAS in Global Security at the Global Studies Institute (GSI) of the University of Geneva, Switzerland. As a Visiting Fellow of the Changing Character of War (CCW) Programme at the University of Oxford, UK, he led research on the theme of the return of conventional warfare. A Senior General Staff Officer and Editor-in-Chief of the *Revue militaire suisse* (RMS), he is also the President of the Officer's Society of Geneva (SMG) and the Swiss Cavalry Officer's association (OG Panzer).

Pascal Wild is an Assistant Professor at the School of Management in Freiburg, Switzerland, where he has specialized in the study of SMEs' internationalization. He is also a PhD candidate at the University of Geneva, and his current research deals with the role of East Asian global cities, and Singapore in particular, in the internationalization of Swiss SMEs to access emerging markets.

Andrey Yukhanaev is an Associate Professor in Strategic Management and International Business. He holds an MBA from Northumbria University, UK, and a PhD from the Russian Presidential Academy of National Economy and Public Administration. Dr Yukhanaev is an active researcher in the areas of internationalization of the firm, FDI in emerging markets, corporate governance and institutional development of the post-Soviet economies.

Jane Yuting Zhuang is a Senior Lecturer teaching Management and Research Methods papers at the Pacific International Hotel Management School (PIHMS), New Zealand. She is also a PhD finalist in Management at the University of Otago, with particular interests in historical cultural clusters and Grounded Theory methodology. Her current research compares porcelain clusters in China, Japan, Korea, the UK and New Zealand.

Abbreviations

2SLS-IV	two-stage least squares instrumental variable
AGOA	African Growth and Opportunity Act
AIIB	Asian Infrastructure Investment Bank
ASEAN	Association of Southeast Asian Nations
AU	African Union
B2B	business-to-business
b/d	barrels per day
BDS	business development services
BJP	Bharatiya Janata Party
BOJ	Bank of Japan
BRIC(S)	Brazil, Russian Federation, India, People's Republic of China, (South Africa)
C4ISTAR	command, control, communications, computers, intelligence, surveillance, targeting, acquisition, reconnaissance
CACM	Central American Common Market
CARICOM	the Caribbean Community
CBS	Community Baboon Sanctuary
CEE	Central and Eastern Europe
CEECs	Central and Eastern European countries
CEMAC	Central African Economic and Monetary Community
CEN-SAD	Community of Sahel-Saharan States
CES	constant elasticity of substitution
CGE	Computable General Equilibrium
COMECON	Council for Mutual Economic Assistance (also known as CMEA)
COMESA	Common Market for Eastern and Southern Africa
CPI	consumer price index
CSRC	China Securities Regulatory Commission
CUSTA	Canada-United States Free Trade Agreement
DDA	Doha Development Agenda
DSGE	Dynamic Stochastic General Equilibrium
EAC	East African Community
EBRD	European Bank for Reconstruction and Development

ECB	European Central Bank
ECOWAS	Economic Community of West African States
EEU	Eurasian Economic Union
EI	economic intelligence
EMSR	emerging market-specific risks
EU	European Union
FDI	foreign direct investment
FOB	freight on board
FOCAC	Forum on China–Africa Cooperation
FOREX	foreign exchange market
FTA	free trade agreement
FY	financial year
GaWC	Globalization and World Cities Research Network
GCC	Gulf Cooperation Council
GDP	gross domestic product
GEM	Global Entrepreneurship Monitor
GFC	global financial crisis
GMM	Generalized Method of Moments
GNI	gross national income
GNP	gross national product
GSP	Generalized System of Preferences
GTAP	Global Trade Analysis Project
GVAR	Global Vector Auto Regression
HS	Harmonized System
IAEA	International Atomic Energy Agency
ICMA	International Capital Market Association
ICT	information and communications technologies
IMF	International Monetary Fund
INC	Indian National Congress
I-O	Input-Output
IS(IS)	Islamic State (in Iraq and Syria)
LDBC	less developed beneficiary country
LDC	least developed countries
LIC	low-income country
mb/d	million barrels per day
MBT	main battle tank
MERCOSUR	Common Market of the South
METI	Ministry of Economy, Trade and Industry
MNC	multinational corporation
MNE	multinational enterprise
NAFTA	North American Free Trade Agreement
NAM	Non-Aligned Movement
NATO	North Atlantic Treaty Organization
NEPAD	New Partnership for Africa's Development
NGO	nongovernmental organization

NISA	Nippon Individual Savings Account
NSA	National Security Agency
OAU	Organisation of African Unity
OECD	Organisation for Economic Co-operation and Development
OLS-FE	ordinary least squares—fixed effects
OPEC	Organization of the Petroleum Exporting Countries
OROB	One Road One Belt
PPP	public–private partnership
PPP	purchasing-power parity
PTA	preferential trade agreement
QQE	quantitative and qualitative easing
R&D	research and development
RCA	revealed comparative advantage
RCEP	Regional Comprehensive Economic Partnership
REC	regional economic community
REER	Real Effective Exchange Rate
REI	regional economic institution
REI	regional economic integration
SADC	Southern African Development Community
SADCC	Southern African Development Coordination Conference
SAM	social accounting matrices
SAP	Structural Adjustment Program
SBRs	state–business relations
SMEs	small and medium-sized enterprises
SSA	sub-Saharan Africa
TCFR	third-country fabric rule
TEU	20-foot equivalent unit
TPP	Trans-Pacific Partnership
TTIP	Transatlantic Trade and Investment Partnership
UEMOA	Union Economique et Monétaire Ouest Africaine (West African Economic and Monetary Union)
UN	United Nations
US(A)	United States (of America)
USSR	Union of Soviet Socialist Republics
VAR	Vector Auto Regression
VECM	Vector Error Correction Method
WMD	weapons of mass destruction
WTO	World Trade Organization
YFR	yarn forward rule
y/y	year on year

1 Introduction

J. Mark Munoz

1 Introduction

Geoeconomics is the dynamic economic relationships of countries shaped by a multitude of intervening factors such as geography, politics, and business. Geoeconomics differs from geopolitics, in a sense that economic thought and action constitute the framework of its implementation. Macroeconomic and microeconomic variables exert a salient influence in its practice.

As a discipline, geoeconomics is associated with American strategist Edward Luttwak who stressed the higher importance of trade and finance among nations over military strength and ideological competition (Csurgai, 1998).

In the past 30 years, the world economy experienced market integration, trade liberalization, aggregation of international financial markets, breakthroughs in technology, communication and transportation, which intensified economic integration and accelerated globalization (Dreher et al., 2008). Total global merchandise trade reached US$18,494 billion in 2014 (WTO, 2015).

Globalization sets the stage for meaningful and intense relationships between countries. Country relationships and agenda are shaped by influences such as quest for power, economic conflict, regionalization, and volatility of resource availability (Leonard, 2015).

With conflicting interests, nations demonstrated hostility in non-traditional ways. For instance, in cases such as Western sanctions against Russia, and trade controls with Iran and Venezuela, governments wielded their power not through military might but economic warfare (Bhatia & Trenin, 2015).

The practice of geoeconomics has been on the rise (Torreblanca & Prislan, 2012). With heightened ability of people, companies and countries to reach out to each other, economic interactions have intensified. However, not all economic interactions prove to be beneficial to everyone. For instance, with the North American Free Trade Agreement (NAFTA), some businesses benefited while others succumbed to competitive and market pressures.

Economic integration among countries paved the way for new political agenda and alignments, strategic alliances and the creation of innovative business models. Countries are aware that strategic alignment through tariff reduction and trade-friendly policies, could lead to economic vitalization and political harmonization. Japan needs to find suitable emerging markets for its products to sustain the pensions and retirement of its ageing populace (Schulz, 2013). As for Britain, joining China's Asian Infrastructure Investment Bank highlights the importance of geoeconomics and an economic relationship in the Far East (Beeson, 2015).

Aside from economic integration platforms, new models and alignments continue to be explored. For instance, the US led discussions on the Trans-Pacific Partnership, China pushed for the Regional Comprehensive Economic Partnership, and Russia aimed to develop the Eurasian Economic Union (Mitachi, 2015). The UK's decision to leave the European Union (EU), or 'Brexit,' led to the redefinition of economic relationships across multiple countries.

Central to geoeconomic relationships across countries is regional economic integration. Due to its importance in the political and economic well-being of a country, it has shaped the agenda in a country's international affairs. In the 1990s, Brazil was the driving force in the creation of the Common Market of the South (MERCOSUR). In 2008, South Africa pushed for the Southern African Development Community (SADC).

Economic integration is a process where linked countries are aligned with a global market (Bekaert & Harvey, 1995). Drivers of economic integration include economic forces and need, and these agreements are subsequently executed through formal means (Muñoz del Bustillo & Perales, 2000).

A country can be engaged in several economic integration initiatives. In the view of Bhagwati and Panagariya (1999), this multitude of agreements appears like a 'bowl of spaghetti,' with overlapping treaties across many countries.

There are diverse ways in which economic integration is formed and executed. Integration may be through exchange modes (i.e. trade and financial) or geographic emphasis (i.e. within the regional economic bloc or outside). The World Trade Organization (WTO, 2011a) indicated six levels of economic integration: trade areas, customs unions, common markets, economic unions, monetary unions, and fiscal unions.

While numerous benefits have been ascribed to regional economic integration, its strongest appeal lies in the positive impact on trade and investment. Economic integration enhances a country's ability to attract investment and aids in its posture in trade negotiations (Büthe & Milner, 2008; Mansfield & Reinhardt, 2003).

Participation in regional economic integration recalibrates a country's political and economic situation. Country convergence results in the synchronization of business cycles at the regional level (Brida et al., 2011). Regional alignments lead to global implications or 'global regionalization' (Capanelli et al., 2010).

Scholars continue to explore the logic and motivation behind the economic alignment of nations. Aggregation of countries is shaped by financial linkages and fiscal regulations (Baxter & Kouparitsas, 2005; De Grauwe, 2006). Market size and level of development give member nations regional power (Schirm, 2010). There is a growing importance of technology and finance in the international agenda of countries (Rediker, 2015). This quest for answers continues given the evolving nature of geoeconomics.

2 International economic architecture

Geoeconomic relationships of countries shape their economic architecture. Strong economic globalization tends to take place at a regional rather than a global level (Artis et al., 2011). Oftentimes, the strongest states in an economic union yield the most influence (Grieco, 1990). Referred to as 'regional hegemons,' these countries use their clout and influence in shaping the political, economic and business agenda. Some countries have 'shaping power' or the ability to define end results and events on the international stage (Szabo, 2015).

Geoeconomics has a profound impact on a nation's trade engagement. Diverse trade issues not addressed in broad multilateral agreements pose opportunities for regional cooperation (Maur, 2011). Among members of an economic bloc, trade tends to increase (Schiff & Winters, 2003). Large trade volume suggests close country linkages (Mourão, 2011). A nation's capacity to trade is determined by international demand, and affects its security and influence (McCombie & Thirlwall, 1994; Gowa, 1994).

The globalized environment redefined business frameworks. There is an emergence of global factories where manufacturers create goods in diverse locations around the world (Gereffi, 1989). Diverse linkages tie in producers, buyers and nations, while global value chains lead to lower operational costs and efficiencies (Gereffi, 1994; Bair & Gereffi, 2003).

With emerging economic alignments and business models, there are new considerations. Geography and size impact volume of trade and growth (Frankel & Romer, 1999). An increase in trade is not exclusively due to tariff reduction (WTO, 2011b); attention needs to be placed on a broad range of influencing factors. Infrastructure has to be assessed along with export capacity, logistics, security, and depth of integration (Romanowski, 2015). Changes in the geoeconomic configuration in the oil industry with the discovery of shale gas and non-conventional energy sources, underscore the need to watch geoeconomic shifts carefully (Blanke & Kaspersen, 2015).

The selected political standpoint and operational policies define a country's geoeconomic future. Trade-related policies and procedures impact country trade volume and can be used as strategic tools to strengthen international power through relationships with other states (Portugal-Perez & Wilson, 2012; Aggarwal & Fogarty, 2004). Institutional frameworks and market regulations shape the extent of country integration (Jansen & Stokman, 2011).

As countries select the best geoeconomic policies, attention to quality, freedom and integration is important. Institutional quality is linked to economic growth (Stroup, 2007). Economic freedom enhances productivity through cost reduction and stimulates efficiency and innovation (Kirzner, 1997; Gwartney et al., 1999). Countries are connected through financial integration as demonstrated by the deregulation of domestic financial markets (Kim et al., 2012).

National integration across countries contributes to benefits such as: global alignments (Baldwin, 2006); economic prosperity (Sen, 1999; Bhagwati, 2004); financial development (Bekaert et al., 2005); capital access and foreign investment (Baker et al., 2004); knowledge gains (Gertler & Levitte, 2005); economic growth, technological flows and the creation of jobs (Kucera, 2002; Flanagan, 2006); leading to growth paths of member nations (Lee, 2012); convergence of income per capita among participating nations (Martin, 1998); and the development of neighboring countries (Resmini, 2003).

Challenges to country integration include: volatility of unstableness in participating developing nations (Krapohl et al., 2014); weakened agglomeration (Crozet & Soubeyran, 2004); dispersal of industries to lower-cost locations (Krugman & Elizondo 1996); and detrimental effects during a financial crisis due to trade and financial linkages, policies, and operational weakness (Kali & Reyes, 2005; Berkmen et al., 2012).

Diverse international economic relationships and circumstances contribute to potentially detrimental scenarios. For instance, there are limitations in intra-regional gains (Burges, 2005). Regional integration among industrialized nations tends to be more successful than in developing countries (Mattli, 1999). In Central Asia, current economic agreement did not promote economic growth among its member countries, with regional cooperation hindered by economic capability, strategic intent, and political agenda (Qoraboyev, 2010; Romanowski, 2015). Countries may experience a contagion, or significant correlation with other nations in times of financial crisis (Forbes & Rigobon, 2002).

With distinct interests and objectives, nations take on diverse geoeconomic postures and respond to integration in different ways. In some instances, internal trade is preferred over external trade (McCallum, 1995). Some countries tend to invest in domestic securities (Lewis, 1999). Others pursue a beggar-thy-neighbor policy (Kronberger, 2002) where their own economic challenges are addressed and those of other countries are neglected.

Geoeconomic action of nations also leads to counteraction from others. Baldwin (1993) introduced a 'domino theory' where economic integration resulted in a series of government and business reactions, including competitive action from other nations. Reduced import barriers encourage investment as a response to foreign competition (Neary, 2002). Domestic competition forces organizations to disperse into new locations (Crozet & Soubeyran, 2004).

A country's selected geoeconomic posture has consequences. Countries with weak geoeconomic ties would not be able to reap important economic, political and business benefits. Countries geoeconomically aligned with unpopular nations may be perceived in a negative light by others, while countries associated with popular nations may gain from positive association. Countries that are geoeconomically influential can leverage their position to create competitive advantages. For example, if Country A is geoeconomically aligned with Country B, a country facing a civil war, its geoeconomic appeal decreases. If Country C, a small emerging nation, has strong ties with a geoeconomic powerhouse, it would be viewed as one with potential and could be poised to reap future economic benefits.

Geoeconomic postures and relationships require careful thought and consideration. Germany demonstrated the importance of geoeconomics in its foreign policy agenda when it took a different standpoint from its European partners and opposed military intervention in Libya to prioritize its economic interests (Torreblanca & Prislan, 2012). The standpoint of European countries on the refugee crisis has had lasting political and economic consequences.

There are at least ten attributes that characterize the contemporary global geoeconomic environment:

- *Dynamic*: geoeconomic relationships are constantly evolving and based on changing conditions. China has taken a proactive role in cultivating relationships in new ways through infrastructure support and finance, loans, grants, and joint ventures in locations in Asia, the Indian Ocean, Africa and Latin America (Khanna, 2015).
- *Evolving*: economic alignments can change quickly as a result of several factors. Trade arguments across countries result in weakened economic ties and policy changes. Oil prices continue to have a profound impact on countries such as Russia, Saudi Arabia, the USA, China, Mexico and Brazil, leading to shifts in consumption, investment, and government policies (Levi, 2015).
- *Politically anchored*: economic relationships are influenced by politics. A nation's political agenda drives fiscal and economic decisions. States are taking an active role in capitalistic endeavors, leveraging company ownership and financial institutions to promote their agenda (Rediker, 2015).
- *Market driven*: market desires and preferences impact the geoeconomic standpoint of countries. Most countries seek to attract investments and boost tourism. They plan for ways to become attractive destinations. Nations compete to penetrate new markets, as seen in the USA's efforts to strengthen relationships with India and China, and Russia's efforts toward business development in Venezuela (Khar, 2015).
- *Fragmented*: regional economic integration results in economic clustering, linking small blocs of countries together while excluding others. In the case of the EU, member countries receive economic privileges that are not available to other nations. The same can be said about NAFTA which economically links the USA, Canada and Mexico in a cohesive manner.
- *Impactful*: the geoeconomic agenda of countries lead to far-reaching consequences. In some regional trade alignments, the larger and more influential countries (core) tend to benefit more than the others

(periphery) (Bremmer, 2015). A nation's geoeconomic action has an impact on the future of key stakeholders—neighboring countries, trade allies, major corporations, small businesses, and country residents. Geoeconomic actions shape the global economic architecture and its economic sustainability.

- *Cohesive*: the geoeconomic strategy of a country is a unifying force that draws countries together. A nation with a well-developed geoeconomic agenda will attract others that share similar goals. Nation-states are motivated to obtain gains from international economic activities while maintaining their autonomy (Gilpin, 2001).
- *Varied intensity*: geoeconomic relationships differ in terms of depth of association. In some cases, economic relationships across countries cover extensive aspects of trade and politics; in other cases the extent of association is limited and superficial. Some economic accords are more comprehensive than others.
- *Misunderstood*: geoeconomics and its implications are commonly misunderstood and underappreciated. Given the fact that it impacts and is impacted by diverse factors, many aspects of its practice are not well understood. The discipline of geoeconomics is evolving and needs to be studied carefully in the coming years.
- *Transformative*: geoeconomics influences business, economics and politics in profound ways. Trade alliances across nations can impact the price of commodities which affects the global economy. This same influence is evident in combating terrorism, international health, environmental conservation, food supply and security, resolving political conflicts, and dealing with global financial crises. Geoeconomics can transform the global economic architecture.

3 Geoeconomics: pros and cons

As in many global endeavors, there are advantages and disadvantages associated with geoeconomic engagement. The advantages include:

- *Economic benefits*: strengthened economic ties with other countries enhance trade among participating nations (Schiff & Winters, 2003). One can marvel at the trade enhancements resulting from the EU and NAFTA.
- *Political harmony*: goal mutuality and economic cooperation set the stage for better understanding and improved political relations with other nations. Through strengthened relationships a country's influence grows (Portugal-Perez & Wilson, 2012).
- *Trade stimulus*: it greases the wheels of trade and stimulates business activities across several business sectors. It paves the way toward progress (Bhagwati, 2004).

- *Efficiency building*: since economic alliances facilitate cross-border exchanges of labor, knowledge, capital, information and services, it provides a framework for the building of operational efficiencies (Gwartney et al., 1999).
- *Cost reduction*: regional economic integration leads to lower tariffs and attractive administrative trade policies that lead to lower business operational cost. It is an avenue for economic betterment through lowered cost (Kirzner, 1997).
- *Capital flows*: geoeconomics facilitates cross-border transfer of capital. It enables nations to move financial resources and investments (Baker et al., 2004).
- *Skill building*: heightened economic integration and enhanced labor mobility lead to skills transfers that are beneficial to business and the economy. Cross-border jobs are created and technological developments are shared (Flanagan, 2006).
- *Technology transfers*: with strengthened economic relationships across countries, research and technologies are conveniently shared across borders. Consequently, new knowledge is gained (Gertler & Levitte, 2005).
- *Wealth creator*: geoeconomics is an avenue for increased business interaction and therefore revenue generation and wealth creation. It has an impact on income per capita (Martin, 1998).
- *Gateway for entrepreneurship*: a well-developed economic alliance across countries can stimulate entrepreneurial intent and activity and lead to economic betterment. For instance, in the case of NAFTA, the established trade agreement motivated Mexican manufacturers to export their products to the USA and Canada. Seeing the success of their counterparts encouraged budding entrepreneurs to follow suit.

While the advantages are quite compelling, there are significant disadvantages:

- *Domineering positions*: some nations have more resources and influence than others. Countries can exert their political and military clout to achieve their goals rather than emphasize economic gains (Szabo, 2015).
- *Uneven benefits*: in geoeconomic relationships not all parties benefit equally. Studies have shown that certain industries gain while others lose in economic integration. This scenario has been evident in the case of lost jobs and income by textile manufacturers in the USA shortly after NAFTA was implemented. In certain cases, economic growth was inexistent (Qoraboyev, 2010).
- *Disagreements*: geoeconomic relationships lead to misunderstanding and conflict. The challenges experienced by Greece tested its relationship with EU member nations and led to many disputes. Geoeconomic alignments pose opportunities as well as dangers (Beeson, 2015).
- *Legal complications*: with heightened business interaction across geoeconomically aligned countries, there is likely to be a rise in cases of business

arguments and legal conflict. Laws may not be clear cut in foreign locations (Khanna & Palepu, 1997).

- *Alienating*: countries in geoeconomic alignment may alienate other countries outside their circle of influence. Some trade blocs have been criticized as operating 'economic fortresses' favoring trade among their member nations and excluding others. In some cases, geoeconomics has led to multipolarity rather than the creation of multilateral relationships (Torreblanca & Prislan, 2012).
- *Lack of clarity*: there remain a number of misunderstood factors shaping and impacting geoeconomics. Organizations lack tools for geoeconomic risk assessment and its integration into strategic plans (Blanke & Kaspersen, 2015). This lack of clarity leads to poor comprehension of the real challenges and opportunities associated with its practice.

4 Emergence of geoeconomics and book structure

With the growing importance of economic relationships on the world stage, the study and the practice of geoeconomics will likely increase in coming years. This book aims to capture diverse viewpoints of geoeconomics and its impact on the world.

The content is beneficial to academics in their efforts to expand research and understanding on the subject. The topic is relevant to managers and entrepreneurs as they seek understanding of the business implications of geoeconomic events. Consultants, international organizations, and government policymakers will find the geoeconomic insights helpful in the identification of strategies and solutions for economic and business challenges.

Following this Introduction by J. Mark Munoz, the book has three parts. Part I is Understanding geoeconomics, with chapters on: Geoeconomics: A review of the research methodologies of trade alliances (Subhajit Chakrabarty); The geoeconomics of global cities: Exploring new avenues for expanding business internationalization (Philippe Régnier and Pascal Wild); Influence of region, country and subnational-region institutions on internationalization of multinational corporations (Wiboon Kittilaksanawong); Geoeconomic spillovers: Are Indian states interconnected in promoting state–business relations? An empirical analysis (Krishna Chaitanya Vadlamannati, Artur Tamazian and Arusha Cooray); Geoeconomics in Central and Eastern Europe: Implications of FDI (Zoltan Gal and Andrea Schmidt); The changing geoeconomics of China's diplomacy in Africa (Richard Aidoo); The nature, impact and lessons of Abenomics (Viara Bojkova); and Where geoeconomics and geostrategy meet: The troubled relations between the European Union and the Russian Federation (David Criekemans).

Part II covers International geoeconomics, and includes the following chapters: Geostrategic economics in the 21st century: China, America, and the Trans-Pacific Partnership (Francis Schortgen); EU trade policy after the

GFC: The geoeconomics of shifting EU trade policy priorities (Louise Curran); Determinants of FDI in the Customs Union of Russia, Belarus and Kazakhstan (Richard B. Nyuur, Andrey Yukhanaev and Alina Amirzadova); The role of regional integration on foreign direct investment in Southern Africa (Jayati Ghosh, Imelda K. Moise and Ezekiel Kalipeni); A case study: Geoeconomics and the Iranian nuclear deal (Jonathon Cini); The impact of geographic factors on economic development: Evaluation of Europe and the Middle East (Hilal Yıldırır Keser and Işın Çetin); Three spheres of geoeconomic advantage in Central America: Transportation, tourism and trade (Michael J. Pisani); and The state of regional integration in Africa: Prospects and advances (Joash Ntenga Moitui).

Part III pertains to Managing geoeconomics, and covers: The evolution of geoeconomics and the need for new theories of governance (Najiba Benabess); Geoeconomics and banking (Hubert Bonin); Geoeconomics of the global arms industry (Alexandre J. Vautravers); The new geoeconomics of energy: A Saudi Arabian case study (Robert E. Looney); Global water geoeconomics: Paradigm shift and emerging challenges (Lakshmi Mudunuru and J. Uma Rao); The geoeconomics of aging (Masud Chand); Geoeconomics and political interference: The case of China's porcelain industry (Jane Yuting Zhuang and André M. Everett); The African Growth and Opportunity Act: International business, relations and politics (Satyendra Singh); and Geoeconomic strategies and economic intelligence (Gyula Csurgai). The book ends with a Conclusion (J. Mark Munoz).

As one of the pioneering and most comprehensive books on the subject, the editor hopes that a heightened global interest in the topic will follow. It is hoped that this book will become a stimulus for more intensive research on the subject and open the doors to innovative solutions for the contemporary economic challenges confronting businesses and nations.

References

Aggarwal, V.K. and Fogarty, E. (eds) (2004) *EU Trade Strategies between Regionalism and Globalism*. Houndmills: Palgrave.

Artis, M., Chouliarakis, G. and Harischandra, P.K.G. (2011) Business cycle synchronization since 1880. *The Manchester School* 79(2): 173–207.

Bair, J. and Gereffi, G. (2003) Upgrading, uneven development, and jobs in the North American apparel industry. *Global Networks* 3(2): 143–169.

Baker, M.C., Foley, F. and Wurgler, J. (2004) *The Stock Market and Investment: Evidence from FDI Flows*. Working paper, Harvard Business School.

Baldwin, R. (1993) *A Domino Theory of Regionalism*. Working Paper no. 4465. Cambridge, MA: National Bureau of Economic Research.

Baldwin, R.E. (2006) *Multilateralising Regionalism: Spaghetti Bowls as Building Blocs on the Path to Global Free Trade*. Working Paper No. W12545. Cambridge, MA: National Bureau of Economic Research.

Baxter, M. and Kouparitsas, M.A. (2005) Determinants of business cycle comovement: A robust analysis. *Journal of Monetary Economics* 52(1): 113–157.

Beeson, M. (2015) Geopolitics versus geoeconomics: The new international order. *The Conversation*. Accessed July 28, 2015. theconversation.com/geopolitics-versus-geoeconomics-the-new-international-order-38824.
Bekaert, G. and Harvey, C. (1995) Time-varying world market integration. *Journal of Finance* 50(2): 403–444.
Bekaert, G., Harvey, C.R. and Lundblad, C. (2005) Does financial liberalization spur growth? *Journal of Financial Economics* 77: 3–55.
Berkmen, P.S., Gelos, G., Rennhack, R. and Walsh, J.P. (2012) The global financial crisis: Explaining cross-country differences in the output impact. *Journal of International Money and Finance* 31(1): 42–59.
Bhagwati, J. (2004) *In Defense of Globalization*. Princeton, NJ: Princeton University Press.
Bhagwati, J. and Panagariya, A. (1999) Preferential trading areas and multilateralism. In *Trading Blocs*, J. Bhagwati, P. Krishna and A. Panagariya (eds) Cambridge, MA: MIT Press.
Bhatia, K. and Trenin, D. (2015) *Challenge One: Economic Warfare*. World Economic Forum Report. Accessed July 15, 2015. www3.weforum.org/docs/WEF_Geo-economics_7_Challenges_Globalization_2015_report.pdf.
Blanke, J. and Kaspersen, A. (2015) Business, like government must master geo-economics. *Brink News*. Accessed July 28, 2015. www.brinknews.com/business-like-government-must-master-geo-economics/.
Bremmer, I. (2015) *Challenge five: The survival of the biggest and the hollowing out of the periphery*. Accessed July 15, 2015. www3.weforum.org/docs/WEF_Geo-economics_7_Challenges_Globalization_2015_report.pdf.
Brida, J.G., London, S., Punzo, L. and Risso, W.A. (2011) An alternative view of the convergence issue of growth empirics. *Growth and Change* 42(3): 320–350.
Burges, S.W. (2005) Bounded by the reality of trade: Practical limits to a South American region. *Cambridge Review of International Affairs* 18: 437–454.
Büthe, T. and Milner, H. (2008) The politics of foreign direct investment into developing countries: Increasing FDI through international trade agreements? *American Journal of Political Science* 52: 741–762.
Capanelli, G., Lee, J.-W., Petri, P.A. (2010) Economic interdependence in Asia: Developing indicators for regional integration and cooperation. *The Singapore Economic Review* 55(1): 125–161.
Crozet, M. and Soubeyran, P.K. (2004) EU enlargement and the internal geography of countries. *Journal of Comparative Economics* 32(2): 265–279.
Csurgai, G. (1998) *Geopolitics, Geoeconomics and Economic Intelligence*. The Canadian Institute of Strategic Studies. Accessed July 20, 2015. opencanada.org/wp-content/uploads/2011/05/SD-69-Csurgai.pdf.
De Grauwe, P. (2006) *Economics of Monetary Union*. Oxford: Oxford University Press.
Dreher, A., Gaston, N. and Martens, P. (2008) *Measuring Globalization: Gauging its Consequences*. New York: Springer.
Flanagan, R. (2006) *Globalization and Labor Conditions: Working Conditions and Worker Rights in a Global Economy*. New York: Oxford University Press.
Forbes, K. and Rigobon, R. (2002) No contagion, only interdependence: Measuring stock market comovements. *Journal of Finance* 57(5): 2223–2261.
Frankel, J.A. and Romer, D. (1999) Does trade cause growth? *American Economic Review* 89(3): 379–399.

Gereffi, G. (1989) Development strategies and the global factory. *Annals of the American Academy of Political and Social Science* 505: 92–104.

Gereffi, G. (1994) The organization of buyer-driven global commodity chains: How US retailers shape overseas production networks. In *Commodity Chains and Global Capitalism*, G. Gereffi and M. Korzeniewicz (eds) London: Praeger, pp. 78–104.

Gertler, M. and Levitte, Y.M. (2005) Local nodes in global networks: The geography of knowledge flows in biotechnology innovation. *Industry & Innovation* 12(4): 487–507.

Gilpin, R. (2001) *Global Political Economy*. Princeton, NJ: Princeton University Press.

Gowa, J. (1994) *Allies, Adversaries, and International Trade*. Princeton, NJ: Princeton University Press.

Grieco, J. (1990) *Co-operation Among Nations: Europe, America, and Non-tariff Barriers to Trade*. Ithaca, NY: Cornell University Press.

Gwartney, J., Lawson, R. and Holcombe, R. (1999) Economic freedom and the environment for economic growth. *Journal of Institutional and Theoretical Economics* 155 (4): 1–21.

Jansen, J. and Stokman, A. (2011) *International Business Cycle Comovement: Trade and Foreign Direct Investment*. DNB Working Paper 319, September. Amsterdam: DNB.

Kali, R. and Reyes, J.A. (2005) *Financial Contagion on the International Trade Network*. Working Paper, Department of Economics. Fayetteville: University of Arkansas, Sam M. Walton College of Business.

Khanna, P. (2015) *Challenge six: China's infrastructure driven alliances*. Accessed July 15, 2015. www3.weforum.org/docs/WEF_Geo-economics_7_Challenges_Globalization_2015_report.pdf.

Khanna, T. and Palepu, K. (1997) Why focused strategies may be wrong for emerging markets. *Harvard Business Review* (July–August), 41–51.

Khar, H.R. (2015) *Challenge four: Competition for gated markets, not natural resources*. World Economic Forum Report. Accessed July 15, 2015. www3.weforum.org/docs/WEF_Geo-economics_7_Challenges_Globalization_2015_report.pdf.

Kim, D.H., Lin, S.C. and Suen, Y.B. (2012) Dynamic effects of financial openness on economic growth and macroeconomic uncertainty. *Emerging Markets Finance & Trade* 48(1): 25–54.

Kirzner, I.M. (1997) Entrepreneurial discovery and the competitive market process: An Austrian approach. *Journal of Economic Literature* 35(1): 60–85.

Krapohl, S., Meissner, K.L. and Muntschick, J. (2014) Regional powers as leaders or Rambos? The ambivalent behavior of Brazil and South Africa in regional economic integration. *Journal of Common Market Studies* 52(4): 879–895.

Kronberger, R. (2002) A cost-benefit analysis of a monetary union for Mercosur with particular emphasis on the optimum currency area theory. *Integration and Trade* 6: 29–93.

Krugman, P. and Elizondo, R.L. (1996) Trade policy and the Third World metropolis. *Journal of Development Economics* 49: 137–150.

Kucera, D. (2002) Core labour standards and foreign direct investment. *International Labour Review* 141(1–2): 31–69.

Lee, J. (2012) Measuring business cycle comovements in Europe: Evidence from a dynamic factor model with time-varying parameters. *Economics Letters* 115(3): 438–440.

Leonard, M. (2015) *Geopolitics vs Globalization: How Companies and States can become Winners in the Age of Geo-economics*. World Economic Forum Report.

Accessed July 15, 2015. www3.weforum.org/docs/WEF_Geo-economics_7_Challenges_Globalization_2015_report.pdf.
Levi, M.A. (2015) *Challenge Seven: The Decline in Oil Prices*. World Economic Forum Report. Accessed July 15, 2015. www3.weforum.org/docs/WEF_Geo-economics_7_Challenges_Globalization_2015_report.pdf.
Lewis, K. (1999) Trying to explain home bias in equities and consumption. *Journal of Economic Literature* 37: 571–608.
Mansfield, E.D. and Reinhardt, E. (2003) Multilateral determinants of regionalism: The effects of GATT/WTO on the formation of preferential trading arrangements. *International Organization* 57: 829–862.
Martin, P.H. (1998) Can regional policies affect growth and geography in Europe? *World Economy* 21(6): 757–774.
Mattli, W. (1999) *The Logic of Regional Integration*. Cambridge: Cambridge University Press.
Maur, J.C. (2011) Trade facilitation. In *Preferential Trade Agreement Policies for Development: A Handbook*, J.P. Chauffour and J.C. Maur (eds) Washington, DC: The World Bank.
McCallum, J. (1995) National borders matter: Canada-U.S. regional trade patterns. *American Economic Review* 85: 615–623.
McCombie, J.S.L. and Thirlwall, A.P. (1994) *Economic Growth and the Balance-of-Payments Constraint*. Houndmills, Basingstoke: Macmillan.
Mitachi, T. (2015) *Challenge Two: The Geopoliticization of Trade Talks*. World Economic Forum Report. Accessed July 15, 2015. www3.weforum.org/docs/WEF_Geo-economics_7_Challenges_Globalization_2015_report.pdf.
Mourão, P.R. (2011) Has trade openness already voted? A panel data study. *Emerging Markets Finance & Trade* 47(5): 53–71.
Muñoz del Bustillo, R. and Perales, B.R. (2000) *Introducción a la Unión Europea: un análisis desde la economía* [Introduction to the European Union: Analysis from an Economic Perspective]. Madrid: Alianza Editorial.
Neary, J.P. (2002) Foreign competition and wage inequality. *Review of International Economics* 10: 680–693.
Portugal-Perez, A. and Wilson, J.S. (2012) Export performance and trade facilitation reform: Hard and soft infrastructure. *World Development* 40(7): 1295–1307.
Qoraboyev, I. (2010) From Central Asian regional integration to Eurasian integration space? The changing dynamics of post-Soviet regionalism. In *EDB Eurasian Integration Yearbook 2010*, Evgeny Vinokurov (ed.). Almaty, Kazakhstan: Eurasian Development Bank, pp. 206–232.
Rediker, D. (2015) *Challenge Three: State Capitalism 2.0*. World Economic Forum Report. Accessed July 15, 2015. www3.weforum.org/docs/WEF_Geo-economics_7_Challenges_Globalization_2015_report.pdf.
Resmini, L. (2003) Economic integration, industry location, and frontier economies in transition countries. *Economic Systems* 27: 205–221.
Romanowski, M. (2015) Geoeconomics in Central Asia. *The Diplomat*. Accessed July 28, 2015. thediplomat.com/2015/07/geoeconomics-in-central-asia/.
Schiff, M. and Winters, L.A. (2003) *Regional Integration and Development*. Washington, DC: World Bank and Oxford University Press.
Schirm, S.A. (2010) Leaders in need of followers: Emerging powers in global governance. *European Journal of International Relations* 16(2): 197–221.

Schulz, M. (2013) The global debt crisis and the shift of Japan's economic relations with Southeast Asia. *Journal of Southeast Asian Economies* 30(2): 143–163.

Sen, A. (1999) *Development as Freedom*. Oxford: Oxford University Press.

Stroup, M. (2007) Economic freedom, democracy, and the quality of life. *World Development* 35(1): 52–66.

Szabo, S.F. (2015) Germany = geoeconomics, US = geopolitics? *The Globalist*. Accessed July 28, 2015. www.theglobalist.com/germany-united-states-difference-geoeconomics-geopolitics/.

Torreblanca, J.I. and Prislan, N. (2012) The ominous rise of geoeconomics. European Council on Foreign Relations. Accessed July 28, 2015. www.ecfr.eu/article/commentary_the_ominous_rise_of_geoeconomics.

World Trade Organization (WTO). (2011a). *World Trade Report 2011*. Geneva: World Trade Organization.

World Trade Organization (WTO) (2011b). *The WTO and Preferential Trade Agreements: From Co-existence to Coherence. World Trade Report*. Geneva: World Trade Organization.

World Trade Organization (WTO) (2015) International trade statistics. Accessed June 21, 2016. www.wto.org/english/res_e/statis_e/its2015_e/its2015_e.pdf.

Part I

Understanding geoeconomics

2 Geoeconomics

A review of the research methodologies of trade alliances

Subhajit Chakrabarty

Trade alliance is an important subject of investigation among researchers of international trade. In this chapter, the author explores the theoretical basis and determinants of trade, and the role of trade alliances. A discussion of methodologies used will follow.

1 The theoretical basis of trade

The earliest theory of trade was mercantilism which implied dominance of weak countries and colonies through trade and restricting the colonies to expand through trade. The theory of absolute advantage by Adam Smith spoke of two countries trading in goods in which countries have advantage of endowments, considering labour as the key factor. The comparative advantage theory by David Ricardo spoke of nations trading on the basis of opportunity cost even if they did not have absolute advantage. Krugman extended it further and reasoned that consumers also have love for variety, hence there is reason to trade beyond comparative advantage and this sought to explain some more of the trade (Krugman, 1980).

The above is largely differentiation based on product. Another differentiation is based on countries. Armington (1969), in drawing up his analysis, made the assumption that products exported by each country are different. As each country has its own differentiated system and tariffs, this assumption was considered acceptable. Armington (1969) indicated that elasticities extended to include micro-elasticity (substitution among third countries) and macro-elasticity (substitution with respect to home-country competition) can be a useful base to estimate trade elasticities (Feenstra et al., 2012).

The third basis of differentiation is based on firm heterogeneity. This challenged distance as a factor (the gravity model). The issue of firm heterogeneity has come up because trade is considered to occur not only among nations but also among heterogeneous firms (Chaney, 2008). Heterogeneity is largely modelled with an extensive margin (the number of firms exporting) and an intensive margin (the average turnover of an exporting firm). Therefore, broadly, three types of differentiation (differentiation with respect to product, with respect to country and with respect to firm) can be drawn on to explain the theoretical basis of trade, given in Figure 2.1.

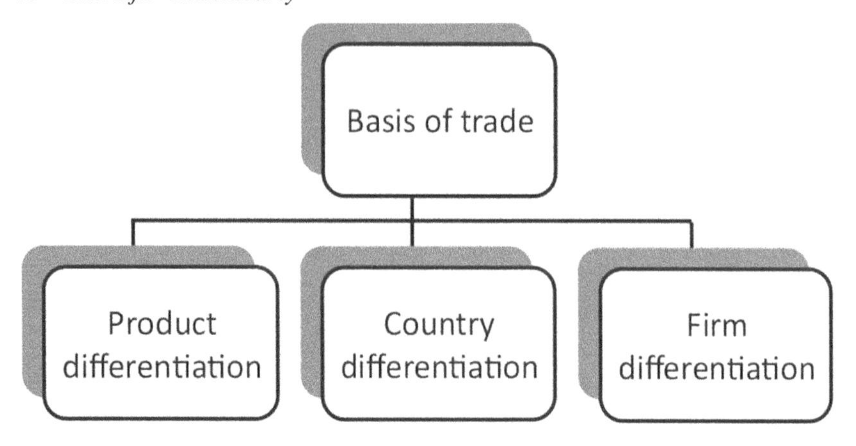

Figure 2.1 Why does international trade happen?

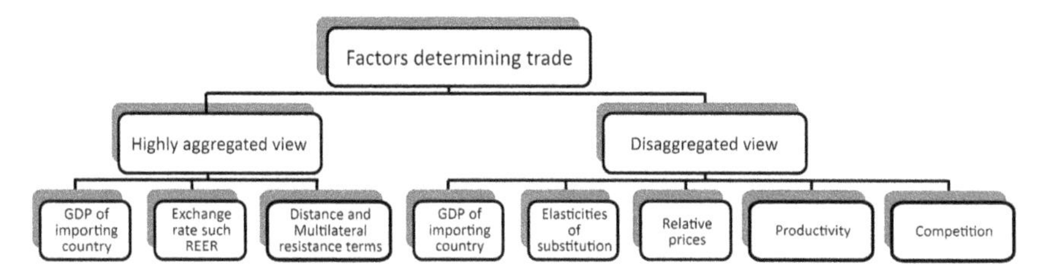

Figure 2.2 What drives trade?

2 Factors governing trade

At a highly aggregated level, the primary factors governing exports are gross domestic product (GDP) of the importing country and the exchange rate, such as the Real Effective Exchange Rate (REER), of the exporting country apart from the trade costs (Rangarajan & Mishra, 2013). The GDP is a proxy for demand. At a disaggregated level, each commodity can be differentiated based on country of origin (Armington, 1969), and in this constant elasticity of substitution (CES) is assumed. Though CES is a fair assumption, there are limitations (Yilmazkuday, 2008). The primary factors governing exports at the highly disaggregated level are the elasticities of substitution (against domestic competition as well as against third-country competition in the foreign market), relative prices and income (Feenstra et al., 2012). When firm productivity is included, the number of exporting firms and the average turnover of the exporting firm need to be incorporated as factors as well. Competitive factors may also emerge at the highly disaggregated level, particularly in a sectoral context (Chakrabarty et al., 2016). This is summarized in Figure 2.2.

A lucid introductory review of the gravity model by Shepherd (2012) alludes to the need to make a closer choice of variables in the case of sectoral models so that they are more relevant, such as choosing sectoral expenditure and income. An example of a paper on the sector model is one that tried to identify the trade theory model behind Botswana's sectors using the Revealed Comparative Advantage Index (Makochekanwa & Jordaan, 2008). A paper on estimating elasticities related to the oil and petroleum sector was presented by Balistreri, Al-Qahtani and Dahl (2009), in which they use bilateral trade and transport costs at a global level and estimate the elasticities using fixed-effects gravity regressions.

3 Foreign trade agreements and trade

Foreign trade agreements are expected to impact trade. Among the major works in this area, a study on the impact of NAFTA and the Canada-United States Free Trade Agreement (CUSTA) on international trade used data for 5,000 commodities (Romalis, 2004). Kehoe (2005) wrote a critique of NAFTA models: the models under-predicted trade growth, especially along the extensive margin. It was observed that there was equilibrium in within-industry variation in plant-level productivity (Bartelsman & Doms, 2000) and that the productivity differences persist over time (Bartelsman & Dhrymes, 1998). Trade shocks induce productivity growth through within-industry reallocation of resources (Pavcnik, 2002; Bernard et al., 2003). Another major study, by Powers (2007), examined the effect of tariff reductions and free trade agreement participation on sectoral imports in a panel with about 75 countries, 25 manufacturing sectors, and three time periods. The panel includes data for sectoral bilateral imports, sectoral preferential tariff rates, sectoral output, GDP and free trade agreement (FTA) participation. Tables 2.1 and 2.2 highlight key information on regional trade agreements and preferential agreements in the world.

The data suggest that most of the regional trade agreements are free trade agreements. Apparently the desperation has been to increase trade volumes

Table 2.1 Regional trade agreements

	Grand total
Customs union	19
Customs union—accession	10
Economic integration agreement	133
Economic integration agreement—accession	6
Free trade agreement	232
Free trade agreement—accession	2
Partial scope agreement	16
Partial scope agreement—accession	1
Grand total	419

(WTO, 2016b)

Table 2.2 Preferential trade agreements

Name	*Type*	*Provider(s)*	*Initial entry into force*
Generalized System of Preferences (GSP)—Australia	GSP	Australia	01/01/1974
Generalized System of Preferences—Canada	GSP	Canada	01/07/1974
Generalized System of Preferences—European Union	GSP	European Union	01/07/1971
Generalized System of Preferences—Iceland	GSP	Iceland	29/01/2002
Generalized System of Preferences—Japan	GSP	Japan	01/08/1971
Generalized System of Preferences—New Zealand	GSP	New Zealand	01/01/1972
Generalized System of Preferences—Norway	GSP	Norway	01/10/1971
Generalized System of Preferences—Russian Federation, Belarus, Kazakhstan	GSP	Belarus; Kazakhstan; Russian Federation	01/01/2010
Generalized System of Preferences—Switzerland	GSP	Switzerland	01/03/1972
Generalized System of Preferences—Turkey	GSP	Turkey	01/01/2002
Generalized System of Preferences—USA	GSP	USA	01/01/1976
Duty-free tariff preferences scheme for least developed countries (LDCs)	LDC-specific	India	13/08/2008
Duty-free treatment for African LDCs—Morocco	LDC-specific	Morocco	01/01/2001
Duty-free treatment for LDCs—Chile	LDC-specific	Chile	28/02/2014
Duty-free treatment for LDCs—China	LDC-specific	China	01/07/2010
Duty-free treatment for LDCs—Taipei, China	LDC-specific	Taipei, China	17/12/2003
Duty-free treatment for LDCs—Kyrgyz Republic	LDC-specific	Kyrgyz Republic	29/03/2006
Duty-free treatment for LDCs—Tajikistan	LDC-specific	Tajikistan	25/10/2003
Duty-free treatment for LDCs—Thailand	LDC-specific	Thailand	09/04/2015
Preferential tariff for LDCs—Republic of Korea	LDC-specific	Korea, Republic of	01/01/2000

Name	*Type*	*Provider(s)*	*Initial entry into force*
African Growth and Opportunity Act	Other preferential trade agreement (PTA)	USA	18/05/2000
Andean Trade Preferences	Other PTA	USA	04/12/1991
Caribbean Basin Economic Recovery Act	Other PTA	USA	01/01/1984
Commonwealth Caribbean Countries Tariff	Other PTA	Canada	15/06/1986
Former Trust Territory of the Pacific Islands	Other PTA	USA	08/09/1948
South Pacific Regional Trade and Economic Cooperation Agreement	Other PTA	Australia; New Zealand	01/01/1981
Trade preferences for the countries of the Western Balkans	Other PTA	European Union	01/12/2000
Trade preferences for Pakistan	Other PTA	European Union	15/11/2012
Trade preferences for the Republic of Moldova	Other PTA	European Union	21/01/2008

(WTO, 2016a)

through the lowering of tariffs, with the multilateral World Trade Organization (WTO) negotiations yet to be finalized. Among preferential trade agreements, the GSP has been the standard preferential access and LDC-specific agreements have served as additional preferential access for the poor countries.

4 Methodologies

Broadly, there are four types of methodologies used in modelling international trade: regression, general equilibrium, game theory and network analysis, shown in Figure 2.3.

The traditional model for aggregate trade flows in a monopolistic competition framework is the gravity model, in which distance is considered a significant determinant. Anderson and van Wincoop (2003) show that this model applies to sectoral trade as well. Feenstra (2004) showed a fixed-effects method of estimation of the gravity equation to generate average border effect of a pair of countries.

Models to understand the impact of FTAs mostly use dummy variables for the FTA and include the tariffs in the multilateral resistance terms. Traditional gravity models of bilateral trade are biased in the presence of trade agreements when they do not account for trade barriers between other trading partners of the importer and exporter, i.e. ignoring the multilateral resistance.

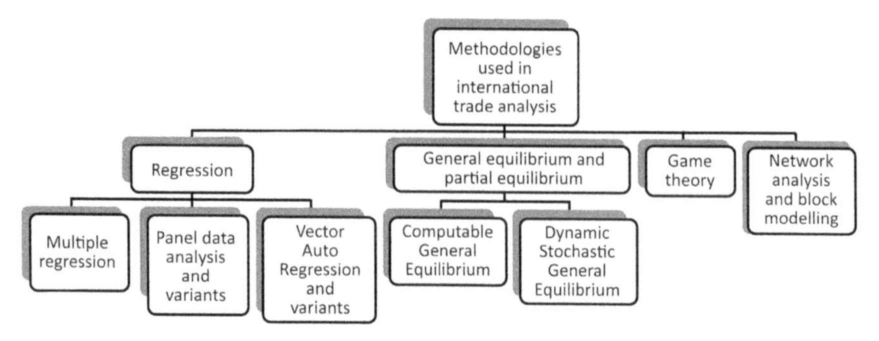

Figure 2.3 Broad methodologies used

Anderson and van Wincoop (2003) showed that exclusion of multilateral resistance terms leads to severe omitted variable bias and also presented a non-linear solution for the multilateral resistance terms. Baier and Bergstrand (2007) provided a linear solution with Taylor's approximation of the multilateral resistance terms. However, Behar and Nelson (2012) examined the multilateral resistance terms in greater detail and one of the conclusions was that the dampening of trade due to multilateral resistance is small for bilateral changes in trade costs, implying that for most analyses of trade agreements between two countries the multilateral resistance can be ignored for practical purposes.

Two popular approaches of trade models are general equilibrium analysis and regression analysis. The general equilibrium models can be static or dynamic. In general equilibrium models, demand and supply meet to reach an equilibrium state for the whole economy with several interacting markets. The Input-Output (I-O) tables are useful in this. An I-O table shows inter-industry relationships within an economy—how output from one sector may become an input to another sector—column entries representing inputs to the sector and row entries representing outputs from the sector. The forerunners of the Computable General Equilibrium (CGE) models are Leontief's (1936, 1941) input-output models and the mathematical programming models of Sandee (1960), and further developed by Manne (1963). Johansen (1960) developed a general model containing 20 cost-minimizing industries and a utility-maximizing household sector. In this model, prices were determined by market equilibrium conditions. It described growth in Norway using input-output data and estimates of household price and income elasticity.

Thereafter, during the 1960s leading economists attempted to refine various theoretical propositions (Arrow & Hahn, 1971). Scarf (1967a, 1967b, 1973) derived an algorithm for computing solutions to numerically specified general equilibrium models. However, the work was largely inspirational rather than practical. Improved databases and computer programs such as General Equilibrium Modelling PACKage (GEMPACK) and General Algebraic Modeling System (GAMS) were then developed. The Global Trade Analysis

Project (GTAP), which uses CGE analysis, has become quite popular worldwide. Hertel (1997) at Purdue University initiated the idea of GTAP where databases (input-out tables, etc.) can be incorporated by collaborators globally. Balistreri and Hillberry (2007) proposed a general approach to structural estimation of CGE trade models. During the last six decades, CGE modelling has been used to determine effects such as on macro-variables (including nationwide or global economic welfare), industry variables, regional variables, labour market variables, distributional variables and environmental variables. The shocks that have been described using CGE modelling during the last five decades are taxes, public consumption, social security payments, tariffs, interferences in international trade, environmental policies, technology, international commodity prices, interest rates, wage-setting arrangements, union behaviour and exploitability of mineral deposits (the Dutch disease). In Dynamic Stochastic General Equilibrium (DSGE) models, time series data of international trade are modelled using a Bayesian approach. This was a major leap in general equilibrium modelling (Fernández-Villaverde, 2009).

Global trade modelling may be carried out using various approaches. One considers global trade data as a base and uses social accounting matrices (SAM). Another considers SAM as the base and extends the model to various countries with the globe as the clearing house. The third approach incorporates the value chain which seeks to eliminate double counting and considers the supply chain. There are a large number of economic variables and the SAM are quite large. So there has been an effort to simplify the variables in the panel so that the model does not become indeterminate.

Traditionally, multiple regression has been used to model international trade at a highly aggregated level. Variants such as ridge regression or lasso regression are seldom used. Lasso-type penalties in panel data regression have been found effective in modelling time-varying covariate effects in international trade models (Hess et al., 2013). Vector Auto Regression (VAR) is now often used in modelling international trade in which a matrix of interrelationships among all the lagged variables is evaluated for significance. Long-term relationships are found using cointegration and the Vector Error Correction Method (VECM). The VAR/VECM approach can also show the impulse response occurring due to a shock. Global Vector Auto Regression (GVAR) can better use panel data regression and is an improvement over VAR (Pesaran et al., 2004; Bussière et al., 2009).

On trade data, four bases are found: gross basis, value-added basis, economic agent basis and game theory basis. The gross basis is the most popular, while the value-added basis has now emerged strongly. The economic agent basis and game theory are less popular. In gross basis, the value of trade is in the gross basis (mostly freight on board, or FOB, value) as reported by nations. However, this does not take into account the value addition. For example, if China imports cotton cloth from India worth US$40, manufactures garments (value addition) and exports to the USA worth US$100, then the gross value of exports will be US$100 for China and US$40 for

India, while the value-added exports will be US$40 for India and US$60 for China. So, the gross value has a problem of double counting. This is rectified in the value-added basis, but accurate value addition matrices are not available for all countries. In the economic agent basis, the initial conditions are specified by the modeller and the 'agents' learn 'behaviour' over time. Simulation and machine learning techniques are applied to understand 'behaviour'. The fourth basis, the game theoretic approach, brings in the negotiation dynamics of international trade (Baldwin & Clarke, 1987; Harrison & Rustrom, 1987). In one-level game theory, a country negotiates with its FTA partner, while in two-level game theory, there can be an international dimension (Level I) for bargaining between international negotiators leading to a tentative agreement, as well as a domestic dimension (Level II) for separate discussions within each group in the country about whether to ratify the agreement or not. Level III can consider the regional dimension.

The use of graph-based models is rare (Benedictis et al., 2013; Batagelj & Mrvar, 2003). A graph is a unique data structure in which the nodes may represent countries (their attributes may be GDP, etc.), while the directed links may represent trade flows in a direction. Stronger links imply stronger flows and highly interconnected regions can be observed. A network analysis of world trade has been presented in Synder and Kick (1979). This seminal work considered block modelling using four types of international networks: trade flows, military interventions, diplomatic relations and conjoint treaty memberships. Block models can help to detect subsets of graphs (such as groups of countries trading intensively among themselves). A few other studies have used graph clustering and block modelling methods in modelling trade data (Batagelj et al., 1999), but not much empirical work has been done on these models.

5 Issues and limitations

Often we hear about the likely impact of some trade alliance, and negotiations and politics base their information source on some 'research' on the

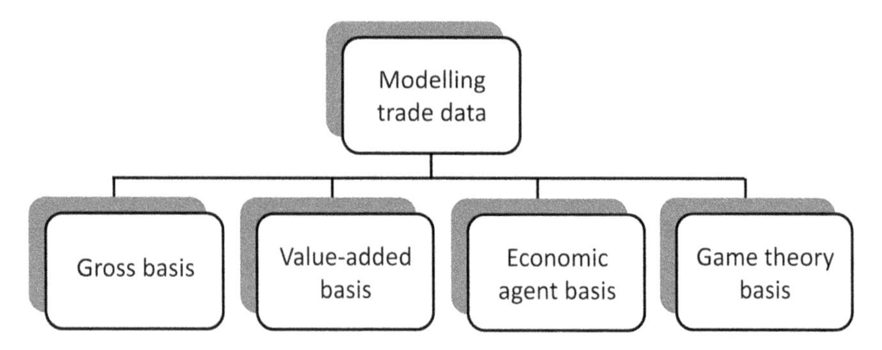

Figure 2.4 Modelling trade data

likely impact. However, the data sources or analytic tools are not without major limitations.

The quality of trade data has been an issue. In fact, the global totals of exports and imports never match! The data are also revised by reporting countries. Sometimes, exporters do not declare the merchandise as per the correct Harmonized System (HS) code; not all goods are physically inspected by customs as a trade facilitation measure. In fact, modellers even consider this mismatch in reported figures through modelling the variance in reported data. So, in some models such as GTAP, the confidence in reported trade data may differ for different countries.

Global services trade is found in the balance-of-payments statistics and is about a fifth of total trade in goods and services combined. Foreign affiliates' trade statistics provide a broader picture of trade in services. A merchandise trade also has a services component in its value chain. More importantly, modelling of both services and merchandise together with their determining factors is not yet integrated properly. Besides this, data on a value-added basis are also not reliably available for all countries.

On methodologies, the regression models depend on assumptions of a linear relationship, multivariate normality, no or little multi-collinearity, absence of auto-correlation and homoscedasticity, which are challenged. At a highly disaggregated level, the trade data may represent a sparse matrix because of zero values for specific products. The large range of products and their differing contexts may present differing variances and non-normal behaviour. The large number of economic parameters and interrelated factors presents a complex situation of mediating and moderating variables. Sophisticated models such CGE depend on parametric assumptions. Underlying functions of the economy are assumed to have specific behaviour; how robust these functions are and to what extent they can be applied to all markets or economies at all points of time, is questionable. Issues of splices in the time series data through policy changes or structural breaks are also not sufficiently modelled in CGE models, where the focus is to find the result of the application of shocks and in what range the impact is spread. Welfare effects represent added difficulties of measurement metrics and multiple objectives. Game theory presents strategic positioning but not historical results. Graph-based models are yet to be fully applied to the whole spectrum of economic relationships.

6 Conclusion

Trade modelling is complex. There are a large number of economic factors and the matrix of relationships is complicated and difficult to estimate. Free trade agreements impact trade but quantifying these 'shocks' to the economy is imprecise. Despite the promise of DSGE and newer research methods, limitations remain. Some parametric assumptions in general equilibrium modelling and the emerging methods need stronger empirical foundations.

Bibliography

Anderson, J.E. and van Wincoop, E. (2003) *Gravity with Gravitas: A Solution to the Border Puzzle*. NBER.

Armington, P.S. (1969) A theory of demand for products distinguished by place of production. *Staff Papers—International Monetary Fund* 6: 159–178.

Arrow, K. and Hahn, F. (1971) *General Competitive Analysis*. San Francisco, CA: Holden Day.

Baier, S.L. and Bergstrand, H.J. (2007, Oct). *Bonus Vetus OLS: A Simple Method for Approximating International Trade-cost Effects Using the Gravity Equation*. University of Notre Dame.

Baldwin, R.E. and Clarke, R.N. (1987) Game-modeling multilateral trade negotiations. *Journal of Policy Modeling* 9(2): 257–284.

Balistreri, E.J., Al-Qahtani, A. and Dahl, C.A. (2009, October). *Oil and Petroleum Product Armington Elasticities: A New-Geography-of-Trade Approach to Estimation*.

Balistreri, EJ. and Hillberry, R. (2007) Structural estimation and the border puzzle. *Journal of International Economics* 72(2): 451–463. EconPapers.repec.org/RePEc:eee:inecon:v:72:y:2007:i:2:p:451-463.

Bartelsman, E.J. and Dhrymes, P. (1998) Productivity dynamics: U.S. manufacturing plants, 1972–1986. *Journal of Productivity Analysis* 9(1) (January): 5–34.

Bartelsman, E.J. and Doms, M. (2000) *Understanding Productivity: Lessons from Longitudinal Microdata*. Finance and Economics Discussion Series 2000–19. Board of Governors of the Federal Reserve System (US).

Batagelj, V. and Mrvar, A. (2003) *Pajek Analysis and Visualization of Large Networks*. Ljubljana, Slovenia: University of Ljubljana.

Batagelj, V., Mrvar, A. and Zaversnik, M. (1999) Partition approach to visualization of large graphs. In *GD'99, LNCS 1731*, J. Kratochvil. Heidelberg: Springer-Verlag, pp. 90–97.

Behar, A. and Nelson, B.D. (2012) *Trade Flows, Multilateral Resistance, and Firm Heterogeneity*, February. Washington, DC: IMF.

Benedictis, L.D., Nenci, S., Santoni, G. and Tajoli, L. (2013) *CEPII Working Paper. Network Analysis of World Trade using the BACI-CEPII Dataset*. CEPII.

Bernard, A.B., Eaton, J., Jensen, B. and Kortum, S. (2003) Plants and productivity in international trade. *American Economic Review* 93(4): 1268–1290.

Bussière, M., Chudik, A. and Sestieri, G. (2009) *Modelling Global Trade Flows—Results from GVAR Model*. Working paper no. 1087. Frankfurt, Germany: European Central Bank.

Chakrabarty, S., Nag, B., Dasgupta, P. and Rastogi, S.K. (2016) Determinants and relationships in sectoral trade: A bilateral model for knitwear clothing. *Thunderbird International Business Review*.

Chaney, T. (2008) Distorted gravity: The intensive and extensive margins of international trade. *American Economic Review*, 1707–1721.

Cruz de Castro, R. (2005) Politics in command: The case of the US proposal for an FTA with the Philippines. *Contemporary Southeast Asia* 27(3): 453–471.

Dixon, P.B. and Parmenter, B.R. (1996a) Computable general equilibrium modelling for policy analysis and forecasting. In *Handbook of Computational Economics* (Vol. 1), H.M. Amman, D.A. Kendrick and J. Rust. Amsterdam: Elsevier, pp. 1–86.

Dixon, P.B. and Parmenter, B.R. (1996b) Computable general equilibrium modelling for policy analysis and forecasting. In *Handbook of Computational Economics* (Vol. 1). Amsterdam: Elsevier, pp. 1–86.

Ensign, P.C. (2003) The impact of North American Free Trade Agreement on women in the United States. *International Journal of Commerce & Management* 13(2): 1–28.

Feenstra, R.C. (2004) *Advanced International Trade: Theory and Evidence*. Princeton, NJ: Princeton University Press.

Feenstra, R.C., Obstfeld, M. and Russ, K.N. (2012) *In Search of the Armington Elasticity*. Retrieved April 4, 2013, from UC Berkeley and UC Davis: www.econ.ucdavis.edu/faculty/knruss/FOR_6-1-2012.pdf.

Fernández-Villaverde, J. (2009) *The Econometrics of DSGE Models*. NBER working paper 14677. NBER.

Harrison, G.W. and Rustrom, E.E. (1987) *Trade Wars and Trade Negotiations: A Computational Approach*. Working Paper no. 8714C. Centre for the Study of International Economic Relations, University of Western Ontario.

Hertel, T.W. (Ed.) (1997) *Global Trade Analysis: Modeling and Applications*. Cambridge: Cambridge University Press.

Hess, W., Persson, M., Rubenbauer, S. and Gertheiss, J. (2013, Feb). *Using Lasso-Type Penalties to Model Time-Varying Covariate Effects in Panel Data Regressions—A Novel Approach Illustrated by the 'Death of Distance' in International Trade*. Working Paper 2013: 5. Sweden: Lund University.

Johansen, L. (1960) *A Multisectoral Study of Economic Growth*. Contributions to Economic Analysis 21. North-Holland Publishing Company.

Kehoe, T.J. (2005) An evaluation of the performance of applied general equilibrium models of the impact of NAFTA. In *Frontiers in Applied General Equilibrium Modeling: Essays in Honor of Herbert Scarf*, ed. T.J. Kehoe, T.N. Srinivasan and J. Whalley. Cambridge: Cambridge University Press, pp. 341–377.

Krugman, P. (1980) Scale economies, product differentiation, and the pattern of trade. *The American Economic Review* 70(5): 950–959.

Leontief, W. (1936) Quantitative input and output relations in the economic system of the United States. *Review of Economics and Statistics* 18: 105–125.

Leontief, W. (1941) *The Structure of the American Economy, 1919–1929*. Cambridge, MA: Harvard University Press.

Makochekanwa, A. and Jordaan, A.C. (2008) *Identifying the Trade Theory Model behind Botswana's Sectoral Exports*. Pretoria: University of Pretoria.

Manne, A.S. (1963) Key sectors of the Mexican economy 1960–1970. In *Studies in Process Analysis*, ed. A.S. Manne and H.M. Markowitz. New York: Wiley, pp. 379–400.

Park, S.-H. and Koo, M.G. (2007) Forming a cross-regional partnership: The South Korea-Chile FTA and its implications. *Pacific Affairs* 80(2): 259.

Pavcnik, N. (2002) Trade liberalization, exit, and productivity improvements: Evidence from Chilean plants. *Review of Economic Studies* 69 (January), 245–276.

Pesaran, M.H., Schuermann, T. and Weiner, S.M. (2004) Modelling regional interdependencies using a global error-correcting macroeconometric model. *Journal of Business and Economics Statistics* 22: 129–162.

Powers, W.M. (2007) *Endogenous Liberalization and Sectoral Trade*, June. US International Trade Commission.

Rangarajan, C. and Mishra, P. (2013) India's external sector—Do we need to worry. *Economic & Political Weekly*, February 16 XLVIII(7): 52–59.

Romalis, J. (2004) *NAFTA's and CUSTA's Impact on International Trade*, December. NBER.
Sandee, J. (1960) *A Long-term Planning Model for India*. New York: Asia Publishing House; Calcutta: Statistical Publishing Company.
Scarf, H.E. (1967a) The approximation of fixed points of a continuous mapping. *SIAM Journal of Applied Mathematics* 15(5): 328–343.
Scarf, H.E. (1967b) On the computation of equilibrium prices. In *Ten Essays in Honor of Irving Fisher*, ed. W. Fellner. New York: Wiley.
Scarf, H.E. (1973) *The computation of economic equilibria*. New Haven, CT and London: Yale University Press.
Shepherd, B. (2012) *The Gravity Model of International Trade—A User Guide*. UN ESCAP.
Siddiqi, W., Ahmad, N., Khan, A.A. and Yousef, K. (2012) Determinants of export demand of textile and clothing sector of Pakistan: An empirical analysis. *World Applied Sciences Journal* 16(8): 1171–1175.
Solís, M. and Katada, S.N. (2007) The Japan-Mexico FTA: A cross-regional step in the path towards Asian regionalism. *Pacific Affairs* 80(2): 279.
Synder, D. and Kick, E. (1979) Structural position in the world system and economic growth 1955–1970: A multiple network analysis of transnational interactions. *American Journal of Sociology* 84: 1096–1126.
White, G.W. (2005) Free trade as a strategic instrument in the war on terror? The 2004 US-Moroccan free trade agreement. *The Middle East Journal* 59(4): 597–616.
World Trade Organization (WTO) (2016a) *Database on Preferential Trade Agreements*. ptadb.wto.org/?lang=1.
World Trade Organization (WTO) (2016b) *Regional Trade Agreements Information Systems*. Retrieved April 20, 2016. rtais.wto.org/UI/PublicMaintainRTAHome.aspx.
Yilmazkuday, H. (2008, July). *Is the Armington Elasticity Really Constant across Importers?* Nashville, TN: Vanderbilt University.

3 The geoeconomics of global cities

Exploring new avenues for expanding business internationalization

Philippe Régnier and Pascal Wild

1 Introduction

This chapter suggests some advances in the study of global city geoeconomics as the role of the international corporate sector has not yet been heavily covered in the existing literature. In addition, it was anticipated that the economic intermediation role of major world cities and others would decline with the new wave of economic globalization and the acceleration of information and communication technologies (ICT)-based instant communication since the early 1990s. However, the exact opposite has taken place, and competitive rankings of global cities have even emerged and resonated worldwide since the turn of the century.

A global city is usually considered as an important node in the global system. This concept is derived from world economic history, development economics and urban geography, but more specifically from sociology since the early 1990s. Inspired by the masterpieces of Saskia Sassen (1991, 2001), it suggests that globalization is facilitated by strategic hubs according to a hierarchical organization of the global trade and financial system.

The study of global cities has been produced by geographers, historians, and sociologists, but its integration in international economics and business studies is a more recent proposal. It was initiated among others by the Global Entrepreneurship Monitor (GEM), and derived from a highly ranked paper by Acs, Bosma and Sternberg (2008) titled 'The Entrepreneurial Advantage of World Cities: Evidence from Global Entrepreneurship Monitor Data". The paper suggests that global cities provide a specific entrepreneurial climate, which has much to do 'with cultural richness, economic diversity, international connectivity and infrastructure excellence that is not available in any city' (Acs et al., 2008, p. 5). Other authors such as Taylor (2004) or Fritsch and Falck (2007) underline that qualitative entrepreneurship features are still lacking in most metropolitan studies. They refer to quality of professional life, mobilization capacity of needed resources, availability of technical supportive services and venture capital, spatial proximity to both customers and suppliers, concentration of industrial knowledge and business regional networks.

Empirical data and evidence have been collected since the late 1990s in the case of multinational corporations and their various modes of presence in global cities. This is particularly true for the three first-ranking global cities worldwide, namely New York, London and Tokyo.

2 Global cities: interdisciplinary approach and theories

It is generally accepted that a global city is a major urban center acting as a node in the world economic and financial system. The emphasis is put on the regional and international linkages of global cities. They are an object of research interest in various disciplines such as geography and urban studies, history, economics, sociology, politics, and more recently entrepreneurship and management.

2.1 Definitions

Considering the historical importance of world cities (Abu-Lughod, 1989; Braudel, 1984; Dollinger, 1970), social sciences have studied the role of cities as economic, historical, geographic, political, and socio-cultural centers (Currid, 2006; Friedmann, 1986; Jacobs, 1969, 1984). While the cross-border intermediation role of cities has been documented by numerous scholars (e.g. Braudel, 1984; Wallerstein, 1974), a new type of network among cities has been identified since the post-1989 new wave of globalization. Today's global cities are major nodes in the world economy (Castells, 1996, 2011; Sassen, 1991, 2001; Taylor, 2004), and master more centralizing power than any city ever had before (Beaverstock et al., 1999; Castells, 1996, 2011; Doel & Hubbard, 2002; Friedmann, 1986; Jacobs, 1969, 1984; Sassen, 1991, 2001; Taylor et al., 2014; Taylor, 2004, 2011).

Since the late 2000s, the GEM data on entrepreneurship-enabling conditions have inspired a new production of scientific articles in geoeconomics (Acs et al., 2008). A new research avenue has emerged aiming at the integration of entrepreneurship combined with the entrepreneurial ecosystems of global cities. Such systems offer high spatial concentrations of services, a density of highly qualified workforce, and access to key resources that can facilitate entrepreneurship and act as business hubs for multinational corporations (MNCs) and small and medium-sized enterprises (SMEs) venturing to distant markets.

2.2 International classification of global cities

The concept of a 'global city' was first promoted at Princeton University by sociologist Saskia Sassen in her book *The Global City: New York, London, Tokyo* (Sassen, 1991). The term 'world city' goes back to the 19th century, describing the control of a disproportionate density of global business activities in the port of Liverpool as suggested by the *Illustrated London News* in 1886. Patrick Geddes also used this term later in 1915 (Doel & Hubbard, 2002). The role of global cities is compared to other categories of cities

(Jacobs, 1969, 1984; Friedmann, 1986), to their involvement in networks of cities (Taylor, 2004), or in terms of high concentrations of services (Acs et al., 2008; Castells, 1996). The first attempt to better categorize and rank global cities was made in 1998 by British academics (Beaverstock et al., 1999). They established the Globalization and World Cities Research Network (GaWC) as a kind of roster ranking cities based on their connectivity through four 'advanced producer services': accountancy, advertising, banking/finance, and law. The GaWC inventory identifies three levels of global cities and several sub-ranks. Since 2004, it has included some new indicators while continuing to rank urban economic factors more heavily than political or cultural ones. Since 2008, the GaWC has suggested the following categorization:

- *Alpha++* cities are London and New York, which are more integrated with the global economy than other cities.
- *Alpha+* cities complement London and New York City by filling advanced service niches for the global economy.
- *Alpha* and *Alpha–* cities link major economic regions to the world economy.
- *Beta* cities link moderate economic regions to the world economy.
- *Gamma* cities link smaller economic regions to the world economy.
- *Sufficiency* cities concentrate a sufficient degree of services so as not to be dependent on world cities.

In 2008, *Foreign Policy*, in conjunction with the Chicago-based consulting firm A.T. Kearney and the Chicago Council on Global Affairs, published a ranking of global cities based on consultation with Saskia Sassen, the *2012 Global Cities Index and Emerging Cities Outlook*. It was noted that the world's largest and most interconnected cities help the setting of global agendas, weather transnational dangers, and serve as hubs of regional and global integration. They are engines of global growth and gateways to intra-regional and inter-regional resources. The main parameters are: 'business activity' (30%), 'human capital' (30%), 'information exchange' (15%), 'cultural experience' (15%) and 'political engagement' (10%). This index is updated every two years. In all rankings, New York, London and Tokyo rank first. Looking at East Asia, Beijing, Hong Kong, Singapore and Tokyo are among the top ten global cities, whereas Seoul (12th), Shanghai (18th), Kuala Lumpur (39th) and Bangkok (42nd) lag behind. Since a couple of years ago, Hong Kong and its inter-connection with south China have seemed to catch up somehow with Tokyo.

2.3 Command and control center

In history, there have been command centers, where important decisions influenced a nation, a region or even a whole continent. For example, Rome was the control center of the Roman Empire. In the ancient Northern European Hanseatic system, a sea-based city would gain importance mainly from trade. This was reproduced later in the West (London, New York), and in East Asia by Hong Kong and Singapore as trading city-states.

Friedmann (1986, p. 69) analyzes the 'spatial organization of the new international division of labor' and the inter-linkages among cities. He suggests a hierarchical categorization of cities between core/primary and peripheral/secondary cities. Later in the 1990s, he focused on their 'economic articulations.' Through the process of globalization, the power of global cities to command and control major world regions increased massively (Sassen, 2001).

While there is some kind of international consensus on the identification of global cities, national and international definitions of secondary cities tend to vary rather substantially depending on the demographics and urban/rural geography of countries.

2.4 Concentration of services

Jacobs (1984) defines dynamic and static cities. Dynamic cities project economic activities as centers of innovation and trade, and concentrate human skills. In contrast, peripheral or static cities do not contribute to overall economic wealth. They are trading houses where goods are only conveyed but with little added value. They tend to remain the 'hinterlands' of dynamic cities (Taylor, 2004).

Due to globalization, Sassen has brought up the concept of inter-connected cities. She identifies global cities as world servicing centers concentrating manufacturing activities and services, with a high propensity for innovation (Sassen, 1991). If we refer to the post-1990s concept of business development services (BDS), it can be argued that global cities offer a high density of BDS, and play crucial functions in corporate internationalization modes.

2.5 Networks of cities

Another focus is to envisage global cities in terms of their linkages to other cities (global and not). Jacobs (1984), Sassen (1991), Castells (1996) and Taylor (2004) adopt a geographic and spatial approach. There is space for cities and transaction flows in the global system. Thanks to ICTs, products and services can be interconnected across borders, independently from their spatial location, and global cities take leadership in this transnational process. Such interconnectivity stimulates within and among global cities a highly entrepreneurial environment based on information, knowledge, creativity and innovation. These concepts are quite distant from the more traditional notions of global cities envisaged as control or command centers.

2.6 Entrepreneurship and globalization

Global cities can be analyzed through various lenses (hierarchical functions, servicing concentration, networking integration), and different typologies can coexist. For example, in the case of Europe, besides London and Paris, several other types of strategic cities coexist in a relatively small spatial geography; Geneva or Zurich are far more global than many others despite their small populations.

Recent conceptual research tries to link urban and geographic studies to other scientific domains such as entrepreneurship: New York can maintain its first-class position as a global city thanks to a special concentration of brains and creativity (Currid, 2006). Based on previous authors (Fritsch & Falck, 2007), leading scholars have started to use the GEM, combining national data surveys for over 80 countries to study the global status of world cities (Acs et al., 2008). The focus is centered on their enabling role of corporate internationalization, mainly MNCs but also, increasingly, smaller firms. Global cities offer a top quality entrepreneurial milieu, which facilitates MNCs and smaller firms to venture into regional and intercontinental markets. Micro-processes interconnect different spaces, time zones, and both real and virtual flows. Using global cities as entry points, interconnections with more 'static cities' in the 'hinterland' seek resource optimization and entry simplification to distant markets. As indicated by Zucchella and Scabini (2007), a firm may benefit from 'strategic enhancement' as follows:

- Easy access to reliable information by means of business-to-business (B2B) associations, service centers and corporate consortia, reduces search costs.
- Knowledge and technological spillovers are possible thanks to high numbers of Schumpeterian imitative processes and high rates of business spin-offs.
- Access to human resources is facilitated, in particular to highly specialized professionals.
- Rapid connections are made available to backward and forward linkages associated with international value chains and large domestic or regional markets.
- A variety of options are offered to share infrastructure, logistics and networks among firms and subsidiaries located close to each other.

2.7 *Theory of global cities*

Existing theories have established that global cities are territorial nodes essential to the sustainable development of world trade and financial flows along global value chains. Furthermore, due to their high concentration of foreign MNCs and affiliates, they provide an exceptional density of specialized services and project various types of entrepreneurship capacities linking their hinterland to regional and world markets.

As global cities offer a wide range of functional and social networks used but also reinforced over time by global MNCs, a small number of Organisation for Economic Co-operation and Development (OECD) transnational

SMEs are making similar utilization of global cities (Fujita, 1998). It remains to be seen how higher flows of foreign SMEs do access global cities as providers of supportive services needed to facilitate their penetration into emerging markets. Thanks to global cities' BDS, SMEs are enabled to increase their level of distant market knowledge and of local business practices. Through appropriate BDS support available in global cities, they can build up local business confidence and limit market risk exposure when initiating business deals with distant/foreign emerging markets. Otherwise, SMEs may face numerous obstacles and waste their limited internal resources in trying to venture far away from home and neighboring markets (Johanson & Vahlne, 1977, 2009).

3 International business management, global cities and SME internationalization

Internationalization of firms has been studied across different research domains such as strategic management, entrepreneurship, international business, organizational theory and small business economics (Bell et al., 2003; Peiris et al., 2012; Ruzzier et al., 2006; Zucchella & Scabini, 2007).

It has been recognized that SME growth is essential for any national economy (Coviello & Munro, 1995) as SMEs are responsible for the vast majority of existing firms, jobs and income creation both in industrialized and developing countries. SMEs perceive growth as a necessity for various reasons, and decide to go international mainly for that purpose (Fujita, 1998). However, internationalizing SMEs have to overcome hurdles such as organizational change, adaptation of strategy, products, marketing and distribution (Ruzzier et al., 2006; Zucchella & Scabini, 2007). They have to cope with challenges such as cultural and language differences, geographical and psychological distance, etc. (Johanson & Vahlne, 1977, 1990, 2009). SMEs active internationally are seen as better performing than non-internationalizing ones (EU-Japan Centre for Industrial Cooperation, 2012). In fact, without good performance, lean management and quality products, survival is very difficult (OECD, 2009). SME internationalization patterns and market entry strategies have been studied (Bell et al., 2001; Bell et al., 2003; Coviello & Jones, 2004; Coviello & Munro, 1995, 1997; Fujita, 1998; Johanson & Vahlne, 1977, 1990, 2009; Oviatt & McDougall, 1994). However, not a single theory has been able to encapsulate the whole SME internationalization process (Bell et al., 2003; Coviello & Jones, 2004; Gankema et al., 2000; Kraus, 2011; Ruzzier et al., 2006; Schueffel & Baldegger, 2008; Zahra & George, 2002b; Zahra, 2005; Zucchella & Scabini, 2007).

3.1 Limitations of MNC theories

SME specialists suggest that theories mainly derived from internationalization of MNCs, cannot be fully applied to SMEs (Ruzzier et al., 2006). Differences in terms of size, internal resources, management, and external outreach strategy make it difficult to apply such theories across the board. However, they may provide a holistic understanding of internationalizing SMEs, for instance by focusing on the costs of transaction to internationalize. The owner location internalization paradigm explains the different advantages for an MNC to go international though the accumulation of intangible assets, the improvement of supply chain management and the mobilization of other productive factors depending on geographical factors (Ruzzier et al., 2006). As SMEs have more limited internal resources than MNCs, the optimal combination of their internal/external resources is crucial. This is where the business hub enabling role of global cities can play a part, even though MNC affiliates and subsidiaries have been the major categories of firms using them with high visibility so far.

3.2 SME internationalization: the Uppsala model

Different models of behaviors have been identified regarding SME internationalization. In the 1970s, SME internationalization was considered a gradual or incremental process. Two models were developed: the 'I-Model' or 'innovation model,' and the 'U-Model' or 'Uppsala model.'

In the I-Model, each SME internationalization step is seen as an opportunity (Gankema et al., 2000), and the main focus is on export capacity (Ruzzier et al., 2006). In general, three steps are identified: (i) pre-export, (ii) initial export, and (iii) advanced export.

The U-Model suggest that a firm increases its international linkages through gradual overseas market learning (Johanson & Vahlne, 1977, 1990). New competences are acquired incrementally to enter new 'psychic distant' markets as the process involves differences in language, education, and business practices.

Both models envisage internationalization as an accumulation of small steps. Stage models have been criticized as being 'deterministic.' However, U-Models in particular have been widely applied and have made a huge contribution to the understanding of SME internationalization.

Since the 1990s, a new type of SMEs has been identified as 'born global' or 'international new ventures' (Bell et al., 2003; Oviatt & McDougall, 1994; Schueffel & Baldegger, 2008). Such firms target global 'lead markets' (Bell et al., 2003) and have global activities from the very early phases of their creation (i.e. some start-ups in ICTs). They have generally high and specific skills and/or proprietary technologies used as competitive advantage. These global start-ups internationalize rapidly and do not fear 'psychic' distances. Definition efforts have been proposed in recent years, and have contributed to the identification of a new research domain in international entrepreneurship, whose boundaries are still being discussed (McDougall-Covin et al., 2014). Bell proposes an integrative model of SME internationalization, which explains the differences between traditional, born global and born-again global firms.

It suggests a causal link between SME internal knowledge and the chosen mode of internationalization.

3.3 SME network and resource-based approaches

SMEs entering distant markets need to consider financial, marketing and organizational implications. In order to shed light on these aspects, two additional analytical models are useful.

The network approach considers any firm as a part of business networks. It looks into the linkages between its business development and the role of external actors. The analysis is derived from the U-Model, as Johanson adopts a network perspective to explain internationalization motives (Zucchella & Scabini, 2007).

The resource-based view is derived from strategic management, and analyzes the use of resources to develop competitive advantages. Resources can be tangible (e.g. capital, facilities), intangible (e.g. patents, knowledge), or in the form of capabilities (e.g. ability to determine entrepreneurial opportunities) (Zucchella & Scabini, 2007). Both approaches consider 'internal' and 'external' resources as the total assets of a firm. The development of both models go 'hand in hand' (Ruzzier et al., 2006).

3.4 SME market entry and BDS

According to Fujita (1998), SMEs generally choose among several modes to enter a market: licensing, subcontracting, know-how and technology transfers, foreign direct investment (FDI), joint ventures, international partnerships and management contracts, mergers and acquisitions. In order to overcome financing limitations and to mobilize other resources, SMEs can get public or private business facilitation from supportive institutions or from B2B linkages (Fujita, 1998; Bell, 2003). Based on the existing literature on BDS, a clear distinction is made between financial services provided by various institutions (accounting and auditing firms, banks, brokers, credit guarantee funds, insurance companies, etc.), and non-financial or technical institutions (coaching, training, legal counseling, technology incubation, scientific and testing services, etc.) (Fujita, 1998). This distinction is usual among academics and practitioners. Banking and other financial services are a world in itself, and all other types of services are 'technical' with various sub-categories. Since post-1989 neoliberal globalization, deregulation and privatization, this divide has been enriched by a second distinction between private and public services, later somehow reconciled by the promotion of so-called public–private partnerships (PPPs), and considered as more efficient to promote SMEs. Since 1999–2001, the concept of BDS has been introduced by leading international agencies and consulting firms, including the OECD and the World Bank. The concept of BDS covers financial and technical services contributing to a friendly entrepreneurial eco-system and a pro-SME regulatory environment facilitating business internationalization. The supply of BDS should be market-driven and with limited public intervention (White, 2001).

3.5 SME internationalization integrative model

Different integrative models have been developed (Ruzzier et al., 2006; Zahra & George, 2002a; Zucchella & Scabini, 2007). An SME can mobilize resources either internally, or acquire them externally. Internal development refers to investment and innovation. External acquisition refers to strategic partnerships in order to 'introduce new products, services and ideas in the market' (Zucchella & Scabini, 2007, p. 126). It involves SME outreach to a wide range of financial and technical inputs provided by business linkages, supportive organizations and/or inter-personal networks.

In order to 'integrate, build and reconfigure internal and external competencies […] the SME depends on managerial processes, position and path dependence' (Zucchella & Scabini, 2007, p. 128). The SME managerial process commands the coordination and integration of resources to enter a market and its local environment. Path dependence concerns SME entrepreneurial learning characterized by its educational and practical experience (SME entrepreneur and senior management). It involves aspects of organizational learning.

Measuring international performance is complex, 'as it may be measured in terms of profitability, growth, export intensity, geographic scope and international precocity' (Zucchella & Scabini, 2007, p. 134).

3.6 SME internationalization to distant markets

SMEs are understood as foreign to a given distant market. The notion of distance can be geographical but also cultural and even psychological. SMEs generally choose among several modes to enter distant markets: licensing, subcontracting, know-how and technology transfers, FDI, joint ventures, international partnerships and management contracts, mergers and acquisitions. Each mode can be conceived in a consecutive and gradual manner, and it has various types of internal financial and organizational implications (Fujita, 1998). A number of studies have been conducted using network and/or resource-based approaches.

3.7 Network approach

Based on the revisited U-Model of Johanson and Vahlne (2009), recent studies analyze 'the process of how an SME actively enters its internationalization-relevant network' (Schweizer, 2013, p. 81). They focus on OECD highly innovative SMEs developing new international networks to distant markets, in particular to Japan and South Korea. The process contains four phases:

Phase 1: Recognition of the existence and liability of outsidership (not being part of the relevant networks)
Phase 2: Identification of the relevant network
Phase 3: Re-bundling of the firm's resources and capabilities
Phase 4: Accessing, managing, and leveraging opportunities identified in the new network

(Schweizer, 2013, pp. 97–98)

Based on the study of internationalizing Malaysian SMEs, the relevant network approach can be explained in more detail (Che Senik et al., 2011). According to this model, an SME network is constituted of supportive institutions (government agencies), business associations and personal relations. Such linkages can initiate awareness, as well as trigger, strengthen, and sustain SME internationalization. They can decrease SMEs' total risk exposure, and increase their level of self-confidence and trust in a selected mode of market entry.

3.8 Resource-based approach

Some authors have investigated the changes in terms of actors, activities and mobilized resources during the SME internationalization process (Nummela, 2002), often combined with the network approach. Nummela, for instance, has studied the internationalization of Finnish manufacturing SMEs and their interaction with external and supportive institutions (business associations, professional consultants, public services, subcontractors, universities). Ojala also underlines the importance of supportive networks in the internationalization process of knowledge-based Scandinavian firms interested to enter the Japanese market (Ojala, 2009). Most available studies tend to focus on software SMEs and the development of linkages with larger clients without taking into account a holistic approach as indicated in Figure 3.1 (Moen et al., 2004; Reuber & Fischer, 1997; Zain & Ng, 2006).

3.9 Knowledge management approach

As part of the resource-based approach, recent studies underline the role of internal/external knowledge mobilization and management, introducing a clear distinction between gradually internationalizing SMEs and globally born SMEs. In the first category, SMEs do mobilize their internal knowledge of proximity markets, where they have started to internationalize during the first five to ten years of the process. Globally born SMEs are, for instance, young high-tech start-ups, which perform in very specific segments of high-tech markets in manufacturing or services, and can (but not always) expand overseas rapidly, including to distant markets.

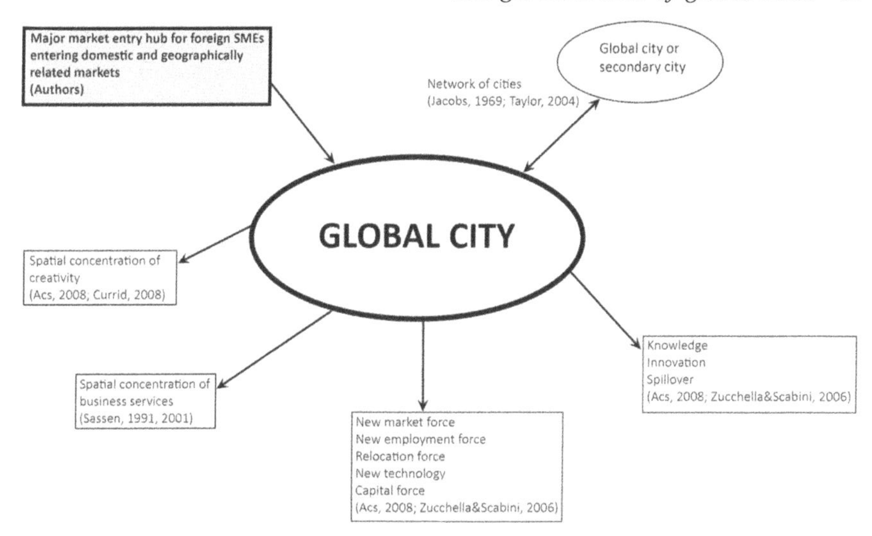

Figure 3.1 SME/global city geoeconomic interlinkages

3.10 Vicarious learning

SMEs may capitalize on internal knowledge accumulated during their initial phases of internationalization, especially vis-à-vis markets of proximity, and then expand gradually to more distant ones in order to connect, in particular, to difficult emerging markets such as in East Asia.

They may also source external knowledge from other SMEs and business networks having already established such connections and accumulated experience locally. Vicarious learning is one of the concepts developed by social cognitive theories developed since the 1960s.

Internationalizing SMEs tend to learn from other SMEs, which are not necessarily direct competitors or may even be active in different sectors. What matters is that these SMEs have already penetrated distant emerging markets, and they may share both their difficulties and success stories. Inter-SME networking is therefore often quite high on the agenda of internationalizing SMEs.

3.11 Implications for SME internationalization theory

No theory has so far captured the whole SME internationalization process. The Uppsala model developed in 1977 and revised in 2009 has remained dominant along three key concepts, as follows:

- SMEs tend to internationalize gradually and incrementally, and seldom to distant markets before having accumulated first-hand experience in foreign markets of proximity. For instance, recent surveys show that companies still tend to internationalize in a gradual and stepwise manner.

For instance, Asian markets often represent Western European SMEs' second export destination behind EU markets of proximity. The number of globally born SMEs remains rather small but is increasing (Baldegger, 2013).

- SMEs have to cope with high risks and transaction costs to reduce the 'distance' of overseas markets. SME network economics shows that SMEs need to identify both functional and social networks to access reliable business information and access distant markets. Such networks are even more crucial to penetrate new emerging and unknown markets, where incomplete and unstable market institutions still prevail.
- Identification and use of functional and social networks by SMEs imply access to territorial and institutional actors providing business intermediation services to approach distant and risky markets, such as in emerging East Asia. Such services are heavily concentrated in global cities, as shown in Figure 3.2.

4 Conceptual framework

This chapter aims to contribute to the construction of a conceptual framework which combines two sources of knowledge, namely global city theories and SME internationalization theories. SME quantitative and qualitative surveys exist in a number of global cities, but they concentrate mainly on the study of domestic SMEs, and consider both domestic and foreign SMEs as only one SME category. In addition, national SME surveys available do not concentrate on major cities exclusively, nor the specific category of global cities. Theories and classifications of global cities have been built so far exclusively based on MNC data. This is due to the magnitude and visibility of

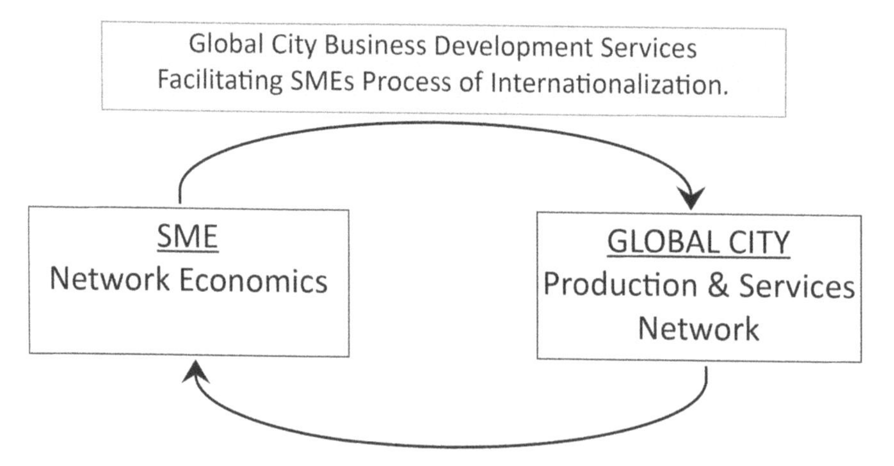

Figure 3.2 A tentative SME/global city conceptual framework

MNC presence in global cities, and by available access to their data through accessible electronic communications worldwide and in each city classified as a global city. A similar exercise extended to internationalizing SMEs present (directly or indirectly) in global cities is much more difficult and remains to be conducted locally and on a comparable global scale.

The cross-fertilization of the two sources of scientific knowledge, namely SME Network Economics and Global Cities, enables the identification of a conceptual framework in order to conduct research on the use of functions and services of global cities by foreign internationalizing SMEs to distant emerging markets.

First, SME internationalization theories as a sub-component of SME economics and management are embedded in small business network economics. This means that such internationalization relies on both functional and social networks to be identified and mobilized through global cities in order to reduce market entry risks and transaction costs.

Second, theories of global cities have established that they represent major hubs of global production and service networks. Parts of these networks are also constituted by dense business interlinkages among global cities within and across continents.

The combination of these two sources of knowledge has led to the proposal that global cities can and do provide services to foreign SMEs, which are integrated in their core functional and social networking capacities to link their hinterland (regional markets) and the global origins of foreign internationalizing SMEs.

Empirically, research work cannot be carried out on a random basis as has been done to measure quantitatively and qualitatively MNC presence in global cities through their affiliates, subsidiaries and representative offices. It has to rely on two sources of SME internationalization data that can be collected: (i) in the country of SME origin, and (ii) in the global city of BDS intermediation, depending on the localization of the distant market and final clients targeted by each specific SME. In the country of origin, it requires a fairly large quantitative and qualitative research apparatus to be able to document the numbers and profiles of local SMEs already in the internationalizing process, and using global cities as trading hubs to reach distant markets.

SMEs use in one form or another the functional services and social networks concentrated in global cities as enablers to access neighboring developed, emerging and/or underdeveloped markets depending on the geoeconomic location of each global city. As a word of caution, the authors do not suggest that all internationalizing SMEs make an exclusive use of global cities to internationalize. Some SMEs may find other routes to access distant markets by themselves, and sometimes more directly than via global cities. However, even though global cities are often perceived by SMEs as costly nodes of business information search and operational intermediation, their reliable ecosystem and specialization of supportive services do enable SMEs to reduce hazards and risks, especially in difficult emerging markets. Such global cities are localized in East Asia, for example, either as major global and regional business hubs such as Hong Kong or Singapore, or as major global and domestic hubs such as Shanghai or Tokyo.

This chapter intends to be an innovative and inspiring contribution to both academics and practitioners interested in the geoeconomics of global cities, already or not yet convinced that such cities are not meant to serve large corporations exclusively, but also smaller firms and middlemen in many visible or invisible manners—as actors of global production networks and value chains. By the time this chapter was finalized, it was becoming more and more obvious by the day that a number of governments and municipalities of global cities were putting in place new strategies, policies and instruments to enhance various forms of collaboration and networking between highly specialized SMEs and start-ups located in different global cities worldwide. An acceleration of geoeconomics among interconnected global cities is expected in the coming years, benefiting both large and small firms with little distinction of origin and nationality.

Bibliography

Abu-Lughod, J.L. (1989) *Before European Hegemony: The World System A.D. 1250–1350*. New York: Oxford University Press.

Acs, Z. (2002) *Innovation and the Growth of Cities*. Cheltenham: Edward Elgar.

Acs, Z. and Armington, C. (2004) Employment growth and entrepreneurial activity in cities. *Regional Studies* 38(8): 911–927.

Acs, Z., Bosma, N. and Sternberg, R. (2008) *The Entrepreneurial Advantage of World Cities: Evidence from Global Entrepreneurship Monitor Data*. GEM research paper.

Baldegger, R.J. (2013) *Swiss International Entrepreneurship Survey 2013: Internationalization Efforts of Swiss Small and Medium-sized Enterprises (SMEs)*. Fribourg/Bern: Swiss Post Finance.

Beaverstock, J., Smith, R. and Taylor, P.J. (1999) A roster of world cities. *Cities* 16(6): 445–458.

Bell, J. (1995) The internationalization of small computer software firms: A further challenge to 'stage' theories. *European Journal of Marketing* 29(8): 60–75.

Bell, J., McNaughton, R. and Young, S. (2001) 'Born-again global' firms: An extension to the 'born global' phenomenon. *Journal of International Management* 7: 173–189.

Bell, J., McNaughton, R., Young, S. and Crick, D. (2003) Towards an integrative model of small firm internationalisation. *Journal of International Entrepreneurship* 1(4): 339–362.

Braudel, F. (1984) *The Perspective of the World*. London: Collins.

Castells, M. (1996) *The Rise of Network Society*. Oxford: Blackwell, 2nd edition.

Castells, M. (2011) *The Rise of the Network Society: The Information Age: Economy, Society, and Culture* (Vol. 1.). Oxford: John Wiley & Sons.

Che Senik, Z., Scott-Ladd, B., Entrekin, L. and Adham, K.A. (2011) Networking and internationalization of SMEs in emerging economies. *Journal of International Entrepreneurship* 9(4): 259–281.

Coviello, N.E. and Jones, M.V. (2004) Methodological issues in international entrepreneurship research. *Journal of Business Venturing* 19: 485–508.

Coviello, N.E. and Munro, H.J. (1995) Growing the entrepreneurial firm market development. *European Journal of Marketing* 29(7): 49–61.
Coviello, N. and Munro, H. (1997) Network relationships and the internationalisation process of small software firms. *International Business Review* 6(4): 361–386.
Coviello, N.E. and McAuley, A. (1999) Internationalisation and the smaller firm: A review of contemporary empirical research. *Management International Review* 39(3): 353–356.
Currid, E. (2006) New York as a global creative hub: A competitive analysis of four theories on world cities. *Economic Development Quarterly* 20(4): 330–350.
Derudder, B. and Taylor, P. (2005) The cliquishness of world cities. *Global Networks* 5 (1): 71–91.
Doel, M. and Hubbard, P. (2002) Taking world cities literally: Marketing the city in a global space of flows. *City* 6(3): 351–368.
Dollinger, P. (1970) *The German Hansa*. London: Macmillan.
EU-Japan Centre for Industrial Cooperation (2012) *Strategies for Promoting the Internationalisation of SMEs in the EU and Japan*, pp. 1–15.
Friedmann, J. (1986) The world city hypothesis. *Development and Change* 17(1), 69–83.
Fritsch, M. and Falck, O. (2007) New business formation by industry over space and time: A multidimensional analysis. *Regional Studies* 41(2): 157–172.
Fritsch, M. and Mueller, P. (2006) The evolution of regional entrepreneurship and growth regimes. *Entrepreneurship in the Region*, 225–244.
Fujita, M. (1998) *The Transnational Activities of Small and Medium-sized Enterprises.* Boston, MA: Kluwer Academic Publisher.
Gankema, H.G.J., Snuif, H.R. and Zwaart, P.S. (2000) The internationalization process of small and medium-sized enterprises: An evaluation of stage theory. *Journal of Small Business Management* 38(4): 15–27.
Jacobs, J. (1969) *The Economy of Cities.* New York: Random House.
Jacobs, J. (1984) *Cities and the Wealth of Nations.* New York: Random House.
Johanson, J. and Mattsson, L.-G. (1987) Interorganizational relations in industrial systems: A network approach compared with the transaction-cost approach. *International Studies of Management & Organization*, 34–48.
Johanson, J. and Mattsson, L.-G. (1988) Internationalization in industrial systems—A network approach. *Strategies in Global Competition*, 287–314.
Johanson, J. and Vahlne, J.E. (1977) The internationalization process of the firm—A model of knowledge development and increasing foreign market commitments. *Journal of International Business Studies* 8(1): 23–33.
Johanson, J. and Vahlne, J.E. (1990) The mechanism of internationalization. *International Marketing Review* 7(4): 11–25.
Johanson, J. and Vahlne, J.-E. (2009) The Uppsala internationalization process model revisited: From liability of foreignness to liability of outsidership. *Journal of International Business Studies* 40(9): 1411–1431.
Johanson, J. and Wiedersheim-Paul, F. (1975) The internationalization of the firm—Four Swedish cases. *The Journal of Management Studies* 12(3): 305–322.
Knight, G.A. and Cavusgil, S.T. (1996) The born global firm: A challenge to traditional internationalization theory. *Advances in International Marketing* 8: 11–26.
Kraus, S. (2011) State-of-the-art current research in international entrepreneurship: A citation analysis. *African Journal of Business Management* 5(3): 1020–1038.

McDougall-Covin, P., Jones, M.V. and Serapio, M.G. (2014) High-potential concepts, phenomena, and theories for the advancement of international entrepreneurship research. *Entrepreneurship Theory and Practice* 38(1): 1–10.
Moen, Ø., Gavlen, M. and Endresen, I. (2004) Internationalization of small, computer software firms: Entry forms and market selection. *European Journal of Marketing* 38(9/10): 1236–1251. doi:10.1108/03090560410548951.
Nummela, N. (2002) Change in SME internationalization. A network perspective. Paper presented at the 28th EIBA Conference 2002, Athens, Greece. Retrieved from http://biblioteca.fundacionicbc.edu.ar/images/6/67/Estrategia_internacionalizacion_9.pdf.
Organisation for Economic Co-operation and Development (OECD) (2009) *Top Barriers and Drivers to SME Internationalisation.*
Organisation for Economic Co-operation and Development (OECD) (2013) *Fostering SMEs' Participation in Global Markets: Final Report*. Paris.
Organisation for Economic Co-operation and Development (OECD) (2013a). *Developing the Potential of Small and Medium-sized Enterprises to Internationalise.* Paris, 1–71.
Organisation for Economic Co-operation and Development (OECD) (2013b). *Fostering SMEs' Participation in Global Markets: Final Report*. Paris, Vol. 33, 1–135.
Ojala, A. (2008) Entry in a psychically distant market: Finnish small and medium-sized software firms in Japan. *European Management Journal* 26(2): 135–144.
Ojala, A. (2009) Internationalization of knowledge-intensive SMEs: The role of network relationships in the entry to a psychically distant market. *International Business Review* 18(1): 50–59.
Oviatt, B.M. and McDougall, P.P. (1994) Toward a theory of international new ventures. *Journal of International Business Studies* 25: 45–64.
Peiris, I.K., Akoorie, M.E.M. and Sinha, P. (2012) International entrepreneurship: A critical analysis of studies in the past two decades and future directions for research. *Journal of International Entrepreneurship* 10(4): 279–324.
Reuber, A.R. and Fischer, E. (1997) The influence of the management team's international experience on the internationalization behaviors of SMEs. *Journal of International Business Studies*, 807–825.
Ruzzier, M., Hisrich, R.D. and Antoncic, B. (2006) SME internationalization research: Past, present, and future. *Journal of Small Business and Enterprise Development* 13(4): 476–497.
Sassen, S. (1991) *The Global City: New York, London, Tokyo*. Princeton, NJ: Princeton University Press.
Sassen, S. (2001) *The Global City: New York, London, Tokyo*, 2nd edition. Princeton, NJ: Princeton University Press.
Schueffel, P.E. and Baldegger, R.J. (2008) *The Process Model of Internationalization and the International New Venture Framework*. Liebefeld/Bern: Growth Publisher.
Schweizer, R. (2013) SMEs and networks: Overcoming the liability of outsidership. *Journal of International Entrepreneurship* 11(1): 80–103.
Taylor, P.J. (2004) *World City Network: A Global Urban Analysis*. Routledge.
Taylor, P.J. (2011) Advanced producer service centres in the world economy. In *Global Urban Analysis: A Survey of Cities in Globalization*. London: Earthscan, 22–39.
Taylor, P.J., Catalano, G. and Walker, D.R.F. (2002) Measurement of the world city network. *Urban Studies* 39(13): 2367–2376.

Taylor, P.J., Derudder, B., Faulconbridge, J., Hoyler, M. and Ni, P. (2014) Advanced producer service firms as strategic networks, global cities as strategic places. *Economic Geography* 90(3): 267–291.

Wallerstein, I. (1974) *The Modern World-System*. New York: Academic Press.

White, S. (2001) *Business Development Services Guidelines.* Cambridge and Washington, DC: Donor Committee for Enterprise Development & World Bank Group.

Zahra, S.A. (2005) A theory of international new ventures: A decade of research. *Journal of International Business Studies* 36(April): 20–28.

Zahra, S.A. and George, G. (2002a) Absorbative capacity: A review, reconceptualization, and extension. *Academy of Management Review* 27(2): 185–203.

Zahra, S.A. and George, G. (2002b) International entrepreneurship: The current status of the field and future research agenda. In *Strategic Entrepreneurship: Creating a New Mindset*, M.A. Hitt, R.D. Ireland, S.M. Camp and D. Sexton (eds) Oxford: Wiley, 255–288.

Zain, M. and Ng, S.I. (2006) The impacts of network relationships on SMEs' internationalization process. *Thunderbird International Business Review* 48(2): 183–205.

Zucchella, A. and Scabini, P. (2007) *International Entrepreneurship—Theoretical Foundations and Practices.* London: Palgrave.

4 Influence of region, country and subnational-region institutions on internationalization of multinational corporations

Wiboon Kittilaksanawong

1 Introduction

The decision of firms to expand operations into foreign markets is one of the most critical strategic decisions because it involves considerable resource commitments and risks. Traditional studies suggest that the industry structure primarily determines a firm's behavior and its long-term performance. The industry-based view thus argues that performance of firms varies due to different characteristics across industries. However, later studies reveal that a firm's internal resources and capabilities are a major source of its sustained competitive advantages. This resource-based view argues that performance of firms varies due to different resources and capabilities across business units of firms. These studies mostly focus on investigating performance of multiple-business firms and effects of industry, corporate, and business units within a single country.

When the firm's operational boundary extends beyond its home country to other countries, further studies find that differences in the institutions across countries mainly contribute to the variation in behavior and performance of multinational corporations (Chan et al., 2008; Kittilaksanawong, 2017; Makino et al., 2004). More recent studies extend the influence of such institutional differences from country-level to lower-level subnational and higher-level supranational regions. These studies reveal that institutional differences indeed appear within a country and determine behavior and performance of a firm's business units in different subnational regions (Chan et al., 2010; Ma et al., 2013). The studies emphasizing semiglobalization also find that formal institutions across supranational regions determine location choices and performance of a firm's internationalization (Arregle et al., 2013; Qian et al., 2010).

These recent studies provide abundant opportunities to discuss further their related problems and challenges. First, how do the institutions of the host country affect the variation of foreign affiliate performance? What are the effects of the level of institutional development of the host countries? Second, how do the institutions across subnational regions within host countries affect the variation of foreign affiliate performance? How do such institutions

interact with the industry, corporate parent, and home country? Third, how do the institutions across supranational regions affect the location choices and performance of multinational corporations? In the context of semiglobalization, what are the performance consequences of the intra- and inter-regional internationalization? The following sections discuss these problems and provide implications for academics, practitioners, and policymakers as the conclusion.

2 Country, industry, and firm effects

In the single country context, the performance of a business unit of firms is largely determined by the business unit itself, followed by the industry, and then by the corporate (McGahan & Porter, 1997). In the multinational context, a foreign affiliate is considered as both an integrated part of its parent firm in the home country and an independent local firm, competing with indigenous firms, while complying with local laws and regulations in the host country (Ghemawat, 2003). Similarly, the performance of foreign affiliates differs across industries in a host country and across countries in an industry. The performance of foreign affiliates is therefore influenced by the parent firm's firm-specific advantages and the host country's location-specific advantages.

Firm-specific advantages come from a firm's unique and valuable resources that create the competitive barriers to its indigenous rivals, and its capabilities to transfer these resources from the parent firm to the foreign affiliate (Kogut & Zander, 1993). Location-specific advantages come from the different factor costs related to capital, labor, and land across countries that make a firm's investment in one location more advantageous than in other locations (Dunning, 1988). Some forms of location-specific advantages may be beneficial to specific firms in a host country. The industry effect is thus country-bound because countries differ in the availability and costs of those production factors, and also in the country's capability. Such differences influence the production costs across industries within a country, and the competitive advantage of the indigenous firms within an industry (Porter, 1990).

3 Effects of national institutions

The strategy and performance of foreign affiliates is not only influenced by such location-specific advantages and country-bound industry effects, but also by institutions in the host and the home country (Kostova & Zaheer, 1999; Peng et al., 2008). Institutions refer to the humanly devised rules of the game in a society (North, 1990). Together with the employed technology, institutions affect transaction and production costs and hence the profitability of firms. Since institutions are highly path dependent and localized processes in a country, their effects on firm performance vary across countries (Makino et al., 2004). While foreign affiliates are pressured to conform to institutions in the host country, they are also obliged to sustain internal consistency by responding to the institutional pressures imposed by their parent firm in the home country (Kostova & Zaheer, 1999).

Host-country governments may provide investment incentives and create a favorable business environment to attract foreign direct investment. They may also implement rules and regulations to limit competition with local indigenous firms and restrict access to local resources, thereby constraining the profit potential of foreign affiliates. To enhance local legitimacy, foreign affiliates may imitate local institutionalized practices to increase the chance of survival and sustainable growth. However, such imitation may instead impede the efficient transfer of firm-specific advantages from the parent firm to its foreign affiliates (DiMaggio & Powell, 1983). The cultural and other institutional distances between the home and the host country may also be a barrier for foreign affiliates in building local business relationships, hence constraining their access to knowledge and other resources of local firms and government authorities (Kittilaksanawong, 2017).

In emerging economies, institutional rules are insufficient, poorly enforced, or even absent (Hitt et al., 2004; North, 1990). Foreign firms are more exposed to the risk of asset expropriation in these economies. They are likely to adopt inferior technology and suboptimal operations in response to underdeveloped property rights and uncertain contract enforcement (North, 1990). These firms have to protect possible unwanted dissemination of their intellectual and proprietary assets. Emerging economies usually lack reliable market information and intermediary institutions, hence increasing transaction costs of foreign firms operating in the market (Khanna & Palepu, 2000). Their operational efficiency tends to be compromised through engaging in local bureaucracies and corrupt transactions.

The performance of foreign affiliates in these economies varies considerably due to the lack of legitimate strategic choices and differences in their ability to cope with institutional idiosyncrasies (Chan et al., 2008). Such institutions may not be able to judge what constitutes legitimate organizational actions. Foreign affiliates are likely to pursue a wider range of strategic actions to circumvent uncertainties in their market transactions (North, 1990). Due to the lack of prior information about these strategic actions, their outcomes are difficult to predict with reasonable accuracy. However, foreign affiliates that have sufficient institutional ability are likely to achieve better performance (Henisz, 2003).

Better-developed institutions are more able to determine what constitutes socially accepted organizational actions (Henisz, 2003; Hitt et al., 2004). Firms are likely to follow legitimate practices with more confidence in the outcome and chance of survival (DiMaggio & Powell, 1983). As such organizational practices are more institutionalized and adopted, the ability of firms to deal with institutional idiosyncrasies becomes less important (Peng, 2003). Foreign affiliates are accordingly likely to experience less variation in their performance. However, when institutions are very well developed, firm-specific capabilities and resources become more important than such legitimacy and institutional ability (Makino et al., 2004). Variations in firm performance will become larger again because firm-level effects are more pronounced than such country-level effects (Peng, 2003).

4 Effects of subnational institutions

The performance of foreign affiliates varies greatly not only across countries with different levels of institutional development but also within countries, particularly within those that are large and that have a low level of institutional development (Chan et al., 2008; Chan et al., 2010; Ma et al., 2013). This effect comes from the embeddedness of foreign affiliates in the institutions of subnational regions within host countries. The governments in certain subnational regions may implement investment policies and offer preferential treatment to attract foreign investors. Subnational regions, particularly within a large emerging economy, may have distinct shared cultural values among society members, which affect the costs of doing business (Tung, 2008). These variations in formal and informal institutions thus create different opportunities and challenges that affect the performance of foreign affiliates.

While regions with well-established institutions can facilitate competitive capabilities of foreign affiliates, those with underdeveloped institutions are likely to pose challenges to their strategic actions and performance (McEvily & Zaheer, 1999). Emerging economies are likely to have greater subnational-region variations than advanced economies, leading to a wider difference in the performance of foreign affiliates (Chan et al., 2010). Governments in these economies are likely to make frequent changes in the policies and rules for investments and operations of foreign firms. As these economies increasingly move toward a market-oriented economy, their subnational-region governments are granted more autonomy and responsibility to develop the regional economy (Li et al., 2014). This process of economic transition creates significant disparity between subnational-region economic developments.

The variation of foreign affiliate performance across subnational regions within host countries is due not only to institutional differences across subnational regions within host countries but also to the interaction effects of industry, parent firm, and home country of foreign affiliates with institutions within subnational regions (Ma et al., 2013). In particular, due to increased decentralization in many emerging economies, subnational-region governments may promote the development of certain industries in a subnational region (Kittilaksanawong et al., 2013; Li et al., 2014). Firms in a subnational region may be more advantageous in certain industries because that region is relatively rich in some specific production factors, including high-quality human capital.

Subnational regions with highly educated talent may facilitate the transfer of firm-specific advantages such as technologies or brands from the parent firm to its foreign affiliates (Kogut & Zander, 1993). However, the cross-border transfer of firm-specific advantages may fail when the intellectual property protection in a subnational region is weak, or when the contractual enforcement law in the region is not effective. High concentration of upstream or downstream industry players helps foreign affiliates access local market knowledge and resources (Tan & Meyer, 2011). The transfer of firm-specific advantages will therefore be discounted in a subnational region that does not have a sufficient number of buyers and suppliers, hence influencing the performance of foreign affiliates embedded in the subnational region.

The home country of foreign affiliates in a subnational region of the host country affects their performance through institutional distance, historical ties, as well as geographic and linguistic distance (Ma et al., 2013). Large institutional distance requires that foreign affiliates heavily adapt their operational practices in the legal and social context within the subnational regions. The benefits from the foreign affiliate's experience in the home regulatory institutions may therefore be compromised. Foreign affiliates may not readily exploit their home-based institutional experience and thus require new organizational learning in culturally distant subnational regions. Historical ties between the home country and a subnational region in the host country may also make operations more efficient, while improving legitimacy (Makino & Tsang, 2011). Besides, geographic and linguistic distance also affects the costs of communication between the foreign affiliate and the parent firm.

5 Effects of regional economic institutions

Supranational regions with stronger economic institutions are likely to attract more foreign direct investment (Dunning, 1988). Governments in these regions are likely to have the policies to make capital investments in the region and to provide various support for economic and market growth. Capital investments shape demand for and supply of resources in the economy, which create positive spillovers for foreign investors and, in turn, influence their strategic behavior and performance (Arregle et al., 2013). These investments provide opportunities for firms to learn and develop new technology and knowledge in the region. Such capital investments also support production expansion, research and development, and human capital development of foreign investors.

Firms often expand abroad by exploiting knowledge and resources of their prior internationalization in the same regions and countries within these regions. Their geographic scope is largely determined by the ability to integrate their firm-specific advantages with the country's location-specific advantages (Rugman & Verbeke, 2005). Such country-specific investments allow firms to create related asset specificity that imposes increasing costs for redeploying assets related to such investments elsewhere in other countries. To increase opportunities to redeploy these assets, firms develop region-bound firm-specific advantages as they expand into more countries within the same region. These advantages allow firms to expand more successfully throughout a region (Arregle et al., 2013). Region-bound firm-specific advantages occur when the firm can integrate its several foreign affiliates within a region through low-cost linking investments in geographic proximity while successfully maintaining local responsiveness in countries within that region (Rugman & Verbeke, 2005).

Such supranational-region expansion critically involves cumulative and time-consuming experiential learning from the market and networks to overcome the liability of foreignness in countries within the region (Johanson & Vahlne, 2009). Successful knowledge development is built on the firm's absorptive capability that requires a degree of proximity between existing and new competences (Cohen & Levinthal, 1990). This sequential organizational learning allows firms gradually to accumulate knowledge and capabilities in proximate countries and use them in new emerging opportunities. Therefore, prior internationalization into a region allows geographically close foreign subsidiaries of a firm to access and share knowledge among them, and facilitates flows of knowledge and learning within firms (Arregle et al., 2013). Due to business networks, the prior foreign direct investment in a region allows the firm to learn and accumulate knowledge from these entries and reduce the liability of foreignness for the firm in its subsequent foreign direct investment in the same region.

Such a regional internationalization strategy therefore allows firms to focus more on markets within their home region, where they are likely to have better access to the country's location-specific advantages (Qian et al., 2010). Firms may also be able to combine these location-specific advantages with their own firm-specific advantages and realize higher performance. This intra-regional strategy reduces various costs relating to coordination, transportation, and knowledge-sharing across different countries. Supranational regions and countries are different in their resource availability and munificence. Inter-regional internationalization strategy may, however, provide firms with more expansive learning opportunities through building, integrating, or reconfiguring such different resources and capabilities (Lee & Makhija, 2009). Various economies may be obtained from applying such more generalized knowledge within host countries having similar institutional environments. Through inter-regional networks, firms may also enhance their operational control and efficiency (Lee & Makhija, 2009).

As firms engage in greater levels of inter-regional internationalization, they face challenges in optimally distributing their resources between the often less costly and more focused intra-regional investments and the continuing inter-regional investments. More focused investment in certain countries and regions may be necessary to mitigate costs and risks of inter-regional internationalization. Therefore, firms are likely to achieve the highest performance at moderate levels of inter-regional internationalization (Qian et al., 2010). As firms increase investments in both intra- and inter-regional markets, they may become overloaded with the increasing number of transactions and operational costs, which may negatively affect performance. Hence, firms are likely to attain better performance from a moderate level of total intra- and inter-regional internationalization (Qian et al., 2010).

6 Discussion and implications

Institutions at country, subnational-region, and supranational-region levels influence the strategy and performance of multinational companies and their foreign affiliates (Arregle et al., 2013; Chan et al., 2008; Chan et al., 2010; Kittilaksanawong, 2017; Ma et al., 2013; Makino et al., 2004; Peng et al., 2008; Qian et al., 2010). The country effects are as influential as industry effects, following affiliate and corporate effects (Makino et al., 2004). Further, the country effects tend to be more salient in institutionally underdeveloped countries, while corporate effects are likely to be more pronounced in developed countries (Chan et al., 2008). The performance of foreign affiliates also varies across subnational regions within a country (Chan et al., 2010). Further, the performance of these foreign affiliates within a subnational region also varies across industries, corporate parents, and home countries (Ma et al., 2013). These subnational regional differences are more influential to the performance of firms particularly in large emerging economies.

In emerging economies, foreign affiliates need to have the ability to handle and overcome their institutional idiosyncrasies (Henisz, 2003). Such ability involves developing direct and indirect ties with governments and other firms. As the institutional environments of subnational regions, particularly in large emerging economies, may vary considerably, firm-specific advantages are necessary, but not a sufficient condition for firms to succeed in these economies. Multinational companies need to formulate more distinct regional strategies for investments in these economies. These strategies should respond to heterogeneities at a subnational-region level instead of a country level. Managers of foreign affiliates must align characteristics of their home country, corporate parent, and industry with those of the subnational regions where their firm's operations are embedded to achieve higher performance.

Governments in emerging economies should advance the process of institutional development, and establish trading agreements and investment regulations to attract inward foreign direct investment, known to increase productivity and create new jobs. Policymakers should be able to identify which subnational regions require specific policies and government investments to attract foreign investors. They should consider whether to consolidate certain industries in one subnational region or distribute them across subnational regions. They should also identify the types of multinational companies that potentially benefit from institutions in each subnational region. Subnational regional governments need to align industry policies with location-specific advantages of the regions (Kittilaksanawong et al., 2013). They should also carefully develop the institutional relationships between the subnational regions and the home governments of multinational companies.

The strategy and performance of foreign affiliates varies within intra- and inter-regional countries (Arregle et al., 2013; Qian et al., 2010). Multinational companies should consider institutional environments at the regional level in their investment decisions. They should view the institutional environments of a country in relation to those of other countries in the same or different regions in their investment decisions. They should capitalize on the coordination and learning benefits to develop region-bound, firm-specific advantages from their investments within a region as a platform for subsequent investments in countries within this region (Arregle et al., 2013). While inter-regional investments may deliver a positive return, these investments should be kept at a low to moderate level (Qian et al., 2010). Particularly, multinational companies that pursue a more moderate degree of total intra- and inter-regional internationalization are likely to achieve higher returns. Policy-makers in the region should improve capital availability, one of the most important regional characteristics, while considering regional integration to increase inflows of foreign direct investment in the region.

Acknowledgment

This work was supported by JSPS KAKENHI grant number 15K03694.

References

Arregle, J.L., Miller, T.L., Hitt, M.A. and Beamish, P.W. (2013) Do regions matter? An integrated institutional and semiglobalization perspective on the internationalization of MNEs. *Strategic Management Journal* 34(8): 910–934.

Chan, C.M., Isobe, T. and Makino, S. (2008) Which country matters? Institutional development and foreign affiliate performance. *Strategic Management Journal* 29(11): 1179–1205.

Chan, C.M, Makino, S. and Isobe, T. (2010) Does subnational region matter? Foreign affiliate performance in the United States and China. *Strategic Management Journal* 31(11): 1226–1243.

Cohen, W.M. and Levinthal, D.A. (1990) Absorptive capacity: A new perspective on learning and innovation. *Administrative Science Quarterly* 35: 128–152.

DiMaggio, P.J. and Powell, W.W. (1983) The iron cage revisited: Institutional isomorphism and collective rationality in organizational fields. *American Sociological Review* 48(2): 147–160.

Dunning, J.H. (1988) *Explaining International Production*. London: Allen & Unwin.

Ghemawat, P. (2003) Semiglobalization and international business strategy. *Journal of International Business Studies* 34(2): 138–152.

Henisz, W.J. (2003) The power of the Buckley and Casson thesis: The ability to manage institutional idiosyncrasies. *Journal of International Business Studies* 34(2): 173–184.

Hitt, M.A., Ahlstrom, D., Dacin, M.T., Levitas, E. and Svobodina, L. (2004) The institutional effects on strategic alliance partner selection in transition economies: China vs. Russia. *Organization Science* 15(2): 173–185.

Johanson, J. and Vahlne, J.E. (2009) The Uppsala internationalization process model revisited: From liability of foreignness to liability of outsidership. *Journal of International Business Studies* 40(9): 1411–1431.

Khanna, T. and Palepu, K. (2000) The future of business groups in emerging markets: Long-run evidence from Chile. *Academy of Management Journal* 43(3): 268–285.

Kittilaksanawong, W. (2017) Institutional distances, resources and entry strategies: Evidence from newly-industrialized economy firms. *International Journal of Emerging Market* (forthcoming).

Kittilaksanawong, W., Chen, X.D. and Duan, C.Q. (2013) What drives the strategic alliance formation of transition-economy small and medium-sized enterprises? The moderating role of intermediary organizations. In *Multinationals and Global Consumers: Tension, Potential and Competition*, T. Chan and G. Cui (eds), Basingstoke: Palgrave Macmillan, 40–57.

Kogut, B. and Zander, U. (1993) Knowledge of the firm and the evolutionary theory of the multinational corporation. *Journal of International Business Studies* 24(4): 625–645.

Kostova, T. and Zaheer, S. (1999) Organizational legitimacy under conditions of complexity: The case of the multinational enterprise. *Academy of Management Review* 24(1): 64–81.

Lee, S.H. and Makhija, M. (2009) Flexibility in internationalization: Is it valuable during an economic crisis? *Strategic Management Journal* 30(5): 537–555.

Li, M., Cui, L. and Lu, J. (2014) Varieties in state capitalism: Outward FDI strategies of central and local state owned enterprises from emerging economy countries. *Journal of International Business Studies* 45(8): 980–1004.

Ma, X., Tong, T.W. and Fitza, M. (2013) How much does subnational region matter to foreign subsidiary performance? Evidence from Fortune Global 500 corporations' investment in China. *Journal of International Business Studies* 44(1): 66–87.

Makino, S., Isobe, T. and Chan, C.M. (2004) Does country matter? *Strategic Management Journal* 25(10): 1027–1043.

Makino, S. and Tsang, E.W. (2011) Historical ties and foreign direct investment: An exploratory study. *Journal of International Business Studies* 42(4): 545–557.

McEvily, B. and Zaheer, A. (1999) Bridging ties: A source of firm heterogeneity in competitive capabilities. *Strategic Management Journal* 20(12): 1133–1156.

McGahan, A.M and Porter, M.E. (1997) How much does industry matter, really? *Strategic Management Journal* 18(S1): 15–30.

North, D.C. (1990) *Institutions, Institutional Change and Economic Performance.* New York: Cambridge University Press.

Peng, M.W. (2003) Institutional transitions and strategic choices. *Academy of Management Review* 28(2): 275–286.

Peng, M.W., Wang, D.Y.L. and Jiang, Y. (2008) An institution-based view of international business strategy: A focus on emerging economies. *Journal of International Business Studies* 39(5): 920–936.

Porter, M.E. (1990) *The Competitive Advantage of Nations.* New York: Free Press.

Qian, G., Khoury, T.A., Peng, M.W. and Qian, Z. (2010) The performance implications of intra- and inter-regional geographic diversification. *Strategic Management Journal* 31(9): 1018–1030.

Rugman, A.M. and Verbeke, A. (2005) Towards a theory of regional multinationals: A transaction cost economics approach. *Management International Review* 45(1): 5–17.

Tan, D. and Meyer, K.E. (2011) Country-of-origin and industry FDI agglomeration of foreign investors in an emerging economy. *Journal of International Business Studies* 42(4): 502–520.

Tung, R.L. (2008) The cross-cultural research imperative: The need to balance cross-national and intra-national diversity. *Journal of International Business Studies* 39(1): 41–46.

5 Geoeconomic spillovers

Are Indian states interconnected in promoting state–business relations? An empirical analysis

Krishna Chaitanya Vadlamannati, Artur Tamazian and Arusha Cooray

1 Introduction

This chapter examines the extent to which state–business relations (SBRs) in one state are influenced by changes in SBRs in other states in India. India offers an interesting case study because of the withdrawal of controls exerted by the central government on investment regulations forcing state governments to become competitive to attract investment. Promoting effective SBRs is key if the state intends to attract foreign and private investment. Therefore, promoting effective SBRs to attract investment and learning by imitating states in which SBRs have yielded significant benefits might explain policy diffusion in SBRs across Indian states. Moreover, in a complex federal democracy such as India, state-level politics are dominated by state-specific issues rather than national issues, which places economic development (such as creating job opportunities) of a state as the focus of a potential electorate. In a country where state capacity is weaker, and where institutional quality varies significantly by state, the question of whether effective SBRs in other states can explain observed variations in SBRs in a particular state, remains open for debate and will hence be explored here.

Why are SBRs important? According to Maxfield and Schneider (1997), effective SBRs capture the formal active interaction and mutual trust between the state and business sector. Accordingly, the basic features of effective SBRs are transparency in the flow of accurate information on both sides, reciprocity of the state, credibility of the state on the delivery of promises, and mutual trust between both sides. Cali and Sen (2011) show that effective SBRs are important for economic growth because they not only help attract investment, but also increase the productivity of investments by eliminating investment policy uncertainties, reducing transactions and coordination costs, thereby minimizing corruption and rent-seeking behavior, and enhancing property rights protection. Thus, effective SBRs have far-reaching social implications as they are not only growth enhancing through attracting investment, but also create job opportunities which form huge political capital for incumbent politicians. In particular, even if investment does not flow in as a result of a state's efforts to improve SBRs, if politicians believe that it does, then this alone could result in diffusion of policies to promote effective SBRs among states. The present study aims to investigate whether there exists diffusion in policies to promote effective SBRs among states in India. To the best of our knowledge, no previous study has attempted to examine the extent of policy diffusion to promote effective SBRs, be it using cross-country or intra-country analysis. This is a gap in the literature that the present study aims to fill.

Spatial econometrics have been used in the existing literature to study in general the extent of competition and policy diffusion in the context of broader economic policy reforms, taxes, labor standards and environmental standards, among others. Focusing on tax competition, Davies, Egger and Egger (2003), Devereux, Lockwood and Redoano (2008), Davies and Voget (2008), Overesch and Rinke (2008), Reulier and Rocaboy (2009) and Klemm and van Parys (2009) find that a fall in the tax rate in one developed country leads to lower tax rates in other developed countries to attract foreign direct investment (FDI).

To the best of our knowledge no study has examined plausible policy diffusion among countries to promote SBRs. Our chapter attempts to fill this gap by specifically focusing on major industrial states in India to examine this question. While Cali, Mitra and Purohit (2011) and Cali and Sen (2011) examine the impact of effective SBRs on economic growth among Indian states, they do not test for the existence of strategic interaction in SBRs, i.e. whether changes in policies to promote SBRs in one state depend on those elsewhere. Using panel data on the SBRs index constructed by Cali and Sen (2011) for 16 Indian states during the 1985–2008 period, we find that improved SBRs in one state are positively correlated with the improvement in SBRs in other states. Furthermore, we find this interdependence to be strong during the post-reform period (i.e. in the post-1990 years). We interpret these results as direct evidence of strategic interstate interactions in promoting effective SBRs. This is because economic reforms during this period have been driven by states due to the withdrawal of controls exercised by the central government in areas related to investment regulations.[1] Since there is a noticeable upward trend in aggregate SBRs over the sample period across the states, we consider this as evidence in favor of policy diffusion which is a result of inter-state competition to improve the prevailing investment climate in respective states and also learning by imitating from other states, especially from the early movers, which have benefited from promoting effective SBRs.

The rest of the chapter is structured as follows. Section 2 describes the data and methods adopted. Section 3 discusses the results and section 4 concludes.

2 Empirical methodology and data

We make use of panel data set across 16 Indian states (see appendix Table 5.3) during the 1985–2008 period (24 years), with the following specification:

2.1 Estimation specification

The baseline specification estimates the SBRs in state *i* in year *t* as a function of a set of exogenous variables Z_{it}:

$$SBR_{it} = \phi_i + \beta Z_{it} + \omega_{it}(1)$$

Where ϕ_i is the state-specific constant and ω_{it} is the error term. The control variables are drawn from the literature on determinants of SBRs and are described below. We also include a lagged dependent variable as it is theoretically plausible that past decisions taken to improve SBRs can influence SBRs in the current period. We thus estimate our models with and without a lagged dependent variable. In line with the spatial econometrics literature, we introduce the prevailing SBRs in other states in year *t* to this baseline model, which is the spatial lag:

$$SBR_{it} = \phi i + \rho \sum_{j \neq i} \varpi_{jit} SBR_{it} + \beta Z_{it} + \nu_i + \eta_i + \omega_{it}(2)$$

Where:

$$\sum_{j \neq i} \varpi_{jit} SBR_{it}$$

is the spatial lag, i.e. the weighted average of SBRs prevailing in other states. For weights, following Davies and Vadlamannati (2011), we utilize:

$$\omega_{i,j,t} = 1 dist_{i,j,t} \sum_{k \neq i} 1 dist_{i,k,t}$$

Note that we use geographic distance in kilometers from state *i* as weights here so that distant states are given smaller weights. Hence, we use 'inverse geographic distance,' not geographic distance.[2] It is, however, important to note that the sum of the weights across the other states for state *i* observation will equal one. This weighting scheme imposes the assumption that states with lower geographic distance receive higher weights. The rationale for using inverse geographic distance as the weight is twofold. First, it is plausible that state *i* pays more attention to what is taking place in the nearby or neighboring states rather than states that are farther away, capturing the diffusion effect of 'imitation.' Second, when the goal of a state is to improve the investment climate to attract investment, this will depend on the elasticity of investments to a given state's policies. Thus, if neighboring state *j* is already attractive for investment relative to state *k* either due to large market size or complementary labor, transport options, and local culture, then a change in neighboring state *j*'s

SBR policies has a larger impact on the allocation of investment than a comparable change in state *k*. This, in turn, would make state *i* more responsive to neighboring state *j*'s SBR policies than to state *k*'s, a difference that is reflected in equation (2) by giving a greater weight to neighboring state *j*. In addition to this, the literature shows that closer countries are more attractive for trade and investment (see Blonigen, 2005), which would imply a greater sensitivity on the part of state *i* to the SBR policies of a neighboring state. In addition, previous literature applying spatial econometrics has also used inverse geographic distance as a weight[3] (see Blonigen et al., 2008; Blonigen et al., 2007; Head & Mayer, 2004). ν_i denotes state-fixed effects to control for unobserved state-specific heterogeneity, η_t denotes time-specific dummies in the panel data set, and ω_{it} is the error term. The models are estimated using the pooled ordinary least squares (OLS) fixed effects (FE) method including state-specific and time-specific dummies with robust standard errors, a method that is robust to heteroskedasticity and serial correlation (Wiggins, 1999). Note that the Hausman (1978) test favors fixed effects over random effects models. We also use the Newey–West method as a robustness check which allows us to compute an AR1 process for autocorrelation (Newey & West, 1987).

2.2 Data

For the dependent variable, we make use of the comprehensive State-Business Relations (SBRs) index constructed by Cali and Sen (2011), based on the pattern outlaid by Cali, Mitra and Purohit (2011), which measures state–business relations in each Indian state *i* in financial year *t* on the dimensions of transparency, reciprocity, credibility, and mutual trust between the state and the industry. In this chapter, we consider the comprehensive SBRs index constructed by Cali and Sen (2011), based on the pattern outlaid by Cali, Mitra and Purohit (2011). The SBRs index data are available on a yearly basis (over the 1985–2008 period) for about 16 industrial states in India. The SBRs index is a comprehensive measure comprising four components capturing:

- Role of the private sector: consists of active presence of business associations; quality of organization structure—whether the organization has a website or not, intensity of the organization's activities, how frequently the websites are updated.
- Role of the public sector: consists of the presence of participating state institutions such as investment promotion agencies, financial development, infrastructure development and tourism development corporations; state government spending on industry development.
- Interaction between states and businesses: includes Besley and Burgess's (2004) labor regulation index capturing the amendments made by respective state governments to the Industrial Disputes Act 1947, reflecting either pro-employer or pro-worker regulations; taxes collected by state governments on stamp duties.

- Mechanisms to avoid collusive behaviors: considers gross output of firms belonging to de-licensed industries as a proportion of total industrial gross domestic product (GDP);[4] transparency in the activities of private sector business associations, measuring the frequency of the publication of annual reports and distribution to its members.

These four components roughly comprise 12 objective indicators. Each variable in the respective components was normalized to one, where higher values of the original variable indicated superior SBRs. These 12 variables were then averaged to determine each of the four components. The four components are then averaged to derive the main SBR index for each of the 16 states.[5] The final index is ranked on a scale of zero (no effective SBRs) to one (effective SBRs).

The vector of control variables includes other potential determinants of SBRs in state i during year t, which we try to obtain from the limited literature on this subject. Since this is the first such study employing spatial estimation of SBRs in India, we follow Cali and Sen (2011) and Cali, Mitra and Purohit (2011) on the determinants of SBRs. Accordingly, the models control for development by including state per capita income (logged) in Indian rupees (in 1999–2000 constant prices), obtained from the Reserve Bank of India's macroeconomic data set.[6] We also include the total population (logged) of the respective states in the absence of data on the labor force. To measure industrialization, we include industry value added in a state's GDP, computed from the Reserve Bank of India's macroeconomic data set. Finally, following Besley and Burgess (2000), we use dummy variables to capture the number of years a political party was in power in each state (i.e. state-specific) in year t. Finally, we also include a dummy variable for 'president's rule' imposed upon the state to capture political uncertainty.[7]

2.3 Endogeneity concerns

The difficulty with the spatial lag is that if SBRs in state i depend on those in state j, and vice versa, the spatial lag is then endogenous. In order to address this endogeneity, we utilize two-stage least squares instrumental variable (2SLS-IV) estimation. Following the standard spatial econometric procedure suggested by the literature, for the instruments we use:

$$\sum_{j \neq i} \varpi_{jit} Z_{jt}$$

i.e. the weighted average of the other states' economic and political variables. However, instead of including all variables, we include only two variables—namely, industry share in GDP and a president's rule dummy variable as described above. The intuition behind using only these two variables is twofold. First, for a given state *j*, its industry share value added and president's rule variables directly impact its SBR policies but are not dependent on those in state *i*. On the other hand, income levels of other states and political parties in other states can influence SBRs in the state in question. For instance, a political party in power in state *i* can follow similar policies introduced by the same party that is in power in state *j*, violating instrument exclusion criteria. Keeping this in mind, we exclude income levels and political variables of other states and retain only industry share in GDP and president's rule in other states (weighted by inverse geographic distance, excluding state *i*) as instruments. Both these variables are correlated with the endogenous variable (as shown from the joint F-statistic from the first stage analysis) but are themselves exogenous, making them valid instruments.

The validity of the selected instruments depends on two conditions. The first is instrument relevance, i.e. they must be correlated with the explanatory variable in question. Bound, Jaeger and Baker (1995) suggest examining the joint F-statistic on the excluded instruments in the first-stage regression. The selected instruments would be relevant when the first-stage regression model's joint F-statistics meet the thumb rule threshold of being above ten (Staiger & Stock, 1997). The more powerful test of a Kleibergen-Paap LM statistic is also used (Kleibergen & Paap, 2006). A Kleibergen-Paap LM statistic above the critical value (10% maximum test size) indicates the rejection of weak instruments. The Hansen J-test is employed to check whether the selected instruments satisfy the exclusion restriction (results provided at the end of the models estimated using 2SLS-IV method).

3 Empirical results

3.1 Baseline results

We present the baseline results in Table 5.1. A summary of the data statistics is presented in appendix Table 5.4. While Table 5.2 focuses exclusively on the post-reform period (post-1990), Table 5.3 examines the results using an alternative weighting matrix in constructing the spatial lag variable. As seen in column (1) of Table 5.1, we capture the results without including the spatial lag in order to check the comparison between our results and other studies on determinants of SBRs. As expected, we find that income levels of the state, industrialization, and state population are associated with effective SBRs after controlling for state-specific fixed effects. On the contrary, we do not find any political variables, other than Indian National Congress (INC) ruling years, that have an influence on SBRs. As expected, political instability has a negative effect on SBRs, albeit being statistically insignificant.

In column (2), we report the same results with the lagged dependent variable. After controlling for the lagged dependent variable, we find that only income levels of the state are positive and significantly different from zero at the 1% level.

In column (3), which forms our main specification, we include the SBRs spatial lag term. Here, we find a positive and significant spatial lag, which is significantly different from zero at the 1% level. To interpret the coefficient on this, a standard deviation increase in the SBRs index of all other states would increase the SBRs index in state *i* by roughly 0.12 percentage points, which is about 131% of the standard deviation of the SBRs index.

As seen in column (4) of Table 5.1, the positive significant effects of the SBRs spatial lag remains robust to the inclusion of a lagged dependent variable. The substantive effect of the spatial lag drops from 0.12 to 0.10 percentage points after the inclusion of the lagged dependent variable. Since the spatial lag is positive, this can be interpreted as evidence of strategic complementarity consistent with the arguments made in section 2. Note that although this is consistent with competition among states to promote effective SBRs to attract investment, it does not rule out the possibility of other ways in which the SBRs in one state can depend on those elsewhere. In addition to yardstick competition arguments presented in section 2, the coefficient on the spatial lag could also capture coordination among states, especially those states that are aligned to the center, to promote SBRs rather than competition, that is, a mutual strengthening of SBRs across borders. Nevertheless, since on average SBRs across states improved over the study period, we interpret our results as suggestive of policy diffusion with the intention to promote SBRs in their respective states.

In column (5), we replicate the baseline regressions with 2SLS-IV estimations. As one can see, the positive significant effects of the spatial lag term remain robust in the IV estimations. In fact, the substantive effects suggest that a standard deviation increase in the SBRs spatial lag is now associated with an increase in the SBRs index in state *i* by roughly 0.10 percentage points, which is about 97% of the standard deviation of the SBR index. After controlling for the lagged dependent variable in column (6), the substantive effect of the SBRs spatial lag falls to 0.07 percentage points. The significant positive effects of the spatial lag term can indeed be interpreted as evidence of strategic complementarity. While strategic complementarity can theoretically result in a race to the bottom, since there is an upward trend in the SBRs index, we interpret the result as evidence in favor of policy diffusion among states to improve their investment climate. Columns (5) and (6) of Table 5.1 also capture the results of the endogeneity tests—the joint F-statistic and Kleibergen-Paap LM statistic reject the null hypothesis. The joint F-statistic from the first stage in both columns (5) and (6) reject the null hypothesis that the instruments selected are not relevant. We obtain higher joint F-statistics (Kleibergen-Paap LM statistic) of 10.65 and 12.48 (21.23 and 18.35, respectively), which are significantly different from zero at the 1% level for the models reported in columns (5) and (6). Finally, the Hansen J-statistic (with p-values of 0.25 and 0.66) shows that the null hypothesis of exogeneity cannot be rejected at the conventional level of significance.

Table 5.1 Baseline results (dependent variable: SBRs index)

	(1) SBRs index OLS-FE	*(2) SBRs index OLS-FE*	*(3) SBRs index OLS-FE*	*(4) SBRs index OLS-FE*	*(5) SBRs index 2SLS-IV*	*(6) SBRs index 2SLS-IV*
Lagged dependent variable		0.745***		0.140***		0.360***
		(0.0406)		(0.0385)		(0.0619)
SBRs index—spatial lag			0.620***	0.540***	0.461***	0.344***
			(0.0160)	(0.0190)	(0.0556)	(0.0542)
State per capita GDP (log)	0.0300	0.0255**	0.00569	0.00865**	0.0119**	0.0148***
	(0.0195)	(0.0108)	(0.00491)	(0.00388)	(0.00598)	(0.00467)
Population (log)	0.232**	0.0639	-0.144***	-0.126***	-0.0474	-0.0569*
	(0.0974)	(0.0556)	(0.0261)	(0.0230)	(0.0427)	(0.0320)
Industry share in state GDP	0.00247***	0.000706*	-0.00030**	-0.00025**	0.000414	9.66e-05
	(0.000739)	(0.000414)	(0.000139)	(0.000117)	(0.000340)	(0.000219)
INC ruling years	0.0203***	-0.00318	0.00360**	0.000991	0.00791***	-0.000522
	(0.00612)	(0.00418)	(0.00145)	(0.00134)	(0.00255)	(0.00187)
Bharatiya Janata Party (BJP) ruling years	-0.00543	-0.00501	0.000356	6.20e-05	-0.00113	-0.00178
	(0.00740)	(0.00445)	(0.00159)	(0.00145)	(0.00200)	(0.00193)
Left Front ruling years	0.00859	0.000706	0.00369	0.00121	0.00495	0.00103

	(1) SBRs index OLS-FE	*(2) SBRs index OLS-FE*	*(3) SBRs index OLS-FE*	*(4) SBRs index OLS-FE*	*(5) SBRs index 2SLS-IV*	*(6) SBRs index 2SLS-IV*
	(0.0115)	(0.00779)	(0.00433)	(0.00414)	(0.00469)	(0.00437)
Regional parties ruling years	-0.00876	-0.00114	0.00239	0.00249*	-0.000484	0.00118
	(0.00629)	(0.00411)	(0.00161)	(0.00149)	(0.00240)	(0.00193)
Political instability	-0.0108	0.00314	0.00245	0.00212	-0.000944	0.00249
	(0.00949)	(0.00622)	(0.00326)	(0.00272)	(0.00389)	(0.00267)
R-squared (within)	0.7318	0.8981	0.9821	0.9864	0.9655	0.9748
State-specific dummies	YES	YES	YES	YES	YES	YES
Time-specific dummies	YES	YES	YES	YES	YES	YES
Joint F-statistics					10.65***	12.48***
Kleibergen-Paap rk LM statistic					21.23***	18.35***
Hansen J-statistics (p-value)					0.2499	0.6589
Number of states	16	16	16	16	16	16
Total observations	357	342	357	342	357	342

Robust standard errors in parentheses *** $p<0.01$, ** $p<0.05$, * $p<0.1$

Table 5.2 Post-1990 economic reforms period results (dependent variable: SBRs index)

	(1) SBRs index OLS-FE	*(2) SBRs index OLS-FE*	*(3) SBRs index OLS-FE*	*(4) SBRs index OLS-FE*	*(5) SBRs index 2SLS-IV*	*(6) SBRs index 2SLS-IV*
Lagged dependent variable		0.732***		0.0893***		0.325***
		(0.0477)		(0.0306)		(0.0758)
SBRs index—spatial lag			0.619***	0.580***	0.506***	0.367***
			(0.0110)	(0.0182)	(0.0568)	(0.0678)
State per capita GDP (log)	0.0472*	0.0348**	-0.000967	0.000569	0.00784	0.0131*
	(0.0262)	(0.0171)	(0.00624)	(0.00631)	(0.00628)	(0.00790)
Population (log)	0.111	0.0587	-0.138***	-0.128***	-0.0921***	-0.0596
	(0.123)	(0.0790)	(0.0249)	(0.0248)	(0.0342)	(0.0401)
Industry share in state GDP	0.00193**	0.000658	-9.20e-05	-0.000119	0.000277	0.000166
	(0.000801)	(0.000529)	(0.000121)	(0.000119)	(0.000300)	(0.000249)
INC ruling years	0.00679	-0.00276	0.00105	0.000253	0.00210	-0.000852
	(0.00612)	(0.00471)	(0.00146)	(0.00149)	(0.00181)	(0.00208)
BJP ruling years	-0.0155**	-0.00456	0.000592	0.000907	-0.00235	-0.00110
	(0.00748)	(0.00470)	(0.00165)	(0.00156)	(0.00216)	(0.00197)
Left Front ruling years	-0.00529	3.23e-05	0.00357	0.00366	0.00195	0.00233
	(0.0151)	(0.00966)	(0.00424)	(0.00439)	(0.00428)	(0.00498)

	(1) *SBRs index OLS-FE*	(2) *SBRs index OLS-FE*	(3) *SBRs index OLS-FE*	(4) *SBRs index OLS-FE*	(5) *SBRs index 2SLS-IV*	(6) *SBRs index 2SLS-IV*
Regional parties ruling years	0.00179	-0.000937	0.00107	0.000780	0.00120	0.000150
	(0.00636)	(0.00485)	(0.00162)	(0.00163)	(0.00189)	(0.00226)
Political instability	-0.0103	-0.00508	0.00428	0.00399	0.00162	0.000664
	(0.00925)	(0.00656)	(0.00318)	(0.00288)	(0.00358)	(0.00304)
R-squared (within)	0.7274	0.8700	0.9845	0.9856	0.9760	0.9701
State-specific dummies	YES	YES	YES	YES	YES	YES
Time-specific dummies	YES	YES	YES	YES	YES	YES
Joint F-statistics					10.13***	9.60***
Kleibergen-Paap rk LM statistic					18.12***	12.51***
Hansen J-statistics (p-value)					0.1482	0.5065
Number of states	16	16	16	16	16	16
Total observations	270	270	270	270	270	270

Robust standard errors in parentheses *** $p<0.01$, ** $p<0.05$, * $p<0.1$

3.2 Results for the post-reform period

In Table 5.2, we drop the years prior to 1991 to capture the economic reform period exclusively. We do this to investigate whether the extent of policy diffusion in SBRs differs between post-reform years and the years prior to reform. One aspect of doing this is that most of the key reform measures were initiated in the early 1990s, including the decentralization of economic decision making to the states allowing states to frame their independent investment policies, which is reflected in the years post-1990. In columns (1) and (2), we report the baseline results without the spatial lag term. As expected, the income levels of the state and industrialization are the main drivers in promoting effective SBRs in the post-reform years. In columns (3) and (4), we find that the SBRs spatial lag term is positive and significantly different from zero at the 1% level. After controlling for the lagged dependent variable, however, the effects of the SBRs spatial lag appear to be marginally higher than in the baseline models reported in Table 5.1. In columns (5) and (6), which are estimated using the 2SLS-IV method, we find the positive effect of the SBRs spatial lag remains intact, and significantly different from zero at the 1% level. After controlling for the lagged dependent variable and endogeneity, the substantive effects of the SBRs spatial lag are marginally higher than those reported in Table 5.1 (which were estimated using all the years in the sample). The effect of the SBRs spatial lag increases from 0.54% reported in Table 5.1, to 0.58%, for instance, in the models estimated using the post-reform years. Note that the endogeneity test results, shown in columns (5) and (6) of Table 5.2, suggest that problems associated with weak instruments have been avoided.

Two points are worth noting in the results reported in Tables 5.1 and 5.2. First, the results suggest that the positive effect of the spatial lag is robust, irrespective of changes in the sample years. This suggests that policy diffusion in promoting SBRs in their respective states was evident from 1985 onwards. The positive effects, however, are slightly higher in the post-reform period after controlling for endogeneity, meaning that the diffusion of policies between states became almost certain during the post-1990 years. Second, in both tables, the size of the coefficient for the SBRs spatial lag variable under the 2SLS-IV estimation method is marginally lower than in the OLS regressions, i.e. the effects are lower when controlling for the potential feedback effect of the SBRs index on the spatial lag variable.

3.3 Results with alternative weights

In addition to the baseline results, we check our results by using alternative weights, wherein we replace distance with a contiguity dummy based on borders shared with other states. This measure basically captures the 'neighborhood effect' and does not consider the location of j to states other than i. Moreover, this measure assumes, for example, that policy diffusion is greater for Bihar from West Bengal than it is from Punjab (this may or may not hold in practice). Using the contiguity measure as a weight, we find the results to be robust, in which we find a strong positive spatial lag of SBRs, which is significantly different from zero at the 1% level. The results also hold when including a lagged dependent variable and estimating the sample for only post-reform periods.[8]

Second, we use:

$$\varpi_{ijt} = \frac{StateGDP_{jt}}{\sum_{k \neq i} StateGDP_{kt}}$$

as a weight, where $StateGDP_{jt}$ is the state-level GDP measured in Indian rupees (in 1999–2000 constant prices). The rationale for using this variable is that GDP (a proxy for market size) is more attractive for investment in states with potentially higher market size (Blonigen et al., 2007; Carr et al., 2001; Coughlin et al., 1991). Our results show that the positive effects of the SBRs spatial lag (weighted with state GDP) remain robust, irrespective of the inclusion of the lagged dependent variable. The 2SLS-IV results also lead to the same conclusion. The SBRs spatial lag shows a positive sign, which is significantly different from zero at the 1% level. The general results are not quantitatively different from those reported in the baseline models in Table 5.1.

Third, we also use per capita GDP as an alternative weighting scheme:

$$\varpi_{ijt} = \frac{StatepercapitaGDP_{jt}}{\sum_{k \neq i} StatepercapitaGDP_{kt}}$$

It should, however, be noted that when using state-level GDP and state-level per capita GDP as alternative weights, we replace the time dummies with a time trend as the spatial lag weighted by these aforementioned variables varies slowly by time and hence is strongly correlated with the time dummies. For example, when moving from the lag for the state Haryana to that of Gujarat, we essentially take the latter's GDP-weighted SBRs out of the spatial lag and replace it with Haryana's. We include a time trend to capture other factors that are not accounted for in the model, such as efficiency gains through technological advancement, as these usually grow over time and can be expected to have a positive correlation with SBRs (Cali & Sen, 2011). The results basically remain unchanged, although the magnitude of the coefficients varies marginally.[9]

These results, which remain robust when using alternative weights (other than geographic distance), provide a consistent picture that is suggestive of strategic complementarity. It clearly suggests that the results do not lend support only for the argument of learning by imitation (i.e. yardstick competition). In other words, if yardstick competition were the only driving force behind our results, then one might expect significant spatial lags for the geographic distance weights but not necessarily elsewhere. These results are not shown due to brevity but are made available in the online appendix.[10] Thus, our results appear to be robust, not only for using alternative sample years, but also for using alternative weights.

3.4 Further checks on robustness

Finally, the baseline specifications are modified to explore the robustness of the main findings. We examine the robustness of our key results in the following way. First, we use an alternative estimation technique to address endogeneity concerns. We therefore replace the 2SLS-IV estimation technique with the Generalized Method of Moments (GMM) estimation technique applied by Arellano and Bond (1991), Arellano and Bover (1995) and Blundell and Bond (1998). The results are based on the two-step estimator implemented by Roodman (2009) in Stata 11. We apply the Sargan–Hansen test for instrument validity, and the Arellano–Bond test for second-order autocorrelation. We treat the lagged dependent variable and our measure of the SBRs spatial lag as endogenous, and all other variables as exogenous. Following the standard spatial econometric procedure, we use the instruments illustrated in section 3.3 and lag them by four years.[11] As before, we include state-specific time dummies and, following Roodman (2009), we collapse the instruments matrix to minimize the number of instruments in the GMM regressions. The results remain mostly unchanged, and the SBRs spatial lag is positive and significantly different from zero at the 1% level. Note the GMM results also remain robust when estimating our sample for the post-reform period.

Second, we utilize a balanced sample by dropping the state of Uttarakhand from our sample. The state of Uttarakhand was carved out from the state of Uttar Pradesh in 2000, thus the data on controls for the 1980s and 1990s are absent, making our sample an unbalanced panel. The results once again do not differ from the baseline models in Table 5.1.

Third, we also control for a center-state alignment by including a dummy variable that is coded as one if the chief minister of the state's party belongs to the same party as that governing at the center (or the leading party of a coalition government at the center from which the prime minister comes) and zero otherwise. We control for the dummy because it is plausible that the central government would like to bring some policy changes at the state level but is hampered by the federal structure. In such cases, the desired policies can be first implemented in those states in which it is in power. On the other hand, if states are in competition to attract investment, then such competition might ensure that other states follow suit in implementing the policy changes introduced by the center in its aligned states. Our results show that after controlling for center-state alignment, the positive spatial lag remains robust.

Fourth, we include a spatial lag of state per capita GDP (weighted by inverse distance) into the models to capture potential omitted variable bias in our model. It is likely that economic development in neighboring states might influence the state in question to promote effective SBRs with the intent to attract investment. Also, given the positive correlation between SBRs and economic development, it might be that our spatial lag of SBRs may be picking up the traditional positive association between development levels of other states. Including the spatial lag of per capita GDP of other states does not alter our main findings. The positive significant effect of the spatial lag variable remains intact even after controlling for a lagged dependent variable, addressing endogeneity and a smaller sample including the post-reforms period.

Finally, we considered a set of specifications that included the weighted average of other states' control variables as control variables, i.e. a *Durbin spatial model*:

$$SBR_{it} = \phi_i + \rho \sum_{j \neq i} \varpi_{jit} SBR_{it} + \beta Z_{it} + \sum_{j \neq i} \varpi_{jit} \beta_2 Z_{it} + \nu_i + \eta_t + \omega_{it}$$

Note that in this case, we were not able to estimate an instrumental variable estimator because we include all of the weighted sum control variables as controls in the model thus leaving us with no excluded instruments. In any case, when doing so, the weighted average of other states' controls was rarely significant (with the exception of population). Nevertheless, the results for the spatial lag of SBRs always remained positive and significantly different from zero at the 1% level when estimating the models with all years and post-reforms years. The results related to the robustness checks are not shown here for the sake of brevity, but are available from the authors upon request. In summary, taken together, the results seem to be robust to sample size, specification, and testing procedure.

4 Conclusion

The aim of this chapter was to present the first set of empirical results exploring the possibility of diffusion of policies to improve effective state-business relations among states in India. We examine this question by using the comprehensive index constructed by Cali and Sen which measures effective SBRs in Indian states on dimensions of transparency, reciprocity, credibility and mutual trust between the state and industry for 16 industrial states, and a spatial econometrics approach. We find a positive and significant spatial lag which is consistent with strategic complementarity in SBRs. Furthermore, this regional interdependence is most evident during the economic reform period, i.e. post-1990. We interpret this as improvements in SBRs across states and over time which are a result of both inter-state competition to attract large-scale private and foreign investment, and learning by imitation. The diffusion of such policies would help improve investment laws, bureaucratic efficiency, the business climate in general and institutional quality of states. Our findings are robust in controlling for endogeneity concerns using the two-stage least squares method. Taken together, these results also remain robust for alternative samples, estimation techniques, and alternative weighting schemes.

The states' attempts at improving SBRs are part of a larger geoeconomic process in India's investment-policy reforms which have been furthered by the dynamics of inter-state competition and learning by imitation. It is very important to develop state–business relations by improving institutions and enhancing public–private mediation in order to develop a sustainable business-led development policy. Under a democratic regime like India a robust state–business partnership requires competent, resourceful and relatively autonomous states, economic bureaucracy and a well-organized private sector. If the business sector cannot constitute itself in the form of various broad-based self-governing entities, the policy concerns of the business elite inevitably become narrow in scope and short-term in nature. A robust state–business partnership not only ensures countries' meaningful participation in the global economy but also enhances the capacity to respond to the socioeconomic demands of their domestic constituents.

Appendix

Table 5.3 States under study

Andhra Pradesh	Haryana	Maharashtra	Tamil Nadu
Assam	Karnataka	Orissa	Uttar Pradesh
Bihar	Kerala	Punjab	Uttaranchal
Gujarat	Madhya Pradesh	Rajasthan	West Bengal

Table 5.4 Descriptive statistics

Variables	*Observations*	*Mean*	*Standard deviation*	*Minimum*	*Maximum*
SBRs index	381	0.475	0.094	0.142	0.740
Spatial lag of SBRs index	384	0.755	0.199	0.000	1.204
State per capita GDP (log)	370	9.583	0.420	8.478	10.643
Population (log)	360	15.436	0.595	14.164	16.811
Industry share in state GDP	376	19.697	6.075	4.052	38.130
INC ruling years	370	0.468	0.500	0.000	1.000
BJP ruling years	370	0.203	0.403	0.000	1.000
Left Front ruling years	370	0.103	0.304	0.000	1.000
Regional parties ruling years	370	0.422	0.494	0.000	1.000
Political instability	370	0.049	0.215	0.000	1.000

Table 5.5 Data definitions and sources

Variables	*Definitions and data sources*
SBRs index	State-Business Relations index coded on the scale of 0–1 where the highest value represents effective state-business relations. SBRs index comprises four sub-indices, namely private sector, public sector, interaction between private and public sector, and avoidance of collusive behavior. The four sub-indices are aggregated into the SBRs index
Spatial lag—SBRs	Own construction as described in section 3.1
Per capita GDP (log)	State per capita GDP in Indian rupees, 1999–2000 constant prices from the Reserve Bank of India, Mumbai
Population (log)	Total population of each state obtained from Indiastat.com
Industry share in GDP	Share of industry in state GDP from Reserve Bank of India, Mumbai
Political parties in power	Dummy for each of the political parties and allies (namely, INC, BJP, Left Front and regional parties) in power in state *i* in year *t* based on the information published by the Election Commission of India
Political instability	Dummy if a state *i* in year *t* has witnessed president's rule

Acknowledgment

We thank Massimiliano Cali for generously making the SBRs index data available. We also thank Massimiliano Cali and Kunal Sen for comments on a previous version of the draft, and Ronald B. Davies and Hannes Öhler for extensive discussion on spatial econometrics.

Notes

1 It is noteworthy that although the central government intervened less and allowed state governments to take decisions during our study period, the direction of competition at times was set by the central government. In other words, states competed to be more liberal because this was the direction that the central government wanted them to take, and it is precisely for this reason that the central government in the liberalization program of 1991 emphasized bringing state governments into the economic decision-making process (for more discussion on this, see Kanta, 2011).

2 It is common to 'row standardize' the weights so that the sum of the weights adds up to one (see Anselin, 1988; Blonigen et al., 2007; and Plümper & Neumayer, 2010).

3 Moreover, using geographic distance as weight also avoids reverse causation problems. For instance, it is hard to argue that SBRs in state *i* would influence geographic distance from other states (excluding state *i*).

4 As highlighted by Aghion et al. (2008) Indian companies are required to obtain licenses from the central government to start business operations. Starting in 1985, certain industries were de-licensed and after 1991, almost all industries (with a few exceptions) were fully de-licensed.

5 The reason for considering only 16 industrial states instead of 28 is based on data availability to construct the SBRs index. In fact, these 16 states constitute about 94% of total population and 93% of India's domestic product.

6 See: www.rbi.org.in/scripts/AnnualPublications.aspx?head=Handbook of Statistics on Indian Economy.

7 President's rule is imposed by the president of India based on the central government's recommendations. Imposing president's rule requires dismissing the state legislative assembly with powers then vested to the state's governor until fresh state legislative assembly elections are called.

8 However, it is noteworthy that our instruments when using contiguity as weighting scheme fail to pass the overidentifying test.

9 In both these cases, our instruments pass the overidentifying tests. The joint F-statistics in the first step are always above the threshold limit of ten which is significantly different from zero at the 1% level.

10 Available at https://sites.google.com/site/krishnachaitanyavadlamannati/publications.

11 As a further check for robustness, we used different versions of lagged values for instruments. We employ a six-year lag structure, and the results remained unchanged.

References

Aghion, P., Burgess, R., Redding, S.J. and Zilibotti, F. (2008) The unequal effects of liberalization: Evidence from dismantling the license Raj in India. *American Economic Review* 98(4): 1397–1412.

Anselin, L. (1988) *Spatial Econometrics: Methods and Models.* Boston, MA: Kluwer Academic Publishers.

Arellano, M. and Bond, S. (1991) Some tests of specification for panel data: Monte Carlo evidence and application to employment equations. *Review of Economic Studies* 58(2): 277–297.

Arellano, M. and Bover, O. (1995) Another look at the instrumental-variable estimation of error-components models. *Journal of Econometrics* 68: 29–51.

Besley, T. and Burgess, R. (2000) Land reform, poverty reduction, and growth: Evidence from India. *The Quarterly Journal of Economics* 115(2): 389–430.

Besley, T. and Burgess, R. (2004) Can labour regulation hinder economic performance? Evidence from India. *Quarterly Journal of Economics* 119(1): 91–134.

Blonigen, B.A. (2005) A review of the empirical literature on FDI determinants. *Atlantic Economic Journal* 33(4): 383–403.

Blonigen, B.A., Davies, R.B., Naughton, H.T. and Waddell, G.R. (2008) Spacey parents: Autoregressive patterns in inbound FDI. In *Foreign Direct Investment and the Multinational Enterprise.* Boston, MA: MIT Press.

Blonigen, B.A., Davies, R.B., Waddell, G.R. and Naughton, H. (2007) FDI in space: Spatial autoregressive lags in foreign direct investment. *European Economic Review* 51(5): 1303–1325.

Blundell, R. and Bond, S. (1998) Initial conditions and moment restrictions in dynamic panel data models. *Journal of Econometrics* 87(1): 115–143.

Bound, J., Jaeger, D.A. and Baker, R.M. (1995) Problems with instrumental variables estimation when the correlation between the instruments and the endogenous explanatory variable is weak. *Journal of the American Statistical Association* 90(430): 443–450.

Cali, M., Mitra, S. and Purohit, P. (2011) Measuring state–business relations within developing countries: An application to Indian state. *Journal of International Development* 23(3): 394–419.

Cali, M. and Sen, K. (2011) Do effective state business relations matter for economic growth? Evidence from Indian states. *World Development* 39(9): 1542–1557.

Carr, D.L., Markusen, J.R. and Maskus, K.E. (2001) Estimating the knowledge-capital model of the multinational enterprise. *American Economic Review* 91(3): 693–708.

Coughlin, C.C., Terza, J.V. and Arromdee, V. (1991) State characteristics and location of foreign direct investment within the United States. *Review of Economics and Statistics* 73(4): 675–683.

Davies, R.B., Egger, H. and Egger, P. (2003) *Tax Competition for International Producers and the Mode of Foreign Market Entry.* Working paper 2006-2019, University of Oregon.

Davies, R.B. and Naughton, H.T. (2006) *Cooperation in Environmental Policy: A Spatial Approach.* Working paper 2006–2018, University of Oregon.

Davies, R.B. and Vadlamannati, K.C. (2011) *A Race to the Bottom in Labor Standards? An Empirical Investigation.* Working paper no. 201123, School of Economics, University College Dublin.

Davies, R.B. and Voget, J. (2008) *Tax Competition in an Expanding European Union.* Working paper 0830, Oxford University Centre for Business Taxation.

Devereux, M.P., Lockwood, B. and Redoano, M. (2008) Do countries compete over corporate tax rates? *Journal of Public Economics* 92(5–6): 1210–1235.

Hausman, J. (1978) Specification tests in econometrics. *Econometrica* 46(3), 1251–1271.

Head, K. and Mayer, T. (2004) Market potential and the location of Japanese investment in the European Union. *Review of Economics and Statistics* 86(4), 959–972.

Kanta, M. (2011) *Economic Liberalization, Electoral Coalitions and Private Investment in India*. Paper presented in Politics of FDI Conference, Niehaus Center for Globalization and Governance, September 23–24.

Kleibergen, F. and Paap, R. (2006) Generalized reduced rank tests using the singular value decomposition. *Journal of Econometrics* 127(1): 97–126.

Klemm, A. and Parys, V.S. (2009) *Empirical Evidence on the Effects of Tax Incentives*. Working Paper WP/09/136, Washington, DC: IMF.

Maxfield, S. and Schneider, B.R. (1997) *Business and the State in Developing Countries*. Ithaca, NY: Cornell University Press.

Newey, W. and West, K. (1987) A simple positive semi-definite, heteroskedasticity and autocorrelation consistent covariance matrix. *Econometrica* 55(3): 703–708.

Overesch, M. and Rincke, J. (2008) *Tax Competition in Europe 1980–2007—Evidence from Dynamic Panel Data Estimation*. Working paper.

Plümper, T. and Neumayer, E. (2010) Model specification in the analysis of spatial dependence. *European Journal of Political Research* 49(3): 418–442.

Reulier, E. and Rocaboy, Y. (2009) Regional tax competition: Evidence from French regions. *Regional Studies* 43(7): 915–922.

Roodman, D. (2009) A note on the theme of too many instruments. *Oxford Bulletin of Economics and Statistics* 71(1): 135–158.

Staiger, D. and Stock, J. (1997) Instrumental variables regression with weak instruments. *Econometrica* 65(3): 557–586.

Wiggins, V. (1999) Comparing XTGLS with regress cluster. Stata Corporation. www.stata.com/support/faqs/stat/xtgls_rob.html.

6 Geoeconomics in Central and Eastern Europe

Implications of FDI

Zoltan Gal and Andrea Schmidt

1 Introduction

The chapter investigates problems of capital accumulation, the features of post-socialist transition, as well as the geoeconomic features of the externally managed and financed integration of post-socialist transition countries of Central and Eastern Europe (CEE) into the global economy and the European Union (EU). The authors would like to use the principles of geoeconomics in order to analyse the Central and Eastern European region and the role of foreign direct investment (FDI) in transformation. The importance of geoeconomics lays in the importance of this method in the globalized world. Geoeconomics gradually replaced geopolitics in the era of globalization. In contrast to geopolitics, it focuses not primarily on the state and its role, but rather on private enterprises (Søilen, 2012). Its focus is on networks not blocs, connections not iron curtains, and transborder ties instead of national territories.

Global financial capital has played an important role in all transition economies. FDI in the banking, insurance and manufacturing sectors is closely connected to the transition process in CEE and has received considerable attention from both a theoretical and an empirical perspective (Estrin, 1994; Csaba, 1995; Bevan & Estrin, 2004). Much less attention has been devoted to the post-transition period and the impact of the crisis on externally financed and dependent transition models in CEE.

Economic transformation in Central and Eastern Europe followed a development path based on FDI and reinvigorated short-term competitiveness. However, it needs to go beyond low costs and counteract the unfavourable effects of external capital and export dependencies. The economic transition fuelled by a neoliberal approach through economic liberalization, marketization, and privatization, overlapping with excessive 'foreignization', created the legal and structural frameworks for the dependent mode of reintegration into the EU and into the global division of labour (Sachs, 1990; Sokol, 2001; Smith, 2002). The most important *historical dependencies* of the CEE region, such as financial, technological and market ones, remain constant. This is complemented by the large energy dependency of CEE countries (CEECs) on Russia. This not only further strengthens the external vulnerability of the region, but also makes re-interpretable the geopolitical and geoeconomic features of the former buffer zone situated between the German and Russian spheres of interest.

Dependencies and the semi-peripheral situation are the direct consequences of relative scarcities in capital and technology. The roots of these scarcities lie in the unfavourable conditions of specialization in the international division of labour. This is characterized by the limited access to resources in the process of capital accumulation, and semiperipheral regions experiencing significant outflows of resources making them unable to follow autonomous growth. As a result, there is a heavy dependence on external resources for both investment and consumption (Arrighi et al., 2003). Gerőcs and Pinkasz (2015) argue that CEECs have been following the pattern of semi-peripheral dependent development since the 1990s. Bartlett and Prica (2015) combine the core-periphery model with under-consumption and secular stagnation models in order to find dependency relationships between core regions in the EU and the three different peripheries (inner, outer and super). They also argue that the eurozone core is also dependent on the export and FDI incomes from the peripheries. The outer periphery of the EU (CEE) and the core countries have the largest dependence on the internal economic ties of the EU.

The chapter analyses the changing geoeconomic position of the CEE region that re-emerged after the change of regime during the 1990s in the context of world-system and dependent-market economy models (Amin, 1977; Nölke & Vliegenthart, 2009). We argue that the FDI-led development path in the CEECs followed the pattern of a semi-peripheral dependent development (Amin, 1977). Nölke and Vliegenthart (2009) present the CEECs as prototypes of a new, dependent variety of capitalism. This is based on strong capital, technology and market dependencies developed during the course of economic transition and integration with the advanced countries of Western Europe through foreign ownership of major economic sectors.

The chapter is organized as follows. First we describe the legacy and the geoeconomic position of the CEE region by introducing the changing geoeconomic framework conditions of the past century. The next section analyses the consequence of the post-socialist transformation and the role of FDI in the economic transformation and its impact on transition economies. The last section examines the effects of the financial crisis of 2008. In summary, we evaluate the presence of foreign capital and the underlying dependencies in the CEE region.

2 Changing geoeconomic position of transition countries in Central and Eastern Europe

The CEE region was a special kind of transitional zone in the past two centuries as it was the target zone of the neighbouring great powers from the East and the West. The trade dependence on the German economy appeared in several geopolitical plans (Mitteleuropa Plan, 1915, and the Nazi ideology of Lebensraum). The main international trade partner of the CEECs was Germany until the end of World War II, providing markets for their (mostly) agrarian products while Germany exploited natural resources of the region. This trade connection was replaced by the Soviet Union with the founding of the Council for Mutual Economic Assistance (COMECON, also known as CMEA) in 1949. By the early 1950s the share of foreign trade with the Soviet Union had become dominant (Schmidt, 2015). Bilateral agreements guaranteed the energy and raw material supply for the CEECs from the USSR while they were mostly paid by industrial products. It also helped the rapid industrialization of the mostly semi-agrarian countries of the region.

The trajectory of CEE differed significantly from that of the West and it was characterized by historical dependencies and perpetual attempts at catching up. The CEE region within the system of capitalist division of labour became the semi-periphery of a transforming West during the early modern age. The 19th and 20th centuries were characterized by three major waves of catching up with the West (Figure 6.1) (Gál & Lux, 2014).

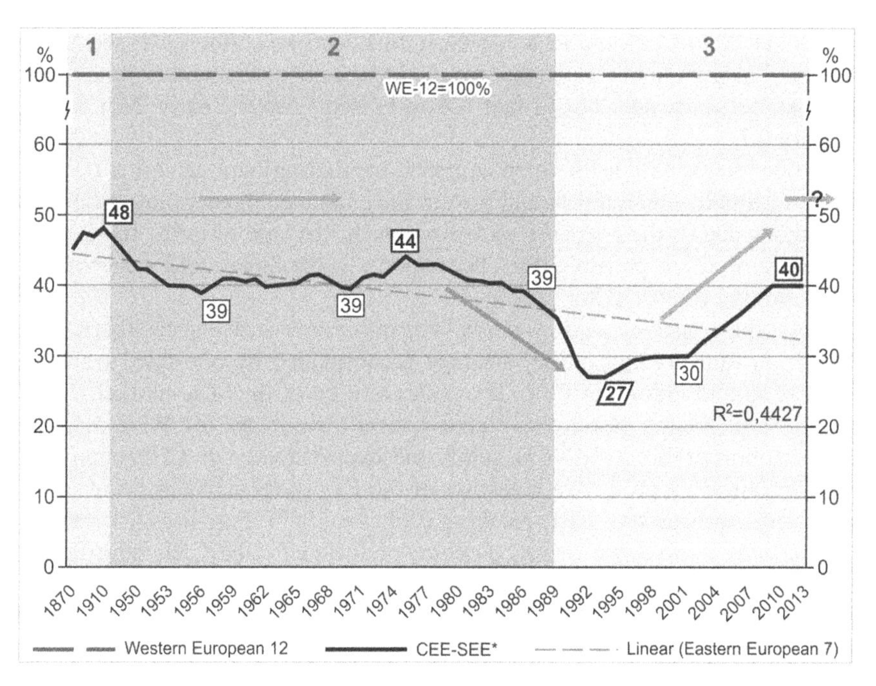

Figure 6.1 Relative development gap between Central and Eastern Europe and Western Europe -12, 1870–2013 (as a percentage of GDP per capita in 1990 Geary-Khamis dollar, WE -12 most developed countries=100%)

(Authors' calculation based on Angus Maddison's database, www.ggdc.net/maddison/maddison-project/data.htm)

1 The *turn of the 19th and 20th centuries* experienced the most successful catching up and the region managed to decrease the development gap significantly.
2 Modernization under the *command economy* with its heavy industrialization and forced capital accumulation policy resulted in moderate convergence of the region in the Soviet block during the 1960s.
3 *Post-communist transformation* and rapid privatization led to a tragic decline of gross domestic product (GDP) and industrial output, and CEE entered a period of half a decade of transformation crisis and stagnation before it started to upsurge gradually.

The deep transformation crisis of the 1990s followed the transition from a command to a market economy. It was the direct consequence of the collapse of Eastern markets, economic decline, unemployment, inflation, doubtful results of privatization and a general decline in living standards. With the return of 4–5% annual growth between 1994 and 2003, per capita GDP reached 35% of the Western European level of development in 2005 (virtually the same level as in 1989), peaking (44%) in 2008 before it began to drop. Our calculation shows that less than half (40%) of the Western GDP per capita level was achieved in Central and South-Eastern European countries. It seems that the development gap between the so-called 'old' and 'new' member states of the EU has not narrowed, but in fact has increased since the early 20th century (Figure 6.1).

In our interpretation the form of access to international capital is tied to a certain geopolitical situation and also to the changing geoeconomic framework conditions due to the course of globalization. In the case of CEE, three major processes were responsible for the region's geopolitical and geoeconomic repositioning (Smith, 2002, 2013).

First, the *transition and economic transformation* with its neoliberal marketization (and foreignization) strategy accompanied by one-sided trade liberalization and inflows of FDI. The incorporation of the huge market with its natural and human resources offered several advantages for Western multinational corporations (MNCs), while the export ability of CEE enterprises was restrained by protective measures of the EU, particularly in those sectors that were important to CEE recovery (Gowan, 1995). Post-socialist transformation was a top-down driven process conducted by the CEE governments and externally assisted by the neoliberal financialization project and by international institutions (the International Monetary Fund—IMF, the World Bank, the European Bank for Reconstruction and Development—EBRD, G7, EU and the North Atlantic Treaty Organization—NATO), which made the institutional aspects of market integration part of an inherently political project of transition (Sokol, 2001; Raviv, 2008).

Second, the international environment in which transformation took place in CEE was shaped by the *economic and financial globalization* providing harsh external conditions to economic and political transformation of the

1990s (Schmidt, 2014). US and EU financial capital was seeking new investment opportunities in the course of financialization and this process was accompanied by the relocation of industrial production of MNCs from developed countries to emerging economies.

The external pressure came from the intertwined virtue of foreign capital and the powerful intervention of international institutions. They created rather strict economic conditions for post-communist countries for their reintegration into the international market economy. As Gowan (1995) argued, the neoliberal economic transformation allowed foreign capital to conquer Eastern European markets and to integrate their captured cheap production lines into the 'hub & spoke' West–East economic relations.

Third, the *Eastern enlargement of the European Union* in 2004, besides being a political project, was committed to the neoliberal, externally dependent, investment-led growth and marketization process. The structural power of EU financial capital has been on the rise, mostly the result of EU policies (Raviv, 2008). This capital flew towards Central and Eastern Europe in the form of FDI even before the accession, but enlargement further stimulated the expansion of MNCs in the new member states.

A key part of the EU's internal interdependencies aims to restructure its global geoeconomic position, creating interdependent trajectories within the EU with the relocation of the more labour-intensive or efficiency-seeking industrial and service value chains to CEE. This internal geoeconomic restructuring within the enlarged EU created new core-periphery relationships that primarily benefit the core, often at the expense of the peripheries. This process hollowed out not only the Mediterranean but even more the Eastern periphery of the EU caused by the resurgence and growing supremacy of the German capital. The Eastward expansion of German capital largely contributed to the global competitiveness of the German economy and to the geoeconomic supremacy of Germany over the EU (Phillips, 2000).

As a result, the main characteristics of this blend of 'imported capitalism' included a relatively fast recovery from transformation crisis but also the dominant role of foreign capital in the process of stabilization. However, foreign investments not only contributed to the modernization of the economy, but also increased its structural and spatial segmentation (Eyal et al., 1998).

3 The role of FDI in CEECs

European and US assistance in reconstruction of the post-socialist region resulted in the appearance of not just foreign capital, but controversial aid programmes launched by the IMF, EBRD[1] and EU, paving the way for foreign private investors. However, both IMF and EU aid programmes, unlike the non-refundable Marshall Plan aid for Western Europe, used their instruments to create the desired goal to open indebted CEECs to FDI.

Foreign investment fundamentally helped the post-socialist countries in shaping the region's diverse development paths. International capital was seeking market opportunities in Eastern Europe at the same time as CEECs started to privatize their state-owned enterprises and the European integration proceeded. The EU's decision to start entry negotiations with selected candidates increased the region's attraction for FDI. During the period of privatization in the indebted countries of CEE there was a far greater cumulative need for external capital than the actual supply of FDI in these economies. As Gerőcs and Pinkasz (2015) argue, this explains the very unequal bargaining position of transition countries suffering from capital shortage vis-à-vis international investors.

FDI inflows into CEE economies have been a vital factor in privatization, and FDI became the predominant type of incoming capital investment in the first stage of the economic transition (Kalotay, 2010) (Table 6.1). Privatization of state-owned enterprises became the cornerstone of economic transition since it shaped the property rights and the corporate government systems. CEECs lacked domestic capitalists with financial resources, therefore privatization opportunities were transferred to foreign investors coming mainly from eurozone countries. Foreign capital was expected to be the engine of transition bringing new capital, new technology, jobs, economic growth and convergence to CEE. However, in low-income countries privatization of state-owned enterprises to foreign investors is considered a negative policy from a development perspective, since 'the family silver was sold' (Easterly, 2001). Furthermore, IMF-led shock therapy required privatization in the middle of the transformation crisis and, therefore, the assets were acquired by foreigners at very low prices[2] (Gowan, 1995).

The shift from state socialism to market capitalism in the second phase of the transition was quickly followed by the transition from industrial capitalism to financial capitalism, in which bank capital became the predominant type of investment after the millennium.

FDI inflows have resulted in dramatic changes of ownership structures, first in the banking and insurance sectors being a forerunner in the privatization process, and quickly followed by manufacturing. In 1994, in the wake of the early transition crises, an overwhelming majority of financial intermediaries in the post-communist countries were still publicly owned. In contrast, in 2007, more than a decade later, private foreign ownership already accounted for about 80% of financial intermediaries' assets in the CEE region. These figures are especially striking when we compare them with the 15% in the euro area. Even the average of non-Organisation for Economic Co-operation and Development (OECD) countries is only 50% (Gál, 2013). The post-crisis external adjustment was followed by increasing state intervention with plans to strengthen local financial structures. As a result, the share of foreign ownership in banking dropped significantly in Hungary and also decreased in Poland and Slovenia (Figure 6.2).

The size and weight of foreign ownership in transition countries can be collected from the EU foreign affiliates and other business statistics for the recent period. The overall share of FDI in the GDP is highest in Hungary

Table 6.1 FDI stocks in CEE countries, 1995–2013 (US$ billion)

Year	*Bulgaria*	*Czech Republic*	*Hungary*	*Poland*	*Romania*	*Slovakia*	*Croatia*	*Slovenia*
1995	0.4	7.4	11.3	7.8	0.8	1.3	0.5	1.8
2000	2.7	21.6	22.9	33.5	7.0	7.0	2.7	2.9
2005	13.9	60.7	61.1	88.2	25.4	29.6	13.3	7.1
2008	44.1	113.2	88.1	157.2	64.8	50.4	28.4	12.0
2009	49.2	125.8	98.9	176.9	69.9	52.5	33.5	11.3
2010	47.2	128.5	90.8	195.4	68.1	50.3	32.3	10.7
2011	47.4	120.6	85.3	174.7	69.5	52.0	28.4	11.5
2012	49.4	136.5	104.0	203.3	76.3	55.1	29.3	12.2
2013	51.2	134.1	108.2	271.7	82.7	58.1	29.9	12.3

(WIR database, Eurostat)

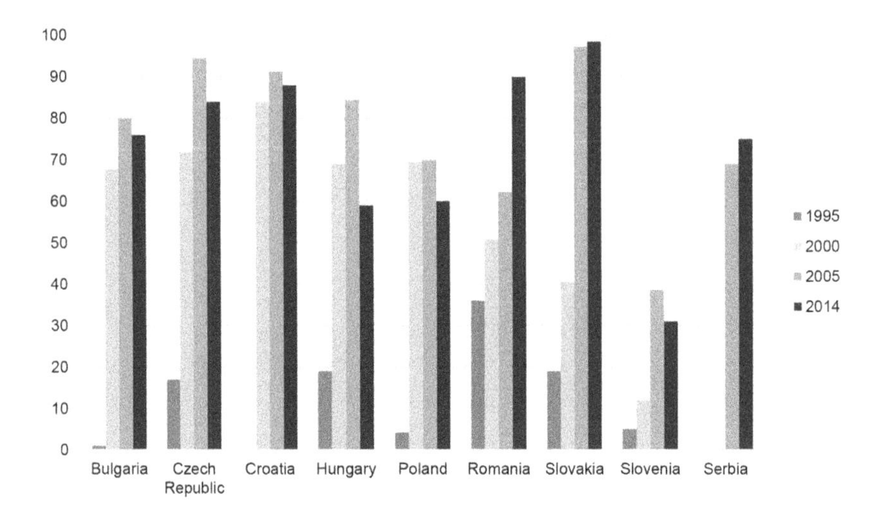

Figure 6.2 Foreign ownership as a percentage of total banking sector assets in Eastern Europe, 1995–2014
(Author's calculation based on data from Raiffeisen International)

(52%) and the Czech Republic (48%), indicating not only the strongest integration of these economies into the EU/global economy but the largest (external) dependencies on MNCs' value chains as well. The share of FDI was lower in Slovakia (32%) and much lower in Poland (25%), which is comparable with the Austrian figure (23%).

The share of foreign affiliates in production value is highest in Slovakia and Hungary, with over 57%, followed by the Czech Republic (Hunya, 2015). Foreign shares in manufacturing production in CEE are dominated by MNCs. Their share in manufacturing is even higher than in the economy as a whole, reaching 80% in Slovakia, almost 70% in Hungary and 67% in the Czech Republic (Figure 6.3). The transition to a market economy helped the growth of the services sector with the increased amount of FDI. From the 2000s, the largest part of this FDI reached was committed to the business and IT services sector.

In terms of the fundamental motives for FDI in the region, these followed first the market-seeking, and later efficiency-seeking strategies. *Market-seeking investments* concentrated on searching for new markets to sell the products or services of the MNCs, while *efficiency(labour)-seeking investment* exploited differences in wages both in labour-intensive production and in knowledge-intensive services (Schmidt, 2015).

The external capital dependency of the region is exacerbated by its manufacturing export dependencies on Western Europe. Economic recovery from the transformation crisis is designed by the IMF to develop trade-led growth, rather than a strong domestic recovery based on domestic consumption. This

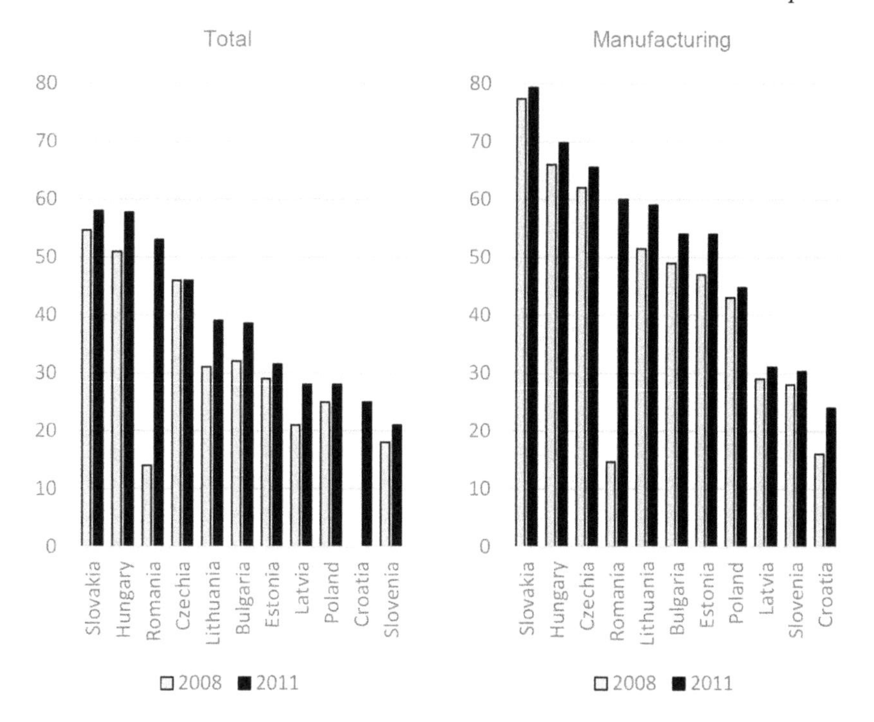

Figure 6.3 Share of foreign affiliates' production value in the non-financial sectors, 2008–11 (%)
Total: all non-financial sectors; Manufacturing: manufacturing sectors.
(Eurostat, foreign affiliates and other business statistics)

exposure to export dependency on EU-15 markets accompanied by industrial relocation of EU-based (mainly German) companies relying upon assembly production, accelerating in car manufacturing and in electronics, integrated CEECs into their global value chains (Smith & Swain, 2010). At the same time, they provided capital in the form of FDI for industrial upgrading to high-tech production (Pavlínek et al., 2009). In this respect, CEE played a significant role in the consolidation of the German (car) manufacturing industries and contributed to their globally competitive position. The capital and export dependencies of CEE were further aggravated by energy dependency on Russia.

4 Impact of FDI on host transition countries

In theory, foreign companies may affect positively the economic performance of the host country (Blomström & Kokko, 1997). FDI has often been viewed as a potential catalyst for the economic transition from a planned to a market economy. It increases productivity and raises the level of competitiveness (Grossman & Helpman, 1991). It can transfer technology and know-how and spread managerial and marketing skills by transactions with domestic firms. It contributes to the restructuring of existing enterprises. However, these positive impacts do not occur automatically. The emergence of '*dual structure*' in transition economies is characterized by deep imbalances between the capitalization knowledge base, market position, and other vital characteristics of foreign and domestic corporations (Hardy, 1998; Barta, 2005). FDI in manufacturing export platforms is considered an economic driving force, although spillover effects remain fairly weak. Despite MNCs occupying all strategic sectors in the transition economies, they may form separate islands in the economy, having very limited contact with domestic enterprises. Moreover, the activity of MNCs can result in *crowding-out* of domestic firms, whereupon MNCs occupy the product and labour markets of local companies (Lux, 2014).

Other controversies emerged in the case of acquisitions by foreigners followed by the closing down of the firms in order to eliminate their Eastern European rivals (Gowan, 1995). There were many privatization cases that were followed by cherry picking of the most valuable assets, general de-skilling as enterprises were 'hollowed out', keeping the lowest value-added activities in the region. Mostly the relatively routine activities were transferred to CEE due to the lower wages for skilled labour there (Myant & Drahokoupil, 2011). As Nölke & Vliegenthart (2009) argue, in contrast to the less regulated liberal market economies (LMEs, e.g. the USA), or the coordinated market economies (CMEs, e.g. Germany), *dependent market economies*' competitiveness is tied to 'a specific type of comparative advantage that is not based on radical innovation (LMEs) or incremental innovation (CMEs), but rather on an assembly platform for semistandardized industrial goods' (p. 679). Contrary to this, market-seeking FDI that targets domestic markets (finance, retail and energy sectors) is more controversial and may be regarded as a risk factor. In the banking sector foreign subsidiaries followed pure commercial rather than economic development principles regardless of the needs of the domestic economy (Raviv, 2008).

Income effects of FDI are very limited as only a small fraction of income from FDI projects is captured by domestic residents (Lane & Milesi-Ferretti, 2007). The growing gap between GDP and gross national income (GNI) is an inevitable result of FDI inflows in transition countries where the gap has been increasing over time, therefore the GDP to GNI ratio is below 100%. This gap in CEECs on average increased from 0.96% to 4.38% of GDP. This is due to an increasing part of the income generated by foreign investment being transferred back to the capital owners' home country.

FDI is expected to bring growth through increased gross fixed capital accumulation and a wealth of benefits to the local economy and the impetus that knowledge from outside may bring to local processes of technological change (Jensen, 2006). Mencinger (2007) finds negative correlation between FDI and growth in CEECs. The privatization incomes are spent on consumption and imports since FDI generates high import and consumption rather than debt reduction. The increase of GDP growth increased the capital outflow as well as trade deficit through the investment, trade and current accounts.

FDI inflows have a direct positive impact on the balance of payments as FDI is prominent in financing high current account deficits. Foreign capital is used to finance investment and ultimately FDI tends to substitute incomplete local financial markets. However, a natural consequence of these inflows has been a large current account deficit as FDI also increases the size of profit repatriation over time. This is related to the fact that some parts of FDI (equity capital, reinvested earnings, dividends, other capital) are mobile.

Rajan et al. (2007) find that developing countries which relied more on foreign finance have grown more slowly than those that used their own savings for investments. They also find that the CEECs in this respect resemble industrial countries where larger inflows of foreign capital boost growth. However, other comparative studies argue that transition countries are more similar to developing than to developed countries in terms of their experiences of hosting FDI (Jensen, 2006).

5 Growing imbalances and the crisis in Central and Eastern Europe

As we have seen, FDI inflows resulted in only a temporary remedy for the indebtedness and current account imbalances of transformation crisis-hit countries in the region. During the 2000s, the growing deficit in current accounts was increasingly financed by inflows of bank capital as the shift from FDI towards credit financing occurred. This process in CEE coincided with the global process of financialization. A new pattern of accumulation, in which profits accrue primarily through financial channels, increased the dominance of financial market actors exerting enormous impacts on firms, states and households (Krippner, 2005; Aalbers, 2008).

From a geoeconomic point of view, the promotion of Euro-Atlantic integration of CEECs was underpinned by the wider financialization-led growth regime (Gowan, 2009). This Atlantic system of financialized capitalism led to excessive borrowing in CEE, increasing indebtedness and real estate bubbles that in the short term generated higher growth rates (Smith & Swain, 2010). Already by the year of EU accession in 2004, few CEECs witnessed a massive debt accumulation. As soon as the privatization opportunities decreased, it led to the reduction of inflow of FDI. At the same time, profits made by MNCs began to repatriate from the region, which resulted in a growing gap in the current account.

Another reason for the growing indebtedness and current account deficit is rooted in the household consumption and mortgage lending that generated huge inflows of foreign credit. The financialization-based consumption model relying on short-term bank capital gradually replaced the FDI-based model in terms of external finance (Figure 6.4).

The credit boom in mortgage and consumer credits fuelled the excessive growth in liabilities throughout the CEE region before the crisis. During this

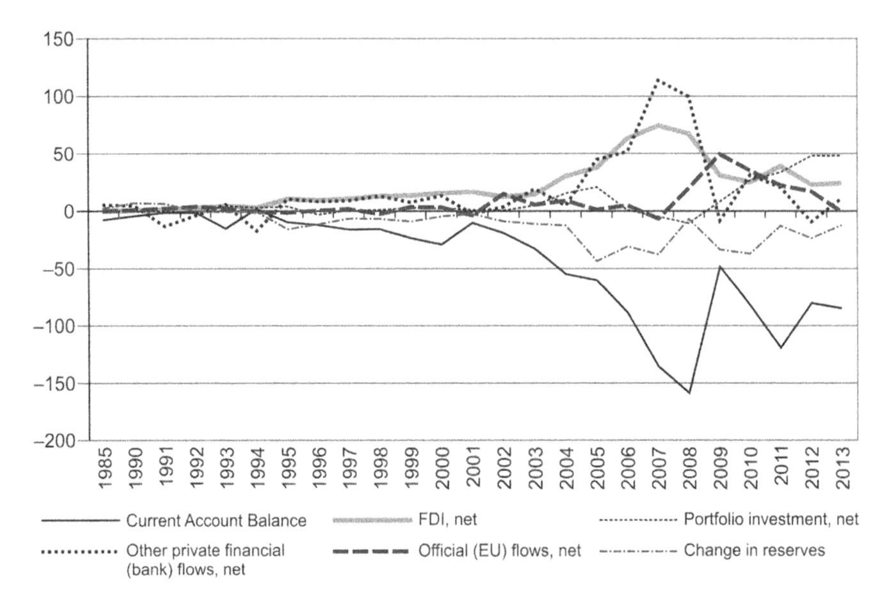

Figure 6.4 Net financial flows and reserves in CEE countries, 1985–2013 (US$ billion) (Compiled by the authors from the IMF *World Economic Outlook*)

period credit growth significantly exceeded the growth rate of domestic deposits, therefore banks' borrowing from external sources increased. As a result the share of deposits within banks' total liabilities may fall significantly. The credit boom-fuelled consumption in many CEECs was extensively financed by the local subsidiaries of foreign parent banks, which entailed a growing dependence on external resources (Gál & Kovács, forthcoming). The share of foreign liabilities in total volumes of liabilities grew from 8% in 2005 to 25% in 2008. Corporate lending developed slowly and the banks increasingly shifted towards the more profitable household lending tapping the upward cycle in the credit boom.

The finance-led growth model further strengthened the ownership, as well as the creditor-debtor control, over CEE. This was able to create very profitable new investment and lending opportunities for foreign banks. Profitability in CEE banking markets during the pre-crisis period was clearly outpaced by that of their Western counterparts (Gál, 2013). In CEECs catching up in the first half of the 2000s was generally accompanied by macroeconomic stability, but most countries of the region became increasingly vulnerable due to the unsustainable trajectories of huge credit booms, high current account deficits and quickly rising external debt.

The household sector's foreign currency borrowing is a recent development in Central and Eastern Europe (commencing in the 2000s), and actually, it soon became the region's equivalent of the subprime mortgage (Figure 6.5). The rapid growth in domestic credit was financed by foreign-owned banks

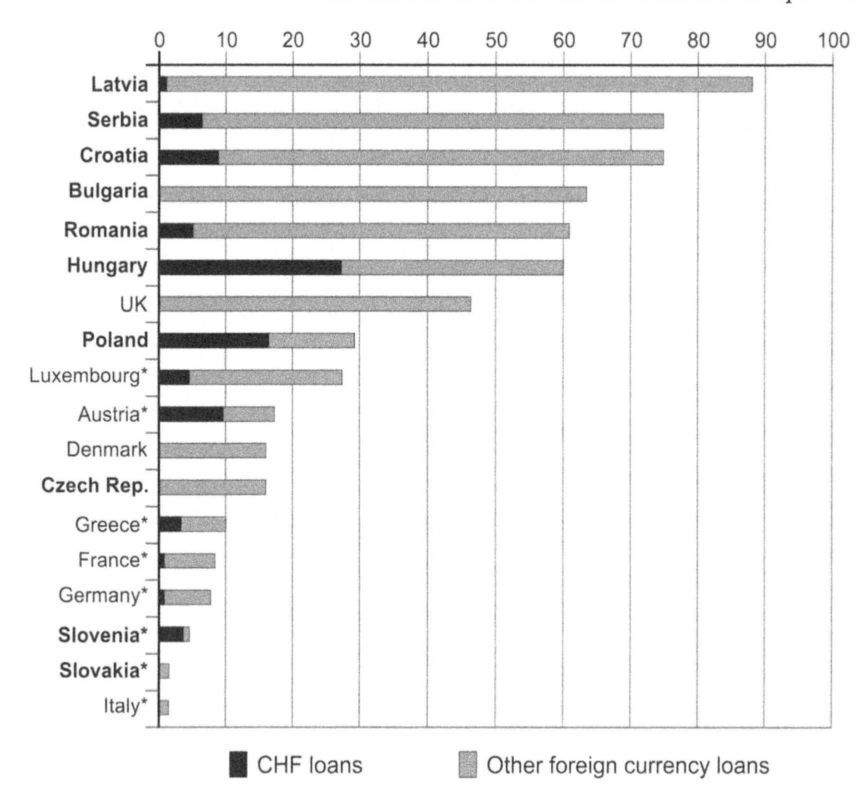

Figure 6.5 Share of foreign currency loans as a percentage of total loans to the non-banking sector in Europe, 2012 (1Q)
Bold: Central and Eastern European countries; * eurozone members; CHF: Swiss franc
(Author's compilation based on data from Raiffeisen International and Swiss National Bank's CHF Lending Monitor)

engaged increasingly in carry trade. Despite their immediate benefits—lower interest rates, longer maturities—foreign exchange loans carry a significant exchange rate risk. Foreign currency indebtedness is a systemic problem with a crippling effect on the whole economy and economic policy in many CEECs (Yeşin, 2013).

As a consequence of this second stage of external capital inflows the CEE region integrated into the geoeconomic structure of the international financial system as a debtor region dependent on importing capital. This increasing dependence on foreign capital led to growing imbalances resulting in transmittance of contagion into CEE and the deepening of the crisis.

The financial crisis in 2008 ended the optimism of the new EU members. It showed the problems of the post-socialist states, as their economies were weak and vulnerable. The attempt to create an economically balanced structure with the accession of new member states had failed. In the run-up to the crisis, the CEECs attracted large capital inflows and some of them built up large external imbalances. However, the crisis years caused not only a decline in capital inflows but also a deterioration of domestic and foreign demand, which led to a deep economic depression in much of the region. The financial crisis was usually explained as an external shock that affected the CEE countries in different ways. However, Bohle (2010) argues that the unfolding crisis in CEE cannot simply be understood as internal adjustments to an external crisis. Rather, the region's integration into the new geoeconomic structures following the collapse of the Soviet bloc created vulnerabilities that unfolded in the recent crisis.

In 2008, the crisis transmitted to the CEE region too, and a year later the previously prospering countries had to experience a double digit decline in GDP while the average decline of the entire region was around 6%. Households with foreign currency debts began to reduce their consumption due to the sudden increase in their debt.

In the first stage of the financial crisis, due to the increased reliance of the banking sector on foreign funding, the risks were associated with the drying up of international finance. A liquidity crisis occurred at the parent banks and was transmitted immediately to their foreign subsidiaries. In the second stage (from mid-2009) the foreign currency indebtedness captured potential spillover effects directly on the host countries affecting all sectors (state, corporate and private households) and resulted in funding withdrawals.[3]

External capital inflow significantly declined and the recovery of both bank capital and FDI flows proved to be a long-lasting phenomenon during the crisis, as a legacy of the foreign-funded credit boom and despite the funding withdrawals since the stock of outstanding financing from foreign banks is still large (26–29%). The current slow economic growth in CEE is linked to low investment activity, both domestic and foreign. Despite the increased domestic savings in crisis-hit countries (Estonia, Latvia, Hungary and Romania), the investments and growth declined because domestic savings were spent on foreign debt repayment rather than investment and consumption (Śliwiński, 2009).

Summing up, we argue that the role of foreign savings in promoting economic growth in the ten CEE countries *was* undoubtedly sustainable only in the short run but was challenged in the long run, particularly during the crisis period. Since the outbreak of the crisis, not only have FDI inflows decreased but also the role of foreign capital in promoting economic growth has had to be revised.

6 Conclusions

The main argument of this chapter was that the global crisis has exposed the systemic vulnerability of the post-socialist neoliberal transition model which failed to decrease the relative development gap between the 'old' and 'new' EU members, and has contributed to growing geoeconomic dependencies of CEE on foreign capital and transnational export platforms.

The economic transformation (with dramatic transfer of ownership and the reallocation of factors of production in favour of foreign investors) and integration model (joining the EU market in a dependent semi-peripheral position), as well as the transition to financialized capitalism (ending up in short-term boom on the expenses of growing indebtedness), created systemic vulnerabilities to wider economic crisis and to the future of economic convergence of the region. The Atlantic system of a financialized capitalist model was transmitted into the CEE region in the form of a creditor-debtor model, which further strengthened Western control over Central and Eastern Europe (Smith & Swain, 2010).

The crisis led to even higher cost of financing and decreasing capital inflows, which will result in greater economic volatility, lower long-term growth and slower convergence with Western Europe. In the crisis aftermath, up to 2030, only moderate economic growth is expected in the region. The average annual growth forecast is 1.93% for CEE and 1.87% for the EU-15 (Gál & Lux, 2014). If this low growth is the case, the existing gap will hardly change and Central and Eastern Europe will remain on the European periphery.

The financially and industrially integrated debtor countries of the region had become locked into the growth trajectories of the core EU countries. In CEE economic restructuring has mainly followed a development path based on FDI, which has reinvigorated competitiveness but now faces the need to transcend the low-income trap, and counteract the unfavourable effects of external capital dependency.

External dependency poses long-term disadvantages for the accumulation of financial, human, and even social capital. Dependent market economies are heavily reliant on external capital, a problem that can be considered an historical weakness of CEE, especially after periodic 'transformation crises' caused by frequent regime change and the accompanying transformation losses (Gál, 2013). Low- and middle-income competitiveness leads to a development trap in CEE: it hinders the formation of new, well-capitalized domestic enterprises, while encouraging skilled workers to move Westwards in pursuit of higher wages—leading to long-term human capital loss and faster ageing in Central Europe, and undermining the potential sources of catching up to the West (Lux, 2014).

In this chapter we have tried to answer the question of why even the most successful CEECs, being highly dependent on foreign capital and on (non-indigenous) MNCs, suffer setbacks from time to time and cannot fill the income gap existing between CEE and Western Europe.

Acknowledgments

Research for this publication has been supported by the National Research, Development and Innovation Office—NKFIH grant #NN 114468 (Change and Continuity in Hungarian Spatial Imaginaries: Nationality, Territoriality, Development and the Politics of Borders).

Notes

1 Est. 1989 in London. *The European Bank for Reconstruction and Development.*
2 Average purchase prices were minimal in CEE: the average amount of foreign equity invested in developed countries was US$18 million, and in developing country subsidiaries it averaged $4 million, while in CEE it has been only $380,000 (Gowan, 1995).
3 CEE/South-Eastern Europe excluding Russia and Turkey lost the funding equivalent of 4.6% of GDP over this period.

References

Aalbers, M.B. (2008) The financialization of home and the mortgage market crisis. *Competition & Change* 12(2): 148–166.

Amin, S. (1977) *Unequal Development: An Essay on the Social Formations of Peripheral Capitalism.* New York Monthly Review Press.

Arrighi, G., Silver, B. and Brewer, B. (2003) Industrial convergence, globalization, and the persistence of the north–south divide. *Studies in Comparative International Development* 38(1): 3–31.

Barta, Gy. (2005) The role of foreign direct investment in the spatial restructuring of Hungarian industry. In *Hungarian Spaces and Places Patterns of Transition*, G. Barta, E. Fekete, I. Kukorelli Szörényiné and J. Timár (eds). Pécs: Centre for Regional Studies, 143–160.

Bartlett, W. and Prica, I. (2015) *Interdependence between Core and Peripheries of the European Economy: Secular Stagnation and Growth in South East Europe.* Paper for first World Congress in Comparative Economics, 25–28 June, Rome. www.researchgate.net/publication/295702854_Interdependence_between_core_and_peripheries_of_the_European_Economy_Secular_Stagnation_and_Growth_in_the_Western_Balkans.

Bevan, A. and Estrin, S. (2004) The determinants of foreign direct investment into European transition economies. *Journal of Comparative Economics* 32(4): 775–787.

Blomström, M. and Kokko, A. (1997) *How Foreign Investment Affects Host Countries.* Policy Research Working Paper Series 1745. Washington, DC The World Bank.

Bohle, D. (2010) East European transformation and the paradoxes of transnationalization. In *Transnational Europe*, J. DeBardeleben and A. Hurrelmann (eds) Houndsmills: Palgrave Macmillan, 130–151.

Csaba, L. (1995) *The Capitalist Revolution in Eastern Europe: A Contribution to the Economic Theory of Systemic Change.* Aldershot: Edward Elgar.

Easterly, W.R. (2001) *The Elusive Quest for Growth Economists' Adventures and Misadventures in the Tropics.* Cambridge, MA: MIT Press.

Estrin, S. (ed.) (1994) *Privatization in Central and Eastern Europe.* London: Longman.

European Bank for Reconstruction and Development (EBRD) (1998) *Transition Report 1998.* London: EBRD.

Eyal, G., Szelenyi, I. and Townsley, E. (1998) *Making Capitalism without Capitalists: Class Formation and Elite Struggle in Post-Communist Central Europe.* London and New York: Verso.

Gál, Z. (2013) Role of financial sector FDI in regional imbalances in Central and Eastern Europe. In *Eurozone Enlargement Challenges for the V4 Countries*, A. Gostyńska, P. Tokarski, P. Toporowski and D. Wnukowski (eds). Warsaw: The Polish Institute of International Affairs, 27–35.

Gál, Z. and Kovács, S. (forthcoming). Role of business and finance services in the Central and Eastern Europe. In *New Driving Forces of Spatial Restructuring and Regional Development Paths in East-Central Europe at the Beginning of the 21st Century*, Gy. Horváth and G. Lux (eds) Abingdon: Routledge.

Gál, Z. and Lux, G. (2014) ET 2050—Territorial scenarios and visions for Europe. *Luxembourg ESPON (European Spatial Planning Observation Network)* 22(8).

Gerőcs, T. and Pinkasz, A. (2015) Debt-ridden development on Europe's Eastern periphery. In *Global Inequalities in World Systems Perspective. PEWS Annual*, M. Boatca, A. Komlosy and H.-H. Nolte (eds) (forthcoming).

Gowan, P. (1995) Neo-liberal theory and practice for Eastern Europe. *New Left Review* 213: 3–60.

Gowan, P. (2009) Crisis in the heartland: Consequences of the new Wall Street system. *New Left Review*, 555–529.

Grossman, G. and Helpman, E. (1991) Trade, knowledge spillovers, and growth. *European Economic Review* 35(2–3), April, 517–526.

Hardy, J. (1998) Cathedrals in the desert? Transnationals, corporate strategy and locality in Wroclaw. *Regional Studies* 32(7): 639–652.

Hunya, G. (2015) Mapping flows and patterns of foreign direct investment in Central and Eastern Europe, Greece and Portugal during the crisis. In *Foreign Investment in Eastern and Southern Europe after 2008: Still a Lever of Growth?*, B. Galgóczi, J. Drahokoupil and M. Bernaciak (eds). Brussels: ETUI aisbl, 37–70.

Jensen, C. (2006) Foreign direct investment and economic transition: Panacea or pain killer? *Europe-Asia Studies* 58(6): 881–902.

Kalotay, K. (2010) Patterns of inward FDI in economies in transition. *Eastern Journal of European Studies* 1(2): 55–76.

Krippner, G.R. (2005) The financialization of the American economy. *Socio-Economic Review* 3: 173–208.

Lane, P.R. and Milesi-Ferretti, G.M. (2007) Capital flows to Central and Eastern Europe. *Emerging Markets Review* 8(2), May, 106–123.

Lux, G. (2014) Can we build location advantages? Local policies for industrial competitiveness. In *Regional Development Policy Scientific Basic and Empirical Evidence*, D. Vuković and H. Hanić (eds). 212 Belgrade Banking Academy, 42–51.

Mencinger, J. (2007) Addiction to FDI and current account balance. In *Dollarization, Euroization and Financial Instability: Central and Eastern European Countries between Stagnation and Financial Crisis?* Marburg: Metropolis Verlag, 109–128.

Myant, M. and Drahokoupil, J. (2011) *Transition Economies: Political Economy in Russia, Eastern Europe and Central Asia*. Hoboken, NJ: Wiley.

Nölke, A. and Vliegenthart, A. (2009) Enlarging the varieties of capitalism: The emergence of dependent market economies in East Central Europe. *World Politics* 61(4): 670–702.

Pavlínek, P., Domański, B. and Guzik, R. (2009) Industrial upgrading through foreign direct investment in Central European automotive. *European Urban and Regional Studies* 16(1): 43–63.

Phillips, A. (2000) *Power and Influence After the Cold War: Germany in East-Central Europe*. Lanham, MD: Rowman & Littlefield, 232.

Rajan, E., Prasad, A. and Subramanian, A. (2007) Foreign capital and economic growth. *Brookings Papers on Economic Activity* 1: 153–230.

Raviv, O. (2008) Chasing the dragon. East exploring the frontiers of Western European finance. *Contemporary Politics* 14(3): 297–314.

Sachs, J. (1990) What is to be done? *The Economist*, 13 January, 23–28.
Schmidt, A. (2014) The economic transformation in Hungary—Detour or impasse. *Politeja* 2: 115–138.
Schmidt, A. (2015) *International Political Economy, The Visegrad 4 States and the Economic Transformation*. Pécs: University of Pécs, Department of Political Science.
Śliwiński, P. (2009) *External Imbalances in CEE-10 Countries and Feldstein-Horioka Puzzle in 1994–2008*, p. 22. http://management6.com/EXTERNAL-IMBALANCES-IN-CEE-10-COUNTRIES-AND-FELDSTEIN-HORIOKA-download-w20677.pdf.
Smith, A. (2002) Imagining geographies of the 'new Europe': Geo-economic power and the new European architecture of integration. *Political Geography* 21, 5647–5670.
Smith, A. (2013) Europe and an inter-dependent world: Uneven geo-economic and geo-political developments. *European Urban and Regional Studies*, January, 20, 3–13.
Smith, A. and Swain, A. (2010) The global economic crisis, Eastern Europe, and the former Soviet Union models of development and the contradictions of internationalization. *Eurasian Geography and Economics* 51: 1–34.
Sokol, M. (2001) Central and Eastern Europe a decade after the fall of state-socialism: Regional dimensions of transition processes. *Regional Studies* 35(7): 645–655.
Søilen, K. (2012) *Geoeconomics*. London: Ventus Publishing ApS/Bookboon.
Yeşin, P. (2013) Foreign currency loans and systemic risk in Europe. *Federal Reserve Bank of St Louis Review* 95(3): 219–235.

7 The changing geoeconomics of China's diplomacy in Africa

Richard Aidoo

1 Introduction

From the 1955 Bandung Conference through subsequent global meetings, to recent events like the Forum on China–Africa Cooperation (FOCAC) summits, Chinese leaders have persistently declared their country's position toward the developing world, and along an evolving Western-dominated global political economy. The words and sentiments expressed in most of these speeches often situate China in juxtaposition to the existing global powers, mostly in the West, and second, pivoted toward the developing world where it has some geopolitical recognition and relevance (Heginbotham & Eisenman, 2013; Dittmer & Yu, 2010). In the developing world, China's history, and diplomatic and development objectives aligned with its Asian, Latin American, and African counterparts. In Africa, Beijing found the opportunity to foster ideological solidarity with countries on the continent, struggling for political self-determination from Western colonialists, and later, helped push back the dominance by the USA and the Soviet Union. Thus, China's engagement in Africa post-1945 was mainly characterized by ideological diplomacy that also featured the supply of military and economic aid, along with high-profile visits by Chinese leaders to express solidarity with the anti-colonial struggles, until its recent resurgence on the continent, particularly at the turn of the millennium.

Today, China's renewed interest in Africa is essentially driven by economic imperatives as its activities and relationships in Africa are mostly defined and sustained through economic objectives established by China and African states. Hence, these economic relationships differ from the ideological contests that Beijing was embroiled in throughout the Cold War era. The configuration of China's new relationships is predominantly shaped by the diplomacy of natural resources, loans, investments, and trade. So, unlike its earlier ideological stint, which significantly recognized the geopolitical presence of China in Africa, and its state-to-state diplomacy, recent engagements feature an emerging geography of economic development, which enables the Chinese state to acknowledge the peculiar national histories and geographies of African economies—geoeconomics.

This chapter reviews and reframes the new and emerging Sino–Africa discourse, which perceives China as a geoeconomic actor that is rather risk averse in its economic engagements—counter to some recent intellectual discourses on China's economic behavior in Africa—and also sensitive to the socio-historic, political and economic causes of the state in Africa. This is particularly so in Africa where politics and economics are in continuous transition. Furthermore, China's geoeconomic activities in Africa prioritize economic over political and security interests, in line with its 'go global' policy—a shift that is in tandem with the ever-increasing economic development pressures on states in Africa. An affirmation of Carmody and Taylor's (2011) 'flexigemony,' a contextualization of how Chinese business actors and operatives generally adapt their strategies and interests to diverse geographies and social spaces in Africa.

2 Shifting narratives in China–Africa relations: from geopolitics to geoeconomics

Over the past two decades, two main narratives have dominated Africa's economic development discourse. First is China's increased diplomacy, and most visibly, economic engagement throughout Africa, which currently has surpassed US$200 billion (Daly, 2014). In Africa, this relationship has been characterized by complementary gains such as the building and rehabilitation of infrastructure, access to loans and other forms of finance, and investments in a wide range of economic sectors. Nonetheless, these gains are often contrasted by the competition that has resulted from the presence of Chinese capital and labor, as domestic workforce and business initiatives across Africa struggle with external economic actors. Along with these challenges, the recent mass migration of Chinese to various African countries has further intensified tensions between locals and Chinese immigrants as the latter's participation in illegal and unregulated economic ventures like small-scale mining or logging often impacts diplomatic relations with China (Hess & Aidoo, 2016).

The second narrative, which has been shaped by the preceding storyline, is Africa's changing development fortunes—the discourse of Africa rising. A far cry from past decades of hopelessness, civil wars, malnutrition, failed states and economies, and epidemics that contribute to high mortality rates, Africa has ostensibly turned a corner in the past decades by posting enviable growth rates, and relatively stable democratic governments that have transformed the continent:

> like night and day: authoritarianism is giving way to accountability. Economic stagnation is turning to resurgence. And most important, despair is being replaced by hope—hope that people can live in peace with their neighbors, that parents can provide for their families, that children

> go to school and receive decent healthcare, and that people can speak their minds without fear.
>
> (Ellen Johnson Sirleaf, in Radelet, 2010, p. 5)

Such anecdotes and rhetoric are undergirded by some statistics. For instance, in 2012 net private capital flows to the region increased by 3.3% to a record $54.4 billion, notwithstanding the 8.8% decline in capital flows to developing countries (World Bank, 2013, as quoted in Chitonge, 2015, pp. 225–226). According to the World Bank (2014), gross domestic product (GDP) in the past decade has shown decent margins, albeit with some volatility in the commodities market (Chitonge, 2015, pp. 225–226). Conversely, others contend that nothing much has actually changed except for the presence of the Chinese who have influenced economies around the continent (Rowden, 2013; Lamido, 2013), signifying vestiges of Afro-pessimism, which continue to linger.

With these two narratives as essential backdrops, the dominant account of China's contribution to the shaping of the path to Africa's recent economic development is also one that shows Beijing's steady shift in strategy—from an ideologically geopolitical stance to a pragmatically geoeconomic posture. To consider China's shifting narratives from geopolitics to geoeconomics in Africa, this chapter concurs with Sparke's (2007, p. 340) assertion that geopolitics and geoeconomics do not necessarily describe distinct geostrategic periods, but are better construed as names for distinct geostrategic discourses. Hence the use of geopolitics, which connotes and conjures the contestation of space to further project political power by the state, can be further conceptualized through contemporary shifts that take into account the spatialization of political, economic and social power that leads beyond geopolitics (Cowen & Smith, 2009)—geoeconomics. Consequently, geoeconomics represents a complex notion: the intersection of economics and finance with global political and security considerations (Cowen & Smith, 2009; Kubarych, 2004). From the 1950s to the present, China–Africa relations have shifted the approach to engagement with the move toward the 21st century. This move features a more nuanced political economic strategy, reflecting the nexus between a rising global economic power and an ever-changing economic region.

The Asia-Africa Conference at Bandung in 1955 set the stage to create a geopolitical balance through South–South cooperation, and the setting of the agenda for the Non-Aligned Movement (NAM), which was to foment relations between China and its neighbors in Asia as well as other members of the NAM, mostly African states. With the Five Principles of Peaceful Coexistence as foundation, China, represented by Premier Zhou Enlai, joined co-conveners Nehru (India), Sukarno (Indonesia) and Nasser (Egypt), to rally the attendees around the political agenda of anti-imperialism with emphasis on noninterference and self-determination. As captured in his closing remarks, Nehru asserted that:

> We are brothers not only because we are Asians and Africans, but also because we are linked by the immeasurable wish for peace, resolute resistance to all dictates, firm determination to raise ourselves from backwardness. I am deeply convinced that we have a great achievement here, not only to the benefit of Asia and Africa, but for the whole of mankind as well.
>
> (as quoted in Vang, 2008, p. 2)

Furthermore, in a bid to position itself on the basis of South–South allegiance, and to project an unequal balance of power in the international system, Deng Xiaoping's address to the Sixth Special Session of the United Nations in April 1974 was resolute in this regard. He classified the international system into 'three worlds,' which consist of the Third World countries from Asia, Africa, and Latin America; and the USA and Soviet Union as the two superpowers that threatened the independence and security of nations through control, subversion, interference or aggression. In this same speech, Deng Xiaoping affirmed China's geopolitical identity as a socialist developing country that belonged to the nomenclature of the Third World, and would never ascend to become a superpower (Xiaoping, 1974, pp. 6–11). In the Third World, together with other African countries, China achieved the goal to establish a timeless geopolitical framework that would serve as a guidepost for future diplomatic relationships with fellow members of the Third World, especially Africa. The functionality of this framework, along with the narrative of South–South cooperation, still holds sway over Beijing's recent continuous attempt to outcompete Western actors in Africa.

Further from the geopolitics of South–South cooperation during the Bandung Conference, and with an end to the cause to extricate imperialism from Africa, China's second entrance into Africa is mainly characterized by a shift away from the proselytization of socialism and anti-imperialism toward issues that pertain to economic self-determination. This rightly complements the post-independent stature of African states. Hence recent complexities of China–Africa relations are underscored by the post-independence shifts that take into account the holistic spatialization of political, economic and social power that transcends the simplicity of geopolitics. As Bandung became 'a symbol of Afro-Asia as a viable political concept' (Larkin, 1971, p. 28), China's engagement with African countries is one that is often perceived as historically well placed. As justifiably put by the former Chinese Foreign Minister Qian Qichen, 'as developing regions that … once suffered the oppression and exploitation of imperialism and colonialism, China and the African countries … easily understand each other's pursuit of independence and freedom and … have a natural feeling of intimacy' (as quoted in Taylor, 2012, p. 24).

The globalization discourse, and contemporary economic arrangements, offered China a renewed opportunity to broaden the narrative with regards to Africa, to include socioeconomic imperatives of global political power, particularly at the turn of the millennium. The FOCAC Summit established this task from its first meeting in Beijing, in October 2000, to its sixth and most recent in Johannesburg, South Africa. As indicated by then Chinese Premier Zhu Rongji at the first FOCAC, China–Africa ties help 'build up our capacity against possible risks, which will put us in a better position to participate in economic globalization and safeguard our economic interests and economic security.' They also 'improve the standing of the developing countries in North-South dialogue so as to facilitate the establishment of a fair and rational new international political economic order' (as quoted in Taylor, 2012, p. 25). This shift in geo-strategy essentially attempts to build on the geopolitical rhetoric at Bandung by adopting the broad frame of geoeconomics, which simply links the 'big picture' with the practical realm of markets (Kubarych, 2004) in an era of global integration.

Lastly, another maturation moment of China–Africa relations that further exemplifies the shift toward a more socioeconomic frame is South Africa's accession to the BRICS—an economic forum (of Brazil, Russia, India, China and South Africa) that is described as less political, but rather a loose constellation of economic interests led by China (Naidu, 2013). Since South Africa's ascent to this forum in 2011 was at the behest of China, it underscores the latter's attempt to broaden South–South economic advancement—a continuation of the quest for solidarity toward self-determination at the Bandung Conference, except that the emphasis is mainly economic rather than political. In spite of the skepticism that South Africa encountered, mostly centered on the robustness and maturity of the South African economy, Naidu (2013) argues that one of the push factors that led to the adding of South Africa, the 'S' in this prominent international relations lexicon, was the geographic representation of Africa in a predominantly South–South economic forum. Undoubtedly, there may be some undertones of global political representation in China's extension of invitation to South Africa; however, there is no contest over the fact that BRICS is an economic forum, and hence this move is mostly construed as a geoeconomic benefit to emerging economic powers.

3 Shifting sands: China's geoeconomics in a changing Africa

In the past decade, China's economic exploits in Africa have been perceived differently from what the latter has encountered with other countries and global institutions, particularly from the West. Comparatively, discourse surrounding Beijing's investments has been distinctive on two fronts: first, Chinese economic engagements in Africa have been characterized as not being risk averse in their diverse investments in Africa, regardless of the political, economic, and demographic terrain. Second, Beijing has been critiqued for extending non-conditional economic investments and other financial terms to African states. This approach to economic engagement of African states is arguably perceived as an encumbrance to structural and institutional reforms in a region of the world known for a dearth of institutions. Thus, China's quest for natural resources has been imputed for propping up recluse political regimes around Africa. Western states and financial institutions like the International Monetary Fund (IMF) and World Bank have been dogged with criticisms of interference in the political and economic development processes in Africa. Hence China's persistent attempt to distinguish its current relations with African economies as ones that are mainly founded on mutual respect and noninterference in the domestic affairs of these polities—both cornerstones of China's diplomacy toward the developing world. These tenets upheld by China in its engagement of African economies have enabled it the flexibility to economically accommodate the different geographies of endowment and uncertainty in Africa.

Though structuralist arguments of uneven relations and exploitation of economies in the global periphery by the core and semi-periphery persist, Africa's economic resurgence in the past decade has dominated the development discourse as sluggish and uncertain economies on the continent have begun to show promise. This nature of economic growth with impressive rates signaled some change in economic fortunes for a continent once deemed hopeless and failing. According to the biannual regional economic outlook of the IMF, growth rates for sub-Saharan Africa were 4.9% for 2013, 5.0% in 2014, and with a projected 4.5% for 2015 (above the global average of 2.5%), which took into account lower commodity prices, and sluggish growth in advanced economies, coupled with China's reduced demand for African commodities due to its own decelerated growth (Adjei, 2015). Additionally, the incremental political progress made by most African states as they embrace democratization and good governance offers a stable investment environment, a far cry from the pervasive and incessant dictatorships that characterized the African political landscape in the 1980s and 1990s.

With such positive political economic developments at the turn of the millennium, China has both contributed to and benefited from this emerging image of Africa. From an insignificant $5 billion in the 1990s to a current total of over $200 billion in trade engagements, Beijing has played a meaningful role in this emerging narrative of Africa rising (Chitonge, 2015; Lamido, 2013), with its insatiable demand for African resources. Alternatively, China has gained from previous structural reforms adopted by African economies upon the insistence of Western countries and financial institutions. Political reforms like the reinstitution of structures of governance, and periodic elections in juxtaposition with fiscal sector reforms encouraged under the Structural Adjustment Programs (SAPs) in the 1980s and 1990s have variedly contributed to some level of stability in the investment sectors of adopter states.

Nonetheless, due to the unstable character of the African political economic environment, and China's flexigemony—its ability to adapt strategies geographically to adjust to specific histories and geographies of African states—intellectual perception gives way to reality. As global economic fortunes have changed with the weakening of the natural resources market, and a faltering Chinese economy, China has reacted by truncating some of its priced investments across Africa (see Table 7.1). As African economies turn to their old ways of excessive borrowing, and over-reliance on natural resources, debt reduces the viability and increases the volatility of these economies, leading to a fall in investor confidence. For instance, debt grew to $20 billion in 2014 with the IMF projecting 3.7% and 2.9% in 2015 and 2016, respectively (Adjei, 2015). This, combined with other socio-political factors within the state, mostly derails or stalls most Chinese-sponsored projects.

Ghana is an instructive case that illustrates Beijing's 'flexigemony' in Africa, investing in small economies like Ghana with incipient oil and energy industries, and predominantly agriculture sectors. Ghana, a former British colony, has generally fostered a dependent relationship with the IMF and World Bank, after years of successive military takeovers and economic stagnation. With persistently poor economic performances, the Rawlings-led Provisional National Defence Council embraced the SAPs from the IMF and the World Bank in the 1990s. Two decades after attempting diverse political and economic reforms, Breisinger et al. (2011) point to Ghana as a prime candidate to champion economic transformation in Africa based on two decades of

Table 7.1 Stalled, failed or canceled China-Africa deals/projects

Year	*Country*	*Investor*	*Sector*	*Project value ($ billion)*
2006	Nigeria	China Railway Construction	Transport	7.5
2007	Nigeria	Gezhouba	Energy	1.4
2007	Angola	Sinopec	Energy	3.4
2008	Nigeria	Sinoma	Real estate	1.4
2009	Democratic Republic of the Congo	Ex-Im Bank	Metals	3.0
2011	Ghana	China Development Bank	Energy	3.0
2011	Libya	China Railway Construction	Transport	4.2
2011	Libya	Sinohydro	Real estate	1.8
2011	Libya	China State Construction Engineering	Real estate	1.3
2011	Tanzania	Jinchuan Group Co. Ltd.	Metals	Not stated
2012	Gabon	Sinomach	Metals	3.0

(*Wall Street Journal*, 2014; Bloomberg News, 2014)

sound and persistent annual growth of about 5%, and projected as the first sub-Saharan African country to achieve the first Millennium Development Goal of halving poverty before 2015. Additionally, Ghana's democratic institutions and governance are known to be some of the most stable across the continent. With political, institutional, and macroeconomic stability, Breisinger et al. (2011) assert that in the past two decades, the return of confidence in the country's creditworthiness and the improvement in investments in the private and public sectors are promising. The prospects were furthered by the discovery of oil in commercial quantities in 2007.

Ghana's progress in economic development came along with China's growing interest in Ghana, as part of its geographically expansive economic interests and engagements across Africa. Though Chinese diplomatic relations were established in 1960 (after Bandung, as Ghana was one of the African countries present at the conference), the relations were largely ideological, backing the then Nkrumah regime in its struggle for independence from the British. In the post-independence era, Ghana–China relations have included economic arrangements. Based on the growing ties between the two countries, and Ghana's socioeconomic and political maturity, Beijing and Accra agreed on a $3 billion oil-for-infrastructure loan deal, which was then the largest of its kind in sub-Saharan Africa. However, owing to falling world market prices in oil, and a political and diplomatic brouhaha over Chinese illegal miners in Ghana (Hess & Aidoo, 2016), Beijing truncated the loan after paying $600 million of the $3 billion (see Table 7.1). In dire need of resources to complete the earmarked infrastructure projects, Ghana did an about-face to the IMF for another reform-based loan of $900 million. This and other examples indicated in Table 7.1 show China's readiness to act on changing domestic political and socioeconomic circumstances to suit its evolving interests in a continent with immense economic and development uncertainties.

4 Concluding remarks

As the narratives surrounding China's vast interests in Africa have evolved over the past decades, it has become evident that China–Africa relations have developed from an ideological perspective toward the more recent economic engagements. The relevance of the ideological connection during the pre-independence era has given way to more pragmatic economic encounters necessary to the post-independence African states. China's emphasis on geopolitical balance in the international community underscored the importance of South–South cooperation during and immediately after the Bandung conference. However, with globalization and the political-economic resurgence of African states, the ability of China to economically adapt to the different geographies and histories in Africa has become a feature of this 21st-century economic engagement. This is even more relevant given the recent downturns in the Chinese economy, as well as the erratic performances of African economies due to the vagaries of the global commodities market. Divergent to the discourse of China's non-conditional loans and investments notwithstanding the risks, China's recent quest to invest and trade in Africa has also come with unforeseen challenges that sometimes led it to rescind its economic interests in particular geographic areas in Africa.

The concept of geoeconomics is especially valuable to the diverse prospective business interests in Africa—a continent that is characteristically known for uncertain socio-political and economic developments. As Kubarych (2004) puts it, geoeconomics simply links the 'big picture' with the practical realm of markets, which is a useful signpost for the era of global economic integration. Like states, the implications for other actors interested in business in Africa include the consideration of the broad socio-political arrangements of the continent or a particular African state of interest. With such understanding, the businesses and investments from China, and other parts of the world that often succeed in Africa, do so with immense abilities to adapt to different spatial contexts. For policymakers and scholars, this means elevating the geoeconomic context over the geopolitical one, which often receives the most attention.

References

Adjei, S. (2015) *Rising Debts in Sub-Saharan Africa—A Threat to 'Africa Arise.'* Retrieved January 5, 2016 from LinkedIn Pulse at www.linkedin.com/pulse/rising-debts-sub-saharan-africa-threat-africa-arise-samuel.

Bloomberg News (2014) China swaps gusto for rigor as it learns from Africa. Retrieved September 20, 2016 from Bloomberg at www.bloomberg.com/news/articles/2014-06-02/china-swaps-gusto-for-rigor-in-africa-as-it-learns-from-mistakes.

Breisinger, C., Diao, X., Kolavalli, S., Al Hassan, R. and Thurlow, J. (eds) (2011) *A New Era of Transformation in Ghana: Lessons from the Past and Scenarios for the Future.* Washington, DC: International Food Policy Research Institute.

Carmody, P. and Taylor, I. (2011) Chinese interests and strategies in Africa. In *The New Scramble for Africa*, C. Padraig (ed.). Cambridge: Polity, pp. 65–94.

Chitonge, H. (2015) *Economic Growth and Development in Africa: Understanding Trends and Prospects.* London and New York: Routledge.

Cowen, D. and Smith, N. (2009) After geopolitics? From the geopolitical social to geoeconomics. *Antipode* 41(1): 22–48.

Daly, J. (2014) In 2014, Chinese-African trade will surpass $200 billion. Retrieved January 5, 2016. oilprice.com/Energy/Energy-General/In-2014-Chinese-African-trade-will-surpass-200-billion.html.

Dittmer, L. and Yu, G. (2010) *China, the Developing World, and the New Global Dynamic.* Boulder, CO: Lynne Rienner.

Heginbotham, E. and Eisenman, J. (2013) *China and the Developing World: Beijing's Strategy for the 21st Century.* New Delhi: KW Publishers Pvt Ltd.

Hess, S. and Aidoo, R. (2016) Charting the impact of subnational actors in China's foreign relations: The 2013 Galamsey crisis in Ghana. *Asian Survey* 52(2) (March/April).

Kubarych, R.M. (2004) Geo-economics injects new uncertainties into troubled markets. Retrieved January 8, 2016. www.cfr.org/international-finance/geo-economics-injects-new-uncertainties-into-troubled-markets/p7039.

Lamido, S. (2013) Africa must get real about Chinese ties. Retrieved January 8, 2016. www.ft.com/intl/cms/s/0/562692b0-898c-11e2-ad3f-00144feabdc0.html#axzz42ksTBuAs.

Larkin, B. (1971) *China and Africa, 1949–70: The Foreign Policy of the People's Republic of China*. Berkeley and Los Angeles: University of California Press.

Naidu, S. (2013) South Africa's accession to the BRICS: Towards the 2013 summit. In *China–Africa Relations in an Era of Great Transformation*, L. Xing and A.O. Farah (eds) London: Ashgate, pp. 185–203.

Radelet, S. (2010) *Emerging Africa: How 17 Countries are Leading the Way.* Washington, DC: Brookings Institution Press.

Rowden, R. (2013) The myth of Africa's rise. Retrieved January 10, 2016. foreignpolicy.com/2013/01/04/the-myth-of-africas-rise/.

Sparke, M. (2007) Geopolitical fears, geoeconomic hopes and the responsibilities of geography. *Annals of the Association of American Geographers* 97(2): 338–349.

Taylor, I. (2012) *The Forum on China–Africa Cooperation (FOCAC)*. New York: Routledge.

Vang, P. (2008) *Five Principles of Chinese Foreign Policies.* Bloomington, IN: Authorhouse.

Wall Street Journal (2014) China takes wary steps in new Africa deal. Retrieved September 20, 2016 from *Wall Street Journal* at www.wsj.com/articles/SB10001424052702303647204579545813194873656.

World Bank (2013) Africa pulse rate: An analysis of issues shaping Africa's economic future. Retrieved September 20, 2016 from www.worldbank.org/content/dam/Worldbank/document/Africa/Report/Africas-Pulse-brochure_Vol8.pdf.

World Bank (2014) Africa pulse rate: An analysis of issues shaping Africa's economic future. Retrieved September 20, 2016 from www.worldbank.org/content/dam/Worldbank/document/Africa/Report/Africas-Pulse-brochure_Vol9.pdf.

Xiaoping, D. (1974) Chairman of Chinese delegation Teng Hsiao-Ping's speech. *Peking Review* 17(16) (April), 6–11.

8 The nature, impact and lessons of Abenomics

Viara Bojkova

1 Introduction

Early in 2013, the newly elected Japanese government of Mr Shinzo Abe began the implementation of a major policy package aimed at addressing the problems of persistent deflation and low growth. This package consisted of three key elements, known as the 'Three Arrows' of Abenomics. These are a mixture of monetary expansion, fiscal stimulus and structural reform of an overregulated economy. Particular attention has focused on the former, which involves a very significant expansion of quantitative and qualitative easing (QQE), linked to its long history in Japan. This chapter outlines the background to the implementation of the Abe programme, the nature of the three components, their impact on the economy to date, likely future direction and prospects for success, and concludes with an assessment of the lessons that other countries might derive from the Japanese experience.

2 'Japan's lost decades' and Abe's policy objectives

Japan's lost decades that followed the 1991 banking crisis were characterised by the lowering of expectations, prices and growth, conditions under which deflationary expectations became self-fulfilling. The crisis, which began with failures of financial institutions and businesses, caused by a high level of speculative investment in property, necessitated the banks assuming major responsibility for various rescue operations and restructuring. To support the economy's escape from a deflationary spiral, the Bank of Japan (BOJ) launched a series of unconventional monetary policies between 2001–06 and 2010, which failed to revitalise the economy. To put an end once and for all to deflation and no growth, Abe introduced a much broader and more radical set of policies in 2013 with the key objectives of:

- Achieving a 2% inflation target via monetary expansion.
- Designing a flexible fiscal policy to act as an economic stimulus in the short term, and in the longer run achieving a budget surplus to reduce public debt.

- Launching a growth strategy to focus on structural reform and private investment to improve long-term growth.

For some, Abenomics represents a monetary regime change similar to that of the USA during the 1930s (Bojkova, 2014). As such, Japan's current policies and developments under the Abe Cabinet, and their regional and global implications, have attracted much interest amongst Western policymakers.

3 Monetary policy—the first arrow of Abenomics

The BOJ has officially used unconventional monetary policies since 2001, and some elements of these since the Great Depression (Bruce & Bojkova, 2014). However, in 2016 it sought to catalyse a bigger and bolder combination of rising prices, higher corporate profits, and increase in wages and employment. The BOJ planned to expand its QQE to maintain the increase of the monetary base at an annual pace of about ¥80 trillion through the purchases of Japanese government bonds, with the provision that purchases could be increased if needed. In addition, from early 2016 the average maturity of the Bank's Japanese government bonds purchases were extended from 7 to about 7–12 years to encourage a smoother decline in rates across the entire yield curve. Moreover, the Bank will, as well as maintaining its purchases of corporate bonds, purchase exchange-traded funds and Japan real estate investment trusts at an annual rate of about ¥3 trillion and ¥90 billion, respectively (BOJ, 2015).

Early in 2016, the BOJ decided to introduce a negative rate on new commercial bank deposits to stimulate lending. In addition, the BOJ has simplified and extended loan periods and eligibility for the Bank's Fund Provisioning Measure to Support Economic Growth (BOJ, 2015). This includes adding a new category—'firms that are actively making investment in physical and human capital'—to the list of 18 possible areas to which financial institutions' investment or lending are recognised as eligible for the Loan Support Programme. This measure has been accompanied by the establishment of a new scheme for purchasing exchange-traded funds at about ¥300 billion in addition to the existing purchases of ¥3 trillion. These are composed only of stocks issued by firms that are making investment in physical and human capital. Thus, from April 2016 the BOJ buys only exchange-traded funds, which track the JPX-Nikkei Index 400.

Overall, the BOJ has launched a massive diversified monetary expansion, and while some argue about the success of the programme, the economy has demonstrated signs of moderate recovery since 2013 despite some risks stemming from global economic conditions and domestic opposition (Bojkova, 2015). The most controversial issue is that of the labour market, where conditions remain tight with a current unemployment rate of about 3.3%, close to 'full employment', and slowly increasing wages.[1] Less controversial is private consumption, which has been fairly resilient, reflecting the improvements in employment and income. Although the nominal and real expenditures declined by 1.3% and 2.3% during 2015, the index of household expenditures for the last five years has shown signs of relatively firm domestic consumption, particularly in spending on food, housing, furniture and household utensils, and medical care (Tables 8.1 and 8.2). It is noticeable that consumption spending shifted to durable purchases and private residential investments in 2014, as both components are most responsive to real interest rate changes.

In the corporate sector, profits have hit record high levels as a result of the lower crude oil prices and the depreciation of the yen. In nominal effective exchange rate terms, the yen had depreciated by more than 20% by early 2015.[2] These developments have benefited both small and large firms, and have increased levels of fixed investment across a broad range of industries. In terms of rising prices, the consumption price index for all items less fresh food

Table 8.1 Change of consumption expenditures, yearly average 2015

Items actual	*Figures (¥)*	*Nominal change (%)*	*Real change (%)*
Two or more-person households			
Consumption expenditures	287,373	−1.3	−2.3
Food	71,844	2.7	−0.4
Housing	17,931	0.1	−0.7
Fuel, light, water charges	23,197	−2.5	0.1
Furniture and household utensils	10,458	−1.6	−3.1
Clothing and footwear	11,363	−5.2	−7.2
Medical care	12,663	−1.4	−2.3
Transportation and communication	40,238	−4.0	−2.1
Education	10,995	0.5	−1.1
Culture and recreation	28,314	−2.2	−4.0
Workers' households			
Disposable income	427,270	0.9	−0.1
Consumption expenditure	315,379	−1.1	−2.1
Average propensity to consume (%)	73.8	75.3[1]	−1.5[2]

Notes: 1 Figure of the previous year; 2 Difference of point between a year.
(Statistics Bureau, Ministry of International Affairs and Communications website, www.stat.go.jp)

Table 8.2 Index of consumption expenditure level (adjusted by number of household members; the first quarter—Q1), 2010=100

Items	*2012 Q1*	*2013 Q1*	*2014 Q1*	*2015 Q1*	*2016 Q1*
General	97.1	100.7	102.7	96.1	92.9
Food	99.5	102.0	103.6	100.4	101.3
Housing	96.9	97.5	108.8	96.3	88.8
Fuel, light, water	97.3	96.2	94.6	92.5	86.0
Furniture, household utensils	105.3	105.9	143.9	107.7	105.0
Clothing and footwear	99.1	102.7	110.8	99.5	91.1
Medical care	102.2	102.1	108.6	101.9	107.8
Transport and communication	95.0	106.2	109.8	101.3	99.0
Education	101.4	106.1	94.8	94.8	98.0
Culture and recreation	93.8	97.7	98.7	89.7	87.0
Others	95.2	99.2	104.6	94.9	90.2

(Statistics Bureau, Ministry of International Affairs and Communications website, Japan www.stat.go.jp)

was 0.0% in November 2015. However, if energy and fresh food prices are excluded, the consumer price index (CPI) has since late 2014 increased at an annual rate of 0.9%,[3] still far below the 2% target. Nevertheless, when all consumption components are considered, a price decline was observed only for transportation and communication services, and to fuel, light and water charges, all due to lower energy prices. The year-on-year rate of change in the CPI excluding energy and fresh food moved above zero in October 2013 and has been positive since then, which arguably marks fairly sustainable inflation which has not been seen in Japan for a long time.

A further positive signal is that nominal gross domestic product (GDP) shifted into an upward trend as the Japanese economy technically managed to avoid a recession in 2015. The gross national income (GNI) has increased even more strikingly, reaching the level of ¥536.9 trillion in the third quarter of 2015, reflecting both an expansion of overseas operations by Japanese firms and a depreciated exchange rate. Real income was also on an upward trend even during the deflationary periods when the nominal income was held back by the falling prices.

Overall, the first arrow of Abenomics achieved a reduction in real interest rates—by lowering nominal rates and raising inflationary expectations—and as such it pushed up both the output gap and inflation, and thus monetary expansion seems to steadily exhibit its intended effects (Bojkova, 2015).

Therefore, the governor of the BOJ, Haruhiko Kuroda, concluded in his speech to the Japan Business Federation (December 2015) that with QQE launched three years earlier, Japan's economy appeared close to completing a true monetary regime change.

4 Fiscal policy and structural reforms—the second and third arrows

The fiscal policy of the Abe Cabinet, described as the second arrow, was launched in January 2013 with the announcement of a ¥10.3 trillion stimulus package, which was complemented in October 2013 by an additional ¥5 trillion. The latter was intended to address any risks of an economic downturn from the planned April 2014 8% consumption tax hike.[4] The supplementary budget implemented specific measures, which during 2014 gave lump-sum benefits to those affected by the tax rise and pay-outs for home buyers, a review of automobile taxation, and measures for reconstruction, disaster prevention and safety (MoF, 2013). In December 2014, a further ¥3.5 trillion was allocated to support the country's lagging regions, small businesses, students and house buyers. Moreover, an important task in 2015 was to take actions to overcome problems with a declining and ageing population, for which the budget was slightly increased by ¥460 billion in FY2015/16 to ¥96.3 trillion.

The government also promoted fiscal consolidation and in 2015 for the first time the issuance amount of Japanese government bonds was planned to fall to ¥30 trillion and the dependence on public debt issuance to decline below 40%. This tendency began in 2013, when the maximum total amount of the Special Deficit-Financing Bonds plus Construction Bonds was ¥40.9 trillion, in 2014 ¥38.5 trillion, and in 2015 ¥36.9 trillion, presenting Abe's medium-term commitment to reduce the dependence on public debt.

The government's target is to bring the primary balance, including national and local government budgets, into surplus by FY2020 and put the debt ratio on a downward trend thereafter (MoF, 2015). However, this still remains to be seen and may prove to be a major obstacle. According to projections by the Organisation for Economic Co-operation and Development (OECD), the primary deficit will be nearly 2% of GDP in FY2020, even considering the delayed second tax hike, with nominal GDP growth averaging 3.1% until FY2022 (OECD, 2015). To tackle this persistent fiscal problem, the government needs to define a credible medium-term strategy supported by a strong institutional framework that would help maintain confidence in Japan's fiscal sustainability.

Despite these fiscal challenges, the packages provided the necessary boost to the real economy via the multiplier effect. The International Monetary Fund (IMF) estimated the real growth of GDP at 0.9% in 2014 and 0.8% in 2015 (IMF, 2014), and a projected 1% in 2016 and 0.3% in 2017 (IMF, 2016). A number of economists have tried to estimate the relative extent to which the monetary and fiscal effects have been channelled through since 2013, but this is difficult to conclude given the extent to which monetary and fiscal effects are entangled (Bojkova, 2015).

The last arrow of Abenomics was launched in June 2014 with a detailed programme of deregulation. The ten key reforms in the 'Japan Revitalisation Strategy' are essential for implementing further changes and increasing growth prospects in addition to the monetary and fiscal stimulus. The list of actions is shown in Table 8.3.

Unquestionably, the long-run structural reforms are critical to the success of Abenomics. Monetary and fiscal stimulus will only have temporary effects if not supported by radical reform, which in itself is targeted to boost GNI per capita by more than ¥1.5 million to ¥5.3 million by 2023.

It may be that the reform programme proves too ambitious, for it will require both extensive debate and consensus from Japanese society. For instance, creating incentives for women to undertake more work and managerial positions (reform 6) would require the existing system of work performance to be fundamentally overhauled, thereby rewarding employees by results, rather than working hours spent.

Moreover, to increase GNI per capita as planned, Japan would need to reverse the decline in the terms of trade that it has experienced due to the emergence of low-cost manufacturing in Asia and a weak Japanese innovation system.[5] Comparatively, Germany's manufactured exports did not experience notable terms-of-trade losses.

The key reforms in the Japan Revitalisation Strategy also ambitiously aim to raise the share of Japan's trade with countries with which it has concluded either an Economic Partnership Agreement or a Free Trade Agreement from 19% in 2012 to 70% by 2018. This will require agreements with key trading partners, such as the USA, China and the European Union, as well as regional trade initiatives such as the US-led Trans-Pacific Partnership. Perhaps quite controversial, from the perspective of traditional Japanese society, is that the trade agreements are expected to introduce structural adjustments in agriculture, a task that will not likely be easily accommodated into Japan's conservative hinterland. However, it must be stressed that there has been little real gain in any of the planned domestic reforms and the vested interests involved are such that it may take longer for any meaningful progress to be made.

5 Impact on the East Asian region and the global economy

As the Japanese economy slowly emerges from deflation and regains momentum, the close interdependence between Japan and the rest of Asia should be strengthening, not only via the currency markets but also through the overseas operations of Japanese corporations. As mentioned, the corporations increased their profits to record highs in 2015 due to the depreciated yen without any increase in the export volume. The trade deficit began to decline at the end of 2014, and up to May 2015, Japan registered the

Table 8.3 Ten key reforms

Key reform	*Actions taken*
1 Enhance corporate governance: aiming for improvements in corporate values	The JPX-Nikkei 400 launched in 2014 followed by a Stewardship Code. A draft corporate governance code requires listed firms to have at least two outside directors on a 'comply or explain basis'
2 Reforms for management of public and quasi-public funds	The Government Pension Investment Fund decided in 2014 to increase the share of equities in its portfolio and reinforce its governance structure
3 Promotion of new business ventures: creating an entrepreneur-friendly environment	The tax system for business start-ups was made user-friendly and promotional measures of crowdfunding were enacted
4 Corporate tax reform: improving business conditions	The effective corporate tax rate was reduced from 34.62% to 32.11% in 2015, and to 31.33% in 2016
5 Stimulate innovation through science and technology, and a 'robot revolution': Japan as a technology frontier	The budget for science and technology, which had been managed by a number of ministries, was centralised in the Council for Science, Technology and Innovation to promote effective R&D
6 Enhancing women's participation and advancement	Additional 400,000 childcare places were added to eliminate waiting lists, together with 300,000 places in after-school care for school-age children. Female employment has risen by 3.9% since late 2012
7 Enabling flexible working practices: improving the talent pool (high-level experts evaluated on actual performance)	Subsidies to maintain jobs are being shifted to promoting labour mobility. Measures against overwork will be reinforced and the Cabinet reviews flexibility and discretionary working-hour systems
8 Attract talent from overseas	Foreign trainees are allowed to stay in Japan for three years; this will be extended to five years
9 A dynamic agricultural policy (structural reforms are planned)	The production quotas for table rice are being phased out over a five-year period by FY2018
10 Strong health care industry and high-quality services	A new health insurance scheme was introduced to give patients faster access to new treatments that are covered by public health insurance (a new institution to manage R&D in health care—created)

(Official website of the Prime Minister of Japan and his Cabinet, www.kantei.go.jp)

smallest deficit, of ¥7.7 trillion, since January 2013. To take advantage of the exchange rate, Japanese firms decided to raise the export prices in yen terms and maintain the export prices in contract non-yen currency terms (more than 60% of all contracts). In this way, they might in the long term be able to increase international market shares without sparking price wars thanks to the monetary expansion.

Regionally, the capital flows from Japan to Asia such as foreign direct investment (FDI) and portfolio investments had been increasing despite the weak yen. The three favourite destinations were China, India and Indonesia. Obviously, there are a number of factors that Japanese corporations take into consideration when making such decisions—lower production costs, higher profit margins, higher yields, expanding domestic markets in Asia and an ageing population[6] in Japan. The opposite effect is also observable where Asian portfolio investments in Japan have been steadily going up since 2013 as Japan implements its growth strategy to facilitate inward FDI, the NISA (Nippon Individual Savings Account) with tax exemption up to ¥1.2 million of stock investments, reduces the corporate tax rate and attracts qualified professionals. With the Revitalisation Strategy in place, Japan will attract more FDI.

Internationally, the focus is on how the correction of excessive appreciation of the yen affects economic activities worldwide, and whether the expansionary policies amount to a competitive devaluation, with some effects on global imbalances. Japan has the world's largest net foreign assets position of ¥113.9 trillion (The World Bank, 2014), most of which is held in US dollars, thus the depreciated rate increases the value of foreign assets in terms of yen. This naturally increases the income from net foreign asset holdings and is visible in the GNI figures, from which Japan's partners also benefit. With this in mind, Abenomics has been developing in a way that minimises negative impacts on Asia and the world, and other countries should learn from it.[7]

6 Conclusions

Overall, Abe's policies have been gradually exerting their effects on Japanese growth, and making some positive impacts on the region and the world, as the analysis has demonstrated. However, assessing the results and lessons of Abe's 'arrows strategy' that might benefit other countries should be done in the context of the diverging global economic conditions that led to separation from the common path of monetary easing. While the Federal Reserve has begun the normalisation of monetary policy in the USA, the European Central Bank, Bank of England and Bank of Japan continue maintaining their accommodative monetary conditions. Although there were similarities among the outcomes of all major central banks' policies—low (even negative) interest rates, depreciated exchange rates, high asset prices, dynamic capital flows, moderate growth rates—one significant distinction of the BOJ's long-run 'unconventional' policies is the diversification of the programmes, targeting specific niche markets as the real economy is a priority, and performing qualitative easing to move Japan to a new phase of higher growth. Moreover, the whole Abe package integrates monetary and fiscal stimulation with a number of structural reforms in a comprehensive way that could be recommended to the European Union.

Notably, full implementation of the structural reforms is urgently needed to foster both growth and income equality along Japan's long-term recovery without any aggravation of global imbalance. For instance, Aoyagi, Ganelli and Murayama (IMF, 2015) estimated a model of the impact of key Abenomics policies on changes in average income and income equality. They found that the expansionary policies that can help move inflation (such as QQE) tend to improve average income growth by up to 1.9%, while increasing female labour participation is found to have a positive impact on income equality by 0.2–0.35%. Such an inclusive growth recovery of Japan is needed both for the success of Abenomics locally and the reduction of the global economy's imbalances.

As the future monetary policies of major central banks increasingly diverge, more capital would be expected to be flowing into emergent Asian markets, which in order to avoid local currency appreciations would flow out in search of safe havens. If such quick money were to flow into Japan, it would have large effects on the Japanese government bonds market and the currency, which might offset some of the BOJ's efforts and damage its credibility. Considering such side effects of major monetary policies and uncoordinated actions, one must admit that the domestic structural reforms are crucial for the lasting success of Abenomics, and a revitalised Japan is of overwhelming importance for the rest of the world in order to set up an excellent example of the measures needed to achieve robust growth and inflation.

Notes

1 Olivier Blanchard (former IMF chief economist) and Adam Posen (Peterson Institute) have recently proposed four measures to force an aggressive wage increase in Japan.
2 Since January 2016 the yen has appreciated by 11% against the dollar (BOJ, 2016).
3 Statistics Bureau of Japan, www.stat.go.jp.
4 The previous National Diet voted the consumption tax rise into law in 2012. While the Abe government was obliged to implement it, in view of the general economic situation, a second increase to 10% was postponed until October 2019.
5 Zhou (2015): the research output traditionally with a stronghold in the Nature Index, Japan dropped in recent years.
6 Due to the ageing population, the household savings rate turned negative in FY2013 for the first time in 60 years.
7 For other studies examining the effects of Abenomics, see Bojkova (2015).

References

Bank of Japan (BOJ) (2015) *Statement on Monetary Policy*. www.boj.or.jp/en/announcements/release_2015/k151218a.pdf.

Bank of Japan (BOJ) (2016) *Outlook for Economic Activity and Prices*. www.boj.or.jp/en/mopo/outlook/gor1604b.pdf.

Bojkova, V. (2014) Current results of Japan's QQE. *GPI Opinion*. www.gpilondon.com/publications/current-results-of-japans-qqe/.

Bojkova, V. (2015) *Abenomics and Japan's Future*. GPI Discussion Paper. www.gpilondon.com/publications/abenomics-and-japans-future/.

Bruce, D. and Bojkova, V. (2014) *The International Financial Integration and Long-term Trends in Japanese Short-term Interest Rates*. GPI Discussion Paper. www.gpilondon.com/publications/international-financial-integration-and-long-run-trends-in-short-term-japanese-interest-rates/.

International Monetary Fund (IMF) (2014) *Regional Economic Outlook Update—Asia and Pacific*. www.imf.org/external/pubs/ft/reo/2014/apd/eng/areo1014.pdf.

International Monetary Fund (IMF) (2015) How inclusive is Abenomics? Working Paper 15/54, C. Aoyagi, G. Ganelli and K. Murayama. www.imf.org/external/pubs/ft/wp/2015/wp1554.pdf.

International Monetary Fund (IMF) (2016) *World Economic Outlook Update*. www.imf.org/external/pubs/ft/weo/2016/update/01/.

Kuroda, H. (2015) *At the Turning Point*. Speech to the JBF. www.boj.or.jp/en/announcements/press/koen_2015/ko151224a.htm/.

Ministry of Finance (MoF) (2013) *Japanese Economy and Policy Measures*. Presentation. www.mof.go.jp/english/public_relations/presentation/pre201310.pdf.

Ministry of Finance (MoF) (2015) Speech on fiscal policy by the minister of finance, Japan. www.mof.go.jp/english/public_relations/statement/fiscal_policy_speech/e20150212.html.

Organisation for Economic Co-operation and Development (OECD) (2015) OECD economic surveys: Japan. www.oecd.org/eco/surveys/Japan-2015-overview.pdf.

Statistics Bureau, Ministry of International Affairs & Communications (n.d.). www.stat.go.jp (accessed 21 May 2016).

The World Bank (2014) Database. www.data.worldbank.org (accessed 5 June 2016).

Zhou, Y. (2015) The rapid rise of a research nation. *Nature* 528(7582): 170–173.

9 Where geoeconomics and geostrategy meet

The troubled relations between the European Union and the Russian Federation

David Criekemans

1 Introduction

In 1990, Edward Luttwak coined the term 'geoeconomics.' He predicted that in some parts of world where the role of military power was diminishing, states would continue to compete within 'a logic of conflict,' but via 'methods of commerce' rather than military methods. In this chapter, it is argued that geoeconomical and geostrategical competition can exist at the same time, and can be mutually supportive. To illustrate this phenomenon, we will study the troubled relationship between the European Union (EU) and the Russian Federation, with particular stress on the period of the third presidency of Vladimir Putin (since May 2012).

Both the EU and Russia had their own rivaling geopolitical project. Geoeconomics was an essential driver in it. First, we will briefly revisit Luttwak's thesis from 1990 and some authors who responded to it. Second, we develop a brief geopolitical and geoeconomic analysis of the relations between the EU and Russia between 1994 and 2012. Third, we investigate in depth the evolution of the relationship between the EU and the Russian Federation, especially focusing on the Ukraine crisis since the end of 2013. Finally, what conclusions can be drawn from this analysis about the interaction and mutual reinforcement of geoeconomical and geostrategic competition?

2 Edward Luttwak's thesis on geoeconomics, and some authors who responded

In 1990, Edward N. Luttwak published his article 'From Geopolitics to Geoeconomics: Logic of Conflict, Grammar of Commerce' in *The National Interest* (Luttwak, 1990). The Cold War was in its last phase. Did this mean that geopolitical struggle had come to an end? Luttwak claimed the methods of commerce are displacing military methods—with disposable capital in lieu of firepower, civilian innovation in lieu of military-technical advancement, and market penetration in lieu of garrisons and bases. States, as spatial entities structured to jealously delimit their own territories, will not disappear but reorient themselves toward geoeconomics in order to compensate for their decaying geopolitical roles. The 'logic of conflict' thus remains, but manifests itself in the 'methods of commerce.'

In 1993, Samuel P. Huntington wrote an essay, 'Why International Primacy Matters' in the journal *International Security*. This analysis came quite close to that of Luttwak. Huntington extended Daniel Bell's assertion: 'economics is the continuation of war by other means' (Bell, 1990). Huntington claimed that in the years to follow, the principal conflict of interests involving the USA and the major powers would likely be over economic issues (especially the relationship with Japan and the EU). Huntington felt that economists are blind to the fact that economic activity is a source of power, as well as 'well-being.' In the realm of economic competition, the instruments of power are productive efficiency, market control, trade surplus, strong currency, foreign exchange reserves, ownership of foreign companies, factories and technology.

A third author who deserves a mention in this regard is Mark P. Thirwell. He also investigated the interconnection between geoeconomics and national security, and asserted in 2010 that if one wants '*to understand many of the most important strategic developments facing the world over the next couple of decades, then you are going to need to devote a reasonable amount of time to thinking about what's going on in the international economy*' (Thirwell, 2010, p. 2).[1] Thirwell lists a number of reasons why geoeconomics is making a come-back since the days of Luttwak: the evolution toward a multi-polar world economy, the potential degradation of the willingness of Washington to continue to supply international public goods needed to sustain a (relatively) smoothly functioning world economy, the rise of the dark side of globalization such as transnational crime, the rise of state capitalism, the financial-economic crisis since 2008 and the age of scarcity (Thirwell, 2010). Previously, Luttwak almost appeared to suggest that in the post-Cold War era, geostrategic struggle would be subservient to geoeconomical strife. In this chapter, however, we claim that *geoeconomical and geostrategic competition can exist at the same time, and can be mutually supportive*. As a case study, we will take the relationship between the EU, traditionally only a geoeconomic actor, and the Russian Federation. Clearly that relationship has undergone a serious transformation, starting from the Ukraine crisis at the end of 2013 until today.

3 A brief geopolitical and geoeconomic analysis of the relations between the EU and Russia between 1994 and 2012

After the Russian internal upheaval and constitutional crisis of 1993, President Yeltsin was able to firmly grasp his political authority in the new country. The roaring nineties turned Russia into a capitalist bonanza. Westernization was the new creed. It is in this political context that the Partnership and Cooperation Agreement of 1994 was signed between the equally new

EU and the Russian Federation. It promised an era of complementary relations, both economically and politically. Shock therapy on the Russian economy resulted in rapid privatization. Huge hyperinflation led to social tensions and gradually degraded the support of the public for further economic reforms. Russia seemed to become weaker instead of rising from the ashes of the Soviet Union. A small elite of oligarchs around Yeltsin also rapidly increased their own political power. Seen from the West, Russia looked less threatening and was retreating from its former sphere of influence. In 1990, US Secretary of State James Baker III had agreed with Soviet leader Gorbachev that the two Germanies could unite and that the former East Germany could even become a North Atlantic Treaty Organization (NATO) member. In exchange, NATO would not enlarge an inch further. Quite the contrary happened. In 1999, the former Warsaw Pact members Poland, Hungary, and the Czech Republic joined the organization. In 2002, seven Central and Eastern European countries joined: Bulgaria, Estonia, Latvia, Lithuania, Romania, Slovakia and Slovenia. In 2009, Albania and Croatia joined. A year earlier, Georgia and the Ukraine had also been considered as NATO members, but the German Chancellor Merkel thought the risk was just too high and 'internal instability' would be imported into the alliance.

Starting from January 2000 onwards, Vladimir Putin became the new (acting) president of the Russian Federation. He wanted to use Russia's national resources to rebuild the country, get rid of the oligarchs, and re-establish Russia as a great geostrategic power. However, much until 2012 Moscow considered NATO to be its geostrategic adversary, not the European Union. By 2008, Russia had become the third most important trade partner of the EU, after China and the USA. Vice versa, the EU was now first in the list of Russia's main trade partners (European Commission, DG Trade 01/08/2008).

Energy constituted by far the most important sector in which the EU and the Russian Federation were interlinked (Vanmaele & Criekemans, 2010, p. 51), but that relationship had come under pressure. It seemed that Moscow was using the 'energy weapon' vis-à-vis those regimes it did not like. From late November 2004 until January 2005, an 'Orange Revolution' swept the important natural gas-transit country Ukraine. The leading candidates were the Western-oriented Viktor Yushchenko and Russia's own candidate Viktor Yanukovych. On December 26, 2004, Ukraine's Supreme Court ordered a second run-off election. This showed a victory for Yushchenko (52% of the vote against Yanukovych's 44%). A dispute began in March 2005 over the price of natural gas supplied and the cost of transit. Russia claimed Ukraine was not paying for gas, but diverting that which was intended to be exported by pipeline to the EU. In January 2006, the dispute reached a new height when Russia cut off all gas supplies passing through Ukrainian territory.

The gas crises between Russia and the Ukraine provoked questions within the EU about the reliability of the Russian Federation as a supplier of energy. This in itself created a growing distrust between both parties, an 'energy security dilemma' (Handke & de Jong, 2007, p. 58). Misperception between both actors created even more problems (Vanmaele & Criekemans, 2010, p. 55). Instead of considering the other actor as a geoeconomic partner, there was more and more mistrust. Within the EU, a debate started for more energy diversification, so as to be less reliant on Russia. Each potential alternative that was developed then was confronted by a Russian counter-proposal (e.g. the debate about a Western Nabucco gas pipeline toward the Middle East versus a South Stream pipeline in the area of the Black Sea).

Ukraine started to symbolize an area where both the EU and the Russian Federation had certain geoeconomic interests of their own. In 2010, however, the Western political forces in the country were defeated after the election of the Russian-backed Viktor Yanukovych as president of the Ukraine. In April 2010, a deal was struck between Yanukovych and then Russian President Medvedev, also known as the 'Kharkiv Pact.' The Russian lease on naval facilities in the harbor port of Sevastopol in the Crimea was extended beyond 2017 until 2042. In exchange, Ukraine received a five-year renewal option for a multiyear discounted contract to provide the country with Russian natural gas. It meant a cheaper energy option in exchange for a crucial geostrategic outpost of the Russian Federation in the Black Sea.

Moscow clearly connected the geoeconomical and the geostrategic dimensions. For the Kremlin, both were intertwined and mutually supportive. In the eyes of Moscow, Ukraine should remain a buffer state of the Russian Federation. On March 4, 2012, Putin ran for a third term as president and won the election with 63.64% of the votes. President Putin had a new plan which was crucial in the re-establishment of the Russian Federation as a geoeconomic powerhouse—the creation of a Eurasian Economic Union (EEU). The goal of the EEU was to create an integrated single market on the Eurasian continent with free movement of goods, capital, services and people. It would provide for common transport, agriculture and energy policies, with provisions for a single currency and greater integration in the future. In this way, the lure of the EU in the West could also be countered. It was, in essence, a geoeconomic counter-project against further economic encroachment by the West of Russia's near abroad. Ukraine became center stage in a geoeconomic struggle between both camps, which would later have serious geostrategic implications.

4 The evolution of the relationship between the EU and the Russian Federation, especially focusing on the Ukraine crisis since the end of 2013

In 2009, the EU proposed an 'Eastern Partnership' to Armenia, Azerbaijan, Belarus, Georgia, Ukraine and Moldova. This entailed cooperation, free trade and financial contributions in exchange for democratic reforms. The planned partnership agreements were intended to facilitate visa-free travel, reduce tariffs and introduce European norms. Although initially a geoeconomic plan, it seemed Brussels also had geostrategic goals with it, although they were not as openly expressed: to limit Russia's influence. Ukrainian President Yanukovych had been negotiating during the second half of 2013 with the European Union. The EU had offered market access and €610 million of financial aid, along with a vague prospect of a €1 billion loan from the International Monetary Fund (IMF). However, on November 9, 2013, Yanukovych met with President Putin. Knowing full well that Kyiv was in the midst of a financial crisis, Moscow was willing to offer €10 billion worth of financial credit. Included in the proposal was membership of the EEU. The EU officials on their part signaled that the Ukraine had to choose—between the deal proposed by Moscow and that of Brussels. As a result of Yanukovych's choice, manifestations of Western-oriented political forces broke out in Kyiv.

The situation worsened in 2014. Based upon a leaked telephone conversation between the American Deputy Secretary of State Victoria Nuland and the American ambassador in Kyiv, it became evident that Washington had collaborated with the Ukrainian opposition leaders. The USA wanted to pull Ukraine into the Western camp, and was disillusioned by the lack of geostrategic thinking of the EU (Criekemans, 2014a). The riots at Maidan square in Kyiv resulted in direct and hard confrontations, leading to deaths and injuries. The EU itself did not respond, but rather an ad hoc coalition of the French, German and Polish ministers of foreign affairs took action. They brokered a new deal whereby Yanukovych and the opposition parties agreed to create a government of national unity and hold new presidential elections at the end of the year. However, street protesters revolted against this deal, forcing the opposition leaders to change position. Meanwhile, Yanukovych fled the country via Crimea toward Russia. Members of Yanukovych's own Party of Regions turned their backs on the president, creating an opportunity whereby the opposition could create a new government.

The idea was suggested that the position of the Russian language would be downgraded in the governance of the country. At the same time, voices started to be heard suggesting that the Ukraine should leave its non-aligned status and apply to join the Western NATO alliance. On March 1, 2014, the Russia Duma gave Putin the authority to 'protect' the Russian population in the Ukraine as long as the emergency situation was going on. In the east of the country, revolts by Russian protesters started in Donetsk and Lugansk, possibly instigated by the Russian secret service. Tensions rose. For Moscow, it was imperative to retain control over the geostrategic port of Sevastopol. At the same time Moscow wanted to signal to the 8 million Russian speakers in the country that it 'stood by their side.' On March 16, 2014, a referendum was organized to effectively secede Crimea from Ukraine. Putin did not plan this secession beforehand. Rather, it was a reaction to his failed 'plan A.'

On March 28, 2014, Putin submitted proposals to the Duma to terminate the legal effect of the Russia–Ukraine agreements, including denouncing the 2010 Kharkiv Pact and the Partition Treaty on the Status and Conditions of the Black Sea Fleet. The Duma approved the move. The failure of Putin's geoeconomic plan seemed to necessitate a firm geostrategic response. Instead of Ukraine becoming a buffer for Moscow, the Russian political and military elite now started to permanently destabilize the east of Ukraine, hoping that the West would blink first and that the new transitional government in Kyiv would collapse under its own weight.

The result was a hardening in the geostrategic relations between the West and the East. More and more actors use the term 'New Cold War' to frame the geostrategic situation that resulted from this. However, both camps are at fault. Russia started to militarize the conflict from May 2014 onwards. Elements of the Russian military secret service started infiltrating the eastern regions of Donetsk and Lugansk, offering military assistance to the rebels in the region. The Kyiv government—later under the presidency of Poroshenko—initially seemed to believe there was a military solution. It even attacked civilian targets, which hardened the stance of the population living in the east. As a result, the American government started supplying the Ukrainians with additional weapons, further fueling the conflict. This made it impossible for the Russians to move back without losing face.

The conflict became internationalized when Russian rebels, probably by accident, downed the Malaysian airliner MH17—which had departed in the Netherlands bound for Asia—with a Buk rocket. Two days later, however, Poroshenko chose to revamp the military option against Donetsk and Lugansk, possibly feeling emboldened by the international outcry against Moscow regarding the downed flight. The reaction of the West no longer came from the EU, but rather from NATO during their Wales summit. It was decided to set up a Very High Readiness Joint Task Force—a high-readiness 'Spearhead Force' able to deploy at short notice. It was to consist of a land brigade numbering around 5,000 troops, supported by air, sea and special forces. The enhanced NATO Response Force will amount to around 30,000 troops. The EU, for its part, followed the US line and initiated economic sanctions against Moscow. A long list of people in the entourage of Putin were placed on a visa-banned list, but also sanctions in the oil industry were imposed—not so much in the natural gas industry, however, since the EU still needed Moscow in that regard. Later on, Brussels declared that it would import 25% less natural gas from the Russian Federation by 2018. That in itself provoked a Russian–Chinese deal for the same volume, be it at lower prices for the Kremlin.

A segmentation between geoeconomics and geostrategy developed in Europe. Brussels had negotiated for years to establish an economic association agreement with Kyiv. However, the technical specialists who were sent out on behalf of the EU were unable to see that such negotiations also had geostrategic consequences for the balance in Eurasia. In the end it was NATO that translated the new geoeconomic situation into an altered geostrategy (Criekemans, 2014b). Relations since have hardened, with both camps feeling compelled to up the ante. Whereas the West's geoeconomic and geostrategic position was sometimes out of sync, Russia seemed better able to integrate both domains, in a negative and defensive spiral. Whereas the Kremlin initially had used geoeconomics to gain a better geostrategical position, Putin reversed this approach well into 2015. From September 2015 onwards, Putin tried to use the geostrategic vacuum in Syria as a lever to enforce a changed geoeconomics. By invitation of the Alawite regime of Bashar al-Assad in Syria, Russia started bombing both Islamic State (IS) and Sunni rebel positions. Moscow portrayed itself as a beacon of civilization against IS. This gamble of Putin should be seen through a geostrategic prism. The Russian Federation tried to portray itself as an alternative security guarantor in the Middle East during a period in which the West was unable or unwilling to play such a role. At the same time, the Kremlin hoped that Western governments would start seeing Russia as an ally against IS, and lower the sanctions. Hence, the geoeconomic containment in which the Russian Federation had found itself since 2014 could be reversed. In the strategy of President Putin, geostrategy and geoeconomics were mutually supportive.

However, the fundamentals of the approach have not yet produced any results. The West still firmly continues its sanction regime against Moscow, although the cracks in it are now firmly visible. At the time of writing, there is a new attempt to start diplomatic negotiations in Geneva between all warring parties except al-Nusra (al-Qaeda in Syria) and IS. If these were to be successful, it is to be expected that there would be some kind of symbolic rapprochement between the East and the West. President Obama signaled his most vocal change of position yet on March 7, 2016, when he suggested that Ukraine was not a core US interest. He indicated that Russia would always be able to maintain dominance in Ukraine because it is a core Russian interest: 'The fact is that Ukraine, which is a non-NATO country, is going to be vulnerable to military domination by Russia no matter what we do.'[2] It is too soon to predict what a new US Administration after the Obama era will do in the dossier of the Ukraine. Obama, on his part, seems to be shifting position in the direction where Vladimir Putin wants him to go. All in all, this shows how intertwined geoeconomics and geostrategy really are, certainly in the international relations of (aspiring) great powers.

5 Conclusions about the interaction and mutual reinforcement of geoeconomical and geostrategic competition

Luttwak seemed to suggest in 1990 that in the post-Cold War era, geostrategic struggle would be subservient to geoeconomic strife. This chapter shows rather that geoeconomical and geostrategic competition can exist at the same time, and can be mutually supportive. One could even claim that those actors in international relations who are able to bring their geoeconomic and geostrategic strategies into sync, have a higher chance of reaching their goals in time. As a unitary actor, the Russian Federation seemed much more able to integrate both compared to the European Union. This led to a situation whereby

Russia in effect was waiting in the Ukraine case for the West to blink first. A similar scenario is developing in the war in Syria. Based upon this analysis, it is clear that the EU itself has a problem. It bases its foreign policy much upon a liberal vision of international relations, and the external dimensions of the internal market. The EU does not seem able to assess the geostrategic consequences of its foreign policy actions. At the same time, it is not yet able to understand the geostrategic developments in its near abroad and develop a policy that tackles this instability. A successful foreign policy needs a geostrategy and geoeconomics that are mutually supportive, not out of sync.

Notes

1 As Thirwell states, the connection between commerce and the power of the state was particularly explicit during the Age of Mercantilism, which spanned the 16th, 17th and 18th centuries. Trade policy was largely about ensuring an excess of exports over imports in order to secure a surplus of the precious metals that were deemed to be crucial to maintaining national wealth and power. It was designed to exploit colonial markets for the benefit of the home power: colonial produce was shipped via home ports before re-export, there were strict controls on the use of foreign shipping, and most long-distance trade was in the hands of state-sanctioned monopolies (Thirwell, 2010, p. 4).

2 Read this source from the news provider *Ukraine Today*, which is actually considered to be pro-Kyiv: uatoday.tv/politics/obama-says-ukraine-will-always-be-vulnerable-to-russian-military-domination-607831.html.

References

Bell, D. (1990) Germany: The enduring fear. *Dissent* 37(4) (Fall), www.dissentmagazine.org/article/germany-the-enduring-fear.

Criekemans, D. (2014a). Grensland Oekraïne: van de opening van de doos van Pandora naar de geopolitieke loopgraven? *Mondiaal Magazine MO**, www.mo.be/analyse/grensland-oekra-ne-van-de-opening-van-de-doos-van-pandora-naar-de-geopolitieke-loopgraven.

Criekemans, D. (2014b). Europa moet veiligheid herdefiniëren. *De Tijd*, 6 September: 58.

Handke, S. and de Jong, J. (2007) *Energy as Bond: Relations with Russia in the European and Dutch Context*. Clingendael International Energy Programme. The Hague: Clingendael Institute, p. 90.

Huntington, S. (1993) Why international primacy matters. *International Security* 17(4): 68–83.

Luttwak, E.N. (1990) From geopolitics to geo-economics: Logic of conflict, grammar of commerce. *The National Interest* 20 (Summer), 17–23.

Thirwell, M.P. (2010) *The Return of Geo-economics: Globalisation and National Security*. Lowy Institute for International Policy, September, p. 43.

Vanmaele, S. and Criekemans, D. (2010) *Geopolitiek van de Energie en de rol van Rusland als motor in mondiale machtsverschuivingen*. Antwerpen: Steunpunt Buitenlands Beleid.

Part II

International geoeconomics

10 Geostrategic economics in the 21st century

China, America and the Trans-Pacific Partnership

Francis Schortgen

1 Introduction

In the 21st century, global economic dynamics and interlinkages appear to have relegated geopolitical calculations and geostrategic designs to secondary importance. The notion of geoeconomics as the *new* geopolitics is a very palpable reality in the contemporary context. It is arguably most powerfully reflected in the deliberations, strategies and calculations surrounding the phenomena of economic regionalism and trade deals in the Asia-Pacific region.

East Asia is poised to assume a leading role in global economic governance in the 21st century. China's expanding regional economic assertiveness, combined with rival conceptions of economic regionalism, compels a more focused assessment of the prospects for increased economic cooperation, integration and competition for strategic influence in the Asia-Pacific region. In normative terms, the notion of regionalism will likely continue to be held hostage in the near-to-medium term by the geopolitical, geostrategic and geoeconomic calculations that will define trans-Pacific relations in the 21st century.

The Trans-Pacific Partnership (TPP) represents an ambitious attempt at deepening Asia-Pacific economic integration in the 21st century. Viewed against the backdrop of Washington's 'Asia Pivot,' it also appears to portend a new dynamic—what the author labeled as *geostrategic economics*. Straddling the intersection of economics and politics, this chapter elucidates the TPP from the perspective of the evolving nature of 21st-century Sino–US relations, with the goal of ascertaining the degree and extent to which the TPP could possibly serve a broader geostrategic purpose for the USA above and beyond geoeconomic and trade considerations.

The chapter first briefly outlines the emergence of geoeconomics as the *new* geopolitics in an international system increasingly shaped by a seemingly irresistible yet also consequential shift in the distribution of global wealth and power. Considering the possibility of America's rebalancing to the Asia-Pacific region—both economically and militarily—being indicative of 'reactive regionalism,' the author proceeds in the following section to give a general overview of the dynamics of East Asian regionalism, and to offer an assessment of the changing nature of American power and influence within the region. Focused on the TTP, the next section discusses the degree and extent to which this proposal is not merely aimed at strengthening the rules of international trade. Specifically, it considers the prospects of the TPP being an integral part of a deliberate US strategy designed to lay the foundation for a new institutional balancing dynamic in the Asia-Pacific region to effectively counter and constrain China's expanding clout. The final section offers brief concluding remarks.

2 Geoeconomics as the new geopolitics

The end of the Cold War, and the attendant demise of the clash of political ideologies—as reflected in Francis Fukuyama's 'end of history' notion—gave rise to a post-Cold War paradigm that appeared to put increasing emphasis on economics, without, however, fully negating the influence and importance of politics and military power altogether. To the extent that this paradigm shift may have engendered apprehension among America's allies, notably in East Asia (De Castro, 2000), speculations over the promises and perils of China's rise ultimately ensured that the post-Cold War-era rivalry was not to remain confined to the economic realm after all.

One could well argue that the transition from geoeconomics to a *new* geopolitics in disguise in the 21st century—particularly when viewed in the context of US–China relations—is not altogether unexpected. However, it certainly begs the question whether it may have been inevitable. While it is not the author's intention here to definitively answer that question, which is a separate research agenda all by itself, a brief overview of economic and political developments related to China's gradual yet sustained expansion of rising influence and power since the 1990s may help to provide a general context for appreciating the possibility of such an evolution.

The first development was the dramatic rise of the Chinese economy, following a revitalization of economic reform and restructuring in the early 1990s which resulted in deepening integration with the global economy and culminated in China's accession to the World Trade Organization (WTO) in 2001. While this represented a critical milestone for China, subsequent achievements have been no less consequential. China cemented its status as an emerging global economic superpower in the second quarter of 2010 when it overtook Japan to become the world's second-largest economy. In 2013, China surpassed the USA as the world's largest trading nation, effectively ranking as the top export partner for 43 nations (up from five in 2000), compared to 31 for the USA. In a further unsettling development, the Chinese economy reportedly emerged as the world's largest economy in late 2014 (adjusted for purchasing power parity), accounting for 16.48% (US$17.632 trillion) of global gross domestic product (GDP) compared to 16.28% (or $17.416 trillion) for the USA (Bloomberg News, 2013). Finally, on

November 30, 2015, the International Monetary Fund (IMF) announced its decision to add the renminbi to the currencies that make up the international reserve asset commonly known as the Special Drawing Rights.

The speed and scope of China's rise, meanwhile, has proven a powerful catalyst for the second development, which has to do with the nature and impact of China's rise in the international system. The degree to which it embraces the role of 'responsible stakeholder' weighs heavily on the prospects of China's stated commitment to a 'peaceful rise' (subsequently replaced by 'peaceful development'). From the vantage point of shared interests, the inevitable reality of China's rise engendered a more pronounced convergence–divergence dynamic. It led to strategic competition rather than strategic partnership and emerged as a dominant analytical framework at the beginning of the 21st century. In fact, the American propensity to misunderstand—and consequently mismanage—the rise of China is as disconcerting an outcome as it is a distinct possibility.

The third development has to do with the emerging geoeconomic and geopolitical realities of an accelerating shift in the distribution of global wealth and power. It is charting a course toward a post-Western world (Zakaria, 2008), replete with a certain degree of hesitation and trepidation at the prospect of a 'new world order' shaped largely by Asia.

While the 2008–09 global financial crisis and its aftermath has invited ever-closer scrutiny of China's rise, it has also served to rekindle questions about the likelihood and ramifications of a relative decline in America's global preeminence. As 'China's global impact is increasingly felt on every continent, in most international institutions, and on many global issues' (Shambaugh, 2013, p. 5), it is increasingly difficult to envision a 21st-century global governance system that continues to reflect merely the ambitions and interests of established powers at the expense of rising powers (Chan et al., 2008; Gray & Murphy, 2013).

Just as the Western neoliberal development approach—commonly referred to as the 'Washington Consensus' model, of which the IMF and the World Bank have long been the institutional standard bearers—has come to be viewed more warily in recent years, it has also fueled speculation and predictions about the inevitable emergence of an alternative 'Beijing Consensus' or 'China Model' (Breslin, 2011; Halper, 2010; Williamson, 2012; Zhao, 2010). Backed by a wide range of trade, financial and development initiatives (Kurlantzick, 2007), such a development may yet prove an appealing and credible alternative to the Western model of modernization. If not at the heart of efforts to create an alternative to the Western-dominated world order, the new BRICS (Brazil, Russia, India, China, South Africa) Development Bank and the Asian Infrastructure Investment Bank (AIIB) certainly compel a critical reappraisal of the institutional structures and Western dominance in the existing system of global governance (Chin, 2014; Khanna, 2014).

With these institutions, China is certainly poised to rekindle the debate over institutional recalibration of the existing international order while simultaneously securing a complementary role in the global economic and financial system. At the same time, owing to China's rising influence, these institutions are also likely to contribute to China's deepening economic and financial integration with Northeast and Southeast Asian economies and, correspondingly, prove a critical factor in China's ability to influence and shape the scope, breadth and depth of East Asian regionalism.

3 America and the realities of East Asian economic regionalism

Regionalism serves as a visible and powerful reminder of competing geopolitical ambitions and designs in the 21st century, just as it was an indelible reality during the Cold War (Jay, 1979). If the breakdown of the bipolar international system after the Cold War provided the initial catalyst, the inevitable fading of the 'unipolar moment' of the 1990s ensured a more focused debate about the resurgence of regionalism and its potential implications for strategic interaction in the 21st-century international system. In the early 1990s, Rosecrance (1991) opined that a concert of nations would present a 'somewhat less unlikely but still uncertain' (p. 379) development of the post-Cold War international system than either a great-power withdrawal, followed by a return to regional sovereignty, or expectations of continued American dominance. At the same time, as a consequence of what he perceived as an inevitable 'overbalance of power' derived from such a concert, 'regions and regionalism will therefore flower in participation with rather than in opposition to the new centralizing tendency in modern world politics and economics' (p. 393).

In the East Asian region, regionalism is 'plainly rampant' (Baldwin, 2008, p. 51). Though trade and non-trade motives remain important catalysts for regionalism, the unfolding geoeconomic, geopolitical and geostrategic dynamics of the 21st century will invariably compel a substantive rethinking of the realities of East Asian regional cooperation, integration and competition. Recent research also asserts that the 'new regionalism' that has been sweeping the East Asian region in the aftermath of the 1997–98 Asian financial crisis is influenced more by political than economic factors. Not only do 'conventional indicators of trade and financial interdependence provide no support for arguments that increasing economic integration has driven the new East Asian regionalism' but the 'political domino effect to date has been more powerful than any economic domino effects' (Ravenhill, 2010, pp. 9, 25). In the post-crisis environment, the dynamics of regionalism became much more formalized and state-driven, shifting toward increased trade and monetary regionalism while simultaneously motivated by a 'desire to limit the influence in the region of the USA and the international financial institutions' (Bowles, 2002, p. 244). Japan's proposal of an Asian Monetary Fund at the height of the Asian financial crisis captures the desire for a relative economic and financial decoupling from the West. Additional initiatives aimed at creating regional self-help and coordination mechanisms, while simultaneously decoupling more concretely from IMF crisis resolution measures (Sussangkarn, 2010, p. 3), included the Chiang Mia Initiative Multilateralization, the formation of Association of Southeast Asian Nations (ASEAN)+3 and the associated ASEAN+3 Macroeconomic Research Office, as well as the attempt to launch an ASEAN Economic Community, announced in late December 2015. At the beginning of the 20th century, Halford Mackinder (1904) outlined the idea of a 'geographical pivot of history.' Judging by widespread expectations of an 'Asian century' or 'Chinese century,' the world might well be on the cusp of a new 'geographical pivot of history.' A vast confluence of political, economic, social and security factors, both endogenous and exogenous, are bound to shape the nature, scope, speed and implications of this 21st-century pivot. Consequently, such a prospect goes a long way toward ensuring that the forces and dynamics of geoeconomics in the 21st century may well assume the role of *geopolitics in disguise.*

4 The Trans-Pacific Partnership as geostrategic economics?

The announcement in 2011 of Washington's 'Asia pivot' was a direct response to the unfolding global power and wealth shift. Acknowledging the Asia-Pacific region as a 'key driver of global politics' in the 21st century, then-US Secretary of State Hillary Clinton declared that 'one of the most important tasks of American statecraft over the next decade will therefore be to lock in a substantially increased investment—diplomatic, economic, strategic, and otherwise—in the Asia-Pacific region' (Clinton, 2011, p. 57). The logic of the proposed rebalancing has subsequently drawn extensive scrutiny, including charges that it may be both unnecessary and possibly counterproductive (Ross, 2012; Kelly, 2014).

The TPP has emerged as an important and integral pillar of a comprehensive American strategy to secure influence and power amid regional efforts to create a new economic integration architecture. According to the Office of the United States Trade Representative, the TPP's main goals—apart from supporting US jobs and economic growth—include bolstering US leadership in the Asia-Pacific region and promoting US values within the context of a global trading system. The latter objective has been unmistakably captured in comments made by President Obama:

> When more than 95 percent of our potential customers live outside our borders, we can't let countries like China write the rules of the global economy. *We should write those rules*, opening new markets to American products while setting high standards for protecting workers and preserving our environment.
>
> (White House, 2015, emphasis added)

The broader question, meanwhile, is whether the conception of the role of the TPP extends beyond trade and regional economic integration. In fact, it seems impossible to disentangle the promotion of the TPP from the geostrategic considerations associated with post-1997 Asian regionalism and the expansion of Chinese influence and power in the Asia-Pacific.

Contemporary trends seem to suggest that, contrary to realist expectations of a concerted effort to constrain China's expanding power, the response of regional economies is 'anomalous from the traditional balance-of-power perspective' (Chan, 2010, p. 387). On closer scrutiny, it becomes apparent that economic imperatives, shaped by explosive regional trade agreement proliferation and deepening intra-regional trade, while not altogether eschewing geopolitical and geostrategic concerns, remain the primary force behind the deepening engagement of China and the East Asian region. From the mid-1990s to the mid-2000s, China emerged as a major export market in merchandise trade for both Northeast and Southeast Asian economies. Meanwhile, the TPP is unlikely to change that dynamic in any consequential way because:

> as the last twenty years have shown, markets and geography are the principal factors behind Southeast Asia's economic integration with China. After all, trade and investment agreements can only facilitate market forces, not fight them. In the end, markets and geography will point Asia toward integrating first and only then will it be in a position to converge with the TPP.
>
> (Nehru, 2012)

Not only has China become a key driver in East Asian intra-regional trade in the first decade of the 21st century, but it has also greatly strengthened production fragmentation among regional economies, which invariably fueled a deepening of trade relations between regional economies.

For the USA, however, the TPP may well constitute a strategic effort to engage with and possibly counter Sino-centric approaches to economic regionalism and institutional balancing underway in the broader Asia-Pacific region. Speaking at the McCain Institute at Arizona State University on April 6, 2015, US Secretary of Defense Ashton Carter's message was highly revealing in that respect:

> you may not expect to hear this from a Secretary of Defense, but in terms of our rebalance in the broadest sense, passing TPP is as important to me as another aircraft carrier. It would deepen our alliances and partnerships abroad and underscore our lasting commitment to the Asia-Pacific. And it would help us promote a global order that reflects both our interests and our values.
>
> (Carter, 2015)

From a geopolitical and geostrategic perspective, the TPP initiative certainly leaves a number of critical questions unanswered. Will it lay the foundation for complementary and multilateralized regionalism, or will it trigger competing regionalism with the potential to increase geopolitical rivalry between the USA and China? Is it an effort to constrain the possibility of further expansion of Chinese influence and power in a region where it is already the dominant regional economic power?

At a time of heightened regional tensions, including most notably ongoing territorial disputes between China and a number of regional economies over the South China Sea, it seems indeed difficult to dismiss the notion that the TPP is not in fact a critical element in Washington's demonstration of commitment to the region and to its allies. Moreover, considering that the terms of the TPP do come, in some cases, at substantial cost to regional economies that have signed on to it, it equally appears to be an attempt at hedging against geopolitical risk. However, the question ultimately will be whether the regional economies will determine that the geopolitical benefits outweigh the economic costs.

5 Conclusion

In 1995, noting the controversy surrounding the consequences of regionalism, Haggard (1995, p. 20) suggested that 'this controversy has obscured the question of why new regional arrangements have arisen at this historical juncture ...' In the context of 21st-century East Asian regionalism, it is hard to ignore that China's rise has effectively ensured that trade has once again come to be subsumed under geopolitics and geostrategy. In particular, it is tempting—and not wholly without reason—to view the TPP as a means to counter a relative shift in US influence over regional developments that in the post-Cold War period have gradually encouraged 'a form of East Asian regionalism that threatens to exclude the US and enhance the position of China' (Beeson, 2006, p. 556).

If prior dynamics of regionalism are any indication, East Asia will witness the emergence of a *balanced* rather than *inflated* regionalism; a regionalism that, while evolving in significant ways from that of the 20th century, will continue to be conditioned by external factors. In pivoting to the Asia-Pacific region, the USA will need to be sensitive to the fact that the dynamics of the *new* East Asian regionalism differ substantively from the regionalism that accompanied the evolving political, economic and security dynamics in Europe after World War II, and to resist the deterministic thinking that China's rise will invariably induce a recalibration of the international system. Failing to recognize the need for new analytical frameworks (Acharya, 2003; Kang, 2003) could well bring about destabilizing geopolitical, geoeconomic and geostrategic consequences, reducing the chances for a more institutionalized regionalism that emphasizes win–win cooperation.

Its nascent liberal multilateralism notwithstanding, China's growing regional clout appears to inexorably transform Asia from a multipolar to a seemingly uni-multipolar region, with an accompanying near-inevitability of possible friction fueled to a large extent by a consequential realignment of global wealth and power and the perceived hegemonic rivalry between a rising China and a USA in relative decline. From a confidence- and trust-building perspective, it is difficult to see how the decision to exclude China from the original TPP negotiations can be viewed by Beijing as anything other than a deliberate attempt to limit China's influence in the 21st-century international system architecture. Such an approach, according to Will Hutton (2006, p. xi), is fraught with danger in itself:

> [China] requires our understanding and engagement—not our enmity and suspicion, which could culminate in self-defeatingly creating the very crisis we fear. China's vulnerability is not widely understood; ... the United States should stay open to China in both our trade and in the realm of ideas.

Even though geoeconomic considerations appear to dominate, the language and thought processes of geopolitics remain ever-present. In fact, it might be most appropriate to view institutional and interactional dynamics in the 21st century increasingly through the lens of geostrategic economics, or geopolitics in disguise. Will the TPP fit this new perspective? Ultimately, time will shed a clarifying light on this question, but in the short term, the TPP appears not so much to project hopes for win–win cooperation as to be grounded in a narrative logic of zero-sum competition.

References

Acharya, A. (2003) *Regionalism and Multilateralism: Essays on Cooperative Security in the Asia-Pacific*. Singapore: Eastern Universities Press.

Baldwin, R.E. (2008) The spoke trap: Hub and spoke bilateralism in East Asia. In *China, Asia, and the New World Economy*, B. Eichengreen, C. Wyplosz and Y.C. Park (eds) New York: Oxford University Press, pp. 51–85.

Beeson, M. (2006) American hegemony and regionalism: The rise of East Asia and the end of the Asia-Pacific. *Geopolitics* 11(4): 541–560.

Bloomberg News (2013) China eclipses U.S. as biggest trading nation. Available at www.bloomberg.com/news/articles/2013-02-09/china-passes-u-s-to-become-the-world-s-biggest-trading-nation (accessed 27 February 2016).

Bowles, P. (2002) Asia's post-crisis regionalism: Bringing the state back in, keeping the (United) States out. *Review of International Political Economy* 9(2): 244–270.

Breslin, S. (2011) The 'China model' and the global crisis: From Friedrich List to a Chinese mode of governance? *International Affairs* 87(6): 1323–1343.

Carter, A. (2015) Remarks on the next phase of the U.S. rebalance to the Asia-Pacific. Available at www.defense.gov/News/Speeches/Speech-View/Article/606660/remarks-on-the-next-phase-of-the-us-rebalance-to-the-asia-pacific-mccain-instit (accessed 27 February 2016).

Chan, L.H., Lee, P.K. and Chan, G. (2008) Rethinking global governance: A China model in the making? *Contemporary Politics* 14(1): 3–9.

Chan, S. (2010) An odd thing happened on the way to balancing: East Asian states' reactions to China's rise. *International Studies Review* 12(3): 387–412.

Chin, G.T. (2014) The BRICS-led development bank: Purpose and politics beyond the G20. *Global Policy* 5(3): 366–373.
Clinton, H. (2011) America's Pacific century. *Foreign Policy* 189: 56–63.
De Castro, R.C. (2000) Whither geoeconomics? Bureaucratic inertia in US post-Cold War foreign policy toward East Asia. *Asian Affairs: An American Review* 26(4): 201–221.
Gray, K. and Murphy, C.N. (2013) Introduction: Rising powers and the future of global governance. *Third World Quarterly* 34(2): 183–193.
Haggard, S. (1995) The political economy of regionalism in Asia and the Americas. In *The Political Economy of Regionalism*, E.D. Mansfield and H.V. Milner (eds) New York: Columbia University Press.
Halper, S. (2010) *The Beijing Consensus: How China's Authoritarian Model Will Dominate the Twenty-First Century.* New York: Basic Books.
Hutton, W. (2006) *The Writing on the Wall: China and the West in the 21st Century.* London: Little, Brown and Company.
Jay, P. (1979) Regionalism as geopolitics. *Foreign Affairs* 58(3): 485–514.
Kang, D.C. (2003) Getting Asia wrong: The need for new analytical frameworks. *International Security* 27(4): 57–85.
Kelly, R.E. (2014) The 'pivot' and its problems: American foreign policy in Northeast Asia. *The Pacific Review* 27(3): 479–503.
Khanna, P. (2014) New BRICS bank a building block of alternative world order. *New Perspectives Quarterly* 31(4): 46–48.
Kurlantzick, J. (2007) *Charm Offensive: How China's Soft Power is Transforming the World.* New Haven, CT: Yale University Press.
Mackinder, H.J. (1904) The geographical pivot of history. *The Geographical Journal* 23 (1): 421–437.
Nehru, V. (2012) Southeast Asia: Will markets and geography trump the TPP? *Carnegie Endowment for International Peace*, July 9. Available at carnegieendowment.org/2012/07/09/southeast-asia-will-markets-and-geography-trump-tpp (accessed 12 March 2016).
Ravenhill, J. (2010) The 'new East Asian regionalism': A political domino effect. *Review of International Political Economy* 17(2): 178–208.
Rosecrance, R. (1991) Regionalism and the post-Cold War era. *International Journal: Canada's Journal of Global Policy Analysis* 46(3): 373–393.
Ross, R. (2012) The problem with the pivot. *Foreign Affairs* 91(6): 70–82.
Shambaugh, D. (2013) *China Goes Global: The Partial Power.* New York: Oxford University Press.
Sussangkarn, C. (2010) The Chiang Mai Initiative Multilateralisation: Origin, development and outlook. Available at ec.europa.eu/economy_finance/events/2010/20100204/2_1_sussangkarn_paper_en.pdf (accessed 15 June 2016).
Williamson, J. (2012) Is the 'Beijing Consensus' now dominant? *Asia Policy* 13(1): 1–16.
The White House (2015) *Statement by the President on the Trans-Pacific Partnership.* Available at www.whitehouse.gov/the-press-office/2015/10/05/statement-president-trans-pacific-partnership (accessed 12 March 2016).
Zakaria, F. (2008) *The Post-American World.* New York: W.W. Norton.
Zhao, S. (2010) The China model: Can it replace the Western model of modernization? *Journal of Contemporary China* 19(65): 419–436.

11 EU trade policy after the GFC

The geoeconomics of shifting EU trade policy priorities

Louise Curran

1 Introduction

The last decade has seen major shifts in the global economic context which have inevitably impacted on the commercial relations between the key actors in the global economy. This chapter will explore how these shifts have impacted on one of the key means by which the European Union (EU) manages its economic relations with its partner regions: external trade policy. From a situation in the early years of this millennium where the EU put a clear focus on multilateral liberalization through the World Trade Organization (WTO) and provided market access to a broad range of developing countries through its Generalized System of Preferences (GSP), it has moved to a strategy providing market access to a smaller number of developing countries and actively pursuing bilateral free trade agreements (FTAs) with favored partners. This chapter will argue that this strategic shift is a reaction to geoeconomic changes, which have made multilateral agreements more difficult and bilateral agreements more politically seductive.

This chapter will map the evolution of EU trade policy over the last decade, starting at the launch of the last multilateral negotiating round—the Doha Development Agenda (DDA)—to the end of 2015. The objective is to identify the key strategic shifts in policy priorities over time and highlight how these shifts can be understood in terms of the evolving geoeconomic context. The chapter draws on existing analysis, policy documents, and speeches by and interviews with the Commission's trade policy executive in Brussels in November 2013 and November 2014.

2 EU trade policy: from multilateral to bilateral

The DDA round of negotiations was launched in 2001. For some time, these multilateral discussions were the priority for EU trade policy. Indeed, there was an informal moratorium on the launching of new bilateral negotiations during the first few years of the Doha Round (Leeg, 2014; Xiaotong et al., 2014). However, the negotiations were difficult and complex, and progress was slow (Curran, 2013). By mid-2006, they were essentially blocked and the EU had shifted its policy priorities towards a mixed approach combining multilateral and bilateral negotiations.

Most observers see the 2006 'Global Europe' initiative as the key manifestation of this policy shift (Antimiani & Salvatici, 2015; Leeg, 2014; Xiaotong et al., 2014). Global Europe reiterated the EU's commitment to WTO negotiations, but also signaled a move towards greater efforts on bilateral negotiations. Negotiating partners were to be chosen on the basis of economic criteria, like market potential, as well as the level of effective protection against EU exports (CEC, 2006). The Association of Southeast Asian Nations (ASEAN), South Korea and MERCOSUR (the Common Market of the South) were identified as priorities on the basis of these criteria, with India, Russia and the Gulf Cooperation Council (GCC) also highlighted as potentially interesting. Although China obviously also fulfilled the criteria, the Commission argued that it 'requires special attention because of the opportunities and risks it presents' (CEC, 2006, p. 11).

Negotiations with MERCOSUR and the GCC were already ongoing before the new strategy, although they have proven long and difficult and are still not concluded. Following Global Europe, negotiations were duly launched with South Korea, India and ASEAN. The Korean FTA negotiations went rather smoothly and the agreement entered into force in July 2011. Others were more difficult. The Indian negotiation proved complicated as several contentious issues emerged (Khorana & Garcia, 2013). They were suspended in 2015. Those with ASEAN proved impossible to achieve on a region-to-region basis and have been transformed into bilateral negotiations between the EU and individual countries—the most advanced of these are with Singapore (concluded in October 2014) and Vietnam (concluded in December 2015).

The Commission issued a renewed strategy—Trade, Growth and World Affairs—in 2010 (CEC, 2010). In a context of economic crisis in Europe, its focus was on trade as a potential motor for growth. It reiterated the EU's commitment to the multilateral negotiations, but also to FTAs. In addition to existing FTA negotiating partners, the potential of the USA, China, Russia and Japan were highlighted. FTA negotiations were subsequently launched with two of these countries—Japan and the USA—as well as with Canada. Furthermore, the EU signaled its intention to focus its special access regime for developing countries—the GSP—on the countries most in need. The outcome was a revision of the GSP such that it excluded several more developed countries, which were 'graduated' from preferential treatment. These included some—Argentina, Brazil, Malaysia and Saudi Arabia—that were in the process of negotiating FTAs with the EU (CEC, 2014).

3 Recent developments—the new Commission and the strengthening of bilateral strategy

The most recent evolution of trade policy followed the accession of the Juncker Commission at the end of 2014. The new trade commissioner—Celia

Malmström, a Swede—launched a review of trade policy and produced a new overarching strategy for the coming years. The strategy, 'Trade for all,' was launched in October 2015 and includes several policy priorities (CEC, 2015). It confirms a less ambitious approach to the WTO and a growing engagement in bilateral FTAs. The EU's bilateral agenda is said to be based on three principles: economics (capacity to deliver growth and jobs), reciprocal high levels of ambition, and consistency in its approach to emerging countries. In the context of the last principle, the strategy explicitly highlights that full reciprocity in market openness will be expected of countries that have been 'graduated' from the GSP. The implicit assumption is that if countries are 'rich' enough to no longer be given preferential access to the EU market, they can be treated as equals in negotiations.

The EU was working on 20 agreements with 60 countries in October 2015, with more in the pipeline (Malmström, 2015). In Asia, in addition to the concluded FTAs with South Korea, Singapore and Vietnam, the EU-Japan FTA is 'a strategic priority' and the investment treaty with China 'a top priority' (CEC, 2015). In Latin America and the Caribbean, FTAs already exist with 26 of the 33 countries, with the main remaining challenge being the negotiations with MERCOSUR. In its neighborhood, the EU seeks to extend Deep and Comprehensive FTAs with Ukraine, Moldova and Georgia to other countries, including Morocco, Tunisia and Jordan. These latter FTAs are primarily political, aimed at stabilizing relations within the region, and thus are not our key focus in this chapter.

The first priority in bilateral negotiations is, however, the Transatlantic Trade and Investment Partnership (TTIP) with the USA. This should build on the existing FTA with Canada, described as 'a ground-breaking agreement' (CEC, 2015). These agreements are likely to be more ambitious and far reaching than those with emerging countries like India or Brazil, where objectives like harmonizing rules on sustainable development and investment are much more controversial (Khorana & Garcia, 2013). The USA is unambiguous about its desire to use FTAs to build new global trade rules. The recently concluded Trans-Pacific Partnership (TPP) is presented as largely about ensuring that these rules are set in line with US priorities (USTR, 2015). Indeed, the negotiations have fostered concerns in other countries, such as China, about their potential to create *de facto* global rules on a bilateral level (Xiaotong et al., 2014).

The conclusion of the TTP in October 2015 changed the geoeconomic context of the TTIP negotiations. The USA's conclusion of an FTA with Asian partners as a priority, coming on top of its 'pivot' towards Asia, fuels fears that the USA no longer sees the EU as a key strategic partner. At the same time, several EU countries, most vocally France, have criticized the USA's engagement and the lack of negotiating offers from their side (*Sud-Ouest*, 2015). At the time of writing, the future of the TTIP negotiations is difficult to predict. As with any long and complex negotiation, there is a risk of further geoeconomic shifts undermining the economic arguments for such agreements, or simply negotiating fatigue. Much depends on the outcome of the 2016 US presidential election.

4 The importance of geoeconomic shifts to the evolution of EU trade policy

When the DDA was launched in 2001, the world was a very different place. Many of the changes in EU policy discussed above can be understood in terms of adaptation of its priorities to the changing geoeconomic landscape. Even before the global financial crisis (GFC) hit in 2007–08, the EU had recognized that it needed to move forward with bilateral efforts to secure market access for its companies and to partner countries chosen on the basis of economic criteria (CEC, 2006). Although the EU has continued to negotiate and conclude FTAs with developing country partners with which it has strong historical trading relationships (such as Peru, Colombia, and the African, Caribbean and Pacific group), these are mainly political projects aimed at securing WTO-compatible market access for historic trading partners.[1] The priority FTAs, from an economic point of view, are with partners whose markets are seen as key to EU companies seeking new opportunities outside a home market with weak growth prospects.

In order to understand the extent of the geoeconomic changes that have occurred since Doha, Table 11.1 presents figures on the evolution of trade over the period 2001–14. It includes 2006 for reference, as it was both the year of the launch of the Global Europe strategy and the year before the brewing

Table 11.1 Changes in trade structures 2001–14

Share of world imports (%)—top ten importers				*Share of world exports (%)—top ten exporters*			
	2001	*2006*	*2014*		*2001*	*2006*	*2014*
EU 27	38.5	38.3	31.4	EU 27	39.6	37.8	32.1
USA	18.7	15.7	12.5	China	4.4	8.1	12.5
China	3.9	6.5	10.5	USA	12.0	8.7	8.7
Japan	5.5	4.7	4.3	Japan	6.6	5.4	3.7
Hong Kong	3.2	2.7	3.2	South Korea	2.5	2.7	3.1
South Korea	2.2	2.5	2.8	Hong Kong	3.1	2.7	2.8
Canada	3.5	2.9	2.5	Russia	1.6	2.5	2.7
India	0.8	1.5	2.5	Canada	4.3	3.2	2.5
Mexico	2.7	2.1	2.1	Singapore	2.0	2.3	2.2
Singapore	1.8	1.9	2.0	Mexico	2.6	2.1	2.1
Total	81.4	79.9	75.3	Total	78.6	75.6	72.4

(ITC Trademap, www.trademap.org, and author's calculations)

GFC began to impact on the world economy. It is evident that the EU's share of world exports and imports has fallen over the time period, but most especially since 2006. In terms of imports, the EU's share was virtually unchanged from 2001 to 2006, while that of the USA fell by 16%. Both fell in the subsequent years by 18% and 20%, respectively. The most notable other change was the rise of China's share of imports, which increased by 68% between 2001 (when they joined the WTO) and 2006, and 62% since then. Japan and Canada also saw their share of world imports fall.

In terms of exports, the EU has also seen its global share fall, including in the 2001–06 period. The rise of China's global export share was even more rapid than that of its import share, increasing by 86% between 2001–06. China overtook the USA to become the second most important world exporter in 2007. It is notable that the USA's loss of export share is entirely concentrated in the first years of analysis, when it fell by 27%. It has been fairly stable since. Other changes of note are the large fall in Japan's export share, especially in the latter years when it fell by 31%, and Canada whose share fell by over 20% in both periods. On the other hand, Russia increased its share by over half in the first few years, but has been fairly stable since, despite joining the WTO in 2012.

In terms of the key trade partners with which the EU has negotiated, or is negotiating, an FTA, clearly an expanding import market would be a motivating factor for such agreements. The situation for the different partners is quite variable in this context. India's share of global imports has seen impressive growth (from a low base). However, two of the key current FTA negotiating partners have become consistently less important (the USA and Japan). Although together they still account for nearly 17% of global imports, that figure was nearly 25% in 2001. Of those countries with an existing agreement, Canada has seen falls in its import share, South Korea has seen consistent growth, Mexico, with which the EU has had an agreement since 2000, has lost share, but has been stable in recent years, and Singapore is close to 2%. If the EU's FTA strategy mainly prioritized expanding import markets, it would have sought an FTA with China. However, the EU has consistently shied away from such a move, although the Chinese side has suggested it (Xiaotong et al., 2014).

Of course, other issues are also important to FTAs, apart from trade growth. The key factors identified in the Global Europe Communication were market potential and level of effective protection for EU exports (CEC, 2006). Table 11.2 provides indicative data for the EU's key trade partners on these market characteristics. Protection includes not only tariffs, but also non-tariff barriers; however, it is difficult to assess the latter in a comparative way. Thus, Table 11.2 only assesses protection on quantitative criteria (average tariffs).

The data indicate that the global economy is becoming more diverse, as the historic economic hegemons—the USA and the EU—become relatively less dominant. From a situation where they represented 60% of the world economy in 2001, they represented only 52% in 2014. Over the same time China's economic weight more than doubled. This fact is obviously a reflection of

Table 11.2 Selected market indicators for key EU trade partners

	% of world GDP			*GDP growth (%)*			*GDP per capita (US$)*			*Average tariff*
	2001	*2006*	*2014*	*2001*	*2006*	*2014*	*2001*	*2006*	*2014*	*2005*
EU	32.0	30.2	26.5	2.2	4.0	1.4	27,260	29,737	30,343	5.5
USA	28.0	27.4	25.4	1.0	3.3	2.4	40,938	45,053	46,405	3.6
China	3.7	5.2	9.1	8.3	5.6	7.3	1,212	1,950	3,863	9.8
Japan	10.4	9.5	8.2	0.4	1.7	-0.1	34,003	36,364	37,595	4.1
India	1.5	1.9	2.7	4.8	12.7	7.3	589	784	1,234	19.9
Canada	2.5	2.4	2.3	1.7	2.7	2.4	33,595	36,679	38,259	5.1
South Korea	1.8	1.9	2.1	4.5	8.9	3.3	15,732	19,528	24,566	12.0
Brazil	1.9	1.9	2.1	1.3	1.7	0.1	4,397	4,865	5,852	12.4
Malaysia	0.3	0.3	0.4	0.5	7.0	6.0	4,785	5,770	7,365	7.3
Singapore	0.2	0.3	0.4	-1.0	7.0	2.9	24,027	31,514	38,088	0.0
Vietnam	0.1	0.1	0.2	6.2	5.2	6.0	558	740	1,078	16.8

(World Bank, World Development Indicators, data.worldbank.org/data-catalog/world-development-indicators)

differential growth rates, which have also enabled China to increase its GDP per capita at an impressive rate. Looking at those countries with which the EU has recently signed an FTA, or is pursuing talks, all Asian partners except Japan (South Korea, Malaysia, Singapore and, most notably, India) have increased their economic weight in the global economy. Brazil has also grown, but at a less impressive rate. The EU's North American partners, Canada and the USA, have both seen a reduction in their economic weight.

A growing market is clearly a motivating factor for an FTA. In this sense all the EU partners shown in Table 11.2, except Japan and Brazil, had growth rates in 2014 that outpaced, often significantly, those of the EU. The situation was slightly different in 2006 when Global Europe was launched, when the EU had a healthy 4% growth rate, although most of the key FTA targets at the time (India, South Korea, ASEAN members) nevertheless outpaced the EU. Wealth is clearly an indicator for consumption and when we look at this indicator, the motivations for the more recent negotiations with Japan, Canada and the USA become clearer. These are simply very rich countries, where the potential market for the relatively high-end products in which the EU excels (Curran & Zignago, 2009) is by definition larger than in growing but still very poor countries like India or Vietnam.

Finally, the question of levels of applied protection is important to the relative gains in competitiveness that EU exporters could expect from an FTA. In terms of this indicator, motivations for FTA negotiations should be highest in India, Vietnam, Brazil and South Korea. However, EU FTAs also seek to address non-tariff measures like technical standards, which also impact on trade. In the case of the EU-Japan FTA, it was estimated that these barriers increased the costs of EU exports by between 10–30%, depending on the sector, and that reducing non-tariff measures to minimal levels would increase EU exports by 50%, more than double the impact of eliminating tariffs (Sunesen et al., 2009).

5 Conclusions—the EU's trade policy in the post-crisis context

The discussion above has highlighted both how the EU's trade policy priorities have evolved since the launch of the last multilateral round of negotiations and how this evolution is a reflection of wider geoeconomic changes. As multilateral efforts floundered in the mid-2000s, the EU, somewhat reluctantly at first, started a series of bilateral negotiations. After the GFC hit, leaving the EU with a legacy of low growth and serious economic difficulties, efforts increased to seek bilateral solutions to increase access to key markets for EU exporters. The choice of new FTA partners since then has been guided by economic principles and the choice of several key partners—India, South Korea, Malaysia—is a reflection of the change in their geoeconomic importance in the world economy. However, these partners are often larger and more powerful than developing countries—like Peru or Colombia—with which the EU has recently finalized agreements. Thus, the political economy of discussions is different and capacity to dictate terms is limited. As one Commission official put it, '*blackmailing a rising power is not a good strategy*' (author interview, November 2013).

The GFC has changed the relative economic importance of the EU and its potential partners. It has also changed the EU's attitude to middle income countries. From a situation in 2001 when the EU provided very wide unilateral market access to developing countries through its GSP, it has focused its trade preferences on a smaller group of low and lower-middle income countries. This has had the effect of concentrating preferences on the poorest countries, but also of increasing the relative level of protection on the EU market for several potential FTA partners, including Brazil and Malaysia. These countries saw tariffs increase on a broad range of products following the revision of the GSP. The latter could therefore be seen as a means of increasing bargaining power with these increasingly important partners.

At the same time, economic size and growth are not the only factors behind the EU's FTA efforts. Politics remains a guiding factor. The EU is not negotiating an FTA with China, in spite of its large size, impressive growth rate and weight in global trade. It has consistently argued that China is a special case, not least because of its very different political system (CEC, 2010, p. 5). Political distance generally has a negative impact on FTA activity (Baldwin & Jaimovich, 2012). Of the existing EU FTAs, only that with Vietnam is with a country with a non-democratic government.

At the same time, the FTA negotiations with the world's biggest democracy—India—have proven far more difficult than anticipated. India has rejected efforts to include non-trade issues like sustainable development and public procurement, due to their very different understanding of the desirability of including such issues in an FTA (Khorana & Garcia, 2013). Thus, on the one hand, the economic rise of the emerging world has led the EU to seek to better integrate with their economies through FTAs, with the objective of improving its own economic prospects. On the other hand, negotiations with the largest emerging nations have been complicated by political factors and very different visions of what an FTA should include. This, in turn, has led to the extension of EU negotiations to more politically and economically similar countries, where the prospects of agreement look better (the USA, Japan, Canada).

What EU trade agreements will emerge in the near future depends on many factors, not least its own capacity to reinvigorate its economy. Just as geoeconomic shifts have changed the EU's vision of its trade partners, so the partners are also reassessing their positions. The EU's economic decline, clearly seen in the figures above, reduces the potential returns of market access and makes it a less attractive FTA partner for emerging nations (McGuire & Lindeque, 2010). As one European Parliament official observed in relation to the India negotiations, '*India wants to be a great power and thinks that the EU can't help them*' (author interview, November 2013). This attitude naturally reduces the motivation of the EU's negotiating partners to make difficult concessions in order to secure agreement.

Note

1 For an explanation of the complexities of WTO-compatible market access for African, Caribbean and Pacific countries, see Erasmus (2010).

References

Antimiani, A. and Salvatici, L. (2015) Regionalism versus multilateralism: The case of the European Union trade policy. *Journal of World Trade* 49(2): 253–276.

Baldwin, R. and Jaimovich, D. (2012) Are free trade agreements contagious? *Journal of International Economics* 88(1): 1–16.

CEC (2006) *Global Europe—Competing in the World.* Brussels: Commission of the European Communities.

CEC (2010) *Trade Growth and World Affairs.* Brussels: Commission of the European Communities.

CEC (2014) *The EU's Generalised Scheme of Preferences (GSP).* Brussels: Commission of the European Communities.

CEC (2015) *Trade for All.* Brussels: Commission of the European Communities.

Curran, L. (2013) The changing governance of international trade and the implications for business. In *Handbook on the Geopolitics of Business*, J.M. Munoz (ed.). Cheltenham: Edward Elgar, pp. 9–20.

Curran, L. and Zignago, S. (2009) *Evolution of EU and its Member States' Competitiveness in International Trade.* CEPII Working Paper 2009–2011. Paris: CEPII. Available at SSRN: ssrn.com/abstract=1532718 or dx.doi.org/10.2139/ssrn.1532718.

Erasmus, G. (2010) Accommodating developing countries in the WTO: From mega debates to economic partnership agreements. In *Redesigning the World Trade Organization for the Twenty First Century*, D. Steger (ed.). Ottawa: Wilfrid Laurier University Press, pp. 363–388.

Khorana, S. and Garcia, M. (2013) European Union—India trade negotiations: One step forward, one back? *Journal of Common Market Studies* 51(4): 684–700.

Leeg, T. (2014) Normative power Europe? The European Union in the negotiations on a free trade agreement with India. *European Foreign Affairs Review* 19(3), 335–356.

Malmström, C. (2015) *Trade for All: Remarks at the European Parliament.* 15 October. Brussels: Commission of the European Communities.

McGuire, S. and Lindeque, J. (2010) The diminishing returns to trade policy in the European Union. *Journal of Common Market Studies* 48(5): 1329–1349.

Sud-Ouest (2015) Traité Transatlantique: 'La France envisage l'arrêt des négociations' [Trans-Atlantic Treaty: 'France considers calling off negotiations']. 28 September, 2–3.

Sunesen, E., Francois, J. and Thelle, M. (2009) *Assessment of Barriers to Trade and Investment between the EU and Japan.* Report for DG Trade European Commission. Copenhagen: Copenhagen Economics.

USTR (2015) The Trans-Pacific Partnership. Leveling the playing field for American workers and American businesses. Available at: ustr.gov/tpp/.

Xiaotong, Z., Ping, Z. and Xiaoyan, Y. (2014) The EU's new FTA adventures and their implications for China. *Journal of World Trade* 48(3): 525–552.

12 Determinants of FDI in the Customs Union of Russia, Belarus and Kazakhstan

Richard B. Nyuur, Andrey Yukhanaev and Alina Amirzadova

1 Introduction

International production has been on the increase for many decades and has become the most salient phenomenon of the global economy (Li & Vashchilko, 2010). Global foreign direct investment (FDI) inflows reached an initial record level of US$1396.5 billion in 2000 (World Bank, 2006). Moreover, the number of multinational enterprise (MNE) parent firms in 2000 was 63,000, associated with 690,000 foreign affiliates. By 2007, the number of MNE parent firms had increased to 79,000 with 790,000 foreign affiliates employing about 82 million people worldwide (Li & Vashchilko, 2010; UNCTAD, 2007). By 2014, global FDI had increased to $1.23 trillion and was projected to reach $1.5 trillion in 2016 and $1.7 trillion in 2017 (UNCTAD, 2015). Accordingly, the demand-stimulating effects of lower oil prices, continued investment liberalisation and promotion measures around the world, the growth prospects in the USA, and the continued high levels of profitability and cash reserves among MNEs would facilitate the global flow of FDI in the near future (UNCTAD, 2015).

The importance of FDI has intensified academic research over the years exploring the impact, determinants and motives of FDI in both developed and developing countries (Dunning, 2002; Asiedu, 2006; Benassy-Quere et al., 2007; Buckley et al., 2007). These studies, to a varying degree of sophistication, suggest that host countries need to have the requisite locational advantages capable of meeting the motives of the investing firms so as to attract substantial FDI (Asiedu, 2006; Dunning, 2002). Moreover, this body of scholarship posits that FDI and the activities of MNCs have a far-reaching positive impact on the host country's overall economic growth and sustainability, especially for developing and transition economies (Cheng & Kwan, 2000; Nyuur & Debrah, 2014). FDI benefits developing and transition economies through the transfer of financial, technological and managerial resources, and through the local allies of global companies that later become self-sufficient with additional operations (Janicki & Wunnava, 2004; Young, 2005).

The underlying argument therefore is that FDI provides a strong stimulus for sustainable economic growth in host countries and offers access to internationally available technologies and management know-how (Benassy-Quere et al., 2007). Furthermore, FDI is considered an important source of capital which complements domestic private investment, creates new job opportunities, enhances innovation through technology transfer, and promotes human capital development through transfer of knowledge and management skills in host countries (Nyuur et al., 2016).

As a result, the attraction of FDI has become a major priority, particularly for developing and transition countries, as FDI is expected to supplement national savings by capital inflows and promote economic development. These positive aspects of FDI form the foundation on which scholars built their argument and encourage emerging countries to dismiss the option of isolating themselves from international trade and capital markets with restrictive policies, by opening up their economies to FDI (Nunnenkamp, 2001). Consequently, almost all countries are pursuing favourable strategies towards the phenomenon as evidenced by the liberalisation of FDI policies and the continuous removal of restrictive policies by countries in order to compete effectively in the attraction of FDI (UNCTAD, 2015). Governments of both developed and transition countries are participating in offering both explicit and implicit incentives in an attempt to attract this foreign capital (Young, 2005).

Notwithstanding, much of this literature is focused more on developed and other emerging regions, with limited studies examining the determinants and motives of FDI in the Customs Union countries of Russia, Belarus and Kazakhstan (Kenisarin & Andrews-Speed, 2008). This scant attention on this region is surprising considering the important role of the region in global events. This study thus seeks to enhance understanding of the phenomenon by examining the role of some indicators in facilitating the FDI phenomenon in the Customs Union countries between 2000 and 2011 (Kenisarin & Andrews-Speed, 2008). The rest of the chapter proceeds with the literature review and hypotheses development section, followed by the methodology section that describes the data collection and analysis. The authors then present the results and discuss the conclusion of the study in the final section.

2 Literature review and hypotheses development

FDI refers to the 'purchase of physical assets or a significant share of ownership (stock) of a company in another country to gain a measure of management control' (Li & Vashchilko, 2010, p. 767). The central logic of the international business scholarship is that firms invest abroad because they possess a superior set of assets compared to host country domestic firms (Sanfilippo, 2015). This perspective is underpinned by the internalisation theory (Caves, 1996; Hymer, 1976) and the ownership-location-internalisation

(OLI) paradigm (Dunning, 1980, 2000). The OLI eclectic paradigm further underscores that firm internationalisation is a function of not only the firm's ownership advantages, but also the locational and internalisation advantages that the firm expects to realise from the international involvement in the host country (Dunning, 2009). The paradigm posits that the interplay of the three independent sets of advantages explains what determines where firms finally end up establishing subsidiaries in the world.

The locational component of the eclectic model provides a framework for assessing the host country determinants of FDI and what makes a location more attractive to a foreign firm. There is substantial empirical research on the locational determinants of FDI that covers both developed (Dunning, 2000) and developing economies (Asiedu, 2002; Benassy-Quere et al., 2007; Buckley et al., 2007). The most dominant determinants found in the literature include market size, market potential and income levels, exchange rate, openness, political stability and trade costs (Liargovas & Skandalis, 2012); availability of natural resources (Asiedu, 2006); quality of infrastructure (Cheng & Kwan, 2000); market growth rate, and government policies (Brewer, 1993; Lall, 1995).

Moreover, other scholars found a strong indigenous technological base, regional trading blocs, language and business culture, tax holidays and exemptions, relative strength of local currency, economic and structural reforms, economic growth, available investment opportunities and the signing of binding multinational investment agreements to be important determinants of FDI in host countries (Buchanan et al., 2012; Dunning, 2002). Additionally, labour costs, investment costs, trade deficit, human capital, tax, inflation, budget deficit, domestic investment, external debt, government consumption and energy use have also been found to influence FDI inflow into a host country (Liargovas & Skandalis, 2012; Vijayakumar et al., 2010). Based on the above theoretical grounding and empirical findings, we explore the impact of host country market size, product growth, level of trade openness, and inflation rate on FDI inflow into the three Customs Union countries (Russia, Kazakhstan and Belarus). Thus we hypothesise that:

H1: Market size has a positive impact on FDI inflow into the three Customs Union countries.
H2: Inflation rate has a negative impact on FDI inflow into the three Customs Union countries.
H3: Trade openness has a positive impact on FDI inflow into the three Customs Union countries.
H4: Unemployment rate has a positive impact on FDI inflow into the three Customs Union countries.
H5: Gross capital formation has a positive impact on FDI inflow into the three Customs Union countries.
H6: The Industrial Production Index has a positive impact on FDI inflow into the three Customs Union countries.

3 Methodology

The data set for this study was obtained in June 2012 from various sources. Specifically, the data for FDI inflows, gross domestic product (GDP), inflation rate, gross capital formation and indicators of trade openness for the three countries were gathered from World Development Indicators published by World Bank. The unemployment rate was obtained from the International Monetary Fund (IMF) World Economic Outlook data, and the Index of Industrial Production for each country was retrieved from the National Statistics Services of Russia, Belarus and Kazakhstan, respectively. The data set covers a 12-year period from 2000 to 2011. This resulted in a total of 36 observations for all three countries over the 12-year period. Following earlier studies (Vijayakumar et al., 2010), we used multiple regression analysis in order to test the effect of the independent variables on a dependent one, as in the model below:

$$\begin{aligned} LFDI_{it} - \alpha &+ \beta_1 LDGP_{it} + \beta_2 INFLATION_{it} \\ &+ \beta_3 OPENNESS_{it} + \beta_4 UNEMPLOYMENT_{it} + \beta_5 IPI_{it} \\ &+ \beta_6 LGCF_{it} + e_{it} \end{aligned}$$

Where:

$LFDI_{it}$ is the log of FDI in current US dollars in country *i* at time *t*.
$LGDP_{it}$ is the log of GDP per capita in current prices (US dollars) in country *i* at time *t* and used as a proxy for MARKET SIZE. A scan through the literature on the determinants of FDI suggests that market size is one of the most significant and widely identified determinants of FDI in host economies (Buckley et al., 2007). The sign is expected to be positive because the larger the market, the more opportunities it offers foreign investors (Resmini, 2000). Moreover, GDP per capita is a measure of the purchasing power of the economy in an internationally comparable way (Liargovas & Skandalis, 2012).
$INFLATION_{it}$ is the inflation rate in the country *i* at time *t*. Inflation rate can be considered as a variable of macroeconomic stability. One of the symptoms of loss of fiscal or monetary control is unbridled inflation. Taking this into account, more stable economies are more attractive for investors. It is therefore expected that high inflation has a negative effect on FDI inflow (Makki & Somwaru, 2004).
$OPENNESS_{it}$ is the trade openness for a country *i* at time *t* measured by the ratio of trade to GDP. It is considered to be a key determinant of FDI inflow. A number of studies have suggested that FDI inflow has a positive association with indicators of 'openness' of an economy (Caves, 1996). According to different studies, foreign investors tend to prefer countries with liberal trade regimes (Resmini, 2000). The level of trade openness is thus expected to positively encourage FDI inflow.
$UNEMPLOYMENT_{it}$ is the unemployment rate in annual percentage for country *i* at time *t*. It is expected that a high unemployment rate presents

foreign firms with available cheap labour. This is particularly the case in situations where companies seek to make use of cheap labour or drive down the cost of operations (Dunning, 2002; Buckley et al., 2007). Thus, emerging and transition countries with a high unemployment rate may be associated with low labour cost, resulting in a positive impact on the magnitude of FDI inflow. We therefore expect the unemployment rate and FDI inflow to have a positive association.

$\boldsymbol{IPI_{it}}$ is the Industrial Production Index in annual percentage for country i at time t. It could be considered a measure of growth prospects of a particular country. The expected sign is positive.

$\boldsymbol{LGCF_{it}}$ is the log of gross capital formation to the percentage of GDP for country i at time t. It is the measure of total investment for each country and includes both private and public sector investment and excludes changes in stocks. According to Vijayakumar et al. (2010), higher gross capital formation leads to greater economic growth. However, a number of studies have not found a clear relation between FDI and gross capital formation in the transition economies. It is thus expected that it could have either positive or negative and significant impact on FDI inflow.

$\boldsymbol{\alpha}$**:** understanding that time is very important in transition economies, a time dummy variable was included in order to allow for shifts of the intercepts over time (Resmini, 2000). e_{it} is the disturbance (error) term over the time t. Some of the variables are in log form in order to adjust for heteroskedasticity (Verbeek, 2008).

4 Results

The analysis was completed using correlations and regression analysis. Table 12.1 depicts the descriptive statistics (means, standard deviations) and correlation coefficients for the independent and dependent variables. The Industrial Production Index has the highest mean of 106.972 and standard deviation is 5.26 in the data distribution. Moreover, except in a few cases, variables are not very strongly correlated as most of the coefficient values are below +/- .60. This eases the concern of multicollinearity presence in the data set.

The results of the multiple regression analysis are presented in Table 12.2, summarising the direct effects of the independent variables and dependent variable (FDI inflow into the Customs Union countries). Model 1 shows the direct effects of the independent variables. The predictive power of the model as denoted by the R^2 value is very strong as it is above the common threshold of 0.1 (Falk & Miller, 1992; Ghauri & Gronhaug, 2010). It shows how much of the variance in *LFDI* is accounted for by the regression model from the sample (Saunders et al., 2012). This indicates that the model explains a high amount (92%) of the variation in FDI inflow into the three Customs Union countries.

The results provide that market size ($\beta=1.766$, $p < 0.001$), unemployment rate ($\beta=0.103$, $p < 0.001$) and trade openness ($\beta= -0.007$, $p < 0.05$) are

Table 12.1 Means, standard deviations, and correlations

Variable	*Mean*	*Standard deviation*	*Min*	*Max*	*1*	*2*	*3*	*4*	*5*	*6*	*7*
1 Log FDI in dollars (LFDI)	9.55	0.80	7.98	10.88	1						
2 Market size (log GDP)	3.59	0.32	3.09	4.12	0. 79	1					
3 Inflation rate (annual %)	19.33	28.53	5.84	168.62	-0.48	-0.39	1				
4 Trade openness	93.25	33.89	48.44	177.89	-0.79	-0.45	0.44	1			
5 Unemployment rate (%)	5.84	3.38	0.60	12.75	0.48	-0.07	-0.32	-0.69	1		
6 Log of gross capital formation (% of GDP)	1.45	0.10	1.26	1.62	-0.19	0.16	-0.04	0.58	-0.62	1	
7 Industrial Production Index (%)	106.97	5.26	90.70	122.10	-0.37	-0.42	-0.01	0.37	0.02	0.10	1

Note: [a]N=36; *p<.05; ** p<.01; *** p<.001.

Table 12.2 Main effects of independent variables on FDI inflow

Variables	*Model 1*		*Hypotheses*	
			Hypothesised direction	*Hypothesis*
	β	*SE*	*Direction*	*Outcome*
Market size (log GDP)	1.766***	(0.209)	H1 (+)	Supported
Inflation rate	0.002	(0.002)	H2 (-)	Rejected
Trade openness	-0.007*	(0.003)	H3 (+)	Rejected
Unemployment rate	0.103***	(0.023)	H4 (+)	Supported
Log of gross capital formation	1.087	(0.705)	H5 (+)	Rejected
Industrial Production Index	0.001	(0.010)	H6 (+)	Rejected
R^2	0.92			
Adjusted R^2	0.90			
F change	56.54			

Note: [a]*N*=36; **p*<.05; ** p<.01; *** p<.001.

significantly associated with FDI inflows into the three Customs Union countries. Although the beta coefficients of market size and unemployment rate are in the direction predicted, that of trade openness is not in the predicted direction. Hypotheses H1 and H4 are thus supported, while H3 is not supported. Additionally, inflation rate ($\beta=0.002$, $p > 0.05$), gross capital formation ($\beta=0.002$, $p > 0.05$), and the Industrial Production Index ($\beta=0.001$, $p > 0.05$) are all positively but not significantly associated with FDI inflow. Thus, hypotheses H2, H5 and H6 are all not supported. These outcomes have important implications.

5 Discussion and conclusion

This study has examined the impact of market size, inflation rate, trade openness, unemployment rate, Industrial Production Index, and gross capital formation on FDI inflow into the Customs Union countries of Russia, Belarus and Kazakhstan. Using a data set from 2000 to 2011, the study tested six hypotheses altogether, with H1 and H3 receiving support while H2, H4, H5 and H6 were not supported by the results. The results contradict the findings of Kinoshita and Campos (2003) that market size does not significantly influence FDI inflow into a host country. However, it confirms the findings of other studies that market size is an important driver of FDI inflow into host countries (Buckley et al., 2007; Resmini, 2000). Unemployment rate is found to have a positive impact on FDI inflow into the region. This finding is suggestive that the region provides a highly qualified, mobile, but cheap workforce (Łahviniec & Papko, 2010; Jensen & Tarr, 2008).

Surprisingly, trade openness is found to have a negative association with FDI inflow into the three Customs Union countries. This finding departs from that of other empirical studies which found significant positive association between trade openness and FDI inflow into host countries (Li & Liu, 2005). Vijayakumar et al. (2010) also found positive but insignificant impact of trade openness on FDI inflow. Arguably, the uncertainties connected with the economies and political regimes of these countries during the selected period may account for this finding. Furthermore, inflation rate, the Industrial Production Index, and gross capital formation are found not to have any significant impact on FDI inflow into the Customs Union countries of Russia, Belarus and Kazakhstan.

These findings make important contributions to the literature. First, there is limited research on the determinants of FDI in this region, notwithstanding the important role of the region in global events (Kenisarin & Andrews-Speed, 2008). By examining the determinants of FDI inflow into the Customs Union countries between 2000 and 2011, this study has therefore filled the gap. Moreover, the findings of the study have enhanced our understanding of the drivers of FDI into the Customs Union countries of Russia, Belarus and Kazakhstan. Moreover, the contrasting findings in this study to those of existing empirical studies have enriched the literature and underscored the contextual relativeness of FDI drivers. Finally, the non-significant effects of some factors imply that not all factors are influential in every host country or region.

References

Asiedu, E. (2002) On the determinants of foreign direct investment to developing countries: Is Africa different? *World Development* 30: 107–119.

Asiedu, E. (2006) Foreign direct investment in Africa: The role of natural resources, market size, government policy, institutions and political instability. *The World Economy* 21(1): 63–77.

Benassy-Quere, A., Coupet, M. and Mayer, T. (2007) Institutional determinants of foreign direct investment. *The World Economy* 30(5): 764–782.

Brewer, T.L. (1993) Government policies, market imperfections and foreign direct investment. *Journal of International Business Studies* 24(1): 101–120.

Buchanan, B.G., Le, Q.V. and Rishi, M. (2012) Foreign direct investment and institutional quality: Some empirical evidence. *International Review of Financial Analysis* 21: 81–89.

Buckley, P.J., Clegg, L.J., Cross, A.R., Liu, X., Voss, H. and Zheng, P. (2007) The determinants of Chinese outward foreign direct investment. *Journal of International Business Studies* 38(4): 499–518.

Caves, R.E. (1996) *Multinational Enterprise and Economic Analysis.* Cambridge: Cambridge University Press.

Cheng, L.K. and Kwan, Y.K. (2000). What are the determinants of the location of foreign direct investment? The Chinese experience. *Journal of International Economics* 51(2): 379–400.

Dunning, J.H. (1980) Toward an eclectic theory of international production: Some empirical tests. *Journal of International Business Studies* 11(1): 9–31.

Dunning, J.H. (2000) The eclectic paradigm as an envelope for economic and business theories of MNE activity. *International Business Review* 9: 163–190.

Dunning, J.H. (2002) *Determinants of Foreign Direct Investment: Globalization Induced Changes and the Role of FDI Policies.* Background Paper for the Annual Bank Conference on Development Economics held in Oslo. Washington, DC: World Bank.

Dunning, J.H. (2009) Location and the multinational enterprise: A neglected factor? *Journal of International Business Studies* 40(1): 5–19.

Falk, R.F. and Miller, N.B. (1992) *A Primer for Soft Modelling*. Akron, OH: University of Akron Press.

Ghauri, P. and Gronhaug, K. (2010) *Research Methods in Business Studies.* Essex: Pearson Education Limited.

Hymer, S. (1976) *The International Operations of National Firms: A Survey of Direct Investment*. Cambridge, MA: MIT Press.

Janicki, H.P. and Wunnava, P.V. (2004) Determinants of foreign direct investment: Empirical evidence from EU accession candidates. *Applied Economics* 36: 505–509.

Jensen, J. and Tarr, D. (2008) Impact of local content restrictions and barriers against foreign direct investment in services: The case of Kazakhstan's accession to the World Trade Organization. *Eastern European Economics* 46(5): 5–26.

Kenisarin, M.M. and Andrews-Speed, P. (2008) Foreign direct investment in countries of the former Soviet Union: Relationship to governance, economic freedom and corruption perception. *Communist and Post-Communist Studies* 41(3): 301–316.

Kinoshita, Y. and Campos, N.F. (2003) Why does FDI go where it goes? New evidence from the transition economies. William Davidson Institute Working Paper No. 573.

Łahviniec, A. and Papko, A. (2010) Unfinished business: Challenges for Belarus on its way to democracy. *European View* 9(2): 253–262.

Lall, S. (1995) Industrial strategy and policies on foreign direct investment in East Asia. *Transnational Corporations* 4(3): 1–26.

Li, Q. and Vashchilko, T. (2010) Dyadic military conflict, security alliances, and bilateral FDI flows. *Journal of International Business Studies* 41(5): 765–782.

Li, X. and Liu, X. (2005) Foreign direct investment and economic growth: An increasingly endogenous relationship. *World Development* 33(3): 393–407.

Liargovas, P.G. and Skandalis, K.S. (2012) Foreign direct investment and trade openness: The case of developing economies. *Social Indicators Research* 106(2): 323–331.

Makki, S.S. and Somwaru, A. (2004) Impact of foreign direct investment and trade on economic growth: Evidence from developing countries. *American Journal of Agricultural Economics* 86(3): 795–801.

Nunnenkamp, P. (2001) Foreign direct investment in developing countries: What policymakers should not do and what economists don't know. Kielerdiskussionsbeitage: Kiel Discussion Papers No. 380.

Nyuur, R. and Debrah, Y.A. (2014) Predicting foreign firms' expansion and divestment intentions in host countries: Insights from Ghana. *Thunderbird International Business Review* 56(5): 407–419.

Nyuur, R.B., Ofori, D.F. and Debrah, Y.A. (2016) The impact of FDI inflow on domestic firms' uptake of CSR activities: The moderating effects of host institutions. *Thunderbird International Business Review*. DOI: 10.1002/tie.21744.

Resmini, L. (2000) The determinants of foreign direct investment in the CEECs: New evidence from sectoral patterns. *Economics of Transition* 8(3): 665–689.

Sanfilippo, M. (2015) FDI from emerging markets and the productivity gap—An analysis on affiliates of BRICS EMNEs in Europe. *International Business Review* 24(4): 665–676.

Saunders, M., Lewis, P. and Thornhill, A. (2012) *Research Methods for Business Students.* Essex: Pearson Education Limited.

UNCTAD (2007) Transnational corporations, extractive industries and development. World investment report. www.unctad.org/en/docs/wir2007_en.pdf (accessed 8 March 2016).

UNCTAD (2015) Reforming international investment governance. World investment report. www.unctad.org/en/PublicationsLibrary/wir2015_en.pdf (accessed 8 March 2016).

Verbeek, M. (2008) *A Guide to Modern Econometrics.* John Wiley & Sons.

Vijayakumar, N., Sridharan, P. and Rao, K.C.S. (2010) Determinants of FDI in BRICS countries: A panel analysis. *International Journal of Business Science & Applied Management* 5(3): 1–13.

World Bank (2006) *India: Financing Infrastructure—Addressing Constraints and Challenges.* Mimeo. Washington, DC: World Bank.

Young, C. (2005) The new FDI environment in East and Central Europe: The response of Hungary's place marketing agenda. *Environment and Planning C* 23: 733–775.

13 The role of regional integration in foreign direct investment in Southern Africa

Jayati Ghosh, Imelda K. Moise and Ezekiel Kalipeni

1 Introduction

Although interregional trade in Africa predates colonialism (Stock, 2013), the promotion of formal interregional integration and cooperation has become an increasingly important part of the economic toolbox to enhance the flow and volume of trade and investment in post-colonial Africa. The past 15 years (2000–15) have ushered in a sense of urgency for interregional trade and integration efforts to spur economic growth and development in Africa. These efforts have involved the creation and/or strengthening the effectiveness of pre-existing regional economic communities (RECs) that vary widely in number of member countries, geographic size, age, history and economic clout. Currently, the African Union officially recognizes eight RECs in Africa, and several second-tier regional associations. In addition to increases in trade, regional economic integration in Africa is supposed to create conditions conducive to increased flows of outside capital or foreign direct investment (FDI), which spur further economic development, flow of innovative ideas, and enhance investment in people (human capital) including enhancements in industrialization processes, technology, and infrastructure development which boost production and accelerate economic development (Ebaidalla & Yahia, 2014; NEPAD, 2013; UNCTAD, 2012). However, despite significant support for and creation of RECs, and generally increased volume of trade within regional economic integration (REI) groupings in Africa over the past three decades, implementation (breadth, depth and quality) has generally been slow and gains in the share of intra- versus extra-regional trade remained low or modest at best but varied across REI groupings (Byiers & Vanheukelo, 2014; Stock, 2013).

The value of intra-region exports as a share of total exports for sub-Saharan Africa's (SSA) five major economic groupings ranged from less than 1% for the Economic Community of Central African States to 18.9% for the East African Community in 2009 (Stock, 2013). As for FDI, Africa's share of global FDI dropped by nearly half, from 5.3% in 1980 to 2.3% in 2000. These generally low levels of intra-regional trade in Africa are often posited as one of the major reasons why Africa retains a marginal role in global trade

(WTO, 2009). Recent evidence suggests that the relationship between REI and FDI is not always straightforward. Impacts may vary based on different types of capital inflows, for example FDI versus foreign portfolio investment (NEPAD, 2013). Further, as the base of sources of FDI broadens, particularly with the coming of new major or emerging global players on the economic scene, including China and India, understanding how REI relates to these different sources of FDI will have value in future economic planning. This chapter examines trends in regional economic integration in Africa, and the relationship between REI and FDI, focusing on Southern Africa and the Southern African Development Community (SADC) region over the past 15 years (i.e. 2000–15).

2 Overview: regional economic integration in Africa and linkages to FDI

During the 1970s and 1980s, there were periods of little or no upward trend in FDI in most African countries. Between 1980 and 2000, however, Africa was viewed primarily as a continent of persistent problems of political and economic instability, social conflict, weak governance and stagnant or declining economic growth with a marginal share of global FDI. This is a post-colonial relic of relations between Africa and the West, and the crushing foreign debt that consumed Africa's disproportionate share of its gross national income (GNI) in debt repayment.

The resulting economic downturn and decline in FDI inflows forced African leaders to mobilize themselves to reverse the declining trend by promoting regional economic cooperation among member countries of individual regional economic groupings. Since then, there has been a proliferation of regional economic groupings in Africa. In order to bring some order and prioritize groupings, the African Union focused on developing eight endorsed RECs as critical building blocks for a future Africa-wide economic union—the African Economic Community, as envisioned in the Abuja Treaty (Baah, 2003; UNCTAD, 2012). Thus, African nations sought to take charge of their own political and economic development affairs first under the Monrovia Strategy in 1979, followed shortly after by the Lagos Plan of Action for Economic Development. The Monrovia Declaration articulated Africa's economic vision of its future, with its strategies incorporated in the Lagos Plan of Action and the Final Act of Lagos in 1980 (Bujra, 2004), which provided the framework and strategies for implementing development programs. Consequently, several RECs emerged out of these efforts. RECs appear to be a rational choice for African countries to reduce dependency on unequal trading relationships with countries from other regions of the world. African countries face many challenges, among them small markets and high costs of doing trade partly due to poor transport and other infrastructure, which are particularly pronounced in landlocked countries (Hartzenberg, 2011; Stock, 2013).

The Community of Sahel-Saharan States (CEN-SAD) has 28 members: Benin, Burkina Faso, the Central African Republic, Chad, Comoros, Côte d'Ivoire, Djibouti, Egypt, Eritrea, Gambia, Ghana, Guinea, Guinea-Bissau, Kenya, Liberia, Libya, Mali, Mauritania, Morocco, Niger, Nigeria, Senegal, São Tomé and Príncipe, Sierra Leone, Somalia, Sudan, Togo, and Tunisia. The Common Market for Eastern and Southern Africa (COMESA), with 20 members, comprises: Burundi, Comoros, Democratic Republic of the Congo, Djibouti, Egypt, Eritrea, Ethiopia, Kenya, Libya, Madagascar, Malawi, Mauritius, Rwanda, Seychelles, South Sudan, Sudan, Swaziland, Uganda, Zambia, and Zimbabwe. The Economic Community of West African States (ECOWAS) has a membership of 15 states: Benin, Burkina Faso, Cape Verde, Gambia, Ghana, Guinea, Guinea Bissau, Côte d'Ivoire, Liberia, Mali, Niger, Nigeria, Senegal, Sierra Leone, and Togo. Finally, SADC has 15 members: Angola, Botswana, Democratic Republic of the Congo, Lesotho, Madagascar, Malawi, Mauritius, Mozambique, Namibia, Seychelles, South Africa, Swaziland, Tanzania, Zambia, and Zimbabwe (see Stock, 2013, pp. 316–321). It is clear that there is considerable overlap in membership, with some countries being members of as many as four RECs, and the economic clout of the RECs also varies considerably (Stock, 2013, p. 320). For the period 2007–11, the members of the top four RECs, CEN-SAD, SADC, COMESA and ECOWAS, had US$778.13 billion, $510.54 billion, $430.90 billion and $311.74 billion in combined gross domestic product (GDP), respectively (UNCTAD, 2013). However, enhancement of trade is not the only goal of regional integration, and RECs have expanded the areas of cooperation to include more economic sectors, natural resources management, cultural exchanges, and politics, governance and security.

African countries export high-value oil-based products outside the RECs while lower-value agricultural goods tend to be traded within the region (Stock, 2013). Thus, the proportion of intra-Africa trade is significantly higher for non-fuel-exporting countries than for fuel exporters. Furthermore, while manufacturing declined in importance in intra-African trade during the first decade of the new millennium, its share in intra-African trade is higher than its share in African extra-regional trade (UNCTAD, 2013).

3 Regional integration in Southern Africa

SADC traces its origins to the Lusaka Declaration of 1980, which founded the Southern African Development Coordination Conference (SADCC). In 1993, SADCC was transformed into the current SADC, a REC comprising 15 members (see above, and Stock, 2013, pp. 316–321). The establishment of SADC revolutionized trade and investment in Southern Africa, helping to unlock the region's economic potential. In addition, the region has enjoyed an extended period of strong economic growth over the past decade. On average, GDP per capita increased by 3% over the past decade (EDIP/GIZ, 2015, p. 17). Following the sharp decline in 2009 due to the global economic recession that also affected advanced economies, economic growth increased slightly from 3.7% in 2012 to 3.8% in 2016, but trailing growth in SSA (IMF, 2015).

While the economic performance of SADC seems to have followed developments in the global economy, further examination of economic growth by country shows some interesting trends. For instance, countries normally strong were the hardest hit by the 2009 economic recession, while some weak economies actually grew during the recession. Botswana, Madagascar, and South Africa were the worst hit, with their GDP shrinking by 7.8%, 4.7% and 2.9%, respectively, while the economies of Zimbabwe, Zambia and Malawi grew by at least 6% (IMF, 2015). After the recession, however, GDP growth recovered and became relatively stable within the range of 2.5–5.5% for most countries with the exception of Mozambique, with growth rates above 9% in 2014 and 2015 (IMF, 2015).

In terms of GDP contribution by country, South Africa dominates the region and contributed 55.5% of SADC's GDP in 2013 even though this marked a 7.5% decrease from 2010. Angola comes in second with a share of 13%, while 'Lesotho and the Seychelles are at the bottom with shares of 0.4% and 0.2%, respectively' (EDIP/GIZ, 2015, p. 17; World Bank, 2013). On average, SADC and most of its countries performed better than the world average, though the region trailed SSA averages. The IMF (2015) suggests that the level of intra-regional trade may be associated with GDP growth rates for SADC. A steep decline in intra-regional trade is observed from 21.4% during 1996–2000 to 12.9% for the period to 2007.

4 Linkages between FDI and regional economic integration

FDI trends are also important because they act as both a driver and outcome of economic performance in SADC. FDI inflows into SADC have increased considerably and steadily from around $64.6 billion in 2002 to peak in 2010 at $245.5 billion after a quick recovery from a steep decline associated with the global economic slump in 2009 (UNCTAD, 2015). FDI inflows declined slightly in 2011 and leveled off at around $230 billion up to 2014. This increasing trend in FDI since 2001 reflects the partial recovery in Africa's share of global FDI stocks after declining from 5.3% in 1980 to 2.3% in 2000 and then regaining to a 2.7% share in 2014 (IMF, 2015). Yet the trend also affirms the continuing marginal role of Africa as an FDI destination. However, the flattening out of FDI inflows since 2010 appears to correspond with a flattening out of, but relatively significant, GDP growth (IMF, 2015), suggesting a positive association between FDI growth and GDP growth.

Closer examination of FDI trends within SADC shows significant variation. South Africa is the dominant economic power, and accounted for 55.5% of FDI inflows in 2013, followed by Angola at 13.0%, and Tanzania at 7.1% (World Bank, 2013). These three countries also showed the widest annual volatility in FDI inflows into SADC between 2003 and 2014. Angola in particular had the most pronounced fluctuations in FDI inflows, despite enjoying higher than 7% annual GDP growth per capita over the past decade (UNCTAD, 2015). South Africa and Mozambique showed a slow, long-term growth trend in FDI inflows despite high annual fluctuations (World Bank, 2015).

There is also significant variation in FDI inflows by source as well as sector. Traditional Organisation for Economic Co-operation and Development (OECD) countries accounted for the bulk of FDI between 2003 and 2014, 73.7%, led by the USA at $45,155 million or 18.7% of total FDI for the period (Bezuidenhout, 2015; FDI Intelligence, 2016). China ranked seventh in FDI share, but together with India and Brazil accounted for 19.2% of total FDI (the East/Global South grouping). Strikingly, when data from the past five years are analyzed, a different picture emerges with growing importance of new investors from the East. While the share of FDI is only slightly higher than for the entire period, India becomes the largest FDI source for investment in SADC from developing countries (second to France)—a total of $25,237.8 million—with South Africa is in second place and China a distant third at $3,477.5 million. Remarkably, South Africa is the biggest African and intra-regional investor in SADC ($17,180.8 million or 7.1% of total FDI for 2003–14), surpassing China for the same period (at $14,455.7 million), and the second largest from the developing region. India and South Africa's contributions illustrate that despite being regarded as a key investor in Southern Africa, 'Chinese investment falls short of media attention and Brazilian investment lags even more' (Hartzenberg, 2011).

There are several possible explanations for the variation in FDI, including the barriers that individual countries have to contend with and what measures they use to address them. For example, to benefit from a REC, a country must be ready to undertake trade reforms to increase its level of trade with its partners. Regional integration, through trade policy reforms, may benefit a country by increasing income levels, exports and trade-to-GDP ratio. In turn, trade reforms may increase exports and facilitate cheaper imports that generate sustainable growth and reduce poverty. Likewise, deep integration can increase regional competitiveness in sectors where economies of scale are easy to achieve. The desire to attract foreign investors has provided a strong incentive for African governments to reform policies and practices (Thomsen, 2005).

As indicated earlier, the relationship between REI and FDI is not straightforward or unidirectional. Effective REI can create conditions and economies of scale that make member countries in the REC attractive to FDI. These conditions include the removal of some trade barriers such as protective tariffs, improvements in banking systems, reducing red tape and generally easing doing business in a country or region, implementing key macroeconomic reforms, reducing corruption, and improving general service delivery (Asiedu, 2006). Development or enhancement of infrastructure such as shared transport corridors that facilitate movement of goods and labor across borders and shared energy for economic development are also important factors. Prior economic conditions, including reasonably high starting levels of economic development to provide purchasing power for finished goods, and development of a trained labor force with the requisite skills are crucial ingredients for economic growth and development. At the same time, the more FDI a region gets because of earlier levels of economic integration and cooperation, the more incentives it provides for further or more profound levels of integration and cooperation across countries (Li & Liu, 2005).

Studies on the relationship between FDI and economic growth and/or REI show mixed results. For instance, studies examining this link across 84 countries from the mid-1980s onwards show the relationship to be increasingly endogenous. FDI promoted economic development directly and also indirectly through interactions with other factors. For instance, interaction of FDI with human capital has positive impacts on economic growth in developing countries, yet FDI relationships with technology gaps have significant negative impacts. Economic development can also respond differently based on type of investment. A study examining impacts of FDI and domestic investment in SSA showed that FDI initially undermined domestic investment mainly through crowding out before producing a positive effect in subsequent years (Adams, 2009). In a study of 22 countries, Asiedu (2006) found that the natural resources endowment of countries as well as size of markets are associated positively with FDI inflows, along with political stability, openness to FDI and reliable legal systems. For instance, Asiedu estimated that reducing corruption in Nigeria to the level of South Africa would be akin to increasing fuels and minerals exports by 35%. However, some studies have observed differences in drivers of FDI for Africa compared to other countries or regions. In one study, a good return on investment and better infrastructure positively influenced FDI in non-SSA countries but had no significant impact in SSA and increased openness produced lower dividends for SSA countries (Adams, 2009), suggesting that SSA and SADC should chart a cautious, regionally appropriate path.

An important source of potential growth for SADC states over the past decade has been the exploitation of service sector opportunities, which are exported both regionally and internationally. There is a consensus that increased export growth leads to overall economic growth. Indeed, the region's attractiveness to foreign investment has improved significantly over the past decade. The advent of peace and tranquility (the end of wars in Mozambique, Angola, Namibia, and the independence of South Africa) and the growth and consolidation of democratic processes in this region support this observation. Rising exports are also related to other gains, like access to larger markets, which in turn enable exploitation of economies of scale, competence gains from technological spillovers and better resource allocation, employment generation and foreign exchange earnings.

By following the market and trade agreement reforms of the 1980s, SADC's FDI inflows rose from $372 million in 1980 to almost 50 times that

($17 billion in 2008) during the past three decades (Mahembe & Odhiamboa, 2013). Likewise, real GDP growth rose from 0.5% in 2009 to over 3% in early 2016. The evidence suggests that there is a strong correlation between economic growth and export performance. The raw materials sector represents the largest share of GDP in this region, contributing over half of GDP in SADC, with about 14% of GDP emanating from agriculture, and over 31% from industry. As for sector drivers of GDP growth, the services sector clearly dominates (55.2% of GDP), followed by industry (30.9%), with agriculture at the bottom (14.1%). Notably, the relative importance of various sectors varies quite significantly by country. For example, while agriculture contributes more than a quarter of GDP for Madagascar, Mozambique and Malawi, it only accounts for 2.09% of Seychelles' GDP. Seychelles generates 82.5% from the services sector, mostly due to its tourism. Likewise, Angola has the greatest share of its GDP from industry (57%), mainly from oil and gas activities and the smallest share from services (32.2%). At the same time, when the sector's contribution is compared—2003 sector contribution to that of 2013—a slight difference is observed. For example, while the services sector increased by two percentage points, the agricultural sector declined by two percentage points (World Bank, 2015).

5 Conclusions

The transformation of SADCC into SADC represents intensification in the level of regional integration from mere regional cooperation to regional integration in multiple sectors. In general, therefore, it seems that this transformation represents responsiveness to both internal and external economic changes that have happened since the 1970s and the growing desire for closer cooperation among member states. Several factors have driven the proliferation of REI in Africa, and for SADC these include the need to improve trade and therefore economic development, to attract FDI, to enhance self-dependence among REC members while reducing dependence on external markets, and to enhance cooperation in various sectors of their economies for mutual benefit. FDI has certainly been beneficial to SADC, in part because of the benefits of REI, which have made the region more attractive to FDI. New investment from China has also played a positive role in this. However, contrary to media reports, intra-regional FDI from South Africa is more important than Chinese trade, and African trade with India is growing faster than trade with China. For SADC, while Africa is becoming increasingly competitive with new investment from China and China has become the largest trading partner for Africa, FDI is still dominated by the West (nearly three quarters over the past 12 years), with the new FDI sources from the East and the Global South contributing at best a fifth of the FDI. SADC is particularly benefiting from intra-regional investment from South Africa, a new and encouraging trend.

Intra-regional investment has offered Africa and SADC new power for more autonomy and fostered the ability to choose among a growing number of potential investors and trading partners than the traditional Western partners and the hegemonic power relations that such trading relations represent. In terms of linkages between FDI and REI, the relationship is two-way: REI creates an environment to attract FDI, and the new FDI catalyzes new economic growth and capabilities that attract more FDI. However, many other factors play a role, including the quality of infrastructure, natural resource endowment, the initial size of the economy, political stability, how welcoming to FDI a country is, and policy/governance issues including openness of society, corruption, strength of the legal system, the quality of the workforce and others. This chapter extends our knowledge of the differentiated impacts of different types of FDI on regional integration and economic development.

References

Adams, S. (2009) Foreign direct investment, domestic investment, and economic growth in sub-Saharan Africa. *Journal of Policy Modeling* 31: 939–949.

Asiedu, E. (2006) Foreign direct investment in Africa: The role of natural resources, market size, government policy, institutions and political instability. *The World Economy* 29: 63–77.

Baah, A. (2003) History of African development initiatives. Paper presented at the Africa Labour Research Network Workshop held in Johannesburg, South Africa, May 22–23. Retrieved on March 20, 2016. www.sarpn.org/documents/d0000407/P373_Baah.pdf.

Basu, A. and Srinivasan, K. (2002) Foreign direct investment in Africa: Some case studies. IMF Working Paper WP/02/6. Washington, DC: International Monetary Fund.

Bezuidenhout, H. (2015) Policy insights 12: SADC investment perspectives in a changing international investment landscape. Retrieved on February 24, 2016. www.econrsa.org/system/files/publications/research_briefs/research_brief_38.pdf.

Bujra, A. (2004) *Pan-African Political and Economic Visions of Development from the OAU to the AU: From the Lagos Plan of Action (LPA) to the New Partnership for African Development (NEPAD)*. Addis Ababa, Ethiopia: Development Policy Management Forum (DPMF).

Byiers, B. and Vanheukelo, J. (2014) What drives regional economic integration? Lessons from the Maputo Development Corridor and the North-South Corridor. Discussion Paper No. 157. European Centre for Development Policy Management. Retrieved on March 20, 2016. ecdpm.org/wp-content/uploads/DP-157-Regional-Economic-Integration-Maputo-Development-Corridor-2014.pdf.

Ebaidalla, M.E. and Yahia, A. (2014) Performance of intra-COMESA trade integration: A comparative study with ASEAN's trade integration. *African Development Review* 26: 77–95.

EDIP/GIZ (2015) *Regional Economic Integration in SADC: Current Status of Key Economic Indicators—Regional Economic Trends*. Johannesburg: German Cooperation and South African Institute of International Affairs, University of the Witwatersrand.

FDI Intelligence (2016) fDi markets: The in-depth crossborder investment monitor from the *Financial Times*. Retrieved on February 16, 2016. www.fdimarkets.com.

Hartzenberg, T. (2011) Regional integration in Africa. Staff Working Paper ERSD-2011–2014, Economic Research and Statistics Division. World Trade Organization. Retrieved on February 26, 2016. www.wto.org/english/res_e/reser_e/ersd201114_e.pdf.
IMF (2015) World economic and financial surveys: Regional economic outlook, sub-Saharan Africa navigating headwinds. Retrieved on March 1, 2016. www.imf.org/external/pubs/ft/reo/2015/afr/eng/pdf/sreo0415.pdf.
Li, X. and Liu, X. (2005) Foreign direct investment and economic growth: An increasingly endogenous relationship. *World Development* 33: 393–407.
Mahembe, A. and Odhiamboa, N.M. (2013) The dynamics of foreign direct investment in SADC countries: Experiences from five middle-income economies. *Problems and Perspective in Management* 11(4): 35–45.
NEPAD (2013) *Annual Report*. Retrieved on February 26. www.nepad.org/system/files/NEPAD_AR_English.pdf.
Stock, R. (2013) *Africa South of the Sahara: A Geographical Interpretation*. New York: Guilford Press.
Thomsen, S. (2005) Foreign investment in Africa: The private-sector response to improved governance. Briefing Paper IEP BP 05/06. International Economics Program, Chatham House, The Royal Institute of International Affairs. Retrieved from www.offnews.info/downloads/BPafrica-fdi.pdf.
UNCTAD (2012) *Trade and Development Report*. Geneva: United Nations.
UNCTAD (2013) *Trade and Development Report: Global Value Chains*. Geneva: United Nations.
UNCTAD (2015) *World Investment Report 2015: Reforming International Investment Governance*. New York and Geneva: United Nations Conference on Trade and Development.
World Bank (2013) *World Development Indicators*. Retrieved on February 1, 2016. data.worldbank.org/data-catalog/Worlddevelopment-indicators.
World Bank (2015) *World Development Indicators*. Retrieved on February 1, 2016. data.worldbank.org/data-catalog/Worlddevelopment-indicators.
World Trade Organization (WTO) (2009) *World Trade Report: Trade Policy Commitments and Contingency Measures*. Geneva: World Trade Organization.

14 A case study

Geoeconomics and the Iranian nuclear deal

Jonathon Cini

A potential new chapter in relations between Iran and the West has been opened, but what were the underlying factors behind the historic nuclear deal of 14 July 2015? Was it about preventing Iran from developing a nuclear weapon? Was it about building trust and bolstering strategic leverage in the region? Or was it simply about economic survival (for Iran) and economic opportunity (for the West)? This chapter will address these questions by considering both the regional geopolitical landscape and the economic motivations of both sides to the deal. It will assume a realist standpoint, ultimately arguing that beyond the stated imperative of constraining Iran's nuclear programme, the main underlying principle was one of geoeconomic interest.

Geoeconomics, in this context, can be broadly defined as the intersection between geopolitics and economics (Cini, 2015). A geoeconomic approach analyses how countries use markets and economics to influence politics; how economic transformations affect power balances; and how geopolitics drives economic shifts. The concept is sometimes used to capture the current retreat from the prevailing logic of liberal globalization that characterized the decades following the fall of the Soviet Union—the widespread belief that increased economic integration would translate into more democracy and stability. Under a hegemonic US umbrella, such a belief was part of the logic of bodies such as the European Union (EU), the Pacific Alliance, and the multilateral system more generally.

However, in today's unstable geopolitical and conflict-strewn environment it appears to be losing ground to more aggressive and targeted forms of economic activity, from protectionism and sanctions to preferential trading regimes and currency wars. The Iranian nuclear deal, with the various economic and strategic logics underpinning it, is an important example of how this geoeconomic perspective can help to explain complex contemporary events.

1 On the surface—arms control

The core objective of the negotiations, for the P5+1,[1] was to prevent or slow Iran's development of a nuclear weapon. To achieve this, negotiators began with the aspiration that Iran would completely shut down its nuclear development programme, and concluded in Vienna on 14 July 2015 by allowing it to continue to enrich uranium at low levels in exchange for economic sanctions relief. Iran's so called 'breakout capability'—the time it would take to produce the required fissile material for a nuclear bomb—has been pushed back to an estimated ten years (*The Economist*, 2015). The International Atomic Energy Agency (IAEA), which was present throughout the negotiations, will play a key role in monitoring and reporting on the status of Iranian nuclear infrastructure.

Many of the Western media have focused on this core objective. The deal, for many, revolved around a normative-security nexus of arms control and the maintenance of peace. In reality, however, it has much wider implications. It is the author's perspective that this arms-control objective informed and was informed by a confluence of strategic and economic motivating factors. These factors, which included the effects of sanctions, economic shifts and changes in the energy market, all interacted in a swirling regional context to shape a backdrop upon which an alignment of interests was reached. Ultimately, it is only through considering these geoeconomic forces that an understanding of the success of a deal can be achieved.

2 A win–win situation—the economic imperative

2.1 Easing the burden

Instead of relying solely on military or hard power, states are increasingly using economic tools to coerce other actors. The interconnectedness of the global economy means that particular countries—those that are economically powerful—are increasingly willing and able to wield economic instruments for strategic ends. This geoeconomic tactic is fast becoming an important function of foreign and security policy (Cini, 2015). Sanctions, as a particularly potent weapon of this new warfare, have devastating impacts on the development, economic integration, and livelihood of the citizens of the target country.

Sanctions leveraged on Iran stretch back to 1979, in response to the Islamic Revolution and takeover of the US embassy in Tehran. Although they continued throughout the 1980s and 1990s, they were significantly escalated in 2006 when the United Nations (UN) passed Resolution 1696 amid suspicions that Iran was attempting to develop nuclear weapons (United Nations, 2006). In the years that followed, however, IAEA reports continued to note a 'substantial' increase in Iran's uranium enrichment capacities (Albright et al., 2013) and the USA and Europe duly tightened sanctions (US Department of the Treasury, 2013). Ceilings imposed on the country's energy exports, together with restrictions on technological imports and ostracization from the SWIFT banking system, began to cut through the centre of the Iranian economy and society (*The Economist*, 2015).

A drop in oil prices in 2014 further compounded budgetary pressures in Tehran (Nephew & Salehi-Isfahani, 2015). As a major current and potential energy supplier—the country houses 15% of the world's oil reserves and 10% of global gas reserves (Paivar, 2015)—it was not spared the effect of the shift in prices. Moreover, it has been suggested that the Organization of the Petroleum Exporting Countries' (OPEC) principal state, Saudi Arabia, may actually benefit from the price drops. More interested in market share than in oil price, Riyadh is prepared to use its substantial financial reserves to bear short-term budgetary difficulties and ensure its continued global reach by letting the market harm emerging competitors (Claes et al., 2015). As a direct economic and energy rival of Iran—OPEC solidarity notwithstanding—the Kingdom wants to prevent any loss of market share to its rival across the Persian Gulf (Claes et al., 2015).

In this context, it is clear that economic issues were one of the paramount interests bringing Iran to the negotiating table. Although President Rouhani's election platform focused on facilitating a reduction in geopolitical tensions and Iranian isolation, there was also a motivation to end the sanctions. The growing economic burden was starting to weigh heavily on the day-to-day life of citizens, and calls to ease the pressure were growing (Fathollah-Nejad, 2013). One could even argue that Iran used a reverse form of geoeconomics, relying on its strongest geostrategic bargaining chip—the threat of a nuclear bomb—in order to ensure economic breathing space.

Concretely, the International Monetary Fund (IMF, 2015) has predicted that lifting sanctions will bring Iran about 5.5% annual growth in gross domestic product (GDP) between 2016 and 2018, and approximately 3.5–4.0% annually in the subsequent years. Perhaps more importantly, it is also estimated that ending the sanctions will result in the return of approximately US $120 billion in accrued foreign exchange reserves frozen abroad for almost a decade (Paivar, 2015). The hope for President Rouhani is that these developments will converge to drive considerable growth and employment, thereby improving stagnating living conditions for Iranian people. The regime also wants to stave off further risk of socio-political unrest, particularly after the 2009 Green Revolution movement.

The pace at which Iran's economy is opening up to foreign direct investment since the deal was penned underscores this and suggests a significant aspiration to be absorbed into the global economy. A week after the deal was concluded Iran announced a proposal to start rebuilding its industries; this included 50 new projects by 2020 valued at $185 billion (Rafi, 2015). These projects will be in the oil and gas, metals and car manufacturing industries, and exporting to Europe is set to begin in the near future, according to Minister Nematzadeh. A week after the deal was concluded Iran announced a proposal to start rebuilding its industries, including 50 oil and gas projects worth $185 billion by 2020 (Rafi, 2015). According to Iranian Minister of Industry, Mines and Trade Mohammad Reza Nematzadeh, Iran will focus on the oil and gas, metals and car industries, and will begin exporting to Europe in the near future.

However, Minister Nematzadeh was also quick to point out that Iran is 'looking for a two-way trade as well as cooperation in development, design and engineering' (Rafi, 2015).

To facilitate this process various meetings have been held after the deal to encourage foreign investment. This includes the Tehran Summit in November 2015. Heralded as a 'once in a lifetime event', the conference brought together a number of international petroleum companies—250 bodies from 33 countries—to discuss potential oil and gas projects in Iran.[2] Shortly thereafter, and for the first time in five years, on 14 February 2016, Iran announced its first shipment of crude oil to Europe, with Deputy Oil Minister Rokneddin Javadi proclaiming the event 'a new chapter' for the oil industry in Iran (Al Jazeera, 2016). On 14 February 2016, Iran announced its first crude oil shipment to Europe in five years, with Deputy Oil Minister Rokneddin Javadi proclaiming the event 'a new chapter' for the oil industry in Iran (Al Jazeera, 2016). The high politics and strategic diplomacy of the deal had potentially changed the course of Iran's economic history.

2.2 A new gold mine?

Aside from the damage to the Iranian economy and society, the sanctions regime also impacted the business interests and economic opportunities of Western companies. This 'double-edged sword' is a recurring feature of economic sanctions: the country employing the weapon often risks damaging the trade and business interests of its own private sector in doing so. As a consequence of sanctions imposed by the USA and European governments, many Western companies—from technology firms to car manufacturers previously present in the region—were forced to shun investment opportunities in Iran (World Economic Forum, 2015).

Similarly, such a scenario can also enable (unwelcome) economic and strategic opportunism from competing states. For instance, Western measures imposed on Iran gave something of a free passage to other countries to enter the market: first individual European economies (before the EU joined the sanctions regime), then China and Russia (World Economic Forum, 2015). Beijing, which was relatively quiet during the nuclear negotiations, markedly increased bilateral trade with Iran during the sanctions period—and although it has recently dipped, it remains about $40 billion annually (Keck, 2013). Thus, Western sanctions helped pave the way for new strategic power alignments between Iran and other regional and global powers, culminating in a negative economic and geopolitical outcome for the USA and the West.

For the P5+1, the new context—notably the call from Tehran for reciprocal trade—was also one of the big draw cards behind securing the deal. The market potential in Iran, particularly in the consumer goods industry, is massive. Iran is the largest untapped market since the opening of China (Kohler, 2015). Western business will also stand to benefit from low oil prices, as well as access to a large population of 77 million, almost the same size as

Germany. Upwards of 50% of the Iranian population has access to the internet, and literacy among the younger population is at approximately 98% (Rafi, 2015). Furthermore, Iran offers a largely untouched $100 billion stock market which is extremely attractive for potential Western businesses and investors (Rafi, 2015).

Unsurprisingly, it has not taken long since the deal for Western companies to make an entry. According to Iran's Deputy Finance Minister Mohammad Khazaei, speaking in Vienna on 23 July 2015, European companies have been quick to invest: 'We are recently witnessing the return of European investors to the country. Some of these negotiations have concluded, and we have approved and granted them the foreign investment licences and protections. Even in the past couple of weeks we have approved more than $2 billion of projects in Iran by European companies' (Reuters, 2015).

This includes a number of companies from France, Germany, Italy and Austria that began talks prior to the deal in anticipation of the sanctions being lifted. One of the recent agreements involved Airbus, which signed a deal to sell 118 planes to Iran worth $25 billion (Johnston, 2016). Combined with increased oil revenues and access to frozen assets, Iranian officials are optimistic that they can achieve significant GDP growth in the coming years (Paivar, 2015). Elsewhere, India has also made positive noises following the deal (Ministry of External Affairs, Government of India, 2015). As the world's fourth biggest consumer of energy and importing over three quarters of its oil and gas, Delhi is understandably keen to diversify its supplier network (Madan, 2015).

With the removal of sanctions on its oil market the International Energy Agency has suggested that Iran can increase production by around 700,000 barrels a day within the first two months (Kohler, 2015). The country is currently producing around 3.1 million barrels per day and, as mentioned above, has already made shipments to the European market (Al Jazeera, 2016). With the global economy stagnating—worldwide growth is forecast to be 3.4% in 2016 (IMF, 2016)—the Vienna deal has been warmly welcomed. China, the engine of the global economy since the global financial crisis, is slowing, and growth may need to come from alternative emerging economies. Iran could be one of the economies to provide this.

3 Order in a shifting region—the strategic imperative

3.1 Increased regional clout

Beyond the economic imperative, an additional motivation behind the Iranian acquiescence appears to be the possibility of breaking from isolation and increasing its geostrategic influence in the region. Since the 2011 Arab Spring movements, Tehran has ostensibly capitalised on mounting instability in the Arab world in order to exert its influence in a number of countries. It is currently heavily engaged in sectarian conflicts in Yemen, Syria and Iraq. Despite the limitations now placed on the country's nuclear programme, its security and clout in the region are more likely to continue growing than ebbing.

If the opening of Iranian markets to foreign investment succeeds in deepening the pockets of Tehran, it could serve to fuel the confrontation that pits it against its regional heavyweight rival, Saudi Arabia. Although this 'battle' revolves around a complex nexus of culture, religion, politics and strategy, economic weight plays a major role (Rafi, 2015). For example, even through years of sanctions Iran still managed to funnel billions of dollars to the revolutionary National Defence Force and paramilitary Shia fighters, key elements of its regional struggle with Riyadh (Farhi et al., 2015). As sanctions are lifted, the possibility of such funding—and hence the reach of the regime—should continue.

Moreover, one of Iran's major beneficiaries, Hezbollah, could also stand to benefit. According to the Council on Foreign Relations, Tehran provides Hezbollah around $200 million of military assistance per year (Farhi et al., 2015). Although this financial support was recently cut back as a result of the sanctions regime and the fall in oil prices, a recovery may prompt a renewal. Similarly, Iran may be capable of ramping up support to other Shia militias in Iraq and Yemen, increasing its regional foothold, but perhaps also exacerbating sectarian conflicts and creating new tensions in the Middle East.

Finally, even if the West manages successfully to limit Iran's nuclear programme for the next decade, once the deal expires, Iran will be entitled—if it chooses to do so—to attain a nuclear weapon (Friedman, 2015). The Obama Administration is walking on a tightrope. It has heavily invested in the idea that by the end of the 10–15-year period Iran will be integrated into the global system as a constructive actor and partner. However, it is easy to imagine a possible reversal of such a situation should a less flexible US Administration and president come to power in 2016, not to mention a deterioration of the regional situation.

3.2 From ostracization to cooperation?

From the perspective of the West, an important strategic imperative was also present. This is especially the case for a US Administration struggling to tackle the various crises engulfing the Middle East and hampered by a lack of domestic appetite as well as a deficit of trust with Arab partners following a decade of US-led wars. The deal thus signifies increased optimism for cooperation with Iran: through increasing economic integration and interdependency with the West, greater trust could be fostered between the two sides, and interests—especially regarding Middle East conflicts—could intersect.

This strategic necessity becomes clear when considering the situation the West faces in the region. Conflicts currently consume much of Syria, Iraq, Yemen, Libya and Afghanistan, and risk spilling over into surrounding states and regions. Complex internal confrontations in the Islamic world pit Sunni against Shia and reaction against revolution, all against the backdrop of a rising Islamic State in Iraq and Syria (ISIS). Iran, the country with the largest Shia population, sees itself as the guardian of all Shia communities, and between the years 2011 and 2014 is thought to have provided approximately $15 billion to $19 billion in support of the Assad Government (Friedman, 2015). Iran has also continued to provide defence spending support to its allies in Iraq and, as discussed above, Lebanon, despite being restricted by sanctions. Furthermore, it has more recently been accused of providing material support for the Houthi takeover in Yemen.

This has led to increasingly overt confrontation with Saudi Arabia, the Sunni hegemon in the region, which acts in a similar way to bolster its proxy allies across the Middle East. With both vying for influence, the West wants to find a way to help restore a balance of power and order to avoid any escalation of this regional 'Cold War'. In 2014, the *New Yorker* published an interview with President Obama, who provided a glimpse into his vision for the Middle East:

> although it would not solve the entire problem, if we were able to get Iran to operate in a responsible fashion—not funding terrorist organizations, not trying to stir up sectarian discontent in other countries, and not developing a nuclear weapon—you could see an equilibrium developing between Sunni, or predominantly Sunni, Gulf states and Iran in which there's competition, perhaps suspicion, but not an active or proxy warfare.
> (Remnick, 2014)

The nuclear deal with Iran provided precisely such an opportunity to rebalance. The agreement would theoretically help to normalise relations between Iran and the West, along with encouraging an economically strong Iran to play a more constructive regional role. Of course, simply signing the deal is not about to turn Iran into an ally: Tehran's own vision of its regional role is primordial, and this will be influenced primarily by regional developments, especially those in Riyadh. However, it does open a window of opportunity for the USA and Iran to discuss common strategic matters. Indeed, the USA is looking for a relationship with Iran that goes beyond mere reconciliation—one that can help find a solution to the Syria crisis and the fight against ISIS. As many voices in the West increasingly call into question the traditional relationship with Saudi Arabia, it has become clear that any efforts to resolve the crises in the region must take Iran's influence into consideration (Nader, 2015). With the Syrian crisis escalating and refugees still streaming towards Europe, some even suggested that the flurry of diplomatic activity to conclude the nuclear deal was directly related to the conflict (Farhi et al., 2015).

4 Conclusion

The deal signed in Vienna attempts to resolve some of these dilemmas. The agreement, although seemingly limited - to curb Iran's nuclear program for sanctions relief - has much broader implications for trade and security in a region mired in conflict (Farhi, Birke, Levitt, Ibish, Freilich and Laub, 2015). A notion supported by Henry Kissinger, as stated in in his book titled *World Order*, for Iran:

> the nuclear issue was treated as one aspect of a general struggle over regional order and ideological supremacy, fought in a range of arenas and territories with methods spanning the spectrum of war and peace—military and paramilitary operations, diplomacy, formal negotiation propaganda and political subversion—in fluid and reinforcing combination.
>
> (Kissinger, 2014)

Iran's geoeconomic objectives are evident: economic strengthening with the prospect of greater influence in the region. It is clear Tehran has a desire to transform itself from a politically and economically isolated country to an emerging power with potentially new geopolitical allies, trade links and worldwide investments. Iran's geoeconomic objectives are evident: economic strengthening with the prospect of greater influence in the region, from being an isolated country to one with new geopolitical allies, trade links and worldwide investments. This clearly illustrates the inherent connection between economics and geopolitics; the nuclear deal will remove the majority of the economic limitations on Iran's capability to project power across the region. From a realist standpoint, we can also suggest that this economic renewal may be converted into hard power. This has the potential to underpin Iran's support as champion and defender of Shia communities in the region.

Similarly, it is clear from the West's perspective that the nuclear agreement has a major geoeconomic component. Its approach was largely based on the belief that increasing economic integration would encourage greater interdependency with the West, improving trust and at the same time ensuring greater democracy and stability—both regionally and globally. Thus, along with the new abundance of economic opportunities for Western business in Iran, the deal signifies an increased optimism for cooperation in tackling conflict in the Middle East, including in the battle over Syria and the containment of ISIS. Whether or not this produces positive outcomes remains to be seen; however, the mere possibility and aspiration of using economics to influence geostrategy in such a way demonstrates the marked shift towards geoeconomic methods in the 21st century.

Acknowledgments

The author wishes to acknowledge the intellectual contribution of Mark Leonard, Co-founder and Director of the European Council on Foreign Relations, Tate Nurkin, Senior Director IHS Strategic Assessments and Futures Studies Center, Domhnall O'Sullivan, Visiting Fellow at the Geneva Centre for Security Policy, and Armin Scheffczyk, Ambassador at ThinkIN

China, who have graciously shared their time and wisdom in interviews that helped shape the content of this chapter.

Notes

1 The five nuclear powers forming the UN Security Council permanent members, plus Germany.
2 See www.tehransummit.com.

References

Albright, D., Walrond, C., Stricker, A. and Avagyan, R. (2013) *ISIS Analysis of IAEA Iran Safeguards Report*. Institute for Science and International Security.

Al Jazeera. (2016) Iran exports first oil to Europe since nuclear deal. Available america.aljazeera.com/articles/2016/2/14/iran-exports-first-oil-to-europe-since-nuclear-deal.html.

Cini, J. (2015) Geo-economic competition: Global disruptions from the new frontline. Geneva Centre for Security Policy. Available www.gcsp.ch/News-Knowledge/Publications/Geo-economic-competition-global-disruptions-from-the-new-frontline.

Claes, D.H., Goldthau, A. and Livingstone, D. (2015) *Saudi Arabia and the Shifting Geoeconomics of Oil*. Carnegie. Available carnegieendowment.org/2015/05/21/saudi-arabia-and-shifting-geoeconomics-of-oil/i8vv.

The Economist (2015) Everything you want to know about the Iranian nuclear deal. Available www.economist.com/blogs/economist-explains/2015/04/economist-explains-3.

Farhi, F., Birke, S., Levitt, M., Ibish, H., Freilich, C. and Laub, Z. (2015) *The Middle East After the Iran Nuclear Deal*. Council on Foreign Relations. Available www.cfr.org/middle-east-and-north-africa/middle-east-after-iran-nuclear-deal/p36963.

Fathollah-Nejad, A. (2013) *Nefarious Fallouts of Iran Sanctions*. Global Research. Available www.globalresearch.ca/nefarious-fallouts-of-iran-sanctions/5345014.

Friedman, B. (2015) *The Geopolitics of the Nuclear Negotiations with Iran*. Foreign Policy Research Institute.

IMF (2015) *Economic Implications of Agreement with the Islamic Republic of Iran: Regional Economic Outlook: Middle East and Central Asia*.

IMF (2016) *Subdued Demand, Diminished Prospects*. Available www.imf.org/external/pubs/ft/weo/2016/update/01/.

Johnston, C. (2016) Airbus signs $25bn deal to sell 118 planes to Iran. BBC. Available www.bbc.com/news/business-35434483.

Keck, Z. (2013) China's trade and investment in Iran plummets. *The Diplomat*. Available thediplomat.com/2013/03/chinas-trade-and-investment-in-iran-plummets/.

Kissinger, H. (2014) *World Order*. Penguin Press.

Kohler, A. (2015) Forget Greece, the Iran nuclear deal is the big news for the global economy. ABC. Available www.abc.net.au/news/2015-07-16/kohler-iran-nuclear-deal-is-the-big-news-for-the-global-economy/6623906.

Madan, T. (2015) India and the Iran deal. Brookings. Available www.brookings.edu/blogs/markaz/posts/2015/07/20-india-iran-nuclear-deal-madan.

Ministry of External Affairs, Government of India (2015) Official spokesperson's response to a question on the Iranian nuclear deal. Available mea.gov.in/bilateral-documents.htm?dtl/25480/Official+Spokespersons+response+to+a+question+on+the+Iranian+nuclear+deal.

Nader, A. (2015) *Iran's Role in Iraq: Room for Cooperation?* RAND. Available www.rand.org/pubs/perspectives/PE151.html.

Nephew, R. and Salehi-Isfahani, D. (2015) *Implications of Sustained Low Oil Prices on Iran*. Columbia Centre on Global Energy Policy. Available energypolicy.columbia.edu/sites/default/files/energy/Implications%20of%20Sustained%20Low%20Oil%20Prices%20on%20Iran_July%202015.pdf.

Paivar, A. (2015) Will nuclear deal really change Iran? *BBC*. Available www.bbc.com/news/world-middle-east-33784480.

Rafi, S. (2015) The Iran deal: It's the economy, stupid. *Asia Times*. Available atimes.com/2015/07/the-iran-deal-its-the-economy-stupid/.

Remnick, D. (2014) Going the distance. *New Yorker*. 27 January.

Reuters (2015) Iran eyes $185 bln oil and gas projects after sanctions. Available www.reuters.com/article/iran-nuclear-industry-idUSL5N10326920150723.

United Nations (2006) Security Council demands Iran suspend uranium enrichment by 31 August, or face possible economic, diplomatic sanctions. Security Council Press Release, July 31. Available www.un.org/press/en/2006/sc8792.doc.htm.

US Department of the Treasury (2013) Treasury announces sanctions against Iran. Available www.treasury.gov/press-center/press-releases/Pages/tg1847.aspx.

World Economic Forum (2015) Geo-economics: Seven challenges to globalization. Available www3.weforum.org/docs/WEF_Geo-economics_7_Challenges_Globalization_2015_report.pdf.

15 The impact of geographical factors on economic development

Evaluation of Europe and the Middle East

Hilal Yıldırır Keser and Işın Çetin

1 Introduction

Development in its simplest form can be defined as an increase in the socio-economic welfare and gross domestic product (GDP) of a given country. A key factor in explaining development is geographical factors—latitude, climate and climate change, geographical location, vegetation and natural resources—which are a country's hereditary characteristics and cannot be changed by man (Brata, 2009). Since economic development plans are unique to a country's geographical factors, these differences have become an important growth consideration.

Geography is a comprehensive field of sciences and studies on human influence and the events affecting it. It can be divided into 'physical' and 'human and economic' geography. Physical geography covers issues such as a country's underground and above-ground resources, their quality and quantity, topographical features, climate, frequency of natural disasters and geographical location. By contrast, human and economic geography studies the distribution and cultural and economic relations of population in a natural environment (Yanar, 2014). Physical geography refers to exogenous factors, whereas socioeconomic geography concerns endogenous factors. Since this study attempts to determine the non-stochastic impact of exogenous factors on economic development, physical geography factors are treated as the basis for geographical factors.

The remainder of this chapter is organized as follows. First, we present a brief summary of the literature on the relationship between geographical factors and economic development. Next, we discuss the basic differences between regions by referencing general geographical features of the Middle Eastern and European regions. Finally, we attempt to estimate the impact of geographical factors specific to these regions on economic development.

2 Geography and economic development

There is a growing interest in the role of geographical features in economic development and regions in which economic activities are conducted. At a global scale, the relationship between differences in economic development and settlement areas is undoubtedly visible. Many studies have adopted various perspectives to examine the relationship between geographical conditions and economic development. The foundation of the literature goes back to Adam Smith's (1776) *Wealth of Nations.* In his book, Smith posits that the physical geography of a region can affect its economic performance and asserts that the economies of coastal regions with easy access to sea trade show better performance than those of inland regions.

However, despite being an issue emphasized by Smith and subsequent economists, the impact of geography on development, and even economic growth until the 1990s, has been largely neglected in macroeconomics (Gallup et al., 1999; Nordhaus, 2006). Relevant studies have assumed that all sections of the world have the same opportunities for economic growth and long-term development. The key reason for these equal opportunities is endogenous factors such as capital, education, technology and political factors, rather than exogenous ones such as geography and population (Nordhaus, 2006). Following the 1990s, macroeconomic studies began accounting for physical geography factors. A seminal work is Gallup, Sachs and Mellinger's (1999) *Geography and Economic Development*, in which they conclude that tropical climates negatively impact economic growth, and excess population on coastal strips has a positive impact. However, they state that tropical climates are closely related to the epidemic of malaria. They analyse the results by region and find that Africa, in particular, is affected by its tropical location and that the spread of malaria is far greater in the region and its share of population on the coastal strip is less. Most of the developing countries are located on the tropical or subtropical (below tropics) regions. Owing to their geographical locations, these countries are subject to damage from pests and parasites, regional diseases, limited water resources and extreme heat. In addition, these countries, with the exception of oil-rich Persian Gulf countries, are poor in natural resources (Todaro & Smith, 2009). Rodrik et al. (2002) examine the relationship between institutions and geography and its effect on income level, and show that geography has an external impact on income level and indirectly affects income depending on the quality of institutions. Nordhaus (2006) examines the effects of geographical variables such as average annual temperature, average annual precipitation, soil categories and remoteness from the sea, and states that geography is important for economic development but is not the sole determinant. Diamond (1997) points to the importance of the natural environment in development. He stresses that the development of countries is contingent on geographical fortune and associates varying developmental levels with geographical conditions.

Recent studies approach geography using various indicators. The commonly used indicators for physical geographical factors that affect economic development are latitude, climate, landlockedness and natural resources.

Latitude is the angular value of the distance for any point on the Earth to the equator, which is the start parallel. There is a systematic relationship between economic development and the latitude on which countries are located. It has been observed that almost all countries situated between the latitudes of 23°45’ north and 23°45’ south of the equator are less developed, while those on the middle and high latitudes have more wealth (Gallup et al., 1999).

Climate is the average of meteorological events such as temperature, humidity, pressure, wind and precipitation, of which precipitation at a certain location over an extended period of time is one of the most effective geographical factors in terms of economic development. Temperature and precipitation can be used to determine natural vegetation, agricultural products, animal species and running water regimes. Therefore, economic activities are generally representative of climate-induced distribution. It has been observed that the development level of countries in tropical regions is often significantly lower than those in regions with a temperate climate. Climate directly affects the diversity of agricultural activities and products, and the distribution of industrial, tourism and economic activities (Dinler, 2008; Higgins & Savoie, 2009).

Landlocked countries are those with no access to open seas, but surrounded by neighbouring land borders. Countries with coasts to the sea and suitable for any type of transportation tend to have higher income and development levels compared to landlocked countries. Landlocked countries are at a disadvantage due to their inability to access the seas. Moreover, these countries are faced with the impossibility of out-migration and the limitations of making infrastructure investments within the border, even though they are at the same distance to the sea as the inland sections of coastal countries (Küçüker, 2000; Gallup et al., 1999). In this case, neighbouring countries play a vital role depending on their geographical conditions and economic development levels, which can affect commercial relationships.

Natural resources are a factor affecting humans and their environment and comprise rocks with mineral ore, oil, coal, uranium, stones used in construction, sunlight, air and water (Başol et al., 2005). The lack of natural resources can negatively affect economic development (Han & Kaya, 2015). Natural resources that can be grouped as underground and above-ground resources constitute raw materials needed for economic activities. For example, iron from underground resources is used as a raw material for the iron–steel industry and rough terrains can be used to construct dams on rivers and produce hydro-electric energy.

3 Basic geographical features: Europe and the Middle East

As seen in Figure 15.1, the European continent extends between 36° and 71° North latitudes in the Northern Hemisphere and from 10° West to 60° East longitudes. Europe, the second smallest continent after Oceania in terms of the area it covers, is surrounded by the Atlantic Ocean to the west, the North Arctic Sea and Atlantic Ocean to the north, the Mediterranean Sea to the south and the Asian continent to the east (Güner & Ertürk, 2015).

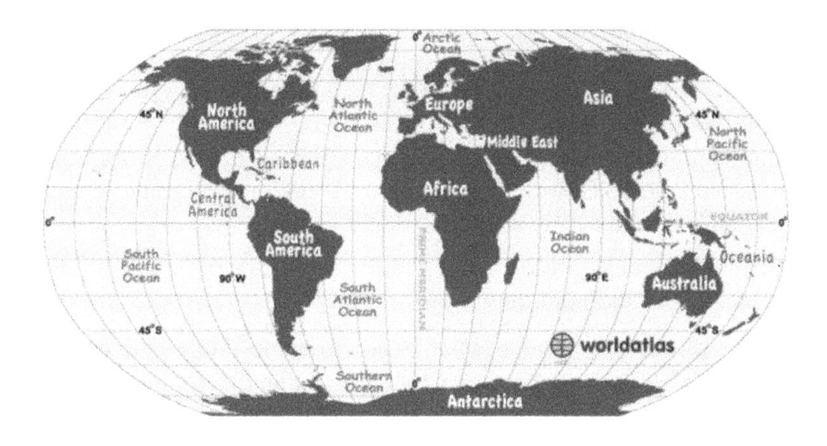

Figure 15.1 World map
(Valnet Inc., www.worldatlas.com, 2016)

Europe experiences various types of climate: the temperate oceanic climate is seen in the north-west, harsh and cold climates are dominant in the north, and terrestrial climate conditions prevail in the middle and east of Europe. The southern part of Europe is under the influence of the Mediterranean climate (Yiğit, 2000). Although a significant number of European countries have coasts to the sea, there are landlocked countries as well (Atasoy, 2010), such as Austria, the Czech Republic, Hungary, Luxembourg, Liechtenstein, Slovakia and Switzerland. In terms of natural resources and underground richness, Europe is highly self-sufficient but dependent on external energy and agricultural resources. However, coal and iron deposits in the north-west of the continent have significantly contributed to the improvement of the industries in the United Kingdom (Atasoy, 2010).

The structure of the Middle East differs from that of Europe in terms of geographical features. The region has high geo- and eco-strategic importance given that it is situated at an intersection of migration and trade, both of which have facilitated globalization since ancient times (Taş, 2012). The Middle East is strategically located between Asia, Africa and Europe, and where the Black Sea connects to the Mediterranean Sea through the Straits and both seas meet the Indian Ocean through the Suez Canal. The Middle Eastern borders run alongside Turkey, Iran, the Persian Gulf, the Arabian Peninsula, Egypt and Cyprus. Its southernmost region descends to 12° N latitude on the coasts of the Arabian Peninsula and the 42° N latitude passes through the farthest point in the north. In the Middle East, the mid-regions cover a narrow area located to the north of the 40° N latitude in Turkey. Therefore, almost half of the Middle East is located in the tropical and the rest is located in the subtropical lower zone of its mid-zone. The common characteristics of these zones are that they are hot and dry. Although the Middle East is not very rich in natural resources, 65% of the known oil reserves are located in this region. The oil reserves in the Middle East meet a significant rate of Europe's and Asia's energy requirements. A total of 36.1% of natural gas reserves are also located in the Middle East.

Undoubtedly, geographical factors alone cannot be used to explain economic development. However, these natural and unchangeable conditions have a significant impact on economic development.

4 Aim, data and methodology

This study adopts data available for 46 countries on GDP, latitude, natural resources, number of neighbouring countries and landlockedness. The objective of the analysis is twofold: detect spatial dependencies using LISA maps and univariate and bivariate Moran's I values and investigate for significant effects on GDP using spatial regression models. The data are analysed using the GeoDa package program. The first stage of the analysis is to examine for spatial relationships in GDP. We tested for spatial autocorrelation using Moran's I statistic and local autocorrelation using LISA maps. The statistics are calculated for 2015.

5 LISA and BILISA maps

LISA cluster maps illustrate regions with significant local Moran statistics and classify them into four groups of spatial correlation (high-high, low-low, high-low and low-high) (Annoni & Kozovska, 2010). In the LISA map, spatial clusters are highlighted using bright colours. The high-high regions are indicated in red, which denotes positive associations with one's own and neighbouring countries' high values of attribute variables. The low-low regions are in blue; here, the positive spatial autocorrelation emerges from one's own and the neighbouring countries' low values.

In addition, BILISA cluster map methods allow us to compare the spatial structure of two indicators and spatial interaction between them. Moran's I for BILISA gives an indication of the degree of linear association between the value for one variable at a given location and the average of another variable at neighbouring locations. BILISA is a correlation between two different variables in an area and in nearby areas (Anselin, 1995).

LISA satisfies the following two requirements:

- for each observation, LISA provides an indication of the extent of significant spatial clustering of similar values around the observation; and
- the sum of LISAs for all observations is proportional to the global indicator of spatial association.

(Anselin, 1995)

6 Spatial regression

In a standard linear regression model, spatial dependence can be incorporated in two distinct ways: an additional regressor in the form of a spatially lagged dependent variable or in an error structure. This can be interpreted as substantive spatial dependence directly related to a spatial model (Anselin, 2003). The estimation of the spatial regression models proceeds on the basis of an iterative procedure that maximizes likelihood (LeSage, 1997).

To begin the process of spatial regression estimation, we first consider the standard Lagrange multiplier (LM)-error and LM-lag test statistics. If neither rejects the null hypothesis, we use the ordinary least squares (OLS) results. In this case, it is likely that Moran's I test statistic will not reject the null hypothesis either.

7 Results

Figure 15.2 is the LISA map for GDP. The map is significant at the 5% significance level. European countries and Yemen are in red. The LISA map detects the locations of spatial patterns for GDP. European countries (except Switzerland) replace the high-high area, indicating that countries with high GDP are surrounded by those with high GDP. For Europe, positive correlation arises from its own and neighbouring countries' high GDP values and its Moran's I statistic is 0.61838 (positive correlation).

Figures 15.3–15.7 depict the relationship between the variables with GDP. The bivariate Moran's I statistics are used to analyse this relationship. To interpret the results, we draw the following hypotheses.

- Hypothesis 1: If a country is between 23° and 45° latitude, its GDP is higher than countries located in the tropics.
- Hypothesis 2: If a country is landlocked, its GDP level is lower than that of countries surrounded by the sea.
- Hypothesis 3: Countries with a large number of neighbouring countries will have a higher GDP level than countries with few neighbours.
- Hypothesis 4: Countries with a temperate climate will have higher GDP than warmer countries.
- Hypothesis 5: Countries with many natural resources will have higher GDP than countries with fewer natural resources.

Figure 15.3 is the BILISA map and shows the relationship between GDP and latitude. Countries denoted in darker grey have high GDP and are located between 23° and 45° latitude; this result supports Hypothesis 1. Countries classified as high-high include Ireland, Denmark, the United Kingdom, France, Belgium, Netherlands, Italy, Germany, Slovenia, Austria, Czech Republic, Poland, Lithuania, Latvia, Estonia, Finland, Norway and Sweden.

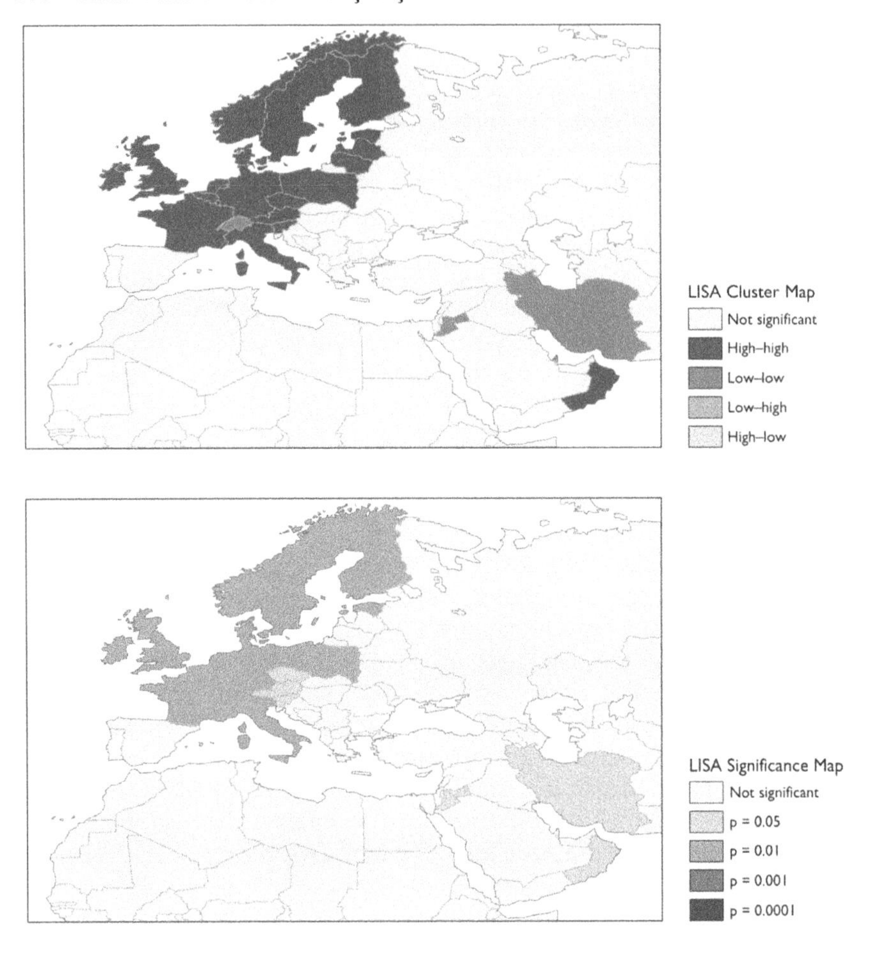

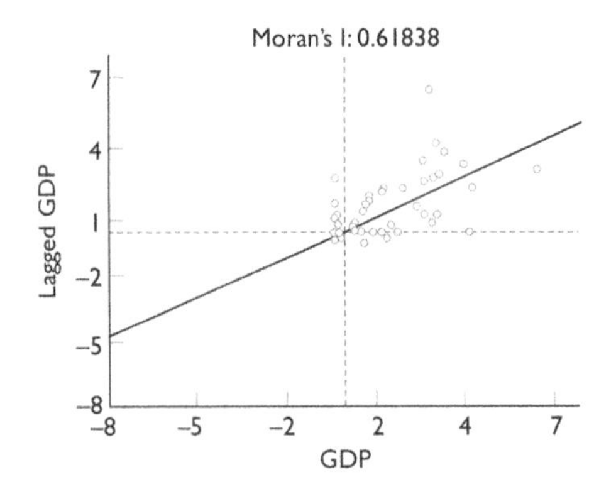

Figure 15.2 LISA map of GDP

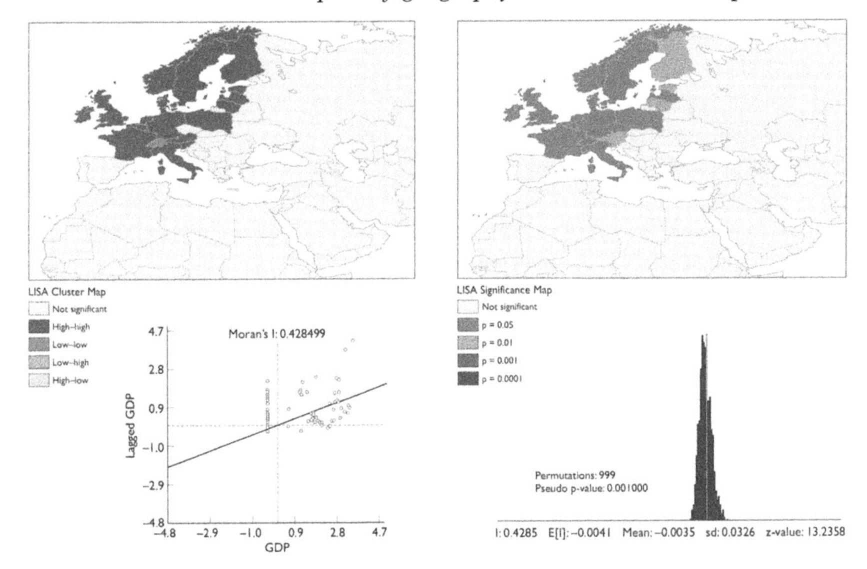

Figure 15.3 BILISA map for GDP vs. latitude

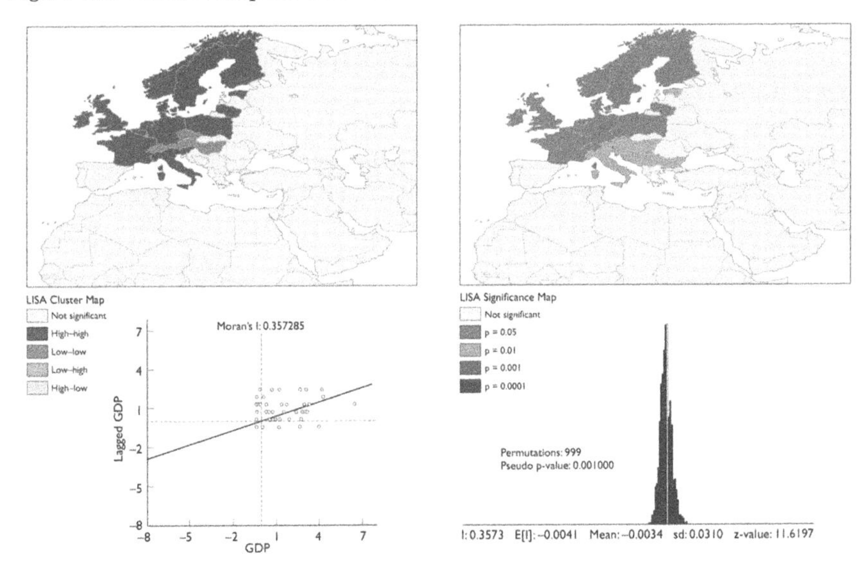

Figure 15.4 BILISA map for GDP vs. landlocked

Switzerland is highlighted in light grey, indicating that its spatial correlation emerges from low GDP with high latitude (except Switzerland). Its Moran's I statistic is 0.521415 and shows a positive correlation between GDP and latitude.

Figure 15.4 illustrates the relationship between GDP and landlockedness. Countries highlighted in red include Denmark, Ireland, the United Kingdom,

France, Belgium, Netherlands, Italy, Germany, Slovenia, Poland, Lithuania, Latvia, Estonia, Finland, Norway and Sweden. These countries have high GDP and are open to the sea. Their Moran's I statistic is 0.309864 and there is a positive correlation between GDP and landlockedness. Switzerland, Czech Republic, Hungary and Austria are in light blue. These countries have lower GDP because they are landlocked (except Austria and Switzerland). This result generally supports Hypothesis 2. There is no significant area in the case of the Middle East as none of its regions are landlocked.

Figure 15.5 demonstrates the relationship between GDP and the number of neighbouring countries. Dark grey indicates that countries with high GDP have more neighbouring countries than the others. These include Denmark, Ireland, the United Kingdom, France, Belgium, Netherlands, Italy, Germany, Slovenia, Austria, Czech Republic, Poland, Lithuania, Latvia, Estonia, Finland, Norway and Sweden. Moran's I statistic is 0.301361, which represents a positive correlation between GDP and the number of neighbouring countries. Light blue shows a correlation between low GDP and a high number of neighbouring countries. Switzerland is light blue, but it has a high GDP level, so except Switzerland, other correlations for countries give us expected results. We thus conclude that countries (except Switzerland) with a higher number of neighbouring countries have high GDP.

Figure 15.6 shows the spatial relationship between GDP and climate. Dark grey indicates that the countries with a temperate climate have high GDP. Countries highlighted in red include the United Kingdom, France, Belgium, Netherlands, Italy, Germany, Slovenia, Austria, Czech Republic, Poland, Lithuania, Latvia, Estonia, Finland, Norway and Sweden. Switzerland, Ireland, Oman and Qatar

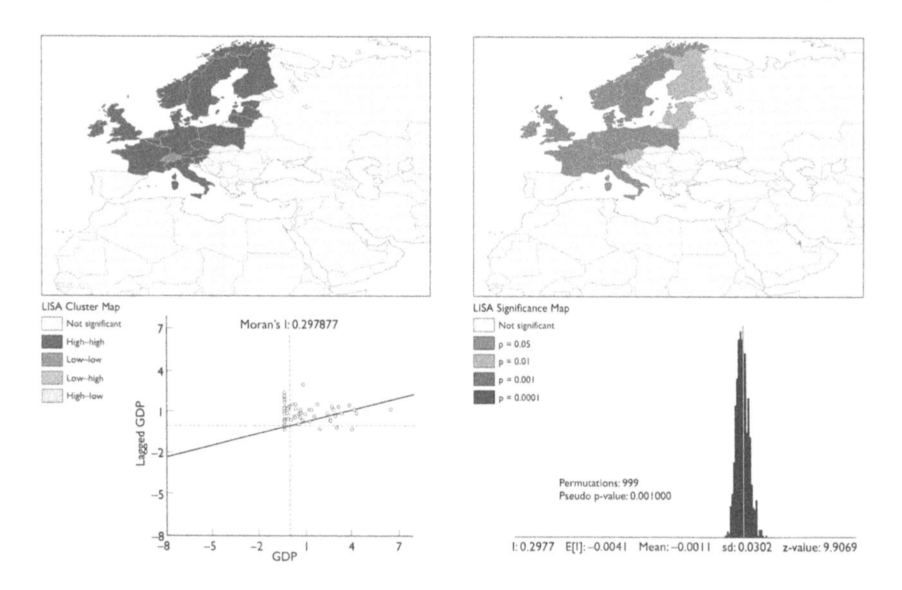

Figure 15.5 BILISA map for GDP vs. number of neighbouring countries

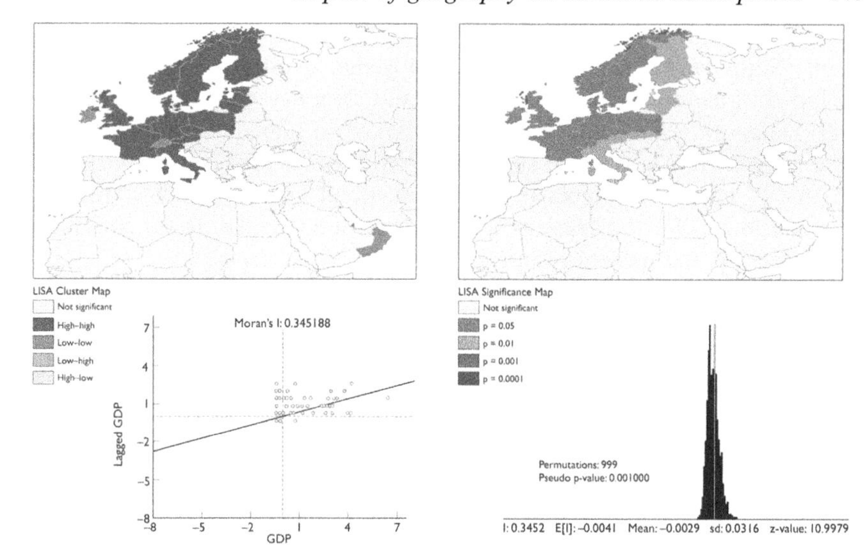

Figure 15.6 BILISA map for GDP vs. climate

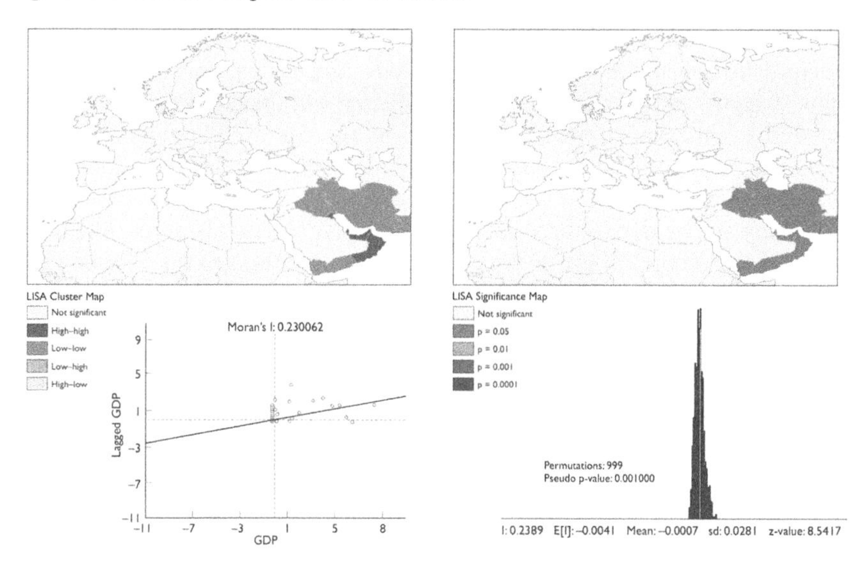

Figure 15.7 BILISA map for GDP vs. natural resources

are marked in light blue and their positive correlations emerge from low GDP and hot climate (except Switzerland and Ireland). Moran's I statistic is 0.264449 and indicates a positive spatial correlation between GDP and climate. Therefore, we conclude that countries with a temperate climate have higher GDP.

Figure 15.7 depicts the relationship between GDP and natural resources. Red indicates that countries with high GDP have natural resources. Countries classified as high-high are Ireland, Iran, the United Kingdom, France, Belgium, Netherlands, Italy, Germany, Slovenia, Austria, Czech Republic, Poland, Lithuania, Latvia, Estonia, Finland, Norway and Sweden. Switzerland, Denmark, Qatar and Oman are marked in light blue, indicating that these regions have a positive spatial autocorrelation between low GDP and the lack of natural resources (except Switzerland and Denmark). Moran's I statistic is 0.230062 and suggests the existence of a positive spatial correlation between GDP and natural resources.

In this study, the growth equation from the basic Solow–Swan model is used. We used the extended model of this. GDP data are used for 46 countries in Europe and the Middle East and we attempted to determine a relationship with latitude, landlockedness, number of neighbouring countries, climate and natural resources. The regression can be written as follows:

$$GDP_i = \alpha + \beta Latitude_i + \gamma Landlocked_i + \delta Neighbour_i + \theta Climate_i + \varphi Source_i$$

Accordingly, we formed three models. First is a spatial linear regression model. This model is distinguished on the basis of two representation types: direct dependence using a distance deterrence function and an exogenous structure by specifying the spatial topology and interaction structure in a spatial weights matrix. To avoid the incidental parameter problem, we estimated the influence of neighbouring locations for each region separately (Florax & Nijkamp, 2003). We use the spatial weight matrix to estimate the OLS spatial regression.

In doing so, we derive three estimation results. The first is applicable to all countries, the second to European countries, and the third to the Middle East. Table 15.1 shows the OLS estimates for all countries. Excluding the constant, all coefficients are statistically significant at the 5% and 1% significance levels. The multicollinearity condition number shows whether the independent variables are correlated with each other. Any value over 30 is considered worrisome. We obtain an OLS estimate of 7.9279, which does not pose a problem. As can be seen in the diagnostics for heteroscedasticity, the Breusch–Pagan and Koenker–Bassett test statistics are significant at the 1% level, indicating strong heteroscedasticity (Table 15.1). Moran's I statistic is 0.117172 and the pseudo p-value is 0.005 and significant at the 1% level, suggesting that the OLS residuals are correlated with each other and, thus, a serious problem. There are two sets of tests to be considered before choosing a spatial regression: the Lagrange multiplier, which tests for the presence of spatial dependence, and the robust LM, which tests for a lag or error in spatial dependence. The second set of tests is a lag or error. Lag refers to a spatially lagged dependent variable and error denotes a spatial autoregressive process for the error term. We first checked the significance of the LM test. Both LM test statistics have p-values of 0.000. Thus, we checked the robust LM (lag) and robust LM (error) and obtained p-values of 0.000 and 0.963. Only the

Table 15.1 OLS estimation R-squared: 0.615 adjusted R-squared: 0.607

Variable	*Coefficient*	*Standard error*	*t-statistic*	*Probability*
Constant	243.46	513.83	0.474	0.636
Latitude	556.056	79.199	7.021	0.000
Neighbour	1504.823	431.123	3.491	0.000
Climate	2719.539	1353.782	2.008	0.003
Landlocked	2384.366	394.096	6.050	0.000
Natural resources	33.569	4.058	8.272	0.000
Regression diagnostics				
Multicollinearity condition number: 7.9279				
Test on normality of errors				
Test	*DF*	*Value*	*Probability*	
Jarque-Bera	2	3908.63	0.000	
Diagnostics for heteroscedasticity				
Test	*DF*	*Value*	*Probability*	
Breusch-Pagan	5	459.345	0.000	
Test				
Koenker-Basset	5	44.0749	0.000	
White	20	197.0809	0.000	
Diagnostics for spatial dependence				
Test	*MI/DF*	*Value*	*Probability*	
Moran's I (error)	0.2937	6.5625	0.000	
Lagrange	1	62.39	0.000	

Variable	*Coefficient*	*Standard error*	*t-statistic*	*Probability*
Multiplier (lag)				
Robust LM (lag)	1	23.81	0.000	
Lagrange	1	38.60	0.000	
Multiplier (error)				
Robust LM (error)	1	0.002	0.963	
Lagrange	2	62.40	0.000	
Multiplier SARMA				

robust LM (lag) test statistic is significant at the 1% and 5% significance levels. Thus, we chose the spatial lag model.

Table 15.2 shows the spatial lag model for all countries. In this model, we have a designated spatial weight file and spatial lag term for GDP (Weighted-GDP). In the estimation output, Weighted-GDP has a positive effect and is significant at the 1% level. All coefficients are positive and have a positive effect on GDP. As a result, the spatial lag model fit improves, as indicated by the higher values of R-squared and log likelihood. The probability in the Breusch–Pagan test (3.2478 with 0.12025 probability) suggests no heteroscedasticity in the model after introducing the spatial lag term.

Table 15.3 represents the spatial lag model for Europe. In the estimation output, Weighted-GDP has a positive effect and is highly significant at the 1% level. The spatial lag model fit improves, thus indicating higher R-squared and log likelihood values. As expected, for Europe, all explanatory variables have a positive effect on GDP.

Table 15.4 shows the spatial lag model for the Middle East. Weighted-GDP in the estimation output has a negative effect and is highly significant at the 1% level. The spatial lag model fit improves, suggesting higher R-squared and log likelihood values. A comparison of Tables 15.3 and 15.4 reveals that the coefficient values for Europe are higher than those for the Middle East. We can say that all explanatory variables are more effective on GDP for Europe than the Middle East.

8 Conclusion

Geographical factors are important in explaining economic development. A country's physical geographical conditions are hereditary and cannot be changed by humans. Economic activities are thus shaped around these basic features. Physical geographical factors that have the most significant effect on economic development include latitude, climate, landlockedness, the number of neighbouring countries and natural resources. These geographical factors vary by region and contribute to differences in the level of development.

A comparison of Europe and the Middle East in terms of latitudes and climatic structure reveals that Europe is situated on the 23°45' North latitude close to the equator and in the temperate zone, which positively impacts economic development. According to the regression results, the impact of climate on development is around the value of 2769.342 in the European countries and 2415.369 in the Middle Eastern countries, and the impact of climate on development is higher in the former. The impact of latitude on development is around 556.056 in the European countries and 358.777 in the Middle Eastern countries; here, as well, the impact of latitude on development is higher for European countries. We found that landlockedness negatively impacts economic development, primarily owing to the inability to provide direct sea access. While Europe appears to have landlocked countries, no such region is found in the Middle East. According to the regression

Table 15.2 Spatial lag estimation (all countries) R-squared: 0,700614

Variable	*Coefficient*	*Standard error*	*z-statistic*	*Probability*
Weighted_GDP	0.394	0.056	6.996	0.000
Constant	6.835	449.78	0.015	0.988
Latitude	368.095	73.544	5.005	0.000
Neighbour	1159.659	375.441	3.089	0.002
Climate	2769.342	720.49	0.948	0.002
Landlocked	3007.687	799.316	3.741	0.003
Natural sources	2.754	0.767	3.443	0.002
Diagnostic for spatial dependence				
Spatial lag dependence for weighted matrix: TM_reg.gal				
Test	*DF*	*Value*	*Probability*	
Likelihood ratio	1	4.4530	0.11730	
Test				
Breusch-Pagan	5	3.2478	0.12025	

Table 15.3 Spatial lag estimation (Europe) R-squared: 0.69877

Variable	*Coefficient*	*Standard error*	*Probability*
Weighted_GDP	0.355	0.035	0.000
Constant	3217.589	417.89	0.000
Latitude	358.777	47.58	0.000
Neighbour	1069.415	511.47	0.001
Climate	2748.311	417.86	0.002
Landlocked	-2589.666	235.88	0.000
Natural sources	4.547	1.458	0.000
Diagnostic for spatial dependence			
Spatial lag dependence for weighted matrix: TM_EUROPE_reg.gal			
Test	*Value*	*Probability*	
Likelihood ratio	3.1478	0.08111	

Table 15.4 Spatial lag estimation results (Middle East) R-squared: 0.67912

Variable	*Coefficient*	*Standard error*	*Probability*
Weighted_GDP	0.245	0.025	0.0000
Constant	50.256	20.361	0.005
Latitude	320.145	41256	0.000
Neighbour	965.411	210.256	0.000
Climate	2415.369	123.698	0.000
Landlocked	–	–	–
Natural sources	11.523	0.258	0.000
Diagnostic for spatial dependence			
Spatial lag dependence for weighted matrix: TM_MIDDLEEAST_reg.gal			
Test	*Value*	*Probability*	
Likelihood ratio test	4.159	0.07412	

results, the parametric magnitude indicating the effect of landlockedness on development is −2589.666 for European countries, indicating a negative impact on development in European countries. The number and characteristics of neighbouring countries also play an important role in the development of countries. In particular in Europe, where landlocked countries exist, the number of neighbouring countries has a greater impact on development; that these countries are developed has a positive effect on the development of landlocked countries. According to the regression results, the impact of the number of neighbouring countries on development is around 1159.659 in the European countries and 965.411 units in the Middle Eastern countries and the impact of the number of neighbouring countries on development is higher in the former. In terms of natural resources, the Middle Eastern countries have a key advantage of economic development given their oil reserves. The regression results also reveal the impact of natural resources on development, which is around 4.547 units in the European countries and 11.523 units in the Middle Eastern countries, indicating a higher impact on the Middle Eastern countries.

References

Annoni, P. and Kozovska, K. (2010) *EU Regional Competitiveness Index*. JRC Scientific and Technical Reports.

Anselin, L. (1995) isites.harvard.edu/fs/docs/icb.topic868440.files/Anselin1995%20LISA.pdf.

Anselin, L. (2003) Spatial econometrics. In *A Companion to Theoretical Econometrics*. Blackwell Publishing Ltd, pp. 310–330.

Atasoy, E. (2010) *Kıtalar ve Ülkeler Coğrafyası*, 2.b. Bursa: Ezgi Kitabevi.

Başol, K., Durman, M. and Çelik, M.Y. (2005) *Kalkınma Sürecinin Lokomotifi; Doğal Kaynaklar*. Muğla Üniversitesi SBE Dergisi, Sayı 14.

Brata, A.G. (2009) *Does Geographic Factors Determine Local Economic Development?* MPRA Paper No. 15817. Online at mpra.ub.uni-muenchen.de/15817.

Diamond, J.M. (1997) *Guns, Germs and Steel: The Fate of Human Societies*. New York: W.W. Norton & Co.

Dinler, Z. (2008) *Bölgesel İktisat*, 8.b. Bursa: Ekin Yayınevi.

Florax, R.J.G.M. and Nijkamp, P. (2003) *Misspecification in Linear Spatial Regression Models*. Tinbergen Institute Discussion Paper, pp. 1–28.

Gallup, J.L., Sachs, D.J. and Mellinger, A. (1999) *Geography and Economic Development*. Working Papers, Center for International Development at Harvard University, CID Working Paper No. 1.

Güner, İ. and Ertürk, M. (2015) *Kıtalar ve Ülkeler Coğrafyası*, 7.b. Ankara: Pegem Akademi Yayınları.

Han, E. and Kaya, A.A. (2015) *Kalkınma Ekonomisi Teori ve Politika*, 7.b. Ankara: Nobel Yayınları.

Higgins, B. and Savoie, D.J. (2009) *Regional Development Theories and their Application*. New Brunswick, NJ: Transaction Publishers.

Küçüker, C. (2000) Yeni Ekonomik Coğrafya ve Kalkınma. *Ekonomik Yaklaşım*.

LeSage, J.P. (1997) Regression analysis of spatial. *The Journal of Regional Analysis & Policy* 27(2): 83–94.

Mellinger, A.D., Sachs, J.D. and Gallup, L. (1999) *Climate, Water Navigability and Economic Development*. CID Working Paper No. 24, September.

Nordhaus, W.D. (2006) Geography and macroeconomics: New data and new findings. *PNAS* (March 7) 103(10): 3510–3517.

Redding, S. and Venables, A.J. (2004) Economic geography and international inequality. *Journal of International Economics* 62, 53–82.

Rodrik, D., Subramanian, A. and Trebbi, F. (2002) *Institutions Rule: The Primacy of Institutions over Geography and Integration in Economic Development*. IMF Working Paper 02/189. Washington, DC: IMF.

Smith, A. (1776) *An Inquiry into the Nature and Causes of the Wealth of Nations.* Oxford: Clarendon Press.

Taş, R. (2012) *Orta Doğu'daki Gelişmelerin Ekonomik Anlamı Ve Küresel, Bölgesel Ve Türkiye Ekonomisi Üzerindeki Potansiyel Etkileri*. Ankara: Turgut Özal Üniversitesi Yayınları.

Todaro, M. and Smith, S. (2009) *Economic Development*, 10th edn. Boston, MA: Addison Wesley.

Yanar, R. (2014) *Kalkınma Ekonomisinin Kapsamı, Kalkınma Sürecinin Ölçülmesi ve Kalkınma Sürecini Belirleyen Etkenler* (Farklı Boyutları ile Türkiye'de Kalkınma), S. Bekmez (ed.) Ankara: Efil Yayınevi.

Yiğit, A. (2000) *Avrupa'nın Sınırları Ve Türkiye'nin Avrupa'ya Göre Konumu*. Fırat Üniversitesi Sosyal Bilimler Dergisi, Cilt: 10, Sayı: 2, Sayfa, pp. 35–50.

16 Three spheres of geoeconomic advantage in Central America

Transportation, tourism and trade

Michael J. Pisani

1 Introduction

Geoeconomics concerns the convergence of geographic space and economic dynamics within the scope of global interactions. This convergence may be conceived broadly on a global scale or more narrowly within a regional scale. This chapter narrows the geoeconomic scale to Central America. As a region, Central America is composed of seven countries; from north to south they are Belize, Guatemala, Honduras, El Salvador, Nicaragua, Costa Rica and Panama. All but Belize trace their modern roots to Spanish colonization (circa 1520s and 1530s) and the concomitant spillovers of centuries of Spanish rule—Spanish language, Spanish legal and mercantile heritage, and culture. The yoke of Spanish imperial authority ended in the early 19th century and these countries, with the exception of Belize, have been independent since. The area of Belize was contested between Spain and England, with England the eventual winner. It was not until 1981 that Belize achieved its independence from Great Britain; hence Belize inherited the cultural and political markers of England (e.g. English language, the Westminster Parliamentary system, etc.).

The Central American nations in this study are not large, though more live in urban environments (see Table 16.1). Even so, Belize is relatively under-populated with only 15 people per square kilometer. On the other end of the population spectrum, both El Salvador and Guatemala have the highest population densities and Guatemala the largest population. As with population, the economies of the region are relatively small, ranging in size from US $1.4 billion (Belize) to $41.4 billion (Guatemala). Nicaragua is the second poorest country in the hemisphere with a per capita gross domestic product (GDP) of $1,470; Honduras also has a per capita income of under $2,000. Panama and Costa Rica boast middling per capita income levels with the remainder in between. Nearly half to three-quarters of the economically active non-agricultural population in the region works under condition of informality. The Central American economies exhibit a large degree of openness to the global market where imports and exports comprise a substantial portion of overall economic activity. The region has varying amounts of

Table 16.1 Basic indicators for Central America

Indicator	*Belize*	*Costa Rica*	*El Salvador*	*Guatemala*	*Honduras*	*Nicaragua*	*Panama*
Area (sq. km)^	22,810	51,060	20,720	107,160	111,890	120,340	74,340
Population^ (in '000s)	309	4,669	6,218	14,341	7,621	5,822	3,678
Population density^# (people per sq. km)	15	95	306	144	72	51	52
% urban^	45	72	64	49	52	57	65
GDP^ (in US$ million)	1,399	36,298	21,418	41,338	15,839	8,938	28,814
Per capita GDP^ (in US$)	4,380	6,910	3,350	2,750	1,890	1,470	8,050
% employment in informal sector+	46.8	43.8	66.4	72.3	75.3	65.7	43.8
Economic openness^*	0.74	0.79	0.69	0.62	1.09	0.85	1.40
% forest area^	60.3	52.8	13.2	33.7	43.2	25.9	62.5

(^ World Bank Indicators; * Human Development Reports, United Nations Development Programme; + International Labour Office, 2009 data)

forested areas (mostly rainforest or mountain pine forest), ranging from 13.2% in El Salvador to over 60% in Belize and Panama.

The confluence of geography and economics has been both an advantage and a challenge for Central America. The challenges include the issues of smallness, in size of the economy, power projection, and colonial legacies of inequality. In this chapter, the focus is on three distinct spheres of geoeconomic advantage related to Central America: (i) East–West transisthmian transportation corridors; (ii) tourism based upon rainforest and biodiversity resources; and (iii) trade augmented by economic integration and informal markets.

2 East–West transisthmian transportation corridors

Since the explorations of Vasco Núñes de Balboa (1513), a shortcut through Central America to connect East and West has been envisioned. The first shortcuts to traverse the area by foot were created in Panama, where the width of the isthmus at its shortest point is less than 40 miles. These early trails helped bring gold and other precious resources from the Americas to Spain during the colonial period. Later, during the California Gold Rush (1849 and later), many retraced the colonial paths from east to west in order to expedite travel to the gold fields. By 1855, this trek could be undertaken by rail with the Panama Railroad Company (McCullough, 1977). Eventually, the railroad was complemented by a canal connecting the Caribbean Sea with the Pacific Ocean. The Panama Canal, first begun by the French (1880), completed by the Americans (1914), was returned to the Panamanians at the turn of the new millennium.

Under the aegis of the Western Hemisphere's continental superpower (1914–99), the Panama Canal linked East and West, permitting trade, communication, and transit. During this time, the Panama Canal was also used as a geopolitical tool of the USA in times of war and peace and the canal fell under the umbrella of the Monroe Doctrine. For example, belligerents of the Allied powers during World War II and Soviets and Soviet proxies during the Cold War were denied access to the canal. Since 2000, the Panama Canal permits transit as mostly a neutral space. However, in 2013 a North Korean ship (the *Chong Chon Gang*) was seized by Panamanian authorities for carrying weapons to Cuba and was released a year later after North Korea paid a fine and the weapons were removed (BBC News, 2014).

As a transportation corridor, 13,874 vessels carrying 340,574,528 tons of goods transited the Panama Canal in 2015, accounting for about 5% of world cargo trade.[1] Three areas of traffic flow account for 89.2% of the vessels transiting the Panama Canal: (i) traffic to and from Asia accounted for 38.5% of vessels transiting the Panama Canal; (ii) inter-Western Hemispheric traffic accounted for 38.0% of vessels transiting the Panama Canal; and (iii) traffic from and to Europe accounted for 12.7% of vessels transiting the Panama Canal.[2] In 2015, the canal could pass vessels carrying up to 5,000 TEUs[3];

however, in 2016 the expanded Panama Canal with parallel larger locks and lock gates came online and can pass vessels carrying between 13,000 and 14,000 TEUs, nearly tripling the cargo-carrying capacity per ship and perhaps doubling the total amount of cargo passing through the canal. The new locks are able to accommodate 98% of container ships (all but the ultra-large container ships), which carry 94% of water-borne trade.[4]

An inter-oceanic transit route through Nicaragua has also been discussed for centuries. Nicaraguan geography allows for river access from the Caribbean Sea via the San Juan River to Lake Nicaragua. From Lake Nicaragua it is a short 11 miles to the Pacific Ocean. This Nicaraguan route was more popular than the Panamanian route to the gold fields of California. Great Britain and the USA even signed a treaty in 1850 (the Clayton–Bulwer Treaty) declaring that if a Nicaraguan canal were to be built, it would be built jointly. Yet, nothing ever came of the dream of a Nicaraguan canal until the contemporary Daniel Ortega-led government of Nicaragua and Wang Jing, a Chinese billionaire, agreed to launch in 2012 a $50 billion project to build a Nicaraguan canal by the Hong Kong Nicaragua Development Group. The project has yet to begin in earnest (as of 2016) (though environmental impact studies have been completed and some local populations in the path of the canal have been removed), because of the falling fortunes of Wang Jing and the Chinese economy and environmental concerns. Nevertheless, the project, if completed, will provide a second transisthmian waterway with an estimated TEU capacity of 18,000 per vessel, accommodating the ultra-large container ships. The prospect of completion for such an undertaking is uncertain in the near future.

3 Tourism based upon rainforest and biodiversity resources

The World Bank reports that the number of overnight international visitors to Central America in 2013 was just over 9 million people, with 58% of these visits for tourist purposes.[5] At the high end, just over one-quarter (27%) of overnight international visitors traveled to Costa Rica and at the other end of the spectrum Belize received 3% of overnight international visitors traveling to Central America. The Central American tourism market is valued at more than $8 billion annually.[6]

However, this does not tell the whole story, as Belize received over 800,000 cruise ship visitors in 2010 and over 1 million visitors annually (Statistical Institute of Belize, 2013). Similarly large numbers of cruise ship tourists call at Honduras, less so for Costa Rica, Guatemala and Panama, but with numbers at about one-third of Belize and Honduras. Cruise ship arrivals are currently small for El Salvador and Nicaragua, but both countries, like the whole region, have enthusiastically embraced cruise ship tourists as a means to generate employment, economic development, and showcase the many ethno-cultural and natural ecosystem-based attractions.[7] These cruise ship tourists typically leave behind about $70 per visitor in the region—important, but not more than $60 million in the most visited country of Belize.[8] Of greater advantage to the economic development of the region are overnight tourist stays that visit, in part, the natural beauty of Central America.

Central America has vast natural tracts of tropical forests and rainforest that contain great diversity in plant and animal life. While over half the national territories of Belize, Costa Rica, and Panama remain forested, the trajectory for maintaining the forest is under heavy economic stress. Human and agricultural encroachment is quickly reducing the size of the forest cover and accompanying flora and fauna. Nevertheless, Central America boasts a high degree of eco-tourism based upon international tourists visiting the remains of the rainforest and the wildlife within.

One prime example of eco-tourism is the Community Baboon Sanctuary (CBS) in Belize. Located in the lush Belize River Valley, the CBS at Bermudian Landing was founded in 1985 to protect the black howler monkey (known as 'baboons' in the local Creole language).[9] The CBS is a registered nongovernmental organization and is managed by the local women's conservation group that not only is pledged to protect the habitat of the howler monkeys, but also promotes sustainable livelihoods and development for the seven allied communities in the river valley. From 800 monkeys in 1985, there are about 4,000 to 5,000 monkeys today allowing for the re-introduction of howler monkeys to other places in Belize where their populations had previously dwindled or collapsed. Initially, the CBS got off the ground with support from a primatologist (Dr Robert Horwich) studying the howlers, and from the World Wildlife Fund and the Zoological Society of Milwaukee. Today, the CBS receives its income from a small tourist fee ($7 or more depending on the length of the tour, including night tours) and grants from the Belize Protected Areas Conservation Trust funded by per-person exit fees ($3.75) attached to international tourism. The CBS receives 25,000 to 30,000 visitors per year, about 90% of whom are international tourists.

The monkeys have been given free rein on a 20-square-mile area of private lands. These contiguous private lands consist of patches of unbroken jungle and are pledged to remain undeveloped in order to sustain the monkey population. In total, about 240 private landowners have voluntarily agreed to work with the CBS. In return, these landowners receive some assistance in farming, animal husbandry, and sustainable livelihood efforts and some of the spillover from eco-tourists visiting the howler monkeys.

Other examples of regional attractions particular to the Central American rainforest and biodiversity resources include the Cockscomb Basin Wildlife Sanctuary and Jaguar Preserve (Belize), barrier reefs (Blue Hole National Monument, Belize; Roatán Island, Honduras), birding (regional), butterfly reserves (regional), rainforest canopy tours (Costa Rica, Guatemala, and Panama), volcanoes (regional), cave tubing (Belize), orchid tours (regional), a sloth sanctuary (Costa Rica), sea turtle conservancy (regional), and so on.

4 Trade augmented by economic integration and informal markets

After economic integration began in Europe in the early 1950s, Central America followed with the introduction of the Central American Common Market (CACM) in 1958. Initial successes promoted economic growth in the region in the 1960s only to be stalled in the 1970s by political turmoil and social revolutions (Rodas-Martini, 1998). The 1980s saw CACM stall and falter (Méndez & Rousslang, 1989) and begin to rebound in the 1990s (Baier & Bergstrand, 2009); yet the 2000s brought a revitalization in trade agreements highlighted with the signing of the Central America–Dominican Republic free trade area with the USA (Jaramillo & Lederman, 2006) (see Table 16.2). Another longstanding Caribbean-based agreement—CARICOM, or the Caribbean Community—which includes Belize, began in 1966, many years before Belize's independence. It has been less successful, results in trade diversion (Viner, 1952; Pisani & Pisani, 2007) and may weaken internal development (Griffith, 2010).

This long experience with economic integration has spurred the region not only to integrate inward, but also seek to integrate outward. The region is very receptive to trade as each country has a trade (or economic) openness index greater than 60%, indicating open space with the global trading community. Central America, in part or fully, has forged trade agreements not only with the USA (the region's primary trade partner), but also Canada, Chile, the Dominican Republic, the European Union, Mexico, Taiwan, and Venezuela. Costa Rica has gone further and entered into free trade agreements with China, Peru, and Singapore.

In the area of goods trade, the World Bank collects international trade information that permits the calculation of revealed comparative advantage (RCA). In essence, RCA is a measure of product competitiveness vis-à-vis the rest of the world for traded goods. An RCA composite score of greater than 1 indicates that a country exports more of the specified product or product group proportionately than the world average. The higher the measure above 1 indicates a higher degree of RCA.[10] Looking at products and product classes with the three highest levels of RCA in Central America divulges the following patterns by country: Belize, animals (8.93), food products (7.10), and vegetables (6.81); Costa Rica, vegetables (3.65), machinery and electronics (2.91), and capital goods (2.52); El Salvador, textiles and clothing (13.13), food products (4.53), and consumer goods (2.47); Guatemala, vegetables (11.00), textiles and clothing (5.04), and food products (4.78); Honduras, textiles and clothing (10.72), vegetables (8.28), and animals (2.30); Nicaragua, textiles and clothing (8.60), animals (8.06), and vegetables (4.04); and Panama, vegetables (2.80), animals (2.60), and fuels (1.81).

Clearly, the region's RCA emphasizes agricultural goods (vegetables, foods, and animals) and textiles and clothing. Agriculture is a mainstay of the region and *maquiladora*-type textile export processing facilities dominate the light industrial sector in El Salvador, Guatemala, Honduras, and Nicaragua.

Table 16.2 Central American economic integration

Economic integration scheme	*Member countries from Central America and year negotiated/signed/established^*
Customs Union	
CACM/SICA*	All (1958)
CARICOM+	Belize (1966)
Free Trade Agreements	
CACM	Chile (1999), Dominican Republic (1998), European Union (2012), Mexico (2011)
CAFTA-DR#	USA (2004)
Canada	Costa Rica (2001), Honduras (2013), Panama (2010)
CARICOM+	Costa Rica (2004), Dominican Republic (1998)
CARIFORUM	Belize-European Union (1998) (via CARIFORUM)
China	Costa Rica (2010)
Peru	Costa Rica (2011), Panama (2011)
Singapore	Panama (2006), Costa Rica (2010)
Taiwan	El Salvador (2007), Guatemala (2005), Honduras (2007), Nicaragua (2005), Panama (2003)
USA	Panama (2007)
Preferential trade agreements	
Belize	Guatemala (2006)
CARICOM	Colombia (1994), Venezuela (1992)
Colombia	Nicaragua (1984), Panama (1993)
Dominican Republic	Panama (1985)
Mexico	Panama (1985)
Venezuela	CARICOM (1992), Costa Rica (1986), Guatemala (1990), El Salvador (1986), Honduras (1986), Nicaragua (1986)

(Foreign Trade Information System, Organization of American States)

Notes: ^May include legacy agreements/institutions. *CACM=Central American Common Market. SICA is the Spanish acronym. #CAFTA-DR=Central American Free Trade Area plus Dominican Republic. +CARICOM=Caribbean Community. CARIFORUM=the forum of the Caribbean Group of African, Caribbean and Pacific States.

Individual countries may also specialize in other products such as electronics in Costa Rica (a result of Intel's advanced computer chip-making operation, which closed at the end of 2014 and was not captured in the reported data) and fuels in Panama related to its oil refining sector, while international services trade such as transit through the Panama Canal and tourism are not recorded in RCA data.

Informality is widespread in Central America, employing nearly half or more of the economically active population. In previous work utilizing the World Bank's Enterprise Surveys for the region, it was observed that a significant relationship exists between firm exporters and the impact of domestic-level informal competition (Pisani, 2015). Exporters from Guatemala and Nicaragua find themselves unencumbered by competition from the domestic informal sector. The opposite occurs in Belize, Costa Rica, El Salvador, Honduras, and Panama, where exporters may be more focused on the global economic environment rather than the local business environment, perhaps providing an opportunity for informal firms to compete against focal firms locally. Research suggests that the informal sector is large in the region and directly impacts unevenly the performance of exporters.

5 Conclusion

This chapter focused on three spheres of geoeconomic convergence—transportation, tourism, and trade—in Central America. Within the geographic space of transisthmian transportation, the Panama Canal is a primary conduit that connects East and West and the Western Hemisphere (North and South). The Panama Canal expansion updates and modernizes this century-old conduit maintaining this Central American transportation advantage. On the horizon is the possibility of a canal transiting Nicaragua providing redundancy (in an era of global terrorism) and increased capacity in the number of vessels and cargo capacity.

Tourism, especially eco-tourism, is a mainstay of Central America. Unique natural assets include rainforests (e.g. jungle, orchids), rainforest wildlife (e.g. birds, jaguars, frogs, sloths), barrier reefs, and abundant rivers and caves. International visitors, from cruise ship tourists to overnight tourists, contribute to employment, economic development, and preservation of eco-tourism environments.

Central America is very open to the global trading environment, actively participating in the global economy and establishing formal ties through economic integration with its primary trading partners. Export specialization in agricultural goods and textiles and clothing is reflected in the region's revealed comparative advantage. This RCA may be tempered by the region's large informal sector. Together, these three sources of geoeconomic advantage—transportation, tourism, and trade—enable Central America to compete in the global economy.

Notes

1 See 'Panama Canal Traffic: Fiscal Years 2013 through 2015,' www.pancanal.com/eng/op/transit-stats/2015/Table01.pdf; and US Department of Transportation, Marine Transportation, 2013.

2 See 'Panama Canal Traffic Along Principal Trade Routes,' www.pancanal.com/eng/op/transit-stats/2015/Table00.pdf.

3 A TEU refers to 20-foot equivalent units, a standard container that is 20 feet long, 8 feet wide and 8.5 feet tall with a volume of 1,360 cubic feet of space.
4 See US Department of Transportation, Marine Transportation, 2013.
5 The remaining visits included travel to visit friends, family, health, religion, or pilgrimage at 19% and business travel at 19% of the total. See the World Bank Indicators, data.worldbank.org/indicators; and United Nations World Tourism Organization, 2013.
6 Ibid.
7 See Bien et al., 2007; and Business Research & Economic Advisors, 2012.
8 Ibid.
9 The information presented for the CBS was gathered from the CBS website (www.howlermonkeys.org) and the author's interview of the director of the CBS and experience in the CBS.
10 The calculations reported were undertaken at the World Bank's World Integrated Trade Solution database available at wits.worldbank.org. Data are for 2012, 2013 or 2014—whichever was the most recent reporting year by country.

References

Baier, S.L. and Bergstrand, J.H. (2009) Estimating the effects of free trade agreements on international trade flows using matching econometrics. *Journal of International Economics* 77(1): 63–76.

BBC News (2014) N. Korean ship seized with Cuban weapons returns to Cuba, February 14. Retrieved March 10, 2016, from www.bbc.com/news/world-latin-america-26210187.

Bien, A., Pratt, L., Seidl, A., Lopez, C.A. and Obando, A.M. (2007) *Cruise Tourism Impacts in Costa Rica & Honduras: Policy Recommendations for Decision Makers.* Report prepared for the Inter-American Development Bank, January. Retrieved March 10, 2016, from www.responsibletravel.org/projects/documents/cruise_tourism_impacts_in_costa_rica_honduras.pdf.

Business Research & Economic Advisors (2012) *Economic Contribution of Cruise Tourism to the Destination Economies: A Survey-based Analysis of the Impacts of Passenger, Crew, and Cruise Line Spending, Volume I Aggregate Analysis.* September. Retrieved March 10, 2016, from www.f-cca.com/downloads/2012-Cruise-Analysis-vol-1.pdf.

Griffith, W.H. (2010) Neoliberal economics and Caribbean economies. *Journal of Economic Issues* 44(2): 505–511.

Jaramillo, C.F. and Lederman, D. (2006) *Challenges of CAFTA: Maximizing the Benefits for Central America.* Washington, DC: The World Bank.

McCullough, D. (1977) *The Path Between the Seas: The Creation of the Panama Canal 1870–1914.* New York: Simon & Schuster.

Méndez, J. and Rousslang, D.J. (1989) Does the Central American common market benefit its members. *Economic Inquiry* 27(3): 473–487.

Pisani, M.J. (2015) *The 'Invisible' Competitor: Informal Competition and Formality in Central America.* Working Paper, Central Michigan University, Mt Pleasant, Michigan.

Pisani, M.J. and Pisani, J.S. (2007) The contemporary Belizean view of the economic way forward: Regional versus global perspectives. *Journal of Belizean Studies* 29(1): 20–37.

Rodas-Martini, P. (1998) Intra-industry trade and revealed comparative advantage in the Central American common market. *World Development* 26(2): 337–344.

Statistical Institute of Belize (2013) *Abstract of Statistics, Belize 2012, Volume 1*. Belmopan, Belize: Statistical Institute of Belize.

United Nations World Tourism Organization (2013) *Tourism in the Americas, 2013 Edition*. Retrieved March 10, 2016, from cf.cdn.unwto.org/sites/all/files/pdf/tourism_in_the_americas.pdf.

US Department of Transportation, Marine Transportation (2013) *Panama Canal Expansion Study, Phase I Report: Developments in Trade and National Global Economics.* Retrieved March 11, 2016, from www.marad.dot.gov/wp-content/uploads/pdf/Panama_Canal_Phase_I_Report_-_20Nov2013.pdf.

Viner, J. (1952) *International Trade and Economic Development*. Glencoe, IL: Free Press.

17 The state of regional integration in Africa

Prospects and advances

Joash Ntenga Moitui

1 Introduction

Over the last decade, Africa has witnessed a changeover in political and institutional structures; the profundity of change, however, remains unclear. A considerable number of African states have marked over 50 years of independence, but without a successful continental integration. This failure is mainly attributed to the absence of authoritative and thought leadership amongst some African leaders. These two concepts form the foundation of 'African Renaissance'. Economists from the World Bank have argued that regional integration in Africa is a consequence of rational challenges 'envisaged' by a continent characterized by small national markets and landlocked countries (Biswaro, 2011). There is a need for Africa to re-evaluate its regional integration through a cost-benefits analysis of the realistic nature of such an arrangement and end result. Regional integration is often used in a confusing manner. It has been used to describe the process and an end state (end product) (Biswaro, 2011). While some definitions emphasize a political dimension, others recognize a spectrum of dimensions. It is not limited to the process of ever increasing and growing cooperation between political actors and is actionable in trade, security, economy, and environmental aspects.

2 Main focus of the chapter

It is evident globally that Africa's integration efforts have thus far been exceedingly unsatisfactory. This is in contrast to other regions that have implemented integration mechanisms and schemes to refurbish economic growth and bolster trade between member countries. Africa's economic development is plagued by dented gross domestic product (GDP) growth, reduced capital inflows, and non-streamlined markets affecting the level of integration within African states (Biswaro, 2011). This 'Achilles heel' seems to cut across the entire continent, in spite of the existence of a continuum of policy plans and visions (Mistry, 2000). The chapter further delves into African Union efforts to build a united Africa in the midst of conflict, and calls for 'self-determination' in countries such as Sudan, and now South Sudan.

There have been continued debates and discussions on the desirability of political integration as a means to the developmental challenge and embedded development footholds facing the continent. The ideological paradigm of pan-Africanism has been taunted by researchers as being political, devoid of the economic component indispensable for political-economic regional integration in the globalized world.

The chapter also explores the linkages between the democratization process and regional integration in Africa, and further focuses on trade (creation and diversion) under the current political arrangements. Tentatively, the chapter introduces a new regional integration model, the institutional model of regional integration, which outlines regional institutions as sources of global governance.

3 Advancements in regional integration

Citing increased challenges due to regionalism and globalization, African leaders have realized the need to further Africa's integration. Since the inception of the Organisation of African Unity (OAU), concerted efforts towards integrating for greater benefits have shown potential. The OAU Charter coupled with the Constitutive Act has termed regional integration as an elaborative act of African unity. The tenets and mechanisms of regional integration within the African context are stipulated within the Lagos Plan of Action and the Abuja Treaty, where they clearly outline economic, political and institutional advances towards regional integration in Africa (Mistry, 2000). The formation of the Commission of the African Union is a step towards advancing the regional integration process given regional economic communities meant to improve trade and increase the global competitiveness of the continent. This core canon forms the 'backbone' of the development agenda for the continent. Through thought leadership Africa's leadership implemented the New Partnership for Africa's Development (NEPAD), a plan that has set Africa's growth and developmental processes in progress.

Globalization has resulted in a paradigm shift in economic environments calling for strategic initiatives to achieve regional integration. Regional economic communities (RECs) have made momentous developments and steps towards trade liberalization and facilitation (Mistry, 2000). The most notable regional integration schemes with diverse trade markets and expansive growth include the West African Economic and Monetary Union (UEMOA), and the Common Market for Eastern and Southern Africa (COMESA) (Mistry, 2000). Meanwhile, the Economic Community of West African States (ECOWAS) boasts of increased levels of labour movement and human capital development within Western Africa (Biswaro, 2011). The Southern African Development Community (SADC), on the other hand, has made colossal efforts to expand its infrastructure. A recent report by the Renewable Energy Policy Network for the 21st century connotes a plan by the SADC to develop and further advance electricity generation through calculated investment of between US$114 billion and $233 billion from 2012–2027. Infrastructure developments have also been upbeat in East African nations such as Kenya. Such advances in the East African Community (EAC) have facilitated movements within EAC promoting trade between member states (Biswaro, 2011). Notably, peace and security through the establishment of protocols and agreement have had step-ups ad infinitum in a continent that witnessed emergent *coups d'état* in the 1980s–90s. In brief, Africa seems to be cementing its position in trade and regional assimilation; however, there is a considerable gap between the main objectives of the regional economic blocs and their potential to achieve the laid down goals, particularly on issues of bolstering greater internal trade, macroeconomic convergence, the capacity of production and physical connectivity. RECs in Africa are characterized by a poor implementation record.

4 Trade policy reforms, trade creation and diversion

Regional arrangements aim at reducing barriers (such as tariffs) to trade among member countries. According to economic theory, free trade will provide citizens with leeway to procure goods and services at affordable and the cheapest prices leading to the reallocation of resources based on comparative advantage. Even with concerted efforts towards liberalizing the trade and markets, the synchronized and integrated sub-regional markets observed are still quite slow. Regional economic communities with respective custom unions denote progressive efforts within shifting stages of progression in instituting free trade areas.

Part of the problem of dismal trade performance is a result of the linear market integration. Under this economic model, there is 'all-round' integration of goods, labour and capital markets, and ultimately monetary and fiscal integration. This model is characterized by a *free trade area*, consequently followed by *a custom union*, a *common market* and eventually an *economic union*. The *political union* is the highest form of regional integration.

Establishing a unified currency is also a regional integration model aimed at maximizing trade liberalization efforts. Sub-regional harmonization of markets within Africa countries has been marked by stunted development due to the complicated nature of trade agreements within these regional economic communities such as UEMOA and the Central African Economic and Monetary Community (CEMAC). Small domestic markets have characterized trade between nations, especially in Central Africa. This is a result of weak production systems within national economies. African economies are also characterized by low incomes, chronic poverty levels and poor administration. They are faced with weaknesses and 'loop-holes' in developing proper infrastructure coupled with limited efforts to reinvent production and trade. African bilateral trade is characterized by creation and diversion, where trade creation refers to a shift in the consumption of higher-cost domestic products in favour of lower-cost products within the participating member countries.

Trade diversion, in contrast, is a situation where a state (member) shifts in the source of imports from lower-cost external tariff sources to a higher-cost source within the regional bloc or participating countries. All these concepts originate after member states agree on a common customs union. Thus, Viner (1950) argues that 'participating countries or the world as a whole may measure the benefits of welfare or losses in the customs union. It may be beneficial if trade creation is predominant and it may lead to losses if trade diversion is dominant'.

Singling out African markets is minimized, while a pooling of resources through regional integration affords greater economies of scale and the capacity for regional production sharing, but runs the twin risk of trade diversion and agglomeration. The monopoly structure of small markets in Africa leads to discouragement which leads to lower investment and the need to widen markets. African countries need to build capacity for regional integration and trade policy development to facilitate effective regional integration (Fischer, 2003). Improving these twin forces, capacity building for regional integration and trade policy development, creates a platform for successful implementation of activities relating to market access and capital flow to Africa. Institutional reforms, both trade-related and legal, are necessary to attract the benefits of macroeconomics of regional integration and to boost growth in economic sectors.

Trade reforms aligned to the World Trade Organization (WTO) are necessary for African emerging economies to conquer the global economy. Such reforms are significant in establishing regulatory and administrative requirements for trade and investment through identifying and removing barriers to private investment and trade. Second, trade reforms are aimed at simplifying important clearance processes and immigration procedures. Third, the process of reforms should entail harmonization of policy and legislation within trade blocs initializing from sub-regional levels (Francis, 2006). Streamlined legal and regulatory frameworks are viewed as viable platforms for attractive foreign direct investment (FDI) and increased trade flows through RECs due to a facilitative and predictive trading environment.

5 The institutional model of regional integration: global governance

Regional arrangements, commonly known as economic communities, have continued to increase globally, bringing into focus the role and nature of regionalism and the effects of 'new regional structures' in influencing global governance and international politics. Antagonists and protagonists of the debate have failed to come to terms with growing concerns about the force, nature and drivers of regionalism vis-à-vis global governance. As one of the earliest researchers in regionalism, Joseph Nye defines a region as consisting of 'a limited number of states linked by a geographical relationship and by a degree of mutual interdependence' (Nye, 1968, p. 7). Breslin and Higgott advance that regionalism represents 'those state-led projects of cooperation that emerge as a result of intergovernmental dialogue and treaties' while regionalization connotes 'processes of integration which albeit seldom unaffected by state policies derive their driving forces from markets, from private trade and investment flows, and from policies and decisions from companies' to a certain extent rather than prearranged government strategy (Breslin & Higgott, 2000, p. 344).

A new institutional form known as regional economic institutions (REI) is rapidly developing also in African nations to govern international regions. In Africa, for example, regional integration has created a form of general regional governance. It is expected that leaders or political actors from a particular region 'speak with one voice', that is, West, East, North, Central or even Southern Africa. There is an association of geographical demographics. Parallel to states' regional bodies are emblems of capitalism and market forces. Notably, REIs are territorial bodies of general governance. Given this, regional institutions in Africa lack two components: coercion and taxation. During past world wars, coercion and taxation were considered vital in an era when involvement in wartime activities created fiscal concerns. The term 'economic' is sustained because it embodies a core hypothesis of the institutional form of RECs. In Africa, regional organizations were founded on economic ties, specifically the provision of economic goods and services, coupled with economic services such as free trade and investment.

A lot of studies have given preference to regional economic communities and declined to focus on the governance of regional institutions and the roles they play in general governance. There is growing literature on the forms of governance that regional institutions such as SADC, ECOWAS and EAC have developed, and that such institutional forms deserve analysis given the significance of RECs in regional and global governance. This chapter aims to advance arguments of new institutional forms of governance in Africa brought about by the African Union and other regional bodies. The African Union, for example, in February 2016 engaged in agreements with the General Conference to withdraw from the International Criminal Court. This brought the perception of 'muscle' in institutional and regional governance. It is imperative to understand the implications of such new forms of regional agreements, decisions, international relations, and their effect on domestic politics. Today, regionalism is viewed as the direction adopted by individual states in tackling issues of trade, resource scarcity, environmental degradation, and terrorism within a 'regional context' (Mistry, 2000). There has been growing concern about 'trans-nationalization and globalization' of problems, thus calling for the need for regional actors to institute a mechanism to curb such a modern Achilles heel. State theory provides the roles and functions of the state with the original core of war, coercion and taxation. In the same way, REIs are involved in extensive activities such as human rights, the security sector, environment and political governance (Krugman, 1993). Nonetheless, institutional creation and death have been the 'hallmark' of Africa's regional integration with RECs, such as the EAC collapse before its eventual 'resurrection' to advance regional trade in East Africa.

6 An 'associational' link between democratization and regionalization

There exists an 'associational' link between democratization and regionalization. More countries globally are more closely developing better networks and trade connections with democratic nations with open and transparent systems. Democracy is widely seen as the most acceptable form of rule. It is a political system where a government of the people in society is determined by respect for liberty and human rights; a people-centred governance system that cuts across political, economic and social aspects without undermining people's liberties and human rights. The question arises of whether democracy is a point of interest in designing and engaging in integration schemes in Africa (Gilpin, 2000).

Citing positioning 'wars' and a scramble for markets in Africa, integration systems have placed stable democracy, political stability and sound economic policies as key factors before integration. The African Union, the most powerful continental body in Africa, reconsiders democracy as a valuable concept towards development. The degree to which the member states of a given regional integration exercise their political freedom determines the extent of regional integration. Another link between democratization and cooperation is made through pointing out the interdependence of the two concepts. The authors contend that substantial evidence shows that democracy diminishes credibility of threat of use of force. In so doing, it promotes regional cooperation and regional integration especially among warring parties. This argument is supported by Crocker et al. (1996), who assert that 'reciprocal interest in sustaining democratic institutions increases initiatives for cooperation and honest exchange of information in the long run promoting transparency, a key component for economic cooperation'.

Regional integration brings increased democratization, which also enhances regional economic and security integration strategies through increased domestic transparency. The impact of pro-democratic ideational forces is substantial for integration. Regional integration schemes have promoted externalization of democratic principles to countries that were earlier seen as being non-democratic (Gilpin, 2000). Gilpin (2000) alluded to the views of Mapuva Mapauva, who argued that democratic policies facilitate economic developments. Democracy, sometimes, is termed as a means or an end to integration, involving decision making, the establishment of rules and regulations, action plans and policies. Dialogue on many integration schemes has been monopolized by government actors and intergovernmental bodies despite the willingness of the citizen to participate in integration processes in Africa. The collapse of the EAC in 1967–77 and its eventual resurfacing using citizen-led democratic processes has led to its current revival with developments in the EAC pointing towards a monetary union (Mistry, 2000).

7 Prospects for the African Union

The transformation of the OAU is more than just a name change. The principal objectives of the African Union (AU) were to integrate and bring about a cooperative continent in handling of 'indigenous issues' that it faced. The AU is more versatile in bolstering good governance, economic development, promotion of human rights and economic development through integration and 'interconnectedness'. The regional body also focuses on promoting the widely accepted form of government-democracy and continental security frameworks through conflict prevention and resolution mechanisms (Mistry, 2000). Unlike the OAU, the AU has intervened in international conflicts and affairs of members in circumstances such as war, genocide, and crimes against humanity (Mistry, 2000). Also, the AU has advocated formally the rejection of unconstitutional changes of government, political assassination and acts of terrorism. The establishment and operationalization of AU practices have moved into a relatively high phase.

8 Pertinence of leadership for advancement of regional integration on the African continent

Disintegration and collapse of regional integration in Africa can also be blamed on the sense of leadership exercised in fostering these regional schemes (McCarthy, 1996). Africa is characterized by poor leadership and misplaced priorities that focus less on Africa's development. In a bid to increase popularity among the masses and the electorate at large, African leaders have only advanced grand ideas and visionary blueprints that have failed to become reality. Thus, Africa's challenges call for a sense of urgency and coordination in action, through regional integration and a sense of pragmatism, through 'thought leadership'.

Developmental challenges require sustainable politico-economic reforms aimed at improving the domestic level as a point to start. The regional level citing its complexity tends to focus on developmental coordination and harmonization of trade policies. For instance, the complementarity of industries within similar trading zones could boost trade between member states such as CEMAC, the Central African trading bloc. Percy Mistry elicits the problem of leadership in African regional integration initiatives by contending that, 'African governments need to be less ambitious and more realistic and pragmatic about the objectives and intermediate targets for integration, taking into account the constraints and capacities of integrating national governments' (Mistry, 2000, p. 566).

9 Future directions

Capacity needs assessment: initializing strategic and calculated regional integration and cooperation in building Africa are the only means towards an effective capacity-building strategy. These would be integral in strengthening collaboration and integration capacity needs. Thus, in the development of regional integration in Africa several components need to be closely evaluated. First is the capacity needs assessment. Through capacity needs assessments, integration experts can deduce capacity gaps and build up priority action plans in the implementation of regional cooperation and integration schemes and mandates of the continent.

Institution for integration, trade policy, development and negotiation: Africa needs to develop a coordination centre for regional integration schemes within the continent. Such a centre, which can be sanctioned by existing regional institutions, such as the AU, can serve as a resource and convening centre for regional representatives, regional and cooperation government actors (relevant ministers), international actors, states, trade and development experts, and negotiators. This should serve as a 'steering wheel' to a common African viewpoint and position in trade policy formulation and negotiations that will stimulate regional integration. The institution's objective would be to offer technical advice to missions, regional organizations and the provision of vital legal expertise when required. Second, it would entail providing legal and advisory support to RECs in drafting necessary legislation to strengthen integration and trade issues. As a research centre, the institution should increase capacity through providing technical assistance using internships and training in professional areas such as trade policy, environmental law, competitiveness assessment, global governance, regional integration, public–private partnerships and negotiation techniques.

Results-oriented training should aim at building national and regional networks or pools of trainers and experts in multilateral trading systems (Kennes, 2001). Such systems should be developed to suit the African market system, not 'blindly aping' Eurocentric models. However, the search for indigenous integration models should not translate to adoption of unsustainable regional integration models. Universities, research centres and think tanks need to develop and sponsor higher-level education studies in trade and payment systems, and trade law. Research efforts should be cemented by a fellowship programme aimed at strategic learning and courses for trade students. There should be industry professional attendance at workshops, conferences, regional trade fairs, economic summits and high-level meetings aimed at networking and developing joint policy through work groups on integration and trade-related issues (Mistry, 2000). The centre should stand as a pillar and regional platform for interactive dialogue in trade negotiations.

The strategies outlined above should induce the materialization of a National Trade Policy Development and Negotiations Centre. Member states within regional economic communities should be compelled to house a functional Integration and Trade Policy Development Unit or Centre (Kennes, 2001). Under the umbrella of the Integration and Trade Policy Development Units and Centres, specialists made up from the public sector (government), private sector (investors, entrepreneurs), civil society (nongovernmental organizations) and think tanks (research centres, advisers) should convene habitually (on a regular basis) for information, briefing and knowledge sharing, and it would also serve as an apparatus for examining developments in regional integration and trade policy. Such an initiative should be all-inclusive and a platform for the AU, African Development Bank, African Capacity Building Foundation and the NEPAD Secretariat to engage all multi-role stakeholders (multi-stakeholder systems) in strengthening the financial infrastructure and renewed efforts in setting up a regional guaranteed payment system to easier facilitate regional and international trade payments (Kennes, 2001). Such initiatives should not only focus on trade-based initiatives but also initiate, support and further physical infrastructure and the development of requisite management capacity. In conclusion, to integrate successfully there is a need to view the benefits of long-term integration as greater than short-term losses that may cause financial disruption in small countries, and devise proper means for compensation.

References

Biswaro, J.M. (2011) *The Quest for Integration in Africa, Latin America and Beyond in the Twenty First Century: Experiences, Progress and Prospects.* Brazil: Fernando Mons Publications.

Breslin, S. and Higgott, R. (2000) Studying regions: Learning from the old, constructing the new. *New Political Economy* 5(3): 333–352.

Crocker, C.A., Hamson, F.O. and Aall, P. (1996) *Managing Global Chaos: Sources of and Responses to International Conflict.* Washington, DC: USIP Press.

Fischer, S. (2003) *Globalization and its Challenges.* American Economic Association Ely Lecture, American Economic Review: Papers and Proceedings, May, Washington, DC.

Francis, D.J. (2006) *Uniting Africa: Building Regional Peace and Security Systems.* Aldershot: Ashgate.

Gilpin, R. (2000) *Global Political Economy: Understanding the International Economic Order.* Princeton, NJ: Princeton University Press.

Kennes, W. (2001) *Strategies for Effective Participation of Developing Countries in the World Trading System.* PSIO Occasional Paper 6. Programme for the Study of International Organizations, Geneva.

Krugman, P. (1993) Regionalism versus multilateralism: Analytical notes. In *New Dimensions in Regional Integration*, J. de Melo and A. Panagariya (eds) Cambridge, New York and Melbourne: Cambridge University Press.

McCarthy, C. (1996) Regional integration, part of the solution or part of the problem. In *Africa Now*, S. Ellis (ed.) London: James Currey and Heinemann.

Mistry, P. (2000) Africa's record of regional economic integration. *African Affairs* 99: 553–573.

Nye, J. (1968) Introduction. In *International Regionalism: Readings edited by Joseph Nye.* Boston, MA: Little, Brown and Company.

Schmitter, P. and Karl, T. (2001) What democracy is … and is not. *Annual Editions*, 103–109.

Viner, J. (1950) *The Customs Union Issue.* Carnegie Endowment for International Peace, pp. 41–55.

Part III

Managing geoeconomics

18 The evolution of geoeconomics and the need for new theories of governance

Najiba Benabess

The study of geoeconomics has been fluid and even contradictory, defined and redefined since Edward Luttwak coined the term in 1990. It has been variously described as a means to achieve strategic geopolitical interests; a process to expand global market integration; and as a remapping of state power in a multipolar world. Some consider the instruments of geoeconomics as tools for statecraft; others consider the powers of statecraft as a support system for commerce. The application of geoeconomic activities has changed from the end of the Cold War as a US strategy to isolate Russia. In the mid-1990s, it was a path for mutually beneficial global interdependence. Yet, at the present time, geoeconomics has become a strategy for political balance, coercion and an end in itself as countries vie to maintain or grow economic dominance regionally or globally.

For those who review scholarly literature, it is possible to imagine the development of applied geoeconomics as divided into three dominant periods. In 1990, Edward Luttwak identified the transition from geopolitics to geoeconomics using the metaphors of war. Firepower, military technology, and garrisons, Luttwak (1990) wrote, would be replaced by capital, technological innovation and markets. His reference point was the isolation and decline of Russian influence as a global superpower. It was economics, not military action, that brought down the Berlin Wall in 1989 and caused the fall of the Soviet Union in 1991.

In the mid-to-late 1990s through the 2000s, a period of relative peace and cooperation between and among developed countries, trade agreements encouraged global integration. This second period was marked by the North American Free Trade Agreement (NAFTA), the establishment of the World Trade Organization (WTO), and trade liberalization. The end goal for these frameworks and multilateral agreements was global commerce. China became the factory of the world. Russia focused on financial reform and industrial development. India's technology sector advanced. US multinational corporations expanded in number and global influence.

Geoeconomic analysis of this period was defined by Pascal Lorot (1999), who noted its applications as a way to protect prized segments of domestic economies while expanding beneficial trade. In 1999 Lorot defined the field of study as follows:

> geoeconomics is the analysis of economic strategies—including commercial—decided by the states in the policy framework to protect their national economy or some well-identified parts of it, to gain mastery of key technologies and/or expand certain segments in the World Markets ... in that their possession or control gives the holder—or state enterprise—an element of power and international influence and contributes to the strengthening of its economic and social potential. Geoeconomics questions the relationship between power and space, but a 'virtual' space or fluidized in the sense that it moves without limits constantly, so this is to say, a space freed of territorial borders and physical characteristics of geopolitics.
>
> (Lorot, 1999, p. 62)

In one sense, a major component of China's state capitalism and Grand Strategy remains, ideologically, in the Lorotian period. China became the leading export nation as a result of 1990s trade agreements under the ideal of market expansion. Its expansion of trade routes into Africa, its monetary policy, and its goal to achieve economic dominance are strategies consistent with global integration. However, it is difficult to associate the third period in geoeconomics with any certainty because some geopolitical experts are once again viewing geoeconomic policies as tools for statecraft. Geoeconomic theory has not yet responded to current events and rapidly evolving activities. Unlike the Lorotian period of the 1990s, the interval from 2001 to 2016 lacks a guiding vision with the noted exception of China's quest for economic dominance. For the USA, this period coincides with the 'war on terror,' diverting its attention from global economics.

From 2001 to 2016, the USA was focused on two wars in the Middle East and the rise of Islamic State in Iraq and Syria (ISIS), lessening policy development in global trade. Experts—even those who may have supported the war on terror—acknowledge the US lack of attention to geoeconomics and its late-coming pivot to Asia (Bremmer, 2016). Regime change in the Middle East may have been intended as an oil war, but, as with the Cold War, economics trumped firepower and troops, only this time US hegemony was the casualty.

Along the same timeline, the emergence of Brazil, Russia, India and China (the BRICs) shifted global economic power eastward, with China rising to the status of the world's second largest economy. In contrast to 1990s ideals, trade agreements became protectionist with an increasing number of restrictive trade measures presented to the WTO every year (Lowrey, 2012). Regional trade agreements also increased during this period, subdividing global integration into regional and strategic partnerships. By the 2010s, exclusionary mega-free trade agreements were in the works, with the US pivot to Asia, the Trans-Pacific Partnership (TPP) and the proposed Transatlantic Trade and Investment Partnership (TTIP). President Obama's now famous remark, '[w]e should write the rules,' (2015) was a direct reference to US opposition to

China's economic domination in the Asian marketplace. TPP 'serves the dual purposes of balancing China's expanding economic influence and deepening U.S. trade and investment ties to the region' (Itagaki, 2016, p. 1). In response, China is negotiating a Regional Comprehensive Economic Partnership (RCEP) which, like the TPP, excludes its primary geoeconomic competitor (Chang, 2015).

However, the USA is behind the ball and, unlike China, has limited ability to open new markets because its international economic role has already matured. China, on the other hand, is expanding imports and exports across the Eastern Hemisphere and South America. Trade agreements are only one tactic in China's Grand Strategy. Its newest tools for growth are infrastructure, finance and transportation.

In 2016, China launched the Asian Infrastructure Investment Bank (AIIB) and the New Development Bank (BRICS bank, with the BRICS now including South Africa). Together, AIIB and the BRICS bank offset reliance on the World Bank and the International Monetary Fund (IMF). AIIB finances construction and development of the One Road One Belt (OROB) initiative. The BRICS bank objectives are to establish partnerships and promote infrastructure in BRICS countries. Both institutions contribute to China's rise toward the status of the world's largest economy.

China's transportation infrastructure demonstrates its ability to expand into new markets. As an overland and maritime transportation route, OROB provides access to markets in the Middle East, the European Union and Russia. Along its maritime routes, OROB connects Quanzhou to Southeast Asia, Bangladesh, India, the Saudi Peninsula and East Africa. OROB secures imports of natural resources which can be transformed into products destined for global markets and increase market penetration throughout the Eastern Hemisphere.

Once again, we can imagine China's emphasis on global integration as the natural extension of the Lorotian period in geoeconomics. However, China departs from 1990s Lorotian trade with a geopolitical twist. While the end goal appears to focus on economic versus political dominance, China's protection of trade interests with assertive military support redefines geoeconomics by turning Luttwak's vision on its head. At the end of the Cold War, economies became weapons, but in the South and East China Seas, as well as in Kashmir, we can see weapons drumming the heartbeat of trade. Increasingly, China's flag not only follows trade, it secures it. Lorot's description of a virtual geoeconomic space 'freed of territorial borders' is not part of China's Grand Strategy. Instead, China is militarizing commerce with maritime territorial claims and troops along OROB trade routes. Is its growing navy and development of advanced weaponry truly intended, as China claims, for defensive and deterrence purposes? If China's end goal is global economic dominance, then perhaps so.

However, the USA, India and Southeast Pacific countries are increasingly concerned about China's military activity. India has been monitoring the presence of the People's Liberation Army along the Kashmir Line of Control. Tensions are rising in the South and East China Seas as China constructs artificial islands with air bases on the Spratly Reefs. In response, international naval exercises and US surveillance drones are escalating Sino–American relations. As a result, a potentially unfortunate change in leading geoeconomic theory may be on the horizon. In 2016, Blackwill and Harris (2016) echoed Luttwak's metaphors of conflict in their book, *War by Other Means.* This is a US-centric argument which, while contributing to the sophistication of applied geoeconomics, blunts its definition into a cudgel of state interests. Unlike the Lorotian definition emphasizing trade and global integration, Blackwill and Harris (2016, p. 15) state, without nuance, '[g]eoeconomics is the use of economic instruments to achieve geopolitical goals.' The Blackwill and Harris contribution to geoeconomic analysis is their identification of seven instruments that could be strategically deployed against political rivals: trade policy, investment policy, economic and financial sanctions, cyber, aid, financial and monetary policy, and energy and commodities carry levers of state control and determinants of success. However, their approach also diminishes benefits of trade and appears to dismiss altogether the fundamental interests of corporations and peaceful commerce. If geoeconomics is to become a weapon of geopolitics, the most likely casualties will be the multinational companies that drive economic dominance in free-market economies. Under a Blackwill and Harris policy, the global economy would be hollowed out from within. Lorot's comprehensive definition of geoeconomics would be replaced with a seven-pointed spear which fragments, rather than unifies, the global economy.

Connectivity is a key to geoeconomic success, as we can see from the rise of China. Fragmentation, on the other hand, simply creates a growing gap between powerful and weak economies. Weak economies are awarded small trade carrots in exchange for geopolitical presence which can wield military sticks against rivals. This sums up the purpose of TPP. The USA will lose some jobs to Pacific Rim countries, but it gains a firm naval presence near the Spratly Reef. This is the unintended consequence of a fragmented Blackwill and Harris geoeconomy. Using geoeconomic instruments against China to conduct 'war by other means' exacerbates political tension and, despite its portfolio of weaponry, may end in a US defeat.

We are on the cusp of a new period in geoeconomics which requires new, more sophisticated schools of thought. Lacking renewed, comprehensive geoeconomic theories of governance, we are now seeing the emergence of militarized commerce. How do we reconcile the Lorot vision of trade against the Blackwill and Harris geopolitical subtext? Can the WTO and United Nations intervene when trade conflict arises, or have both institutions become obsolete? Does the potential direction of geopolitically driven geoeconomics lead to, as suggested by Mark Thirlwell (2010), a zero-sum approach?

Calling for a new theory in geoeconomic governance obliges at least one concept as a starting point for further discussion. With the emergence of militarized commerce, the global trade community needs to define expectations for peaceful free trade, as well as potential consequences in response to hostility in the form of a 'rules of trade engagement' concept. Mark Leonard (2015) touches on this in a World Economic Forum report, *Seven Challenges to Globalization*, although the recommendation comes without detail. Rules of trade engagement policies would be embedded in trade agreements, identifying military exclusion zones, territorial protections, or, if failing consensus on either of the aforementioned, coordinated military patrols in economic trade corridors. Rules of trade engagement policies should form the foundation principles of agreements to prevent a geopolitical conflict. The overlap of smaller trade partners in many agreements such as the TPP and RCEP may ensure large economies, including China, India and the USA, are party to regional concerns, such as the militarization of the South and East China Seas. The threat of military engagement encourages an environment of non-engagement. It decreases the likelihood of militarized commerce because, as we now know, trade trumps war. In a multipolar geoeconomic world, the most powerful nations depend on each other to survive and risk self-inflicted economic consequences in a sustained campaign against a key economic partner or rival.

No matter what new theories emerge, it is important to remember that as the study of geoeconomics matures, we should anticipate a fluid, changing field, evolving in areas not yet considered or imagined at all. As geoeconomic activity increases and becomes more complex, we will need to expand areas of inquiry and dissect issues more thoroughly. We will need to think of the rise of geoeconomics less as a chronology and more as a complex, rapidly changing evolutionary process with unexpected competitions and transmutations in the global order. Nothing is static. Any strategy can unravel on a moment's notice.

References

Blackwill, R. and Harris, J. (2016) *War by Other Means: Geoeconomics and Statecraft*. Cambridge, MA: Belknap Press of Harvard University Press.

Bremmer, I. (2016) *The Age of Geoeconomics: Choices for Japan & the US in a G-Zero World*. Japan Society.

Chang, G. (2015) *TPP vs. RCEP: America and China Battle for Control of Pacific Trade*. The National Interest.

Itagaki, S. (2016) *The Trans-Pacific Partnership in the Asia-Pacific*. The National Bureau of Asian Research.

Leonard, M. (2015) *Geo-economics: Seven Challenges to Globalization*. World Economic Forum Report.

Lorot, P. (eds) (1999) *Introduction à la géoéconomie*. Paris, France: Institut européen de géoéconomie, Economica.

Lowrey, A. (2012) An increase in barriers to trade is reported. *The New York Times*, June 22.

Luttwak, E.N. (1990) From geopolitics to geoeconomics: Logic of conflict, grammar of commerce. *The National Interest* 20: 17–23.

Obama, B. (2015) *Statement by the President on the Trans-Pacific Partnership.* The White House, Office of the Press Secretary.
Thirlwell, M. (2010) *The Return of Geoeconomics: Globalisation and National Security.* Sydney: Lowy Institute for International Policy.

19 Geoeconomics and banking

Hubert Bonin

1 Introduction

In the 1970s–90s, living within an economy structured along the division between East and West, Third World and developed countries, and specialisation, the banking and financial marketplaces faced internal competition, technological changes, liberalisation processes, commonplace risks, volatility and crises. Since the turn of the 21st century, they have endured new revolutions leading to strategic and managerial challenges. Linked economies built an actual globalised world of money flows. Petro-dollars and classical Asian dollars were joined by the upsurge of 'Chinese dollars' and the osmosis between the 'rich world' and that of competitive emerging countries. Beyond market banking, already deeply inserted into worldwide exchanges, every classical activity (the foreign exchange market, or FOREX, management of means of payment, commercial and investment banking, retail banking, wealth management, asset management) had to be conducted in a 'regional' (continental) or even globalised way within interdependent settings.

'National' banking and cities were at stake. Significant challenges occurred. On one side, there were attempts to dismantle tax evasion, secret accounts and fraud. On another side, there was a need to confront accounting and balance-sheet silos, new regulations, matters of compliance and processes of transparency. Geopolitics and geoeconomics challenged organisational operations in new ways, reshaping the practise of management and banking, corporate cultures, and defying economic patriotism and the political aspiration of countries to dispose of their 'national' banking bigwigs. Business history of banking cannot escape the reconstitution of the interactions between the practise of banks' strategies, and the several levels and issues of geoeconomics (Solberg Soilen, 2012) throughout the activities of banks and market places (Bonin, 2009, 2013; Fratianni, 2009).

The growing worldwide integration of banking and tools of management should have favoured a soft management of globalised finance, because cooperative programmes blossomed in order to ease the circulation of money, data and orders. Private law and business habits have commenced a powerful convergence even in countries where there are tight state laws and unorthodox practices. These scenarios demand levels of influence. On a more global level, the life of banks and finance institutions cannot but depend on rules, interventions, and financial support. First, by the International Monetary Fund (IMF). Second, by the World Bank Group, on a world scale, or by the European Central Bank (ECB), on a continental level. These organisations legitimise osmosis between banks, and experts of these institutions engage in cooperative actions. For all these reasons, interwoven networks of technical and business cooperation forged a far more integrated world of geo-banking. It is reliant on fluid supply chains, harmonious and balanced gains and profits, agility, and resiliency against disruptions.

2 Dependence upon geopolitical fireplaces

With instant and complete information on one side, and respect of 'common rules' about good practices on the other side, there exist 'black faces' in financial forces. The geoeconomy of banking is rich in contradictions. For example, it practises universal finance, through worldwide circulation of money and credit, and a global clearing of financial exchanges. This mainly takes place in London with eurobonds as the cornerstone and technical gearwheel of derivatives and new market products, but this harmony is broken down by inefficient or unadjusted practices. Far from being more 'intelligent' than its predecessors, the 21st century was also shaken by debt crises. Argentina in 2001–05 (with a loss of 70%) and 2014, and Greece in 2008–10 disturbed the world of state bonds because of their insolvency and banking crises. A dozen countries were the main contributors in the recent history of sovereign defaults, regardless of their size. Each time what was at stake was not only their insolvency, but its effects on global trust among bankers and institutional lenders or bearers of bonds (investment funds). Such fireplaces fueled concerns about the liquidity of the banking economy. Many big banks bore bonds of failing countries, as was the case for European banks owning Greek bonds.

The structure of geo-finance was weakened by sudden rifts and risks of marketplace earthquakes. The efficiency of the key tools of the financial markets was questioned: the three big credit rating agencies (Standard & Poor's, Fitch, Moody's) in charge of assessing the main financial products (government bonds, corporate bonds, municipal bonds, preferred stock and collateralised securities, such as mortgage-backed securities and collateralised debt obligations) (Sinclair, 2005) proved their shortcomings in the sub-prime boom and the bonds of many 'second-tier' countries. The capital of talent and art of watchfulness of the two international 'clubs' of creditors supervising the sovereign debts (the Paris Club for public debt, since 1956; the London Club for corporate debt, since 1970) were submitted to critics. They had to go on acting as firefighters from two 'euro-centrist' market places to rescue the soft functioning of markets, and to alleviate the charge on key activities of banks, asset management and commercial banking.

A harmonious life of the finance world cannot be guaranteed because of the absence of a legal framework, system and authorities able to impose the completion of decisions involving bad debts, bonds and sovereign debts. This scenario leads to unending lawsuits by 'local' courts on 'global' finance—for example, a court case in a US state because creditors are based there. This was the case for the Argentine debt in 2010. No multilateral framework may be applied to the restructuring of sovereign debt because of the right of each state to manage its own debt. In the United Nations Organization system, decisions by the main stakeholders of globalised market places have to be negotiated harshly on the field for years (i.e. Argentina or Greece).

Reforms are maturing at the turn of the 21st century as a result of efficient but long discussions. Since 1995, experts at the Organisation for Economic Co-operation and Development (OECD), have convinced key actors to commit to conceived 'collective action clauses'. One of them is the International Capital Market Association (ICMA) established in 2005 by the merger of two previous associations. This organisation acts as a self-regulatory organisation gathering issuers, primary and secondary market intermediaries, asset managers, investors and capital market infrastructure providers, who grapple with a comprehensive range of regulatory, market and practice issues at the core of the international debt capital markets. This led to the 'collective action clauses in sovereign bond contracts', enhanced by the ICMA, the IMF (its promoter since 2002) and all big stakeholders of the globalised finance markets (Gelpern & Gulati, 2008; IMF, 2002). Such a step fosters a positive impact on the geoeconomics of banking. Collective action clauses help overcome creditor coordination problems by allowing important terms of the bonds to be amended by a defined majority of holders. They facilitate debt restructuring by making amendments binding all holders, including the dissenting minority. They eliminate contract rights through majority voting without any court supervision and outside a rules-based statute.

Geopolitics obviously triggered these successive crises: either third-worldist and nationalist governments played with the international investor community beyond its limit, or connivance predominated as big-wigs (the USA mainly, or the UK) favoured countries that were re-joining (Angola, Argentina) or sticking (Nigeria) to the capital-friendly community. The evidence of such indulgence is gathering momentum through the recent crisis of oil and mineral commodities prices, caused by the Chinese uncertainties in 2015–17. A huge crisis of liquidity is pending among the petro-countries and the oil and mining companies. This opens the door to bad debts, insolvencies, and dwindling value of portfolios of asset managers and investment or sovereign funds rich in oil and mining corporation stocks. The worldwide financial system does not lack liquidity, but such a crisis paves the way to localised crisis for some banks (as lenders and asset managers) and financial investment institutions. The Chinese banking system will undoubtedly face a crisis when the authorities, along with the need for international credibility, lead to a thorough reshuffling of balance sheets to reach some realistic figures.

However, stakeholders do not wish to impose sectarian and immediate rules and reforms. The soft cleaning up of balance sheets will predominate, as has been the case in Greece. The word 'renegotiation' epitomises real practices among the European and worldwide authorities and clubs. The geoeconomy of banking needs fine-tuned actions to avoid dire shocks that would cultivate distrust and lead to panic similar to that of 2008.

3 Dependence on geopolitical balances of power

Commercial and investment bankers and asset managers have to take into account the balance of power cemented around 'the dollar economy'—as with the pound sterling before World War I or 1931. Despite its floating rate since the 1970s, it has imposed its rules and hegemony on stakeholders of world business. Its advantages are obvious: fluidity of currency transfers, homogeneity of values of reference, easy counterparts to market operations; FOREX markets rely on the dollar (64% in 2015) far more than the euro (20%) and the pound (4.7%). The dollar is the basis for direct loans to banks by oil companies, states and rich transnationals. These take place through repurchase agreements (*repos*) on government securities, and commercial paper money markets. Sovereign funds are big subscribers of high-yield bonds in dollars. Banks are bent to favour the US dollar in their operations and balance sheets because Asian and petrodollars constitute thick layers of worldwide assets. However, banks also have to respect the desire of several partners of the global money market to use the euro and the yuan/renminbi, because others want to counterbalance such hegemony. The Chinese even spearheaded the Asian Infrastructure Investment Bank from 2016 to short-circuit the World Bank Group, which had been connected with the US poles of decision and financing, and to assert its new scope of economic 'regionalism'.

The day-to-day fate of the US dollar and its volatility through each economic, diplomatic or political 'crisis' also demand lucid reaction to tackle the huge assets expressed in that currency. No bank can escape an overhaul of its commitments to alleviate risks. Geopolitics intervened in the geo-dollarisation of banking. In the wake of the crash, bankers discovered in 2011–16 that they were reported to the US Justice Department and their US dollar activities were monitored. Large fines were imposed on banks because of their bad practices during the 2004–07 boom. US banks were the main victims of such a judiciary move against banks, and had to extract about US$100 billion out of their coffers (and provisions). European bankers discovered that they had to pay significant fines as well. Banks did not consider enough the implications of the International Emergency Economic Powers Act of 1977, or the Sarbanes–Oxley Act of 2002 regarding corporate criminal law. Some were accused of having drug cartels as customers. Others had opened their Swiss safes to US tax evaders. These banks accepted fines reluctantly for they would have lost their licence to continue working in the USA. They would have needed to close their doors there, impacting global business with their affiliates and clients. There is in fact an overall authority over geo-banking, not for regulation *ex-ante*, but for sanctions *ex-post*, and it lies with US litigation.

In the geoeconomic context, the USA asserts 'extra-territoriality' for any operation achieved in US dollars. This appears as a sacred principle which no supra-authority might oppose. If the eurozone, for example, were to impose a reverse demand, one might imagine retaliation that could destroy transatlantic business. An unequal balance of power predominates in geo-finance gatekeeping. Intensive negotiations were necessary for several years before an agreement on market derivatives was reached in February 2016. The Commodity Futures Trading Commission and the European Commission forged a common framework for transactions on derivatives products. Both zones admit the value of each supervisory process and decision, whatever the nationality of the stakeholders involved, and a level of parity. Public attorneys and business lawyers have been constantly resolving compliance issues in the USA, generally through private agreements, crowned by gigantic fines ranging from several hundred million dollars to a few billion. European banks have to incorporate into their strategic schemes, their tactics and their balance sheet the prospect of such fines. The geoeconomics of banking might appear unbalanced in favour of US hegemony: altogether it is a "judge and be judged" scenario.

4 Dependence on political cooperative strategies

Banks and financial companies are working within the frames of regulatory rules. From the 1990s, projects have matured in favour of internationalised rules, mainly what has been called 'the Basel rules' (*Basel I* and *II*). These rules proportion between key assets and counterparts on the availability to prop up liquidity of balance sheets. However, national rules prevailed. The transnational rules were applied reluctantly, balance sheets were often tricky—as appeared in the Lehman Brothers case (with thick 'off-balance sheet' lines, dissimulating actual risks). The massive securitisation helped to gather into the same bond securities spread along the scale of risks, whilst the rating agencies in charge with their assessment were not independent-minded or actively lucid enough. The geoeconomies of banking depended deeply on the US overall mindset on the paradigms of finance markets. They blossomed in a transatlantic way because they found ideological allies and links in Europe. In the USA, a strong wave of opinion ended among bankers and the supervisory or governing authorities in favour of almost free banking and the 'financialisation' of business (Epstein, 2005). Deregulation and the creeds into the virtues of the 'new financial instruments' prevailed. This explains the Gramm–Leach-Bliley Act which reneged in 1999 on the Glass–Steagall Act of 1933, and the Commodity Futures Modernization Act in 2000, which rejected any federal regulation over the derivatives markets.

Owing to the success of neoliberalism in Europe, such fads crossed the Atlantic. It was an era of commonly shared regulation in favour of deregulation and of free market banking. The influential role of the Institute of International Finance since its creation in 1983 exemplifies this move. It mandates 450 institutions involved in finance, to collect data and to supply subjective information about innovative products to think tanks, lobbyists and committees of the International Settlements Bank about reforms of the banking system. The International Swaps and Derivatives Association has also been active as a leverage force to convince the authorities (Commodities Futures Trading Commission, etc.) of the efficiency of self-regulation of new finance markets. This helped draw the lines of geoeconomics of market banking. The system was successful in 2003–07, then became fiercely controversial. It led to disputes because of the lack of lucidity among many big bankers (Bonin, 2011).

Since the 2007–08 crash, precepts of 'resolution', of risk management and of conformity have been hardened (*Basel III* for banks and for insurance companies, and European directives *MIFID I* from 2004 and *II* from 2018 for securities markets managed by about 300 platforms, etc.). However, pressure groups, experts' controversies, and the national ministries acted to put a brake on these moves. This multiplied the poles of decision and reference. The European Commission and Parliament pushed their own sets of rules (Banking Union rules, MIFID). London struggled hard to preserve its autonomy of regulation for the sake of the attractiveness of the City as the clearing place of a globalised economy of banking. It put itself outside the process of the continental Banking Union. London goes on taking profit from its ambiguous relations with off-shore financial centres, causing risks of hidden fault-lines (Rajan, 2010) in asset management. This helps avoid 'naming and shaming' processes against opaque practices. The USA sustained reforms on their own side (the Dodd–Frank Act in 2010), with ups and downs in their completion, and have kept their influence within the meetings of the G20 and the Basel Committee on Banking Supervision.

Because of these centrifugal forces, a fragmented geoeconomics of banking resulted from such divisions in theory, reform and regulation—as the IMF may only intervene to refinance state debts and bonds (in Greece). The central banks (the Fed, the Bank of England, Japanese Central Bank, and the ECB, mainly, supervising 123 banks since November 2014) have injected dozens of billions of dollars or euros by purchasing bonds and qualified assets borne by banks of their area of influence, within the 'quantitative easing' scheme. The map of geo-banking therefore lacks clarity and homogeneity, which sometimes fuels uncertainty and volatility, and for Europe euro-scepticism about the effectiveness of cooperative action.

A crucial field is cooperation against fraud. National rules on banking secrecy blocked cooperation for an efficient struggle against tax evasion and moreover against money laundering. On the first point, Switzerland and Luxembourg agreed to open their doors to share data, through bilateral fiscal conventions. Tax havens (Piolet, 2015) are more and more submitted to transparency rules, like Panama which was lifted in 2016 from the 'blacklist' of states established by the Financial Action Task Force (FATF). With its 36 members, it sets standards and promotes effective implementation of legal, regulatory and operational measures for combating money laundering, terrorist financing and other related threats to the integrity of the international financial system. It monitors the progress of its members in implementing necessary measures, reviews money laundering and terrorist financing techniques and counter-measures, and promotes the adoption and implementation of appropriate measures globally. In collaboration with other international stakeholders, FATF works to identify national-level vulnerabilities with the aim of protecting the international financial system from misuse (FATF, 2016). On the second point, opaque fund transfers and deposits of illicit funds in bank accounts are common, and it traces suspect movements by actors of shadow markets (drugs, counterfeiting, arms for terrorism) (Unifab, 2016; Biersteker & Eckert, 2007). This scenario became a key geopolitical issue involving geo-banking. Circuits of means of payment are increasingly being targeted.

5 Issues of competitiveness and rankings: economic patriotism and geoeconomics of banking

The competition among worldwide market places remains the issue in this century, through 'the fight for financial supremacy' (Einzig, 1931). The 1980s–90s opened windows of opportunity to big national players. They jumped over the strategic train of globalisation, along all the banking activities. Deutsche Bank absorbed Morgan Grenfell in the UK in 1989 and Bankers Trust in the USA in 1998. It was crowned Derivatives House of the Year in 2003 by the magazine *Risk*. Many of them imitated investment banks and practised market banking in Europe, the UK and the USA, or developed offshoots in wealth management and retail banking. A globalised business model was shared by those intending to join the co-leadership of world banking. It was supposed to be 'the end of geography' (O'Brien, 1992). Royal Bank of Scotland-Greenwich Capital was just second to Lehman Brothers for sub-prime credit in the USA in 2007, whilst Citicorp extended its retail banking network all over Europe. The crisis blew away this model and the map of geo-banking. Through a drastic refocus on key activities and markets, which led to dwindling balance sheets, beyond the fall of a few leaders the fate of markets was at stake. Frankfurt endured the constriction of several mixed banks, and even Deutsche Bank ended oscillating in 2015–16. Paris and London endured dire years of rebuilding the basis of their leaders, and Barclays gave up its dream of being a global bank. Both cities resisted, and even BNP Paribas took over the Belgian leader Fortis in 2009.

Ambitious schemes were scrubbed away. In all countries the surviving leaders sold affiliates or activities that lacked muscle, rubbing off the myth of an actual universal bank practising universal banking all over the world. Even Barclays launched the sale of its powerful affiliate in Africa, ABSA, in 2016–17.

The geoeconomics of banking became more 'embedded' in traditional and promising markets: Spanish BBVA and Santander (Guillen & Tschoegl, 2008) across the Atlantic in Latin America; HSBC in Asia and Western Europe; Standard Chartered in Asia and Africa; Nomura in Japan and Asia after having failed to revive the activities of Lehman Brothers in Europe in 2008–12. The result of this reshuffling is clear. Even if GE divested its financial services affiliate and Wells Fargo remains a domestic bank, US institutions asserted their strength, through banks, investment banks (Goodhart) and hedge funds.

London kept its edge through its predominance in FOREX (40% market share), market banking (efficient nanosecond exchanges, clearing markets and high-frequency trading), asset management and stock exchanges. It preserved its own judiciary processes, to sanction international banks and bankers that bypassed the rules on the Euribor and Libor markets (Serious Fraud Office). Barclays in 2005–09 managed cartels, in parallel with the sanctions already fixed in 2013 by the European Commission and the US Commodity Futures Trading Commission: the City struggled to preserve its domain against the eurozone. It imposed stricter regulation and taxation to remain the most attractive world location for issuing, clearing and market banking. Other places need to redefine their strong points and adapt their allocation of resources alongside this, to respect the ratios of permanent funds/assets.

The perception of banks or insurance companies as flags of economic patriotism scrambling over all the areas of geo-finance still prevails, but reality and regulation rules are now predominating. No more piracy (off-shore and off-balance sheet), less container ship and lighter cargoes (retail banking, investment banking), and even yachts (private banking) and clippers (mergers and acquisitions banking): the geoeconomy of banking adapted itself to more lucid and balanced management of risks and resources. The idea of a stand-alone corporate and investment bank strategy has been given up by the big banks, like BNP Paribas. Assets are cut (from one fifth to a third) and a refocus on key markets and customers was imposed as a priority to reach the ratios imposed by the *Basel III* rules, all the more for 'systemic banks' along European patterns.

Each market place still fights in favour of its 'champions' and for its attractiveness among talent pools. The association Paris Europlace and the Treasury act in France to entertain a few big banks, asset managers and insurance companies, because, despite cooperation and Europeanisation, each country feels the need to keep a few tools and symbols of its independence. It is an issue of capital of expertise and revenues in commissions, of highly qualified jobs, of technical impacts and of internal platforms of services (Venzin, 2009) to business processes and outsourcing. Mergers and acquisitions teams have had to be transnationalised to accompany the cross-border mergers. More and more technical centres have moved abroad (i.e. India, Singapore). Teams (banking market rooms, means of payments systems) and directions are often a mix of nationalities, with transnational heads.

6 Conclusion

The World Economic Forum (2015) picked up *Seven Challenges to Globalisation* which sums up the challenges of geoeconomics in the mid-2010s, and insisted on 'economic warfare'. Despite so many international institutions contributing to cooperation, competition among currencies, market places, centres of geopolitical power, transnational banks, investment funds, asset managers and insurance companies has been spurred by the restructuring of the overall economy and the balance of power drawn by emerging countries and technological levers of the world. Issues of financial sovereignty and territoriality are still at stake even if the customers of financial institutions are so much globalised. At the moment, no one can anticipate the fate of the balance of banking and financial powers between the city and continental market places when the Brexit process takes place in the coming years.

Bibliography

Bastidon-Gilles, C., Brasseul, J. and Gilles, P. (2010) *Histoire de la globalisation financière. Essor, crises et perspective des marchés financiers internationaux*. Paris: Armand Colin-U.

Biersteker, T. and Eckert, S. (eds) (2007) *Countering the Financing of Terrorism*. London: Routledge.

Bonin, H. (2009) La géographie historique de la finance. In *Géographies de la finance mondialisée*, C. Dupuy and S. Lavigne (eds) Paris: La Documentation française, Les Études, 19–34.

Bonin, H. (2011) *Des banquiers lucides dans le boum et la tempête? (2004–2010)*. Paris: Textuel.

Bonin, H. (2013) Banks and geopolitics: Issues of finance connections. In *Handbook in the Geopolitics of Business*, Joseph Mark Munoz (ed.) Cheltenham and Northampton, MA: Edward Elgar, pp. 125–138.

Brender, A. and Pisani, F. (2009) *La crise de la finance globalisée*, Paris: La Découverte, 'Repères'.

Caprio, G. (ed.) (2012a). *Handbook of Key Global Financial Markets, Institutions, and Infrastructure*. New York: Academic Press-Elsevier.

Caprio, G. (ed.) (2012b). *The Evidence and Impact of Financial Globalization*. New York: Academic Press-Elsevier.

Cassis, Y. (2006). *Capitals of Capital. A History of International Financial Centers, 1780–2005*. Cambridge: Cambridge University Press.

Cassis, Y. and Bussière, E. (eds) (2005) *London and Paris as International Financial Centres in the Twentieth Century*. Oxford: Oxford University Press.

Clark, G.-L. and Wöjcik, D. (2007) *The Geography of Finance. Corporate Governance in the Global Marketplace*. Oxford: Oxford University Press.

Einzig, P. (1931) *The Fight for Financial Supremacy*. London: Macmillan. www.fatf-gafi.org/about.

Epstein, G. (2005) *Financialization and the World Economy*. Cheltenham: Edward Elgar.

Financial Action Task Force (FATF) (2016) *Terrorist Financing. FATF's Strategy on Combating Terrorist Financing*.

Fratianni, M. (2009) The evolutionary chain of international finance centers. In *The Changing Geography of Banking and Finance*, P. Alessandrini, M. Fratianni and A. Zazzaro (eds). London: Springer, pp. 251–276.

Gelpern, A. and Gulati, M. (2008) Innovation after the revolution: Foreign sovereign bond contracts since 2003. *Capital Markets Law Journal* 4(1): 85–103.

Goodhart, C. and Schoenmaker, D. (2016) *The United States Dominates Global Investment Banking: Does it Matter for Europe?* Bruegel Policy Contribution, March, 06.

Gordon, C. and Wöjcik, D. (2007) *The Geography of Finance. Corporate Governance in the Global Marketplace.* Oxford: Oxford University Press.

Guillen, M. and Tschoegl, A. (2008) *Building a Global Bank. The Transformation of Banco Santander.* Princeton, NJ: Princeton University Press.

IMF (2002) Collective action clauses in sovereign bond contracts. Encouraging greater use. www.imf.org/external/np/psi/2002/eng/060602a.pdf.

Mishkin, F. (2013) *Economics of Money, Banking & Financial Markets*, 10th edition. New York: Pearson Series in Economics.

Mosley, L. (2003) *Global Capital and National Governments.* Cambridge: Cambridge University Press.

O'Brien, R. (1992) *Global Finance Integration: The End of Geography.* London: The Royal Institute of International Affairs—Pinters Publishers.

Piolet, V. (2015). *Paradis fiscaux, enjeux géopolitiques.* Paris: Technip.

Plihon, D., Couppey-Soubeyran, J. and Saïdane, D. (2006) *Les banques: acteurs de la globalisation financière.* Paris: La Documentation française.

Rajan, R. (2010) *Fault Lines: Hidden Fractures Still Threaten the World Economy.* Princeton, NJ: Princeton University Press.

Roy, S., Ingo, W. and DeLong, G. (2012) *Global Banking*, third edition. Oxford: Oxford University Press.

Sinclair, T. (2005) *The New Masters of Capital: American Bond Rating Agencies and the Politics of Creditworthiness.* Ithaca, NY: Cornell University Press.

Solberg Soilen, K. (2012) *Geoeconomics.* London: Bookboon.

Unifab (2016) *Counterfeiting & Terrorism, Report 2016.* Paris.

Venzin, M. (2009) *Building International Financial Services Firm. How Successful Firms Design and Execute Cross-Borders Strategies.* Oxford: Oxford University Press.

World Economic Forum (2015) *Geo-Economics. Seven Challenges to Globalisation.* Geneva: Global Agenda Council on Geo-Economics. www.weforum.org.

20 Geoeconomics of the global arms industry

Alexandre J. Vautravers

This chapter will focus on the three trends impacting the economics behind the contemporary global arms market. It aims to link the various themes and areas of research on the arms industry. It will demonstrate that today, many armies are strong only on paper. True power and defence lie with the ability to develop, equip and even export sophisticated weapon systems. The conclusions will show that this can be interpreted as a new form of monopoly of legitimate violence. It replaces the traditional national model on a global scale.

After defining the scope and limitations of this paper, the chapter will first examine the historical origins of the arms industry and the trends since the fall of the Berlin Wall. The chapter will then look at the economic weight and market of the industry today. Third, an exploration of prospects of development will be presented given the rise of new actors in the East.

1 Arms 'silos' and limitations on research

The debate and study on the global arms industry is profoundly segmented—as, for example, research on strategic weapons. It is therefore possible to find studies on the themes of procurement, arms trade (linked to the first), disarmament, ethics and international humanitarian law, foreign military sales and political/military alliances, technology transfer, embargoes, weapons trafficking/smuggling and organised crime, terrorism, technological development, public/private sector economics, defence budgets, gun rights/lobbies and, to be thorough, gender and domestic violence issues. The problem is that little of this *corpus* of research and literature actually interfaces.

This siloed thinking is regrettable because not only are the publications fragmented, but so are research and policies regarding arms production. The conclusions of one thread of research regularly contradict the conclusions of another branch. Activists and policymakers alike often react by mixing issues that have little in common—such as the links between the national production of arms for legitimate self-defence, authorised by the United Nations (UN) Charter in its Article 41, and gun laws, domestic violence and even suicide issues. This chapter will demonstrate that links exist between the different themes listed above. Some of these have strong geoeconomic or geopolitical implications—such as the maintenance of technological 'clusters' in the defence sector—while others are essentially policy or opinion driven.

It should also be mentioned that most literature amalgamates both topics and data from extremely different types of weapons, and therefore arms-manufacturing industries. For the purposes of this research, a distinction between small arms, conventional arms, and strategic weapons or weapons of mass destruction (WMD) is made. Not only are the historical roots of these three industries very different, but so too are the legal regimes under which these weapons fall. It is also noteworthy that there is a large disparity of thought on political and policy issues relating to the transfer and use of weapons. This chapter will demonstrate how the development of the Arms Trade Treaty in the closing days of 2014 has blurred these traditional distinctions even further.

Evidently, the topic of manufacturing and sales in the arms industry is charged with great emotion. Given its assumed weight in armed conflict, national governance and international relations, it should come as no surprise that many authors, researchers and even think tanks are clearly biased and offer argumentation for policy, rather than objective research on the topic. Only a marginal discussion on the ethical or moral aspects of the arms trade will be provided, given the limited scope of this chapter.

The latter point is further exacerbated by the fact that precise data on the arms industry are difficult to obtain. Many arms manufacturers are state owned. They therefore do not necessarily publish their figures openly. They may function in ways that do not conform with the logic of the liberal economy, regarding pricing, for example. Many may work in close coordination with the interests of other public entities. Not to mention the grey areas and black market that exist in such an industry.

It is noteworthy that most 'arms manufacturers' today—even among the state-owned entities—rarely exclusively produce weapons. The vast majority of firms produce civilian manufacturing goods or deliver services, or have diversified in 'dual-use' technologies. It is therefore difficult to completely separate the arms industry from the high-tech sector, IT/electronics, heavy industry, or in other cases shipbuilding. To boycott products or investments of arms-producing firms, one of the recurring objectives of anti-arms trade campaigners, is therefore both unrealistic and dangerous.

2 From sovereignty to interdependence

Describing the roots of today's arms industry would be a research topic in its own right, and owing to the diverse nature of the industry today, its diverse models both economically and regionally speaking, not to mention its opportunistic nature, or the evident links with governments and political will, it is probably a vain effort. There is a preponderance of other issues, such as the lack of regulation, the grey and black markets, or the secrecy that surrounds many arms deals.

Until the Industrial Revolution of the mid-19th century, the arms industry developed in an extremely liberal fashion. There was little regulation, not to mention border controls. Engineers and experienced military officers served other countries as the concept of the 'nation-state' only progressively developed with the French revolutionary wars, and mandatory conscription. Certain European regions—Toledo in Spain, Liège in Belgium, Châtellerault in France, the Rhineland or Bavaria in the German states, Woolwich and Enfield in the UK—became famous for their arms manufacturers and exported widely throughout Europe. These were organised during centuries in a decentralised or domestic system of manufacture (Vautravers, 2001). It should be added that even today, the arms sector is not regulated by the World Trade Organization (WTO) agreements.

The development of the 'nation-states' and large conscript armies led to the creation of royal or state arsenals and manufacturers. This started as early as the 14th century in the area of shipbuilding (Portsmouth). It developed in the 17th century with the development of firearms and especially cannon (Bourges). The development of public arms manufacturing supports Max Weber's theory of 'the monopoly of all legitimate violence'. In the late 19th century, many private producers were organised into factories—led by several dynasties: Krupp, Schneider, Renault—and were increasingly nationalised in the early 20th century. For example, the French 'Popular Front' conducted a substantial and well-documented privatisation campaign starting in 1936 (Giovachini, 2000).

Due to the increase in cost and the pace of technological development, state ownership and funding became increasingly necessary for the development of heavy and high-tech weapons—from tanks to wireless communication. The scale rose to massive proportions during World War II, with the increased involvement of state research laboratories often with the mobilisation of academics and researchers—leading to the development of electronic warfare, cryptology, guided or ballistic missiles and, naturally, WMDs.

From an historical perspective, the first half of the 20th century, during which the majority of arms manufacturers were state owned, can be viewed as parenthetical (Vautravers, 2003). The high cost associated with the maintenance of this industry, even during peacetime when it is by definition working at one third or less of its full wartime capacity, has been one of the drivers of privatisation.

Another strong trend towards interdependence has been the European integration process. This played an important role in the Military Assistance Program that closely supported the Marshall Plan in the 1950s. Strong incentives, military loans and access to military sales, both surplus and fresh from the factories, were provided when European countries joined the North Atlantic Treaty Organization (NATO) and agreed to standardise their hardware. World War II demonstrated that small countries, each with their autonomous command and political leadership, their respective units, procedures, communications, hardware and industry, would not be able to resist uniformed and centrally led Warsaw Pact forces. The model for NATO was the Alliance of 1944–45, in which the member states would only have a choice between the equipment agreed upon jointly. Some measure of specialisation was therefore needed, so as to overcome the redundancies associated with traditional national arms procurement: France was to specialise in the development of lightly armoured vehicles and light tactical fighters, as well as guided missiles; the United Kingdom would specialise in heavy armour, bombers and all-weather heavy fighters; Belgium would develop its traditional industry of small firearms; Italy would develop its small arms and aeronautics industry. When Germany joined NATO, it would be encouraged to develop armoured vehicles.

The gradual decrease in American arms subsidies and the end of the Bretton Woods system led to further integration among European arms developers. It has also led to the purchase of increasing amounts of American hardware—particularly aircraft, ships, artillery and guided weapons. These two trends were exemplified by the increasing number of European joint projects—some more successful than others (Jaguar, Alpha Jet, Tornado, Milan, FH77)—and the large number of US-designed combat aircraft purchased by European aircraft-producing nations in the 1970s (Phantom, Starfighter, Bronco, Tiger, Falcon). It could be argued that the latter managed to redress the transatlantic balance of payments, since at that time the USA was suffering a twin deficit. In other words, the European countries paid back the Marshall Plan during the 1970s–80s.

Under stress from the lack of European agreements, and from US sales pressures, the French and British arms manufacturers have increasingly turned to Southern, Middle Eastern or Asian markets in order to find outlets for their products, to lengthen their production runs and therefore amortise their development costs. Some weapons have even been designed specifically for the export market. Nationalisation and sovereignty have now given way to privatisation, interdependence and trade.

3 The global arms industry and the West

This trend was reinforced by the end of the Cold War, given the reduction in military budgets and the professionalisation of most European armies—forcing these countries to spend the vast majority of their budget on wages, when most of it used to be devoted to procurement. The reduction in the size of these professional armies has also made national arms production increasingly inefficient. Indeed while technological progress is making most weapon systems obsolescent in five to ten years when they could remain in frontline service for a decade or two during the Cold War, keeping up with technical innovation while producing ever smaller runs of *matériel* has become economically ruinous. The French example is telling: the Leclerc main battle tank (MBT) and the Rafale multirole fighter have suffered over a decade of delays, and their unit cost has substantially risen in this time—without even counting the costs associated with having to financially support the national manufacturers during all of this time.

Several European firms have encountered these challenges and have either consolidated, or merged under the pressure of their national governments. Others have diversified and, eventually, sold their arms subsidiaries. The early 1990s saw a substantial reshaping of the US arms sector under President Bill Clinton—epitomised by the Boeing/McDonnell Douglas merger in 1995. This was followed by a European-wide effort, culminating in the establishment of the European Aeronautic Defence and Space Company (EADS) in 2000. Despite these waves of mergers, armament production has largely remained decentralised and in its traditional manufacturing basins. Evidently, social and political pressures are essential to maintain employment in these areas and political lobbying has therefore substantially increased (Vautravers, 2015).

A third wave of consolidation took place under the presidency of George W. Bush. Today, the ten largest global arms manufacturers generate 58% of the revenue of the 100 largest producers. This totalled only 39% in 1990. Of these 100 largest firms in 1991, only 19 are left today. At the same time, the global defence market has risen from US$126 billion in 1991 to $192 billion in 2000, and $419 billion in 2010 (Dehoff & Dowdy, 2013).

While the restructuring in the USA has considerably diminished the number of systems under development and in service, such rationalisation has not taken place in Europe yet. While in the USA only a single combat aircraft is being developed, and two types of 'legacy' aircraft are still being produced, in Europe at least four types have been developed in parallel. The politicisation of these programmes, and the implications for these governments' autonomy in matters of foreign policy and military intervention, has meant that the UK and Italy have had to spend vast amounts of their procurement budget for the European joint programmes (i.e. the Eurofighter Typhoon) while at the same time making provision for the transatlantic F-35 Joint Strike Fighter (Vautravers & Foppiani, 2011).

The escalation of costs of individual weapon systems has meant that most European countries are no longer autonomous in arms production, or even in the capacities that they own. Belgium and the Netherlands have foregone all their MBTs and rely on international cooperation, should their troops need support on the ground.

Arms exports—in turnover volume—are essentially in the hands of five countries: the USA, Russia, Germany, France and the United Kingdom. Together, they represented 77% of the exports between 2004 and 2008 (SIPRI, 2016). This share has gone down to 74% during the 2009–13 period, due to the rise of exports in emerging countries and due to Russia's substantial increase in arms exports, rising from 24% to 27%. In this context, German exports have sunk from 10% to 7%. France has gone down from 9% to 4%. British exports have gone down from 4% to less than 3% in the last four years.

4 Markets moving East

The West's lack of investment and disarmament policies has, since the 1970s, promoted exports and foreign sales. In recent years, this scenario led to donations to former Eastern countries as well as North African or Middle Eastern nations. During the oil crisis and the 'détente' period, the USA, UK and France became increasingly dependent on foreign sales to develop their own national weapon systems. The design of major programmes such as the British Challenger tank, or the US Kidd-class destroyers, were originally destined for Middle Eastern customers. The 1970s oil crisis also fuelled a considerable arms race in the Persian Gulf. For two decades, the oil-rich Gulf states have been the main outlet, both for state-of-the-art weapons to be tested by proxies, and for second-hand equipment to be liquidated from the producer's inventories.

At the same time, emerging nations such as Brazil, Russia, India, China and South Africa (the BRICS) are expending considerable effort to develop their own national arms industry. They are trying to become more autonomous and using the development of sophisticated weapon systems (guided missiles, armoured fighting vehicles, combat aircraft) as a matter of national pride and sovereignty. It can be argued that these efforts have proven costly and only marginally successful, as demonstrated by several high-end aircraft programmes, such as the Japanese F-2 or several types of Indian MBTs. It is observable that dependency on key technologies, developed by the Western-led consortia mentioned above, and supported by the USA, NATO or Russia, has overall increased. Evidently, the interdependence of military capabilities, industrial capacity and foreign policy decisions, and cooperation and multinational/combined operations is a current reality.

While most developing countries today have the capability of producing small arms—often replicas or adaptations of Kalashnikovs, former Soviet designs, or a number of Western weapons produced under licence—only a handful have developed truly national designs. During the 1960s, several countries developed industrial capacities for the maintenance, licenced production and upgrade of conventional weapon systems, such as tanks or aircraft. It is from these capacities that many countries have been able to design and build their own heavy and sophisticated weapons in the 1980s and 1990s. In some cases, factories were relics from the British Commonwealth or the Warsaw Pact—as in Canada, India or most Central European countries. Embargoes have also encouraged many developing countries to develop these capabilities: from China to North Korea, Iran or even South Africa. In other cases, strategic political decisions to lower the dependency on Western arms suppliers have led to a determined and often costly effort. Successful examples include Israel, Brazil, South Korea, Turkey or Singapore.

The jump from conventional arms production to the development of strategic arms, or 'proliferation', is encouraged not only by national pride and the desire for autonomy and independence. In many cases an existential threat by large and powerful neighbours, coalitions or superpowers, can only be opposed by a military alliance or by the possession of WMDs—in particular nuclear weapons. As these are in a league of their own, and their usefulness has been the subject of much debate, this issue will not be pursued in this chapter. Suffice it to say that nuclear weapons, without their appropriate vectors—which are in principle conventional weapons: bombers, missiles or artillery systems, for example—may be relegated to a sheer symbolic or rhetorical value.

In 2010, Asia superseded the Middle East as the largest spender on and importer of arms. The tensions and arms race between India and Pakistan are not new, but in the last decades, they have spread from conventional to small arms, and more recently to strategic weapons as well. A new arms race can be seen developing between China and other Asian aspiring regional powers. This has resulted in increased spending in both Koreas, Japan, Australia, Vietnam, Thailand and the Philippines, without even having to mention Taiwan.

This shift, in the context of the ruinous global 'war on terror' waged in the Middle East, has encouraged a US strategic shift—turning away from counterinsurgency, stabilisation or 'small wars' to a renewed focus on conventional conflicts and weapons. Indeed, the USA is trying to oppose a military-political coalition to the development in China of advanced multi-role air superiority fighters, potentially stealth aircraft, as well as half a dozen types of guided missile destroyers, capable of providing escort to a carrier battle group.

5 Geoeconomic perspectives

It is evident in this chapter that the global arms market is increasing—in particular in the area of conventional arms. Defence budgets are rising globally and in Asia in particular. For the first time since the fall of the Berlin Wall, even European defence budgets are increasing again, in real terms and as a percentage of their gross domestic product (GDP). Interdependence will increase in the West, in parallel with political integration in Europe. In times of hardship, international tension and armed conflict at its borders, the significance of European countries possessing key strategic military capabilities, and the ability to sustain them through development, retrofit and production, will gain in significance.

If the periodicity of disarmament and rearming phases is confirmed, the next decade should see substantial increases in procurement—if only to replace the large fleets of platforms, from MBTs to radios, designed for the most part before the end of the Cold War. The substantial quantities of hardware still available may constitute the object of many retrofit programmes in the developing world, but such programmes will be as costly as the purchase of newer systems, while never able to rival them in terms of performance, precision, protection or stealth.

The next decade will see an increase in the offer of light and conventional weapons, given the development of arms industries in several developing countries. The supremacy of the large arms-producing nations, however, will not be challenged, owing to the fact that they also offer military training, intelligence and, in many cases, political support and legitimacy to their clients. It can be argued that China will gain in strategic as well as political and economic influence. It is joining the 'club' of countries able to sell a comprehensive range of arms, from simple firearms to highly complex weapon systems, while at the same time possessing a strategic wildcard, in the form of a *veto* in the UN Security Council.

The numbers published regularly and followed closely by activists and research institutions (Stockholm International Peace Research Institute (SIPRI), Federation of American Scientists, Organisation for Economic Co-operation and Development) are perhaps of limited value, given that they posit the arms industry can be studied as any other item of trade. Ranking countries on their foreign military sales only reflects the quality of their industry: a single stealth F-35 fighter naturally costs more than hundreds of thousands of small arms imported from a developing nation. Politically and strategically, however, these high prices can be justified by the situation of dependency and the partnerships they create.

The increasing unit cost of weapon systems and the emphasis on network-enabled operations and network-centric warfare, computers and C4ISTAR (command, control, communications, computers, intelligence, surveillance, targeting, acquisition, reconnaissance), will support the trend of growing interdependence between Western countries within NATO, but will also make client states increasingly strategically dependent. The establishment of stricter regulation on the international arms trade will also make developing countries more politically and economically dependent on their suppliers. This can be seen as the foundation of a new monopoly of legitimate violence, on a global scale and in the hands of the 'international community'—or the few who are powerful and influential enough to speak in its name.

References

Dehoff, K. and Dowdy, J. (2013) *Managing a Downturn: How the US Defense Industry Can Learn from the Past*. McKinsey & Company. www.mckinsey.com/client_service/public_sector/latest_thinking/mckinsey_on_government/mckinsey_on_defense.

Giovachini, L. (2000) *L'armement français au XXe siècle*. Paris: Ellipses.

SIPRI (2016) The five largest exporters of major conventional weapons (2004–2008 and 2009–2013) and their main recipients (2009–2013). books.sipri.org/product_info?c_product_id=475 (last accessed 27 March 2016).

Vautravers, A. (2001) L'innovation dans le secteur de l'armement en Suisse: Marchés publics, sociétés mixtes. In *Innovations. Incitations et résistances—Des sources de l'innovation à ses effets*, H.J. Gilomen, B. Veyrassat and M. Müller (eds) Bern: Chronos.

Vautravers, A. (2003a) L'Innovation dans le secteur de l'armement en Suisse: Marchés publics, sociétés mixtes. In *Innovations. Incitations et résistances—Des sources de l'innovation à ses effets*, H.J. Gilomen, B. Veyrassat and M. Müller (eds) Bern: Chronos.

Vautravers, A. (2003b) Mondialisation et armements: la parenthèse nationale. In *Expansion—Intégration—Invasion. La globalisation, aspect central du changement économique et social depuis le Moyen Age*, H.J. Gilomen, B. Veyrassat and M. Müller (eds) Berne: Chronos.

Vautravers, A. (2004) *L'Armement en Suisse, de 1850 à nos jours. Carrefour des armées, de la politique et de l'économie.* University of Geneva. PhD dissertation.

Vautravers, A. (2015) Fighting for oil in the skies: The case of the KC-X Tanker Program (Boeing vs. EADS). *Journal of Transatlantic Studies*, Special Edition: Aviation.

Vautravers, A. and Foppiani, O. (2011) The joint strike fighter: Between technological challenges, political-industrial competition, and reality. *Crossroads* 10(1). www.webasa.org/pubblicazioni/crossroads2011-1.pdf (last accessed 27 March 2016).

21 The new geoeconomics of energy

A Saudi Arabian case study

Robert E. Looney

1 Introduction

In recent years, geoeconomics has re-emerged as a promising approach in understanding national economic policymaking (Blackwell & Harris, 2016). In contrast to geopolitics which adopts more of a realist approach, and is more concerned with the interaction between a state's policies and the geographic context in which they occur, geoeconomics is based more on neomercantilism and focuses on the interaction between economic strategies and economic power (Du Plessis, 2013). Also, in sharp contrast to geopolitics with its emphasis on military capacity as a source of national power, geoeconomics associates national power with economic strength.

In this regard, the standard geoeconomic assessment of oil producers (Claes et al., 2015) envisions a country's economic power as stemming from its hydrocarbon reserves, accumulated wealth, and the ability to extend this power through market manipulation and/or financial means. Of course, other elements (Hsiung, 2009) such as human and technological resources, and competitiveness can be included for a more comprehensive picture. Ultimately, however, any attempted measure of geoeconomic power, and ranking of countries' relative strength on this dimension, will be inherently arbitrary. Also limiting our ability to gauge the level of or changes in the amount of geoeconomic power possessed by a country at any time is the fact that it is a concept of stressing a potential capability, often never used.

On the other hand, there is no question as to when the occasional adoption of geoeconomic policies has taken place. The massive amounts of financing (Parasie & Soloman, 2015) provided by Saudi Arabia (and other Gulf oil producers) to Egypt following the Arab Spring overthrow of Hosni Mubarak in January 2011 led many observers to conclude that the Kingdom had started to use its vast financial resources to shape the region, direct political developments and mold strategic relationships (Khan, 2014). A closer look at Saudi policy actions over time, however, suggests the Kingdom has selectively turned to its geoeconomic strength to compensate for its much lesser military strength (Chauvin, 2010). For years, this arrangement defined the Kingdom's relationship with the USA (Council on Foreign Relations, 2015).

If they could be quantified, the likely measures of geoeconomic power in Saudi Arabia and other major energy-producing countries would be much more volatile than comparable figures for countries with more diversified economic structures. For example, in the current context of depressed oil prices, geoeconomic scores (based on oil revenues and reserves) of major oil producers, especially in the developing and emerging worlds, would have undergone a sharp reduction.

Saudi Arabia, for example, is highly dependent on oil revenues for its government budget, and while the country does have abundant financial reserves, amounting to US$623 billion at the end of 2015 (Al-Khatteeb, 2015), these are being depleted at a fairly rapid rate with no end in sight. Specifically, by the end of 2015 Saudi Arabia's Monetary Agency had withdrawn $70 billion (Bianchi, 2015) in funds managed by overseas financial institutions. The Kingdom's foreign reserves had also fallen by almost $73 billion since oil prices slumped (Ali, 2015). The International Monetary Fund has warned (IMF, 2015) that if this trend were to continue, the Kingdom would be bankrupt by 2020.

The view that Saudi Arabia has suffered a major decline in its geoeconomic power is reinforced by the fact that the country's swing producer status, and thus the country's ability to influence oil prices, has been transferred to US shale producers (Godoy, 2015). Other factors said to reduce Saudi Arabia's geoeconomic power include the likely worldwide reduction in oil use stemming from concerns over global climate change, the slowing of the world economy below its long-term trend and the slow-down in Chinese economic growth, all reducing the future demand for oil.

On the supply side, abundant shale deposits in the USA and other countries will conceivably put a price cap on oil, perhaps as low as $40 a barrel (Kumar, 2016). These developments, along with Saudi Arabia's security commitments, have led one observer to ask '[h]as there ever been an oil state as overleveraged at home and overextended abroad?' (Cooper, 2016). This quote harks back to an earlier observation by King Faisal in the early 1970s before the oil boom that 'just in a single generation the country had moved from riding camels to riding Cadillacs … the next generation could be riding camels again' (Osman, 2013).

In the sections that follow, it is argued that the conventional view of declining Saudi Arabian geoeconomic strength capable of securing short-run gains in oil prices, revenues and regional stability provides an incomplete depiction of reality. In its place, a new geoeconomics of energy is developed. While recognizing the short-run elements of national power emphasized by the conventional geoeconomics, the new geoeconomics stresses the ability of a country to pursue policies in its long-run interest even when it appears to be losing its short-run geoeconomic leverage. In contrast to the conventional assessment of Saudi Arabia's geoeconomic decline, the new geoeconomics, by considering geoeconomic power from an inter-temporal perspective, contends that recent developments in world oil markets have temporarily enhanced

Saudi Arabia's geoeconomic power, enabling the Kingdom to fundamentally alter its development strategy.

2 The Saudi Arabian setting

In geoeconomic terms, Saudi Arabia has been a paradox over the years. The country's austere Wahhabi sect of Islam contrasts sharply with the highly advanced corporate efficiency of its gigantic state-owned oil company, Saudi Aramco. It is a country of enormous wealth, but often has an unemployment rate for Saudis of 15 to 24 years of age reaching 30% (Murphy, 2011). While its government has spent billions to upgrade the educational system and improve the country's human capital, private employers still complain that the lack of a qualified Saudi workforce keeps them almost entirely dependent on foreign labor (Gulf Business, 2013).

Given the country's lack of democracy, widespread corruption, massive income disparity and small monarchial elite linked to a fundamentalist religious establishment, Saudi Arabia seemed primed, at the time of the Arab Spring, for instability and revolution. Yet, thanks largely to its geoeconomic strength, and the ability of officials to use this effectively, the Kingdom did not become another Arab Spring casualty.

The Saudi Arabian government's response to the 2011 encroaching threat of the Arab Spring dramatically illustrates the flexibility provided by the country's geoeconomic strength. The government's approach entailed a massive expansion in government spending and the size of the state sector in the economy. The bulk of the stimulus spending went to wage increases for workers in the public sector, critical infrastructure upgrades, housing, utilities, health and education (Wigglesworth, 2011).

The cost in new spending for 2011 alone is estimated at $50 billion, with total expenditures adding up to at least $130 billion over several years (Wigglesworth, 2011). The government followed these initiatives with steps to strengthen the regime's traditional alliance with the Wahhabi religious establishment by providing additional support for the religious police and missionary work abroad.

Another sign of the Kingdom's geoeconomic strength is that the country stepped up assistance to countries like Jordan, Bahrain, Oman and Egypt, which are considered critical to regional stability. The Egyptian case is particularly insightful. A week after Mubarak stepped down, Saudi Arabia announced the establishment of a development bank to help the Egyptian economy recover and orient it toward long-term investments. One month later, the Saudis agreed to lend the country $4 billion in emergency funding, which included a $1 billion deposit to Egypt's Central Bank (Oxford Business Group, 2012).

While the government's massive spending increases may have kept the Arab Spring at bay, little was done to free up the political system or address broad-based concerns regarding corruption—both of which fueled Arab Spring uprising in other countries (Winter, 2013). Because of its stepped-up public spending since 2011, the government is likely to find itself locked into higher levels of outlays that are unsustainable over time.

Even when oil prices appeared to be stabilizing at over $100 a barrel, there were serious concerns that, given the Kingdom's longer-run fiscal capacity, the country's traditional development was not sustainable. In 2011, Brad Borland, head economist of Jadwa Investment in Riyadh, starting with realistic assumptions concerning future oil prices, developed a stark view (Jadwa Investment, 2011) of the country's fiscal future. Specifically, the Jadwa forecast noted that if current population and domestic consumption trends continued, there would be less oil for future export without a massive increase in new exploration and development of very high-cost fields, which an increasingly cash-strapped Saudi Aramco might not be able to afford.

Barring any major upheavals or wars, the Jadwa forecast concluded the country was unlikely to face major fiscal constraints in the next decade. This picture changed dramatically over the longer term, as rapidly increasing domestic energy usage was expected to impact exports sharply at around the same time as Saudi Aramco's production levels were expected to level off or begin declining.

Looking into the future from its 2011 vantage point, Jadwa's assessment concluded it was possible for the Kingdom to avoid a fiscal crisis, but doing so would require draconian and widely unpopular policy reforms, such as removing energy subsidies. Even more difficult, the country would have to find a way to increase its share of global oil production, perhaps at the risk of breaking up the Organization of the Petroleum Exporting Countries (OPEC).

As for OPEC, Jadwa saw the battles between Saudi Arabia and Iran becoming more contentious every year, with Saudi Arabia's push to expand oil production repeatedly met by Iranian resistance. As it stood in 2011, Jadwa felt Saudi Arabia had some sway in OPEC because of its excess capacity, but the difficulty and cost of bringing new production online might cause this leverage to vanish in the not-too-distant future.

The Jadwa model sheds considerable light on the factors underlying the 2014 oil price collapse. It also goes to the heart of Saudi Arabia's geoeconomic power, and the Kingdom's willingness to use that power to maintain its longer-run growth path.

3 The 2014 oil price collapse

The 2014 oil price decline was one of the more dramatic market events in recent years. In June 2014, the price of oil was around $115 a barrel. By December, the price had declined by more than 40% to slightly below $70 a barrel. Despite several short rallies, by March 2016 the price had declined to around $40 per barrel or by more than 70% below its June 2014 price (Krauss, 2016).

A number of factors contributed to this decline. In particular, demand was falling off faster than anticipated, and the shale boom in the USA was increasing oil supplies much more quickly than had been previously forecasted.

In this new oil market setting, OPEC appears to have concluded it was in the cartel's best interests to abandon its traditional goal of supporting the price of oil. In its place, OPEC opted for maintaining its market share. No doubt this changed position reflected the cartel's concern over lost market share to producers, especially shale benefiting from the higher oil price provided by OPEC, but not incurring the costs of the necessary production cut-backs.

As of March 2016, oil prices have seen little inclination to return to their June 2014 levels. The Economist Intelligence Unit was forecasting an average of $40 a barrel through 2016, rising to $67.50 in 2018 (Economist Intelligence Unit, 2016). Other major forecasts were all in this range. In early 2016, there was still a considerable surplus of oil on the market with US output declining by 0.3 mb/d y/y, but Iran's output was steadily rising and predicted to reach pre-sanctions levels by Q3 2016.

4 Saudi motivations

If one of the Saudi motivations in refusing to cut production was to use its geoeconomic power to maintain the Kingdom's market share by crippling US shale production and development, then its actions must be considered a qualified success. Low current and anticipated future prices and short investment horizons are causing many new developments to be put on hold. Rig (oil and gas) count keeps falling. It stood at 476 on March 18, 2016, compared to 1,069 one year earlier (American Oil and Gas Reporter, 2016). Near-term output data are starting to show activity decline. In December 2015, production fell by 80,000 b/d compared to November, the first decline since 2008. It fell a further 70,000 b/d in January 2016. Average production is forecast at 8.7 mb/d in 2016, and 8.5 mb/d in 2017, compared with 9.4 mb/d in 2015 (Ausick, 2016). Supporting the market share theory, Saudi Aramco, for purely geoeconomic reasons, has been undertaking a major investment program (Claes et al., 2015) to expand the Kingdom's productive capacity and share of the global oil market (Reuters, 2015).

5 Declining geoeconomic power

Saudi Arabia's industrial strategy entailed the development of a wide variety of hydrocarbon-based industries. While good for the Kingdom's diversification goals, this strategy may result in increasing constraints on Saudi Arabia's ability to use its hard-won geoeconomic power. Specifically, production cuts might result in feed-stock shortages for these industries forcing expensive temporary shut-downs for lack of critical input. In addition, there is a good chance the Kingdom's geoeconomic power to maintain a favorable range of oil prices may be on the decline.

As noted earlier, the original 2011 Jadwa forecasts suggested Saudi finances would remain viable under reasonable assumptions concerning oil prices.

Beyond that, the country will face a long-run fiscal deterioration. Even as government expenditures rise to accommodate a much larger population and honor past commitments, oil exports and revenues will decline due to increased domestic oil usage, domestic fuel subsidies and the rising costs of bringing new oil to market. Given this, Jadwa estimates an escalation in oil prices per barrel from $90.7 in 1995 increasing to $175.1 in 2025 and $321.7 by 2030 simply to balance the government's budget.

The 2015 price was considerably below the forecasted requirement for a balanced budget. Barring a major supply interruption, and given the development of shale resources in the USA and around the world, given their cost structure and ability to quickly begin production on a scalable level, oil prices above $50 a barrel, the marginal costs of efficient producers and production levels (Harder, 2016) sufficient to meet global demand may be the new oil price ceiling.

Summing up, the new realities in global oil markets, specifically the shift from oligopolistic to competitive environments, brought on by shale, will erode much of Saudi Arabia's geoeconomic power. The Kingdom will remain a major producer, but will largely lose control over influencing global oil prices. This fact, combined with diminishing returns to its traditional development model and the likelihood the Kingdom will be unable to amass reserves comparable to the levels reached before the 2014 oil price collapse, dictates the Kingdom will need to shift its development strategy if the country hopes to continue its prosperity into the future.

6 Strategy for the future

As it contemplates reforms, the Saudi royal family can expect to face a number of challenges. The first set centers on the issues fueling the Arab Spring uprisings in other parts of the region: unemployment, housing shortages, and Shiite unrest. The second set, which will largely define the ability of the Saudi government to respond to these threats, involves the great uncertainty over the government's longer-run fiscal capacity. In charting out a new development strategy for the Kingdom, it is first necessary to recognize that many of the country's domestic problems, both economic and political, stem from the nation's demographics. The country's population has grown from around 15 million in 1990 to over 31 million in 2015 (World Bank, 2016). While not particularly high by international standards, these demographic changes create a major problem in an emerging economy whose comparative advantage is in capital-intensive petroleum and petrochemicals, where job creation does not progress in line with overall growth. The limited potential of the country's agricultural sector, which would ordinarily absorb many of the new entrants to the labor force, is a further complication. In addition, Saudi Arabia's educational system has not effectively responded to the needs of a modern, private sector economy, leaving most graduates sorely under-skilled.

The government has addressed the country's skills shortages through subsidizing university education for large segments of the population (Ottaway, 2012). Unfortunately, this approach has fallen short of expectations due to the poor quality of most degrees (Nolan, 2011). Significantly, 90% of Saudis currently in prison have university degrees (Chatham House, 2011).

As noted previously, unofficial figures suggest that youth unemployment is as high as 30%. This fact has so far been obscured by the safety nets provided by strong family networks and the state—a situation that is unsustainable. In the short run, the government's attempts to address unemployment have centered on the 'Saudization' (Looney, 2004) of the private sector, an approach that attempts to persuade domestic employers to substitute Saudi workers for often much less expensive foreign workers. In the longer run, the government is making massive investments in infrastructure and, more specifically, the creation of 'new economic cities.'

While Saudization programs have gone through a number of refinements over the years, they have never lived up to their promise of creating broad-based employment opportunities for the Kingdom's young and rapidly growing workforce. Specifically, the original Saudization plans called for replacing nearly 320,000 foreign workers with Saudis between 1995 and 2000. Instead, the foreign workforce expanded by 58,400 during this time. In the early 2000s, Saudi Arabia's consultative legislature, the Shura Council, decreed Saudi nationals must comprise 70% of the country's workforce by 2007 (Randeree, 2012). As of 2016, Saudis still account for less than 10% of private sector employees (Haider, 2016).

Rather than create jobs for Saudis through substitution for foreign workers, an alternative approach is to create new jobs. In this regard, the 'new economic cities' program initiated in 2007 has much greater potential for creating jobs for Saudi workers. The program builds on the success of Jubail and Yanbu, industrial cities created from scratch in the 1970s. These cities have been responsible for the successful development of downstream industries, such as petrochemicals. To date, the two cities have created 107,000 jobs and 233 industries, many of which are major exporters.

The 2007 'new cities' (Thorold, 2008) program aims to replicate these earlier successes on a bigger and faster scale, this time with an emphasis on preparing Saudi Arabia for a post-oil future. The new cities are to propel the Kingdom to the next level of development—a knowledge-based economy much less dependent on oil revenues. Each city will have a mix of industries designed to diversify the economy and generate jobs. Based on an initial fiscal commitment of $400 billion, the program is designed to create a broad spectrum of private sector investments.

The new cities program is especially important given Saudi Arabia's grim future fiscal outlook noted above. The cities offer the opportunity of a transition away from a state-centric development model dependent on massive public expenditure, to one relying more on private sector investment and job creation.

The implications are clear. The Saudis face a rapidly closing window to transition to an economy less dependent on oil and more capable of self-sustained, job-creating growth. The good news is the new cities program could potentially kick in before the more painful effects of fiscal crisis set in.

7 Conclusions

Using the country's geopolitical power in the conventional sense worked well for Saudi Arabia over the years. Saudi's spare capacity and its role in affecting oil prices created a relatively stable and lucrative world oil market in which the Kingdom could thrive. As with most models, however, changing circumstances and environments gradually weakened the country's geoeconomic-based development model. To continue the country's prosperity, the Kingdom will need to transition from its current public sector-led economic model to one that is fundamentally market-based. More openness and competition are needed to force improvements in productivity and a more efficient allocation of the Kingdom's resources.

These changes will shift the Kingdom from a patrimonial to an entrepreneurial society. This will not be an easy or smooth transition and could take several generations to complete (Looney, 2016). However, the country's recent use of its remaining geoeconomic power—preserving the Kingdom's oil market share—has at least bought the country time to make these necessary changes. Without this transition the Kingdom would have likely been trapped in a downward spiral of very limited geoeconomic power, increased indebtedness, falling rates of investment and expanding rates of unemployment.

References

Ali, A. (2015) IMF: Saudi Arabia running on empty in five years. *Al Jazeera*. Accessed at www.aljazeera.com/news/2015/10/imf-saudi-arabia-151022110536518.html.

Al-Khatteeb, L. (2015) *Saudi Arabia's Economic Time Bomb*. Brookings Institution. Accessed at www.brookings.edu/research/opinions/2015/12/30-saudi-arabia-economic-time-bomb-alkhatteeb.

American Oil and Gas Reporter (2016) U.S. rig count. Accessed at twitter.com/TheEIU/status/710421964876226561.

Ausick, P. (2016) U.S. oil production to fall by almost a million barrels a day by 2017. *24/7 Wall Street*. Accessed at 247wallst.com/energy-economy/2016/01/12/us-oil-production-to-fall-by-almost-a-million-barrels-a-day-by-2017/.

Bianchi, S. (2015) Saudi Arabia withdrew billions from markets estimates show. Bloomberg. Accessed at www.bloomberg.com/news/articles/2015-09-28/saudi-arabia-has-withdrawn-billions-from-markets-estimates-show.

Blackwell, R.D. and Harris, J.M. (2016) The lost art of economic statecraft. *Foreign Affairs*. Accessed at www.foreignaffairs.com/articles/2016-02-16/lost-art-economic-statecraft.

Chatham House (2011) The political outlook for Saudi Arabia. Accessed at www.chathamhouse.org/publications/papers/view/178077.

Chauvin, N.M.D. (2010) *The Rise of the Gulf: Saudi Arabia as a Global Player.* Konrad Adenauer Stiftung. Accessed at www.kas.de/wf/en/33.19450/.

Claes, D.H., Goldthau, A. and Livingston, D. (2015) *Saudi Arabia and the Shifting Geo-Economics of Oil.* Carnegie Endowment for International Peace. Accessed from carnegieendowment.org/2015/05/21/saudi-arabia-and-shifting-geoeconomics-of-oil/i8vv.

Cooper, A.S. (2016) How Saudi Arabia turned its greatest weapon on itself. *The New York Times.* Accessed at www.nytimes.com/2016/03/13/opinion/sunday/how-saudi-arabia-turned-its-greatest-weapon-on-itself.html?_r=0.

Council on Foreign Relations (2015) CFR backgrounder: U.S.-Saudi relations. Accessed at www.cfr.org/saudi-arabia/us-saudi-relations/p36524.

Du Plessis, F. (2013) *US Shale Gas Boom, Geo-economic Implications for the US and Russia.* Mindmekka Publications. Accessed from www.academia.edu/11933420/.

Economist Intelligence Unit (2016) Structural shifts. Accessed at twitter.com/TheEIU/status/710421964876226561.

Godoy, E. (2015) Shale drives uncertain new geoconomics of oil. Inter Press Service. Accessed at www.ipsnews.net/2015/10/shale-drives-uncertain-new-geoeconomics-of-oil/.

Gulf Business (2013) Saudi Arabia needs to provide job skills to its youth. Accessed at www.gulfbusiness.com/articles/analysis/saudi-arabia-needs-to-provide-job-skills-to-its-youth/.

Haider, S. (2016) Standard work contract soon. *Saudi Gazette.* Accessed at saudigazette.com.sa/saudi-arabia/standard-work-contract-soon/.

Harder, C. (2016) Shale sector hampered in role of producer. *Wall Street Journal.* Accessed at blogs.wsj.com/moneybeat/2016/03/15/shale-sector-hampered-in-role-of-swing-producer-energy-journal/.

Hsiung, J.C. (2009) The age of geo-economics, China's global role, and prospects for cross-strait integration. *Journal of Chinese Political Science* 14, 113–133.

IMF (2015) *Regional Economic Outlook: Middle East and Central Asia.* Accessed at www.imf.org/external/pubs/ft/reo/2015/mcd/eng/pdf/menap1015.pdf.

Jadwa Investment (2011) *Saudi Arabia's Coming Oil and Fiscal Challenge.* Riyadh: Jadwa Investment.

Khan, M. (2014) *The Gulf and Geoeconomics.* The Atlantic Council. Accessed from www.atlanticcouncil.org/blogs/menasource/the-gulf-and-geoeconomics.

Krauss, C. (2016) Oil prices: What's behind the drop? Simple economics. *The New York Times.* Accessed at www.nytimes.com/interactive/2016/business/energy-environment/oil-prices.html.

Kumar, D.K. (2016) U.S. shale's message for OPEC: Above $40, we are coming back. Reuters. Accessed at www.reuters.com/article/us-usa-oil-shale-idUSKCN0W20JH.

Looney, R. (2004) Saudization: A useful tool in the Kingdom's battle against unemployment? *Journal of South Asian and Middle Eastern Studies* 27(3): 13–33. Accessed at calhoun.nps.edu/bitstream/handle/10945/40857/Rel_JSAMES_04_article.pdf?sequence=1.

Looney, R. (2016) *Lengthy Oil Slump Could Force Saudi Arabia's Hand on Economic Reforms.* World Politics Review. Accessed at www.worldpoliticsreview.com/trend-lines/17769/lengthy-oil-slump-could-force-saudi-arabia-s-hand-on-economic-reforms.

Murphy, C. (2011) *Saudi Arabia's Youth and the Kingdom's Future.* Washington, DC: Woodrow Wilson International Center. Accessed at www.wilsoncenter.org/sites/default/files/Saudi%20Arabia%E2%80%99s%20Youth%20and%20the%20Kingdom%E2%80%99s%20Future%20FINAL.pdf.

Nolan, L. (2011) *Managing Reform? Saudi Arabia and the King's Dilemma*. Doha: Brookings. Accessed at www.brookings.edu/~/media/research/files/papers/2011/5/saudi-arabia-nolan/05_saudi_arabia_nolan.pdf.

Osman, T. (2013) *The Saudi Spring*. Project Syndicate. Accessed at www.project-syndicate.org/print/tarek-osman-on-saudi-arabia-as-a-constitutional-monarchy.

Ottaway, D.B. (2012) *Saudi Arabia's Race Against Time*. Washington: Wilson Center. Accessed at www.wilsoncenter.org/sites/default/files/saudi_arabias_race_against_time.pdf.

Oxford Business Group (2012) *The Report: Egypt 2012: Economy*. Accessed at www.oxfordbusinessgroup.com/egypt-2012-0.

Parasie, N. and Solomon, J. (2015) Gulf states pledge aid to Egypt, U.S. balks. *The Wall Street Journal*. Accessed from www.wsj.com/articles/gulf-states-pledge-additional-12-billion-in-aid-to-egypt-1426262660.

Randeree, K. (2012) *Workforce Nationalization in the Gulf Cooperation Council States*. Doha: Georgetown University School of Foreign Service. Accessed at repository.library.georgetown.edu/bitstream/handle/10822/558218/CIRSOccasionalPaper9KasimRanderee2012.pdf?sequence=5.

Reuters (2015) Saudi Aramco reiterates it will spend to keep leading oil position. Accessed at www.reuters.com/article/saudi-arbn-oil-plans-idUSL5N0Y24WR20150512.

Thorold, C. (2008) New cities rise from Saudi desert. BBC. Accessed at news.bbc.co.uk/2/hi/middle_east/7446923.stm.

Wigglesworth, R. (2011) Saudi Arabia: Spend it while you can. *Financial Times*. Accessed at blogs.ft.com/beyond-brics/2011/12/27/saudi-arabia-spend-it-while-you-can/.

Winter, L. (2013) *Jordan and Saudi Arabia After the Arab Spring*. Ft Leavenworth, KS: Foreign Military Studies Office. Accessed at fmso.leavenworth.army.mil/documents/Jordan-Saudi-Arabia-After-Arab-Spring.pdf.

World Bank (2016) *World Development Indicators*. Accessed at databank.worldbank.org/data/reports.aspx?source=world-development-indicators.

22 Global water geoeconomics

Paradigm shift and emerging challenges

Lakshmi Mudunuru and J. Uma Rao

1 Introduction

Water is indispensable for human survival. Its scarcity had begun to be felt during the middle of the last century and the warning bells are ringing louder now. Accessible freshwater is 0.1% of the total freshwater and 0.003% of the total of all water on the planet (Golay, 2009).

This quantity of water has not changed over several thousands of years but the population has grown manifold (Iyer, 2001). Further, the Himalayan glaciers are severely affected due to global warming. Unless we act quickly there is the danger of a severe drinking water shortage (Gore, 2006).

In addition, there are wide spatial and temporal variances in its availability and demand (David-Harden et al., 2007). The United Nations predicts that by 2025, 1.8 billion people will be facing absolute water scarcity (Lovelle, 2015). The world's aquifers are being depleted at an unsustainable rate (Agarwal & Narain, 2005).

Nations, realizing its critical importance, have been working out strategies for securing, protecting and conserving their water resources, but face one reality—water knows no boundaries. There are 263 rivers around the world that cross the boundaries of two or more nations, and an untold number of international ground water aquifers. The catchment areas that contribute to these rivers comprise approximately 47% of the land surface of the Earth, include 40% of the world's population, and contribute almost 80% of fresh water flow (Wolf, 2009). So, countries must and do share water, which influences their economic and political relations with one another.

2 Water and international relations

River water sharing can have both internal and external (international) dimensions, such as the USA sharing the waters of the Colorado River with Mexico and several states sharing the waters allocated to the USA among themselves (Richards & Singh, 1996). In fact, internal compulsions can impact a country's stance on sharing its waters with other countries; for example, in India the state of West Bengal insists on having a say on the country sharing the Ganges' water with Bangladesh.

The other side of the coin is Pakistan's insistence on rigorously adhering to the terms of the Indus Treaty about the quantum of waters to be shared. Any concession in this regard could not only raise national tempers in Pakistan but could facilitate many projects to be taken up in Kashmir which would improve relations between that state and India, which, it is believed, Pakistan perceives to be against its interests (Iyer, 2005). In some instances, water is used as a bargaining chip (Karaev, 2005).

The relative geological location also has a bearing on the water-sharing relationships between countries, i.e. the 'upper riparian-lower riparian' geopolitics of international rivers (Linnerooth, 1990). States may sometimes link water issues to other issues (Katz & Fischhendler, 2011).

Water could determine relations between many countries in Asia. China controls the Tibetan plateau, the source of most major rivers of Asia (*The New York Times*, 2007) and this is a cause of concern in many Asian countries. The cordial relations between countries can be adversely affected by water issues, as between Turkey and Iraq (Turunc, 2011).

Existing political differences may sometimes make water sharing very difficult. For example, India's relations with China and Nepal.

There have also been instances where water has been shared in a mutually beneficial manner (Wolf, 2003). Water issues can be multi-dimensional which makes their resolution all the more difficult (Abhukhater, 2002). Established regional water hegemonies are being questioned, resulting in conflict (Rahman, 2011). Finally, water has the potential to bring about revolutions (International Committee of the Red Cross, 2015).

2.1 River water sharing—conflicts and resolution

A river water conflict starts when a country that shares a river basin with another starts building development projects within its own territory, on the commonly shared river, without consulting the other country. This leads to objections from the other country, creating tensions and regional instability.

However, international water disputes get resolved. Where treaties have been entered to resolve water disputes, they have stood the test of time—even treaties between bitter enemies. These treaties provide for joint management, surveys, sharing of information, water allocation, dispute mechanisms, etc. The Mekong Committee has functioned since 1957. The Indus River Commission functions although wars have occurred between India and Pakistan. The ten countries sharing the Nile are negotiating over cooperative development of the basin (Wolf, 2009).

2.2 Water and the legal regime

The growth of non-navigational uses of international watercourses, many of which were 'consumptive' in nature, increased the likelihood that different states' uses would conflict with one another. For example, one state's dam could interfere with another's navigation or flood its territory; development of extensive irrigation by an upper riparian may leave insufficient water for a lower riparian's established or prospective uses; water discharges from an upstream state's pulp mill may harm a downstream country's fishery; agricultural or industrial pollution could entirely destroy a river's ecosystem; and so forth. Increasingly, therefore, questions arose as to the rights and duties of states in the event of such conflicts (McCaffrey, 2010).

There is no binding water law or effective institutional mechanism to resolve international water disputes. The 1997 Law of the Non-Navigational Uses of International Watercourses, which gives priority to the use of international watercourses to satisfy basic human needs, including the provision of safe drinking water and water required for basic subsistence food production, could not come into force, as it did not get the necessary ratifications. Hence theories, principles and treaties govern the field.

Theories, principles and treaties in vogue are:

- Equitable Utilization Theory: according to this theory, water is to be equitably utilized. What is equitable is a difficult question and has to be decided on a case-by-case basis with specific reference to the facts of each case.
- Equitable Apportionment Theory: it does not lend itself to precise definition, but in essence it postulates that water resources have to be shared equitably, but not equally.
- The Helsinki Rules, 1966: these rules have commanded a large degree of approval, adopted as the basic principle of the equitable utilization of the waters of an international drainage basin (Shearer, 1994).

3 International treaties

As there is no binding water law or effective institutional mechanism to resolve international water disputes, nations have had to enter into treaties, bilateral or multilateral (Brownlie, 2008).

The Transboundary Freshwater Dispute Database project, including an online collection of 145 of these treaties, shows that the legal management of transboundary rivers is still in its conceptual infancy (Wolf, 2001).

3.1 Trade in water

> The capital intensity and economies of scale associated with surface water supply have profound economic and social implications. They foster public provision of a surface water supply rather than individual, self-provision.
>
> (Hanemann, 2006, p. 75)

The relatively high cost of transporting a unit of water compared to its actual price has discouraged any significant bulk transfers of water thus far except in a very few areas. The Australian Stock Exchange is in the process of conceptualizing the idea of forming a futures market to sell abstraction rights in Australia (Kouyoumijian, 2012).

Environmental economist Richard Sandor predicted a US water futures market (Medill, 2015). International trade in bottled drinking water and beverages exists but is very small from a volume perspective and is irrelevant. Bulky international water trade hardly exists (Hoekstra, 2010). What instead happens is acquisition of water rights and virtual trade in water.

3.2 Virtual water trade

Virtual water is the volume of water used to produce a commodity and so is virtually embedded in it. When this commodity is exported, the water associated is exported and when it is imported, the water is imported. Water-stressed countries in the Middle East and North Africa import water-intensive crops and virtual water and so reduce their demand for water. Export of water-intensive commodities, on the other hand, raises national water demand and could add to water scarcity. This happens in the USA and Australia.

Trade patterns can thus influence patterns of water use and scarcity. It is estimated that international trade reduces global water use in agriculture by about 5% (Hoekstra, 2010).

The USA, Canada, Thailand, Argentina and India are the top virtual water exporters, and Sri Lanka, Japan, the Netherlands, Republic of Korea, and China are the top five water importers (Hoekstra & Hung, 2002). The water footprint is the sum of the internally used water resources of a country plus its virtual water imports, minus its virtual water exports. This figure could be used to determine the trend in world water resources usage (World Water Council, 2004).

4 Water—two ideologies

The right to water and the right to sanitation were recognized implicitly in the Universal Declaration of Human Rights of 1948, in the International Covenant on Economic, Social and Cultural Rights of 1966 and in Article 6 of the International Covenant on Civil and Political Rights which enshrines the Right to Life.

The first explicit recognition of the right to water at an international level was made at the United Nations Water Conference, at Mar del Plata in 1977. Constitutions of many countries like Bolivia, Uruguay and South Africa have explicitly incorporated this into their respective constitutions (Golay, 2009).

Is water an economic commodity, or is it a human right not subject to commodification? The Dublin Principles, at the 1992 International Conference on Water and the Environment say that water should be recognized as an economic good (Hanemann, 2006).

It is argued that only the market forces can bring supply and demand into harmony and only pricing will drive water use down and reduce water scarcity (David-Harden et al., 2007). The other view says water belongs to the Earth and all species, and therefore must not be treated as a private commodity to be bought, sold, and traded for profit; global freshwater supply is a shared legacy, a public trust, and a fundamental human right, and therefore a collective responsibility (Petrella, 2007).

The combination of increasing demand and shrinking supply has attracted the interest of the global corporations that want to sell water for a profit (Barlow & Clark, 2011). It is said that the privatization brigade is led by huge transnational corporations which started their efforts with water systems in Third World countries where they wanted to pose as saviors (David-Harden et al., 2007).

It is reported that the Wall Street banks and multibillionaires are buying water all over the world (Yang, 2016). Companies like True Alaska that own the rights to vast stores of water may charge what the market can bear, and spend as little as they can get away with on maintenance and environmental protection. With energy, or food, customers have options. There is no substitute for water (*Newsweek*, 2010). Privatization of water has broader implications than simple efficiency. For example, water needed for agriculture may be transferred to industry where it may be more effectively used and may fetch a better price (Cullet, 2009). The debate rages over the future of water.

5 Pricing and conservation of water

All over the world, water is still owned by the state and supplied free (Hanemann, 2006). Most Irrigation Acts in India have implicitly presumed the absolute rights of the state over water resources (Saleth, 1994). Water is treated differently from other commodities, say oil, coal, or other minerals. The prices that most users pay for water include only the cost of its supply (Hanemann, 2006). Cost of a vital element—scarcity of water—is not included as a part of its price and in the price of goods produced with it (Hoekstra, 2010). A consciousness of the scarce and precious nature of this resource is hardly likely to be fostered by free supply (Iyer, 2003).

Free supply of water in agriculture, which accounts for two-thirds of the world's water use, leads to inefficient use of water. Pricing water closer to its cost is central to water conservation (Postel, 1997). In India, the world's third largest food producer, charges are nominal and do not influence farmers' decisions (Postel, 1997). The entrenched view of ground water as a private source has led to widespread development of ground water markets (Moench, 1998). According to the International Water Management Institute, a quarter of India's harvest could be lost in the near future because of aquifer depletion (Barlow & Clark, 2011). The situation is no better in many advanced countries (Postel, 1997).

Water prices in urban areas too must be raised to include all elements of its cost. Taxing excessive groundwater pumping is another option (Postel, 1997), but some provision must be made for supplying water required for meeting minimum personal needs at affordable cost.

Raising water prices will be a politically unpopular decision but cannot be shirked. The public must be made aware of the need to use water efficiently and to conserve it. Practical and beneficial methods of water conservation can be designed (Postel, 1997).

6 Pollution and climate change

The present rates of water pollution all over the planet and the resultant climate change will have a profound effect on the world's water systems; many water bodies will see increased water flows before they are drastically reduced. The present water resources of many countries as well as the problems they face will change, which will upset the present political and economic relations.

Serious efforts have begun to address pollution and environmental issues and to give international water law a broader perspective within a legal framework more attuned to sustainable development and water shortage than hitherto (Birnie & Boyle, 2004). Societies need to 'buy' disaster insurance by investing in the protection of watersheds, floodplains, and wetlands (Postel & Mastny, 2005).

Bolivia's proposal to the United Nations to accept a Universal Declaration of the Rights of Mother Earth along the lines of the Universal Declaration of Human Rights, could lead to a serious rethinking of standard environmental laws and approaches towards maintaining a balance between humans and nature (*Economic and Political Weekly*, 2012).

7 Need for a global perspective on water

Water issues today have implications that cross national or basin boundaries. Further, the democratization of information about water trends, urban stress and emerging issues has led to a paradigm shift. It calls for a global outlook towards water, with an understanding of the local, regional and national concerns. Thus, water issues are global as well as local. Hence, stakeholders play a significant role in deciding global water futures. The following are important:

- Global climate change induced by human activity at the local level.
- Local water pollution affects waters of other nations.
- The increasing presence of multinationals in the drinking-water sector.
- National plans for inter-basin water transfers involving two or more nations.
- Virtual water trade and savings made possible by it.
- The effects of water footprints of one nation on another.

Water's increasing tendency to become a geopolitical resource will influence the power equation among nations (Hoekstra, 2006).

8 Conclusion

So what needs to be done?

- At the global level

  1 An agreement on all-inclusive water pricing that covers the full cost of water.
  2 A water label for water-intensive products to make consumers aware of its water history.
  3 A disposal tax on goods that cause water pollution, to cover associated costs.
  4 Regulations about maximum allowable levels of water use.
  5 A business code for water multinationals.

(Hoekstra, 2006)

The imbalance between international trade agreements and the absence of international agreements on sustainable water use means trade disputes hold sway over the water conversation. This imbalance must be corrected.

At the national and regional levels water policies must factor in virtual water trade (Hoekstra, 2010).

- At the national and regional levels:

  1 Identifying and utilizing skilled, experienced and impartial negotiators for resolution of disputes.
  2 Parties to the disputes must be patient and be willing to support the long process of negotiations.
  3 Ensuring that the riparians themselves drive the negotiation process.
  4 Strengthening water resource management institutions between nations to provide the necessary institutional framework.
  5 Involving all stakeholders—nongovernmental organizations, farmers and indigenous groups in the resolution process.
  6 Creation of an international body for the resolution of water conflicts must be contemplated seriously.

(Wolf et al., 2006)

Surface water and ground water are part of the hydrological system. Ground water availability is very much affected by the availability of surface water and hence an integrated approach is necessary (Sripada, 2003). The 'public trust doctrine,' a legal principle which means that though the state has absolute sovereignty over its territory, such sovereignty cannot be used to the detriment of its own people, is relevant. While the public trust doctrine reflects the internal dimension, customary international law reflects the principle of 'good neighborliness'—i.e. states have a duty to other states (Postel, 1997). Adequate water for personal needs must be made a fundamental right.

If globalization is the corporate-driven agenda, an agenda for corporate control, then localization is the countervailing people's agenda for protecting the environment, survival and livelihood (Shiva, 2005a). Local communities should have incentives to conserve and maintain water resources. Community rights must be established for ecological sustainability and also to usher in a more democratic rights regime (Shiva, 2005b). The scholarly work of Elinor Ostrom, who was awarded the Nobel Prize in Economics in 2009, on how communities cooperate to share resources lies at the heart of the debates today about resource use, the public sphere and the future of the planet (Walljasper, 2011).

References

Abhukhater, A. (2002) On the cusp of water war: A diagnostic account of the volatile geopolitics of the Middle East. *Peace and Conflict Studies* 17(2): 377–419. Retrieved January 11, 2016 from nsuworks.nova.edu/pcs/vol17/iss2/4/?utm_source=nsuworks.nova.edu%2Fpcs%2Fvol17%2Fiss2%2F4&utm_medium=PDF&utm_campaign=PDFCoverPages.

Agarwal, A. and Narain, S. (2005) *Dying Wisdom: Rise, Fall and Potential of India's Water Harvesting Systems.* New Delhi: Centre for Science and Environment.

Barlow, M. and Clark, T. (2011) *Blue Gold: The Fight to Stop the Corporate Theft of the World's Water.* New Delhi: LeftWord Books.

Birnie, P. and Boyle, A. (2004) *International Law and the Environment*. New York: Oxford University Press.

Brownlie, I. (2008) *Principles of Public International Law.* New York: Oxford University Press.

Cullet, P. (2009) *Water Law, Poverty and Development—Water Sector Reforms in India*. New York: Oxford University Press.

David-Harden, A., Naidoo, A. and Harden, A. (2007) *The Geopolitics of the Water Justice Movement*. Retrieved January 19, 2016 from www.bradford.ac.uk/social-sciences/peace-conflict-and-development/issue-11/PCD-Issue-11_Article_Water-Justice-Movement_Davidson-Naidoo-Harden.pdf.

Economic and Political Weekly (2012) If mountains and rivers could speak. *Economic and Political Weekly* 47(2): 9.

Golay, C. (2009) *The Right to Water*. Retrieved January 5, 2016 from www.cetim.ch/legacy/en/documents/report_6.pdf.

Gore, A. (2006) *An Inconvenient Truth*. New York: Rodale Inc.

Hanemann, W.M. (2006) The economic conception of water. In *Water Crisis: Myth or Reality?* P.R. Peter, M.L. Ramon and M.L. Luis (eds) London: Taylor and Francis Group, pp. 61–91.

Hoekstra, A.Y. (2006) The global dimension of water governance: Nine reasons for global arrangements in order to cope with local water problems. Retrieved February 1, 2016, from waterfootprint.org/media/downloads/Report_20_Global_Water_Governance_1.pdf.

Hoekstra, A.Y. (2010) *The Relation between International Trade and Freshwater Scarcity.* Retrieved December 17, 2015 from www.wto.org/english/res_e/reser_e/ersd201005_e.pdf.

Hoekstra, A.Y. and Hung, P.Q. (2002) *A Quantification of Virtual Water Flows between Nations in Relation to International Crop Trade.* Retrieved December 20, 2015 from waterfootprint.org/media/downloads/Report11.pdf.

International Committee of the Red Cross (2015) Bled dry: How war in the Middle East is bringing the region's water supplies to breaking point. Retrieved January 30, 2016 from www.icrcproject.org/app/water-in-middle-east/PDF/executive-summary.pdf.

Iyer, R.R. (1999) India three treaties conflict-resolution: Three river treaties. *Economic and Political Treaty* 34(24): 1509–1518.

Iyer, R.R. (2001) Water charting, a course for the future-I. *Economic and Political Weekly* 36(13): 1116.

Iyer, R.R. (2003) *Water Perspectives, Issues and Concerns.* New Delhi: Sage Publications.

Iyer, R.R. (2005) Indus Treaty: A different view. *Economic and Political Weekly* 40(29): 3140–3144.

Karaev, Z. (2005) Water diplomacy in Central Asia. *Middle East Review of International Affairs* 9(1): 63–69. Retrieved March 1, 2016 from www.rubincenter.org/meria/2005/03/karaev.pdf.

Katz, D. and Fischhendler, I. (2011) Spatial and temporal dynamics of linkage strategies in Arab–Israeli water negotiations. *Political Geography* 30(1): 13–24. Retrieved December 24, 2015 from sites.hevra.haifa.ac.il/katzd/wp-content/uploads/sites/49/2015/01/katz-fischhendler-2011-linkage-strategies-in-Arab-Israeli-water-negotiations.pdf.

Kouyoumijian, M. (2012) *Selling Water in the Futures Market: In Search of a Spot Price in the UK.* Retrieved November 15, 2015 from www2.cirano.qc.ca/~kouyoumm/pdf/other1.pdf.

Linnerooth, J. (1990) The Danube River Basin: Negotiating settlements to transboundary environmental issues. *Natural Resources Journal* 30 (Summer), 629–660. Retrieved November 23, 2015 from lawschool.unm.edu/nrj/volumes/30/3/10_linnerooth_danube.pdf.

Lovelle, M. (2015) *GRACE Satellite Mission Indicates Global Groundwater Diminishing*. Retrieved January 10, 2016 from www.futuredirections.org.au/publication/grace-satellite-mission-indicates-global-groundwater-diminishing/.

McCaffrey, S.C. (2010) *The Law of International Watercourses.* New York: Oxford University Press.

Medill (2015) Sandor predicts a U.S. water futures market. Retrieved Medill Reports Chicago on November, 18, 2015 from news.medill.northwestern.edu/chicago/sandor-predicts-a-u-s-water-futures-market/.

Moench, M. (1998) Allocating the common heritage—Debates over water rights and governance structure in India. *Economic and Political Weekly* 33(26), A-46–A-53.

Newsweek (2010) The race to buy up the world's water. Retrieved from www.newsweek.com/race-buy-worlds-water-73893.

The New York Times (2007) Averting water wars in Asia. Retrieved November 23, 2015. www.nytimes.com/2007/06/26/opinion/26iht-edchellany.1.6335163.html.

Petrella, R. (2007) *The Right to Water Results from the Right to Life.* Retrieved January 13, 2016 from www.cmo.nl/epa-uk/pdf/source_5_water_is_a_human_right.pdf.

Postel, S. (1997) Implications of public policy. In *Last Oasis: Facing Water Scarcity.* New York: W.W. Norton & Co. Retrieved March 5, 2016 from southeastaquatics.net/resources/pdfs/Implications%20for%20Public%20Policy%20by%20Postel.pdf.

Postel, S. and Mastny, L. (2005) *Liquid Assets: The Critical Need to Safeguard Freshwater Ecosystems*. Retrieved February 17, 2016 from www.worldwatch.org/system/files/WP170.pdf.

Rahman, M.A. (2011) *The Geopolitics of Water in the Nile River Basin*. Retrieved January 2, 2016 from www.deqebat.com/pdf006/NILE_Basin_01.pdf.

Richards, A. and Singh, N. (1996) *Two Level Negotiations in Bargaining over Water*. Retrieved November 11, 2015 from people.ucsc.edu/~boxjenk/waterisi.pdf.

Saleth, R.M. (1994) Towards a new water institution—Economics, law and policy. *Economic and Political Weekly* 29(39), A-147–A-155.

Shearer, I.A. (1994) *Starke's International Law*. New York: Oxford University Press.

Shiva, V. (2005a). *Earth Democracy: Justice, Sustainability and Peace*. New York: South End Press.

Shiva, V. (2005b). The first and the last commons. *Yojana* 49(6): 6–8.

Sripada, S. (2003) Legal aspects of ground water management in India. *Andhra University Law Journal* 4(1).

Turunc, H. (2011) *Turkey's Global Strategy: Turkey and Iraq*. Retrieved December 6, 2015 from eprints.lse.ac.uk/43503/1/Turkey's%20Global%20Strategy_Turkey%20and%20Iraq(lsero).pdf.

Walljasper, J. (2011) *Elinor Ostrom's 8 Principles for Managing a Commons*. Retrieved March 15, 2016 from www.onthecommons.org/magazine/elinor-ostroms-8-principles-managing-commmons.

Wolf, A.T. (2001) Water and human security. *Journal of Contemporary Water Research and Education* 118(1): 29–37.

Wolf, A.T. (2003) *Conflict and Cooperation: Survey of the Past and Reflection for the Future*. Retrieved November 29, 2015 from webworld.unesco.org/water/wwap/pccp/cd/pdf/history_future_shared_water_resources/survey_water_conflicts_cooperation.pdf.

Wolf, A.T. (2009) A long term view of water and international security. *Journal of Contemporary Water Research & Education* 142(1): 67–75. Retrieved February 12, 2016 from onlinelibrary.wiley.com/doi/10.1111/j.1936-704X.2009.00056.x/pdf.

Wolf, A.T., Kramer, A., Carius, A. and Dabelko, G.D. (2006) *Water Can Be a Pathway to Peace, Not War*. Retrieved January 21, 2016 from www.wilsoncenter.org/sites/default/files/NavigatingPeaceIssue1.pdf.

World Water Council (2004) *Virtual Water Trade—Conscious Choices*. Retrieved January 21, 2015 from www.worldwatercouncil.org/fileadmin/wwc/Programs/Virtual_Water/virtual_water_final_synthesis.pdf.

Yang, J. (2016 [2012]). The new 'water barons': Wall Street mega-banks are buying up the world's water. Retrieved January 20, 2016 from www.globalresearch.ca/the-new-water-barons-wall-street-mega-banks-are-buying-up-the-worlds-water/5383274.

23 The geoeconomics of aging

Masud Chand

The combination of declining birthrates and rising life expectancies in most countries of the world is leading to a major global demographic transformation. This transformation combines a decrease in the relative number of the young, while simultaneously seeing an increase in the relative number of the old. Taken together, these trends are causing an unprecedented aging of populations worldwide.

Aging refers to a situation where the median age of a country/region rises due to prolonged life expectancy and/or declining birth rates. While aging is taking place across most countries of the world, it has been more apparent in developed countries so far. The pace of aging is accelerating, and the absolute numbers of senior citizens in developing countries are predicted to outstrip those in developed countries by 2025. By 2050, the worldwide population of people over 60 will reach 2 billion. Three fourths of them will be residents of developing countries (UN, 2009; Australian Institute of Health and Welfare, 2012; Hayutin, 2007). The pace of this change means that emerging economies will have much briefer periods to adjust and establish the infrastructure and policies necessary to meet the needs of their rapidly shifting demographics. It also means that unlike developed countries, they might need to cope with getting old before they get rich (World Economic Forum, 2012).

We start by explaining the importance of aging and the reasons behind the aging process globally. We then study the causes and effects of aging in a number of regions in the world. We look at the world's largest economic entity and one of the regions worst affected by aging, the European Union (EU). We examine the situation in what is currently the most aged country in the world, Japan. We study the world's single largest national economy (not adjusted for purchasing power parity—PPP), the USA. We also study the four BRIC economies, Brazil, Russia, India and China. We then synthesize some themes that emerge from our analysis and conclude by pointing out the geoeconomic implications of our findings for governments and societies.

1 Importance of aging

Aging populations lead to a number of challenges for businesses, societies, and governments, including slowing economic growth, poverty among the elderly, issues of generational equity because of rising wealth transfers from the working age to the retired population, inefficiency in labor markets as the labor supply gradually decreases, and unsustainable pension and public transfer systems as the dependency ratio (the ratio of the non-working to the working population) rises (Chand & Tung, 2014). Over time, these changes can cause major shifts in the geopolitical situation worldwide, as rapid aging combined with differential aging rates in different regions lead to a situation where different countries' growth rates and populations stagnate or start declining at different rates.

By 2050, in some fast-aging European countries such as Germany, Spain, and Italy, the share of the elderly population will be over 35%, while in industrialized Asia-Pacific countries like Japan, South Korea, and Singapore, it will be approaching 40% (Center for Strategic and International Studies, 2011; World Economic Forum, 2012). The World Economic Forum has pointed to aging as one of the five major global risks in the coming decades, and the National Intelligence Council (2012) has identified aging as one of the four key 'megatrends' that will shape the world in 2030.

2 Reasons for aging

There are three major drivers of aging that together are driving the trend toward aging worldwide. These are as follows (World Economic Forum, 2012):

- *Declining fertility*: the world's total fertility rate—that is, the number of children born per woman—fell from 5 children per woman in 1950 to roughly 2.5 today, and is projected to drop to about 2 by 2050. As families have fewer children, the older-age share of the population naturally increases.
- *Increased longevity*: globally, life expectancy increased by two decades since 1950 (from 48 years in 1950 to 1955 to 68 years in 2005 to 2010), and is expected to rise to 75 years by 2050.
- *Falls in mortality rates came before falls in fertility*: in the early phases of demographic transition, large cohorts were born and survived mainly because mortality, especially among children, tended to decline before fertility fell. Those cohorts are now reaching working age and older ages, and their ranks will swell. However, as fertility rates subsequently fell, the size of the follow-up cohorts shrank. In developed countries in particular, post-World War II baby-boom cohorts are reaching older ages, with fewer younger-aged cohorts following.

We now take a look at the causes and effects of aging in different parts of the world.

3 Aging across different regions

The EU has one of the lowest fertility rates in the world at about 1.6. However, this rate includes significant differences across member countries. These range from a near replacement level of 2.1 in some Northern European and Scandinavian countries, to a rate of 1.3 in some Central and Southern European countries. Given this regional disparity, we look at examples of four large EU economies from different regions: Germany, the largest country in the EU; Spain, one of the largest countries in Southern Europe which also had Europe's longest period of right-wing dictatorship; Poland, the largest post-communist Central European country; and the UK, the largest Northern European country.

3.1 Germany

Germany has one of the lowest fertility rates in Europe, at about 1.4 children per woman. For population demographers, 1.4 is a key fertility number—at this rate, the population of a country will drop by half in 50 years. Within Germany, the former East Germany had the lowest rate in Europe. Germany has one of the highest rates of childlessness in the world, and the child-free lifestyle has become widely accepted. The results of the Population Policy Acceptance Survey show that people in Germany have very low desired fertility, and this is mostly due to the high share of those who would like to remain child free (Dorbritz, 2008; Kotowska et al., 2008).

3.2 Poland

Poland also has a very low fertility rate, similar to Germany's at 1.4. Women in Poland are still young mothers relative to women in other EU countries and usually have their first child before reaching 30 years of age. However, increasingly most women are choosing to have only one child. The fertility rate has stabilized since about 2003, after falling continuously since the fall of communism in 1990 (Hoorens et al., 2011). The lower fertility rate might be explained by the decrease in the number of married couples, as well as the increasing age of marriage.

3.3 Spain

Spain had one of the highest fertility rates in Europe in the 1960s to 1970s, reaching nearly three children per mother. However, starting in the mid-1970s, fertility rates experienced one of the steepest drops in all of Europe, reaching a low of 1.15 children in 1998 (Grant et al., 2004; Delgado et al., 2008). Although the fertility rate has not risen above the replacement level of 2.1 children per woman since 1981, it has seen a slight increase since 1998 and now stands at just under 1.5 children per woman, far short of the replacement level.

Under Franco, traditional family values were imposed upon Spanish society, with women restricted to traditional roles within the household, large families encouraged, and contraception and divorce prohibited. In the post-Franco era, family decisions were left to individuals. Factors responsible for the low birth rate include the increasing opportunities in education and employment available to women after the Franco era, the higher proportion of women in the workforce, protracted adulthood and changing cultural values (such as increasing secularization and delayed age of marriage).

3.4 UK

Among all the countries in the EU, the UK has had one of the largest turnarounds in total fertility rates since 2001. The fertility rate declined to a low of 1.6 in 2001, but has since rebounded strongly to 2.0 in 2009. The government emphasis on increasing employment in the 1980s and 1990s was coincident with continued falling fertility rates; the subsequent increases in public spending on free education and childcare, increases in income for low-earning families through the working family tax credit, and increases in the length of maternity leave, are associated with the period of rising fertility rates since the early 2000s (Hoorens et al., 2011).

Overall, in the EU, by 2030, the working-age population is expected to contract in nearly all European countries. For example, the European Foresight Platform predicts that by 2025, there will be only three people employed for every retired person in the EU compared to four employed persons today. By 2050, this number is expected to drop further to only two people employed for every retired person. Together, these changes would mean that European countries increasingly need to gear their economies and societies for an older and possibly shrinking population.

3.5 Japan

Japan has one of the highest proportions of elderly citizens in the world—in 2015, they accounted for 25.9% of the population (Statistics Japan, 2016). The Japanese Health Ministry (2011) estimated that Japan's population will decrease by 25% from 127.8 million in 2005 to 95.2 million by 2050. In Japan, there were 9.3 people under 20 for every person over 65 in 1950; by 2025 this ratio is forecast to be 0.59 (UNC, 2011).

A number of factors have contributed to the trend toward small families: high costs, late marriage, increased participation of women in the labor force, small living spaces, education about the problems of overpopulation by the government in Japan's postwar boom period, and the high costs of child education (*The Economist*, 2011). United Nations (UN) demographers project that Japan needs between 13 million to 17 million new immigrants by 2050 in order to prevent a collapse of its existing pension system; however, in the past 25 years, only 1 million foreigners have been allowed in as immigrants

(Bloom & Canning, 2007; Population Reference Bureau, 2008). The rapid aging of Japan and its corresponding shrinking population could have major geopolitical consequences as younger emerging economies rapidly overtake the Japanese economy and cut into its competitive advantage.

3.6 USA

From the post-World War II period, the USA was unusual among industrialized countries in having a relatively high fertility rate near or above the replacement rate of 2.1. European countries, as previously discussed, were typically below that rate, sometimes far below it. However, figures from 2012 reveal that since the great recession of 2008–09, the fertility rate in the USA has dropped sharply, to about 1.9, below that of countries like Sweden, France, and the UK (*The Economist*, 2012). This could be because losses of income during the recession compounded by the housing crisis have caused young people to postpone marriage and having children.

3.7 Brazil

Brazil has undergone one of the most dramatic demographic shifts over the past 50 years. The fertility rate has been reduced from six children per woman on average to fewer than two. The latest figures show that the fertility rate stands at just over 1.8 children per woman (World Bank, 2012). The declining fertility rate stems from the country's rising standard of living and the urbanization of its population (Foley, 2000; Deaton & Paxson, 1994; Longman, 2004). Demographers also point to the influence of the hugely popular soap operas in that country that glorify small families. In the most popular of Brazil's *telenovelas* these days, the characters are often rich and urbane and have few children, if any at all (Foreno, 2012). This puts increasing pressure on the welfare state that Brazil is beginning to build.

3.8 Russia

The population of Russia peaked at about 150 million in 1991, just before the breakup of the Soviet Union. Russia has a combination of low birth rates, and abnormally high death rates unseen in any other developed country which caused Russia's population to decline at a 0.5% annual rate, or about 750,000 people per year, from the mid-1990s to the mid-2000s. The UN warned in 2005 that Russia's then population of about 143 million could fall by a third by 2050 if trends did not improve (Eke, 2005). Russia has among the highest rate of abortions in the world, which could be contributing to the low fertility rates. Official statistics put the number of abortions at 989,000 compared to 1.7 million births in 2010, though unofficial sources put the figures for Russian abortions much higher (Haub, 2011).

3.9 China

Between 1982 and 2012, China's total fertility rate fell from 2.6 to 1.56, well below the replacement rate. This was partly as a result of the one-child policy that was introduced in 1978 and implemented in 1979. Because very low fertility can become self-reinforcing, with children of one-child families often wanting only one child themselves, China probably has to contend with a long period of low fertility, regardless of what happens to its one-child policy (*The Economist*, 2012). While the government scrapped the policy in 2016, the very low fertility rates will most likely persist especially in the richest parts of the country, because of changing lifestyles and increasing child-rearing costs. According to the UN, China's population will fall from 1.34 billion in 2010 to below 1 billion by 2060, assuming the fertility rate does not recover (UNC, 2011).

China is aging at an unprecedented pace. Because fewer children are born as the overall population grows older, its median age will rise to 49 by 2050, compared to the US forecast of 40. This trend will have profound financial and social consequences. It means that China could have a bulge of pensioners before the country has developed the means of looking after them. Unlike the situation in the developed world, China might grow old before it gets rich (*The Economist*, 2012).

3.10 India

India is the only BRIC country whose population is not aging rapidly. Its fertility rate of 2.58 means that it has a growing and relatively young population, which is forecast to overtake that of China by about 2022 (Basu, 2007). There is, however, a wide variation of fertility across states. States in the north have fertility rates in excess of 3.5 (similar to rates in Ghana, Nigeria, or Laos), while states in the south have rates of about 1.9 (similar to that of Sweden) (*Times of India*, 2012).

India expects to reach the population stabilization fertility rate of 2.1 at 1.65 billion by about 2060, caused mainly by the slower than expected fertility decline in the northern states (Population Reference Bureau, 2011). As large cohorts of young Indians enter the workforce, in the coming decades India should reap the benefits of the demographic dividend—a situation where a large cohort faces the twin benefits of smaller subsequent cohorts (because of declining fertility) and a small elderly cohort (because of previously high mortality rates).

4 Policy measures to improve fertility rates

In response to the continuing decline in birthrates, leaders of several industrialized and emerging economies have proposed financial incentives to encourage women to bear more children. Numerous types of policies have been proposed and implemented: direct cash bonuses for having children (Singapore, Russia), allowances for stay-at-home parents (Germany, France), generous paid maternity leave and job security policies for parents (France, Norway, Sweden), state-sponsored matchmaking services (Singapore), fertility treatments (South Korea), relaxing the limits on the number of children allowed (China), and limits on working hours and overtime for parents with young children (Japan) (Chand & Tung, 2014).

5 Looking to the future

An increasingly older population: globally, we will see a rise in the proportion of the elderly in the population both in absolute and relative terms. In the 25 years from 2002 to 2027, the elderly population of China will increase from 7% to 14% of its total population, while Japan's will rise from 20% in 2010 to 38% by 2050 and South Korea's from 9% to 38% between 2005 and 2050 (UNC, 2011; Japanese Ministry of Internal Affairs and Communications, 2012). This could have important geopolitical consequences, since the elderly population, unlike its preceding cohorts, will be one of the richest and healthiest in human history, and could drive consumption and investment patterns for the rest of the economy. Government expenditures in aging countries would shift from areas such as education and infrastructure to healthcare and welfare for the elderly.

Divergence fertility rates in the EU could lead to viability issues: the significant variation in the demographic outlook across Europe could pose a serious threat to the economic and political viability of the EU, since fast-aging countries with lower fertility levels will tend to have shrinking working-age populations while simultaneously having to support higher social expenditures for their elderly. Thus while the population of Northern Europe stays relatively stable, and the dependency ratios rise modestly, Southern and Central Europe will soon see falling populations, rapidly shrinking working-age populations, and fast-rising dependency ratios. Together, these changes could mean that these countries will have a hard time funding their social welfare systems, without either a large rise in taxes or a cut in services. Since both of these options are politically unpalatable, they may require more wealthy and relatively younger Northern European countries to aid them further. Since this is most likely unacceptable to Northern European countries, this divergence of fertility rates, if left unchecked, could in fact lead to further strains on the unity of the EU (Chand & Tung, 2014).

Immigration challenges: countries with projected labor shortages could partly manage the challenge by allowing greater immigration. However, even in these countries, there is still widespread concern about the cultural impact that large-scale immigration could have. For example, in Germany, increasing concerns are being expressed that Turkish immigrants have not integrated into German society but have chosen to establish their own parallel social systems (Chand & Tung, 2014). Fears of the 'Islamization of Europe' brought on by increased migration from Middle/Near Eastern and other Muslim countries exist to a certain degree in most other European countries (National Intelligence Council, 2012). These concerns may have been exacerbated by the recent large-scale influx of refugees and migrants from Syria and Iraq, and by the 2015/16 New Year incidents involving organized sexual assaults against German women by what seemed to be newly arrived asylum seekers from the Middle East.

The issue of attracting and integrating immigrants is an even greater challenge in rapidly aging countries without a tradition of immigration, such as South Korea and Japan. Given the very homogenous population in both countries, fundamental societal changes will have to be made to accept large-scale immigration, of which presently there is no evidence.

6 Conclusion

The rapid aging of societies, in both industrialized and emerging economies, will have a major impact on the geopolitical and geoeconomic situation in the coming decades. The differential aging of countries within the EU could put pressure on the viability of the union itself—in some ways, we can already see the beginnings of this, as the relatively young Northern European countries are increasingly reluctant to bail out their rapidly aging Southern and Eastern neighbors. The issue of immigration is also increasingly important, as aging societies try to ameliorate the effects through immigration, but this brings up contentious issues of immigrant integration and assimilation into the host society, and the best ways to do this. As societies become more diverse because of immigration, issues of diaspora identity and loyalty, and their relationship to their countries of origin and residence, need to be further investigated and indeed rethought. The issue of immigration becomes even more important for rapidly aging East Asian countries that do not have a culture of immigration, such as Japan and South Korea.

The pension and social security systems of industrialized countries are coming under increasing pressure because of rising dependency ratio rises. Unless a national-level consensus is formed on a combination of higher taxes and lower benefits that is needed to maintain these benefits, this could lead to political disturbances in the affected countries. In some ways the problem is even more acute in emerging economies that are attempting to build welfare states now while their population is beginning to age rapidly.

As societies age and their population grays and begins to decline, the geopolitical and geoeconomic balance of power could shift over time. As countries like China, Japan, and South Korea rapidly age, while countries like India stay relatively young, it could affect their level of influence in transnational bodies like the International Monetary Fund, World Trade Organization and the World Bank, thereby affecting international standards guiding multilateral trade and financial systems worldwide. Another interesting possibility is that as China and the industrialized Asia-Pacific age more rapidly than the USA, the gradual shift in geopolitical power to that region might slow or even begin to reverse over time. The decline of the US share of the global gross domestic product (GDP) since World War II might slow down or even reverse as it ages slowly compared to its major economic competitors. If China actually grows old before it becomes rich, this could affect its growing clout in transnational organizations.

The rapid aging of global populations is leading to unprecedented changes in the geoeconomic environment. Managing these changes will require balancing national and international obligations on immigration, fiscal policy, creating and managing new relationships between businesses and governments, and changes in multilateral organizations. In this chapter, we have provided a short overview of the challenges that global aging is causing in different parts of the world. The process of rapid aging, however, is both long term and largely unprecedented, and managing its consequences will require a dynamic approach. It is vital for business scholars to realize that this discussion will be interdisciplinary in nature and involve different business, government, and social levels as they address what could be the defining societal issue for the first half of the 21st century.

Biography

Australian Institute of Health and Welfare (2012) How do we compare? www.aihw.gov.au/australias-welfare-2011-in-brief/chapter-6/#t1a.

Basu, K. (2007) India's demographic dividend. Accessed from news.bbc.co.uk/2/hi/south_asia/6911544.stm.

Bloom, D. and Canning, D. (2007) Demographic change, fiscal sustainability and macroeconomic performance. *Public Policy and Ageing Report* 17: 18–23.

Center for Strategic and International Studies (2011) *Global Aging Initiative.* Accessed on January 5, 2012, from csis.org/program/global-aging-initiative.

Chand, M. and Tung, R.L. (2014) The aging of the world's population and its effects on global business. *Academy of Management Perspectives* 28(4): 409–429.

CIA (2011) Public debt. In *The World Factbook*. United States Central Intelligence Agency.

Coleman, D. and Dubuc, S. (2010) The fertility of ethnic minority populations in the United Kingdom, 1960s–2006. *Population Studies* 64(1): 19–41.

Deaton, Angus S. and Paxson, C. (1994) Saving, growth, and aging in Taiwan. *Studies in the Economics of Aging* (University of Chicago Press), 331–362.

Delgado, M., Meil, G. et al. (2008) Spain: Short on children and short on family policies. *Demographic Research* 19(27): 1059–1104.

Dorbritz, J. (2008) Germany: Family diversity with low actual and desired fertility. *Childbearing Trends and Policies in Europe* 19(17): 557–598.

The Economist (2011) Into the unknown. Accessed from www.economist.com/node/17492860.

The Economist (2012) China's Achilles heel. Accessed from www.economist.com/node/21553056.

Eke, S. (2005) Russia's population falling fast. *BBC News.* Accessed from news.bbc.co.uk/2/hi/europe/4125072.stm.

Foley, D.K. (2000) Stabilization of human population through economic increasing returns. *Economics Letters* 68(3): 309–317.
Foreno, J. (2012) Brazil's falling birth rate. Accessed from www.npr.org/2012/01/15/145133220/brazils-falling-birth-rate-a-new-way-of-thinking.
Grant, J., Hoorens, S., et al. (2004) *Low Fertility and Population Ageing: Causes, Consequences and Policy Options*. MG205, Santa Monica, CA: RAND.
Haub, C. (2011) Russian birth rate continues to rise. Accessed from prbblog.org/index.php/2011/04/22/russian-birth-rate-continues-to-rise/.
Hayutin, A.M. (2007) Graying of the global population. *Public Policy and Ageing Report* 17: 12–17.
Hoorens, S. et al. (2011) *Low Fertility in Europe: Is there Still Reason to Worry?* RAND (MG-1080). www.prb.org/Articles/2009/braziltfrdecline.aspx.
Japanese Health Ministry (2011) Accessed from www.stat.go.jp/data/jinsui/pdf/201102.pdf.
Japanese Ministry of Internal Affairs and Communications (2012) Trends in population. Accessed from www.stat.go.jp/english/data/handbook/c02cont.htm.
Kotowska, I. (2008) Remarks on family policy in Poland in view of the rise in fertility and labour market participation of women. *Social Policy* 8: 13–19.
Longman, P. (2004) The global baby bust. *Foreign Affairs*, 64–79.
Lutz, W. and Skirbekk, V. (2005) Policies addressing the tempo effect in low-fertility countries. *Population and Development Review* 31(4): 699–720.
National Intelligence Council (2012) *Global Trends 2030: Alternative Worlds*. Accessed June 13, 2013, from www.dni.gov/files/documents/GlobalTrends_2030.pdf.
Population Reference Bureau (2008) World population highlights. *Population Bulletin* 63.
Population Reference Bureau (2009) *Brazil's Fertility Falls Below Two-Child Average*. Accessed from www.prb.org/Publications/Articles/2009/braziltfrdecline.aspx.
Population Reference Bureau (2011) *The World at 7 billion*. Accessed from www.prb.org/pdf11/world-at-7-billion.pdf.
Russian Federal Statistics Service (2011) *Russian Life Expectancy*. Accessed from www.perepis-2010.ru/news/detail.php?ID=7049.
Statistics Japan (2016) Populations and households. www.stat.go.jp/english/data/nenkan/1431-02.htm.
Times of India (2012) Fertility rate in India drops by 19% in 10 yrs. Accessed from articles.timesofindia.indiatimes.com/2012-04-01/india/31269775_1_fertility-rate-population-stabilization-national-population-policy.
United Nations (2009) *World Population Ageing. Department of Economic and Social Affairs*. Population Division. Accessed on April 29, 2012, from www.un.org/esa/population/publications/WPA2009/WPA2009_WorkingPaper.pdf.
University of North Carolina (UNC) (2011) Institute on aging. Accessed on January 5, 2012, from www.aging.unc.edu/infocenter/data/quickfacts.html.
World Bank (2012) Indicators for Brazil. Accessed from www.tradingeconomics.com/brazil/indicators-wb.
World Economic Forum (2012) *Global Population Ageing: Peril or Promise?* Accessed from www3.weforum.org/docs/WEF_GAC_GlobalPopulationAgeing_Report_2012.pdf.

24 Geoeconomics and political interference

The case of China's porcelain industry

Jane Yuting Zhuang and André M. Everett

(The materials for this chapter are derived from the authors' ongoing examination of this cluster. The analyses are drawn primarily from the thesis, 'Grounded in Heritage: An Exploration of Traditional Cultural Clusters in China—The Case of the Jingdezhen Porcelain Cluster.')

1 Introduction

China, as the World Factory (Zhang, 2006), experienced high annual gross domestic product (GDP) growth rates of above 8% over 20 years, achieved primarily through monetary policy. Strategic government actions entailed buying US treasury bonds and linking to the US dollar in order to depress the value of the yuan and thereby take advantage of international trade. As a result of its biased intervention towards leveraging the exchange rate and inflation, China experienced very high inflation rates since the 1990s, forcing the Chinese currency to appreciate and lose its price advantage in exporting, inducing large multinational enterprises (MNEs) to relocate their production activities to other emerging markets such as Vietnam, Thailand, and India. Because this disastrous turn in the export market had a significant internal impact on the Chinese economy, China turned inwards to focus more on its internal demand, which is similar to the strategy played by the Japanese government after 2007's financial crisis (Buckley & Strange, 2015; Schulz, 2013). For instance, the GDP growth rate in 2015 dropped to 6.9%, a historical low point over the past 25 years (Magnier, 2016). China is not well prepared for this economic 'winter,' with disasters in the property and stock markets following each other. As a consequence of the government introducing a stock index 'circuit breaker' inappropriately for four days, US$5 trillion disappeared during the stock market crash in the summer of 2015 (Burgos, 2016). Mr Xiao, the head of the China Securities Regulatory Commission (CSRC), resigned while accepting direct responsibility for misleading policies and subsequent failures in market leveraging (Jourdan, 2016). After several policy failures, the total debt in China reached 260% of annual GDP (Magnier, 2016). This situation significantly impacted the confidence of foreign and domestic investors and led to a net outflow of $175 billion in capital between

July and September 2015 (Worrachate, 2016). US rating agency Moody's subsequently downgraded their outlook on China to negative (Simpson, 2016). The top-down style of decision making and direct intervention in national-, regional-, and local-level economic development set the backdrop for most of the interaction between the public and private sectors in China. An important question is: How can industries and businesses survive misleading political interference?

China has a number of famous millennium industries—ones that have survived at least a millennium. They are labor intensive with high standards of creativity and craft skills. One of them is porcelain. Ceramics discovered in the country through archaeology appear to have been used primarily for ceremonies as early as 24,000 BC (Guire, 2014). Ceramics, along with stoneware, iron, and copper tools, illustrate the development of human civilization. This industry globally has provided significant technological breakthroughs that facilitate division of the living standards of human societies into eras. Porcelain was first produced in China. It has a history of over 2,200 years, commencing early in the Han Dynasty (206 BC–220 AD). The location of the porcelain industry in Jingdezhen was named 'Chang-nan,' meaning 'South of the Long River (Chang-Jiang).' Jingdezhen porcelain was extensively transported to the rest of the world beginning in the Tang Dynasty. The world recognized that the best porcelain was made in 'Chang-nan' and morphed the name of the small town producing porcelain into the word 'china,' subsequently applying the term to the whole region and nation we now know as China.

The porcelain industry of Jingdezhen survived over 400 imperial reigns and is an example of an industrial model for sustainability. Since the time of the Song Dynasty (960–1279 AD), there have been semblances of division of labor in Jingdezhen. For instance, the porcelain production procedure developed into a series of 72 steps and functioned similar to a production line. It had an industrial standard and clear division of labor. The production formulas for porcelain clay, firing techniques, design of shapes and patterns, glazing techniques, and materials have been reinvented, developed, and improved throughout history. No one museum or library in the world could retain and manage them all. The masterpieces made from the royal kilns in Jingdezhen are kept by national museums and sell as antiques at auction houses for millions of dollars. Industrial terminology developed in the industry in Jingdezhen led to the emergence of a technical language spoken by the insiders of the industry.

So, how does this story relate to political interference and geoeconomics? This chapter will base its discussion on the in-depth investigation of a single longitudinal phenomenon to examine the consequences of, and adaptations to, political interference from the municipal government led by former mayor Mrs Shu Xiaoqin, utilizing the Grounded Theory Methodology with data collection conducted through in-depth interviews within the industry. The meaningful links to geoeconomics will be discussed in the concluding section.

2 Research design and methodology

The Grounded Theory Methodology design adopted for this research is based on Glaser's approach to guide data collection, data analysis, and literature review (Glaser, 1992). Grounded Theory is a methodology that systematically guides data collection and analysis with the purpose of discovering theory (Glaser & Strauss, 1967). It is one of the most popular qualitative methodologies, accepted by top journals in the areas of business studies, nursing, medical science, computer science, and some social sciences, and has been deemed essential in qualitative research (Creswell, 2007; Myers, 2013; Saunders et al., 2016; Silverman, 2011a, 2011b). The methodology is designed for both qualitative and quantitative researchers to analyze qualitative data while emulating the rigor and logic of quantitative approaches. Grounded Theory Methodology fits with most data collection methods. To Glaser, all is data (Glaser, 2007), and researchers can be innovative in the ways that they design their frameworks for data collection, in contrast to Strauss and Corbin's alternative approach to Grounded Theory, which is more about following standard procedures (Strauss & Corbin, 1990). In the Grounded Theory Methodology, field literature will not be reviewed before the emergence of the theory from a substantive area (Glaser, 1992).

The principal data collection method for this research is in-depth interviews. The advantage of an in-depth interview is that it allows exploration of the possibility of investigating more comprehensive reasons behind a participant's point of view towards a social phenomenon. It covers issues and problems of discussion through open-ended questions. For in-depth interviews, a snowball effect takes place in that the two-way communication directs the questions to be asked in sequence.

Phenomena arising from an industrial cluster are often complicated. The causality of a particular phenomenon might be multiple, and in the case of the Jingdezhen porcelain cluster, many of these causes are embedded in the local culture and are less obvious to an external observer. Good in-depth interview skills might be able to dig deeper into the issues, enabling more comprehensive analysis by surfacing rich contextualized data from the field. Glaser (1998) encouraged conducting interviews without a recorder to improve efficiency. However, not recording interviews in the Grounded Theory Methodology poses substantial risk of the researcher being unable to recall statements precisely after long, intensive interactions on non-predetermined paths. Fernández (2004), who adopted Glaser's approach, documented his interviews with recorders and manual note-taking during the interviews to mitigate risk.

The analysis and coding framework for this research is built upon the original model by Lehmann (2001) as modified by Fernández (2004, p. 84) and further developed by the researchers to fit the empirical reality of the Jingdezhen porcelain industry (Zhuang, 2011, p. 62). A data library was created as a new construct to serve the purpose of storing inputs that the researcher could not process while staying in the field. At times, interviewing and coding to reach data saturation required staying on-site, which was limited due to both time and budget constraints. In addition, a repository for the substantial amount of extant literature, including a vast historiography, was also created to ensure data saturation and the emergence of theory. This construct is for the entire project, while information concerning the political interference is drawn exclusively from current interview data.

3 Data collection and analysis

For this particular portion of the overall project, the data set consists of 24 interviews recorded in the field with field notes from 11 interviews that could not be recorded, supplemented by notes taken in the field reflecting the reality of the Jingdezhen porcelain industry during a one-month stay. Interviews were conducted and transcribed in Chinese; total processing time for each interview (including preparation, transcription, coding, and theoretical analysis) was approximately 22 hours. Seven interviews and four interviewees from the field notes directly referred to misleading government policies instigated and managed by the former mayor Mrs Shu. The data on political intervention in the local economy from interviews link direct with three government policies: (i) the closing down of the ten state-owned factories

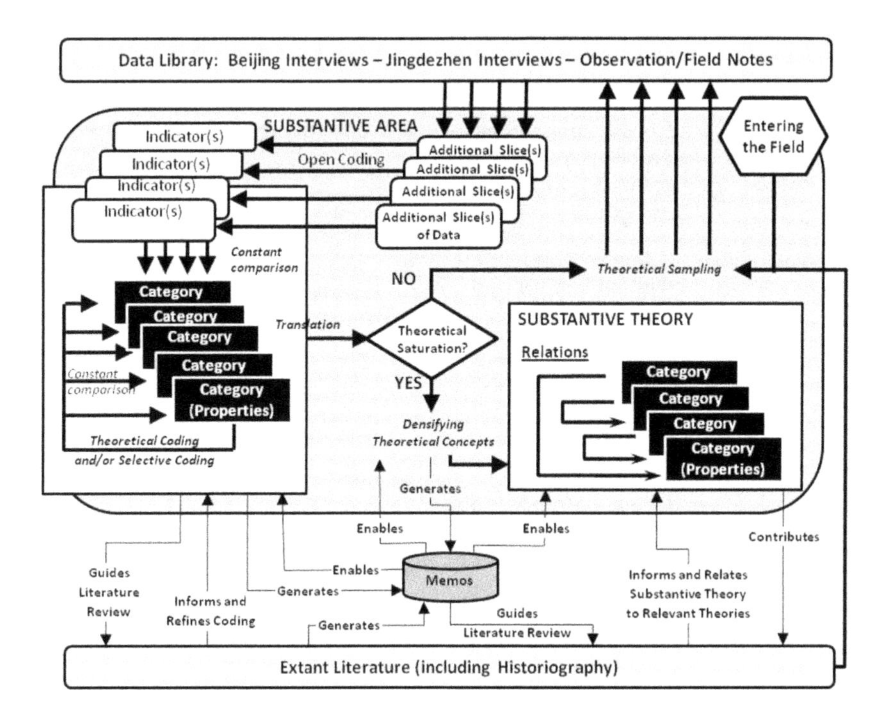

Figure 24.1 Modified Grounded Theory Methodology framework (Zhuang, 2011, p. 62)

(mentioned in six interviews plus by five interviewees from field notes); (ii) moving porcelain workshops to Xindu (mentioned in 13 interviews and by five interviewees in the field notes) and marketing to Jinxiuchangnan (mentioned in two interviews); and (iii) relocating to China Porcelain Town (one interview with in-depth details).

Coding was carried out entirely in English based on Chinese transcripts. The coding process followed the modified framework from Figure 24.1. The three figures representing the substantive theory emerged from the Jingdezhen porcelain cluster related to government interventions indicating that business practitioners have more in-depth insights than the government in developing the local economy. Table 24.1 compares local government interventions with the expectations of the public, including those of business owners and workers within the industry gathered from the interview data regarding issues such as government intervention, in particular regarding Mrs Shu and the issues of closing the ten state-owned factories and the planning of the new markets. Table 24.1 indicates all the issues covered by the interviewees. There was intentionally no single targeted question regarding public expectation and

Table 24.1 Government intervention vs. public expectations

Issues	*Government actions*	*Expectations by the public*	*Met?*
Relocation of markets	Remove some markets and retain others, fooling the public	• Credibility • Execution • Consistency	No
City and district planning	Construction design problems found in planned porcelain markets	• Scientific planning • Long-term orientated • Sensible and functional design with integrity	No
Real estate/rental	Stress on housing, without control over rental price	• Rental price monitoring and paperwork regulation • Protect backbone industry	No
Communication with public	Very little, and only with famous artists	• Take advice from the public as a whole without bias and take actions accordingly	No
State-owned factories	Dissolution, led by former mayor Mrs Shu, without taking care of deployed workforce	• Protect the factories • Maintain distinctive features and advantages • Employ scientific management	No
Copyright	Protect famous artists with food supporting system, without protecting reproductions	• Fairness to every craftsman/artist • Seriousness about faking and bribery—protect city image and the industry	No

local government satisfaction. What the government planned is in parallel to what the public expected. The corruption issue of Mrs Shu was mentioned many times. The interests of Mrs Shu conflicted with the local public for her personal benefit. Public opinion was not heard and incorporated into the economic development of the industry.

Figure 24.2 compares the three government-planned markets (Xindu, Jinxiuchangnan and China Porcelain Town) with the local embedded markets in terms of sustainability. The interview data were gathered from Xindu, Jinxiuchangnan and China Porcelain Town. In the interviews, the local businesses revealed the evolution of the situation behind the scenes. It was uncovered that the government planned the new wholesale and retail markets in Xindu, Jinxiuchangnan and China Porcelain Town in early 2000 due to safety issues of operating kilns in residential zones. However, the three planned business complexes are far from railway and bus stations and accommodation. It is very inconvenient for buyers to get public transportation or a taxi to the new markets. The government then announced a deadline in television and radio broadcasts to remove the old markets of Shaojiwu and Fanjiajing. A significant number of shop owners bought properties in the new markets and started planning their move. The government's economic planning conflicted most radically with the interests of the villagers in Fanjiajing. Many lost their income as a consequence of the market removal. By the end of this story, the government had failed to remove the old markets. The people who had

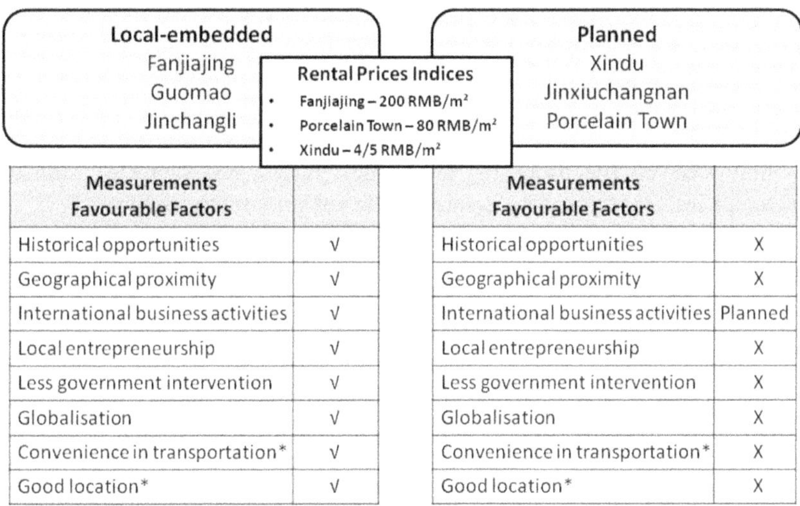

Measurements Favourable Factors	
Historical opportunities	√
Geographical proximity	√
International business activities	√
Local entrepreneurship	√
Less government intervention	√
Globalisation	√
Convenience in transportation*	√
Good location*	√

Measurements Favourable Factors	
Historical opportunities	X
Geographical proximity	X
International business activities	Planned
Local entrepreneurship	X
Less government intervention	X
Globalisation	X
Convenience in transportation*	X
Good location*	X

* Items emerged from data. "Convenience in transportation" includes close to accommodation, railway, bus station, and waterway – Changjiang (water power, clay soil, transporting wood and porcelains)

Figure 24.2 Comparison between local embedded and government-planned markets

bought properties in the new markets returned, suffering great financial losses due to reduced rent prices for their new properties in the planned zones.

4 Discussion

Findings from Beeri and Navot's (2013) research in Israel indicate that corruption is embedded in the governmental system rather than in the behavior of the individuals involved. The problems in the decision-making process by the municipal government exacerbated the mistakes made by the former mayor Mrs Shu. In the process of reforming the ten state-owned factories, Mrs Shu's decisions led immediately to a significant number of people becoming unemployed from the production lines of the closed factories, and created great social pressure and tension in the families that lost their primary source of financial support. She had a choice of either improving the efficiency of the state-owned factories, or slowing down the transformation process to enable the business community to assimilate the unemployed population. She picked the most radical way in order to avoid responsibility for what would appear to be inadequate or delayed performance. The same story has recently been repeated in the failure of stock market leverage in the summer of 2015 through early 2016 by Mr Xiao, the former head of the CSRC. It is not the specific individuals, but rather the political bureaucracy in China that supports the abuse of decisions by political leaders at all levels. In order to improve the quality of decision making in the public sector, strategic partnerships with professional entities might benefit the government with a more holistic view in analysis and evaluation (Conteh, 2013; Wang & Li, 2014). The delivery of order and information from the national government to regional governments and subsequently to municipal governments could become misleading through multiple layers of authorities, especially when implementing urgent decisions (Thompson, 2014). There is a possibility that when Mrs Shu received the order to reform the state-owned factories, sufficient noise crept into the system to create significant miscommunication.

Geoeconomic relationships at the municipal, regional, national and international levels have impacted the porcelain industry. As a key emerging market, the lessons learnt through the development of the Chinese economy could contribute to the development of other emerging markets, especially those sharing similar cultural characteristics (such as Vietnam, India, and various Association of Southeast Asian Nations, or ASEAN, countries). Corruption in the bureaucratic political system impacts on MNEs' foreign direct investment (FDI) decision making under the measurement of political risk. It also neglects the development of local businesses, especially in new industries that are not locally embedded well enough to survive independently. On the other hand, the story told by the Jingdezhen porcelain cluster indicates that governments should respect the history and culture of traditional clusters, which have their unique ways of surviving and developing; without in-depth understanding of a cluster's life cycle and culture, no intervention is better than 'blind' intervention. Studying the success of local traditional clusters can provide useful lessons to local, regional, and national decision makers, particularly where success was generated within the context of a particular national culture or philosophy. Strategies developed from specific traditional clusters will be easier to understand and apply, and success is more likely to be imitated within a similar historical and cultural context.

The comparison of performance between the government-planned markets and locally embedded markets indicates that the markets which emerged naturally, driven by demand, have stronger resilience capability. The businesses in the Jingdezhen porcelain industry are highly intelligent in understanding political interference and over time developed the capability to avoid misleading political intervention in the development of the local industry. Even during the financial crisis in 2008, local businesses revealed a high level of confidence in the future development of the Jingdezhen porcelain industry. The interviews also surfaced evidence of a high degree of tolerance towards uncertainty and difficulties. People in the industry put their faith in the history of their cluster, which survived over 2,000 years. There is faith in the local business atmosphere, especially in the culture of porcelain arts and production. This spirit of craftsmanship rooted in the local culture is hardly visible in many modern industries. Creating one vase might take half a year to a year for the best artists. They also accept the significant risk that a vase might break before they send it away for firing, during firing, after an unsuccessful firing, or during any of the multiple transport processes. The nature of the industry teaches the lesson of passion with patience. This spirit of craftsmanship is now rarely found in China, instead having been inherited by the Japanese (notably including in the ceramics industry, which features in another phase of this research project).

5 Conclusion

Through a narrow investigation of political interference in the Jingdezhen porcelain cluster, based on in-depth interview data, two factors emerged as part of the substantive theory. The two factors highlight: (i) the relationships between the municipal government and the business community; and (ii) the linkage of political action with public reaction. Analysis through the Grounded Theory framework indicates that misleading policies take place in China and around the world, with the typical top-down bureaucratic approach occurring in the Jingdezhen porcelain industry. However, this industry overcame such policies and their consequences through a high level of local business confidence even during major crises. This business confidence is not trained, but inherited from its history and the porcelain production culture.

Geographical economics is constructed in its spatial, social and cultural context. Geoeconomic relations within China and across borders have impacted this industry. In history, the Jingdezhen porcelain cluster is a significant contributor to the marine and land Silk Road since the Tang

Dynasty. Its connection within China and across borders has impacted not only the expression of arts and design but also the business dynamics of the local industry. It is highly sensitive to the economic conditions and the trends of demand internally and externally, enabling a relatively remote inland city to maintain success and survive for over 2,000 years. In the Jingdezhen porcelain reproduction market, there are Islamic vases with Islamic patterns, Japanese kitchenware with Japanese designs, and various coloring techniques and patterns that cross a number of dynasties. With a self-emerged system of industrial labor division (e.g. the 72 steps), Jingdezhen is actually a world factory of porcelain. The lesson delivered by the Jingdezhen porcelain cluster to businesses and industries in general is that industrial resilience is inherited through history and proven through crises. Unless an industry has been through a full life cycle, it is hard to judge its resilience. Industrial culture builds the confidence of participating businesses against interference. Profitability might drive the industry into a developed and mature stage, but only culture can help industry overcome decline and revive itself. Business attitudes towards political intervention in historical cultural clusters are shaped by two factors: (i) acceptance of the political reality; and (ii) consistent creation of good work in the absence of government support. Information from the second phase of data collection in the field (in 2014) indicates that the extraordinary performance of local embedded markets helped overcome the policy failure in Jingdezhen. Since the industry has grown significantly in comparison to 2008, the government-planned porcelain plazas are fully occupied due to overall market expansion. However, instead of replacing the locally embedded markets, the new markets became mere extensions of the existing ones.

The size of the industry, the quality standards it achieved and the duration of its history make the Jingdezhen porcelain industry unique and complicated. Studies searching for the 'gene' of resilience can be broken down into several social sciences: history, sociology, archaeology, anthropology, arts, material studies, antiques, ceramic production, and business. Reaching a comprehensive understanding of an industry becomes impossible without longitudinal and multi-disciplinary approaches. A long-term and multifaceted viewpoint and assessment can help in the sustainability and geoeconomic success of an industry.

References

Beeri, I. and Navot, D. (2013) Local political corruption: Potential structural malfunctions at the central-local, local-local and intra-local levels. *Public Management Review* 15(5): 712–739.

Buckley, P.J. and Strange, R. (2015) The governance of the global factory: Location and control of world economic activity. *Academy of Management Perspectives* 29(2): 237–249.

Burgos, J. (2016) China names new securities regulator head after $US5 trillion stock exchange rout. *Financial Review*, February 23. Retrieved from www.afr.com/markets/

equity-markets/china-names-new-securities-regulator-head-after-us5-trillion-stock-exchange-rout-20160222-gn0sik.

Conteh, C. (2013) Strategic inter-organizational cooperation in complex environments. *Public Management Review* 15(4): 501–521.

Creswell, J.W. (2007) *Qualitative Inquiry & Research Design: Choosing Among Five Approaches.* London: SAGE.

Fernández, W. (2004) Using the Glaserian approach in grounded studies of emerging business practices. *Electronic Journal of Business Research Methods* 2(2): 83–95.

Glaser, B.G. (1992) *Basics of Grounded Theory Analysis.* Mill Valley, CA: Sociology Press.

Glaser, B.G. (1998) *Doing Grounded Theory: Issues and Discussions.* Mill Valley, CA: Sociology Press.

Glaser, B. (2007) All is data. *The Grounded Theory Review* 6(2): 1–3.

Glaser, B.G. and Strauss, A.L. (1967) *The Discovery of Grounded Theory: Strategies for Qualitative Research.* Chicago, IL: Aldine.

Guire, E.D. (2014, May 19) History of ceramics. Retrieved from ceramics.org/learn-about-ceramics/history-of-ceramics.

Jourdan, A. (2016, February 20) China removes stocks regulator head after market woes. Reuters. Retrieved from www.reuters.com/article/us-china-regulator-csrc-idUSKCN0VT03J.

Lehmann, H.P. (2001) *A Grounded Theory of International Information Systems.* PhD thesis. Auckland, New Zealand: University of Auckland.

Magnier, M. (2016, January 9). China's economic growth in 2015 is slowest in 25 years. *The Wall Street Journal.* Retrieved from www.wsj.com/articles/china-economic-growth-slows-to-6-9-on-year-in-2015-1453169398.

Myers, M.D. (2013) *Qualitative Research in Business & Management*, 2nd edn. London: SAGE.

Saunders, M., Lewis, P. and Thornhill, A. (eds) (2016) *Research Methods for Business Students*, 7th edn. Harlow: Pearson Education.

Schulz, M. (2013) The global debt crisis and the shift of Japan's economic relations with Southeast Asia. *Journal of Southeast Asia Economies* 30(2): 143–163.

Silverman, D. (2011a) *Interpreting Qualitative Data*, 4th edn. London: SAGE.

Silverman, D. (2011b) *Qualitative Research*, 3rd edn. London: SAGE.

Simpson, J. (2016, March 3) Critics fear Beijing's sharp turn to authoritarianism. BBC News. Retrieved from www.bbc.com/news/world-35714031.

Strauss, A. and Corbin, J. (1990) *Basics of Qualitative Research: Grounded Theory Procedures and Techniques.* Newbury Park, CA: SAGE.

Thompson, D.F. (2014) Responsibility or failures of government: The problem of many hands. *American Review of Public Administration* 44(3): 259–273.

Wang, C. and Li, X. (2014) Centralizing public procurement in China: Task environment and organizational structure. *Public Management Review* 16(6): 900–921.

Worrachate, A. (2016) China's $175 billion outflow wasn't investor flight: BIS. Bloomberg, March 6. Retrieved from www.bloomberg.com/news/articles/2016-03-06/china-s-175-billion-outflow-wasn-t-investor-flight-bis-says.

Zhang, K.H. (ed.) (2006) *China as the World Factory.* London: Routledge.

Zhuang, Y. (2011) *Grounded in Heritage: An Exploration of Traditional Cultural Clusters in China—The Case of the Jingdezhen Porcelain Cluster.* Master's thesis. Dunedin, New Zealand: University of Otago.

25 The African Growth and Opportunity Act

International business, relations and politics

Satyendra Singh

1 Introduction

The African Growth and Opportunity Act (AGOA) relates to boosting exports from sub-Saharan Africa (SSA) to the USA by eliminating tariff barriers as many African nations lack economic development and competitiveness in international markets. The AGOA preferential agreement, signed into law by the US Congress in 2000, was designed to import products tax-free to the USA from the 40 African member countries. However, the AGOA is a nonreciprocal agreement between the USA and developing countries which the USA uses as foreign aid tools and policies that are allowed under World Trade Organization (WTO) Special and Differential Treatment (Zappile, 2011). Although the USA is a member of the WTO which seeks to promote globalization of the world economy, the AGOA presents additional eligibility requirements and conditions for the African nations (Mushita, 2001). The AGOA has three nontrade-related and politically instigated eligibility criteria. That is, a member country: (i) has established or is making continual progress toward establishing a market-based economy; (ii) does not engage in activities that undermine the USA's national security and foreign policy interests; and (iii) does not engage in gross violations of internationally recognized human rights or provide support for international terrorism (Jones & Williams, 2012). These member countries also need to demonstrate the rule of law, political pluralism, the right to due process, a fair trial, equal protection under the law, economic policies to reduce poverty, increased availability of healthcare, educational opportunities, expanded physical infrastructure, promotion of the development of private enterprise, and formation of capital markets through micro-credit or other programs (CSF, 2014). Failure to adhere to these requirements can lead to severe consequences. The AGOA was initially due to expire in 2008 but was extended to 2015.

The purpose of this chapter is to examine the effectiveness of the AGOA's trade agreement with the USA and its impact on economic activities, trade barriers, international relations and politics. Specifically, the chapter highlights and proposes strategies in the five areas—financial liberalization, export diversification, rules of origin, trading bloc, international relations (USA vs.

China)—where the AGOA appears to be ineffective and thus has failed to contribute significantly to quality of life in SSA.

2 Financial liberalization

Financial liberalization is the availability of foreign capital to reduce the costs of financing and increase investment and business development. In the African context, however, it has the three main barriers: legal, indirect, and emerging market-specific risks (EMSR) (Bekaerta, 1995). Legal barriers relate to a different legal system for foreign and domestic investors, affecting ownership restrictions and taxes. Indirect barriers are the differences in available information, accounting standards, and investor protection. The EMSR barriers include liquidity risk, political risk, economic policy risk, and currency risk. Africa needs substantial investments in infrastructure through financial liberalization and barrier elimination to create an environment conducive to growth. In fact, the main constraint for many small and medium-sized enterprises (SMEs) is the difficulty in accessing finance (Kira, 2013). Thus, elimination of the financial barriers should encourage foreign direct investment (FDI) and manufacturing activities in African nations (Klein & Olivei, 2008). Financial liberalization and FDI are positively related.

The AGOA has the goal to promote trade, investment and economic cooperation between the USA and AGOA member countries, but it needs to address the factors restricting FDI. Although removal of the restrictions on financial liberalization or FDI alone may not lead to automatic success, at least it can allow foreign firms to use existing capabilities. African nations also need to ensure that they have adequate infrastructure, human capital, and technical assistance to attract foreign firms and FDI (Zappile, 2011). Other macroeconomic methods such as a minimal state role in the economy, adoption of nondiscriminatory policy and a favorable corporate tax regime can also attract FDI (Loewendahl, 2001). When financial institutions are strong, the strategy of financial liberalization can create incentives for FDI, attracting capital, technology, managerial skills and international networks (Lall & Narula, 2004). As such, FDI is desirable as it is more stable than the short-term cash flows that could be volatile and disruptive (Stiglitz, 2000). Therefore, it is necessary to determine what level of financial liberalization is most beneficial to African nations. Amendments should be suggested in the renewal of the AGOA to strengthen African nations' financial institutions. The concept of strong financial institutions combined with the strategy of financial liberalization can create incentives for sustainable FDI.

3 Export diversification

The AGOA agreement has so far primarily benefited the oil-based member countries such as Nigeria, Angola and Gabon (Shapouri & Trueblood, 2003). Although the energy sector has accelerated economic growth in Africa and should remain the primary focal point of the AGOA as evidenced by the export of oil-related products, many argue, given about 80% of all exports were to the USA in 2012 (Sanchez, 2014), that much of this trade would occur regardless of the AGOA. The sole dependence on the export of energy-related products has limited the AGOA's economic impact on the rest of the African nations (Coon, 2013). The low-income African nations have yet to fully capitalize on the benefits of the AGOA due to the exclusion of some products such as rice and peanuts which do have comparative advantage but are unable to be exported due to the USA's trade preference policies (Karingi et al., 2010). Clearly, the major problems facing member countries are how to diversify and increase exports (Ackah & Morrissey, 2005). So export diversification should also focus on low-income African nations that do not have energy-related products that are in high demand perennially.

The AGOA was intended to liberalize the trade in the SSA region, but it has failed to do so. Many African nations' exports depend on only a couple of commodities such as oil and apparel, creating a significant need for export diversification. African nations do export textile apparel to the USA, but they account for only 7% of total exports to the USA, exemplifying the need for export diversification. True, South Africa has recorded growth in both sectors—oil and apparel—but other nations have lagged behind due to poor infrastructure and lack of communication systems. In this regard, the AGOA does offer technical assistance and capacity-building training to eligible African nations and encourages their governments to: (i) liberalize trade policies; (ii) engage in financial and fiscal restructuring; and (iii) increase agribusiness linkages among small private sector businesses (Williams, 2014). However, Africa's trade capacity and technical assistance are insufficient. In fact, very few African nations have the capability to facilitate AGOA-inspired international trade even if there were no trade barriers.

Developing countries need to diversify into new export categories and reduce the dependence on the export of traditional primary commodities only. In addition to oil and apparel, agricultural products are important export commodities and can be a major source of employment and foreign exchange. In fact, the AGOA member countries' agribusiness provides over 70% of employment in SSA, equivalent to 40% of SSA's gross domestic product (GDP) (World Bank, 2010). Yet, agricultural products account for only 2% of the total products exported from SSA to the USA under the AGOA agreement (USITC, 2005). Clearly, agriculture-based nations have not benefited much from the AGOA.

4 Rules of origin

Rules of origin prevent non-eligible member countries from redirecting their shipments through a member country to the USA. For non-apparel products, the AGOA requires a minimum value addition of 35% which can be met through production in the home country or outsourcing materials from other member countries or the USA. Up to 15% of the 35% may also be imported from the USA to produce the product (Flatters, 2007). Some perceive that the 35% requirement is too high and that it creates bias against small firms in low-income countries (LICs), because the requirement may restrict access to the most efficient producers and penalize the utilization of low-cost labor in the production process.

However, apparel products can be made only from yarn and fabric produced in member countries or in the USA, under what is called the yarn forward rule (YFR). The rule supports development of local spinning and weaving industries in member countries to increase competitiveness of their apparel industries. However, LICs, where the possibilities for local sourcing are limited because most developing countries are small, are particularly disadvantaged by the YFR relative to larger countries (Moyo & Page, 2010). Thus, LICs may have to shift from a low-cost source of input to a high-cost source, reducing the benefits of export under the AGOA. Further, it is almost impossible to establish an integrated production structure across countries in a global economy when the YFR constrains the ability of local firms to integrate into global and regional production networks. In the global economy, flexibility in outsourcing is the key to international competitiveness (Evbuomwan, 2007). In fact, the YFR increases the costs of production by constraining access to inexpensive input and thus undermines the ability of local firms to compete in international markets. Imposing artificial restrictions on fabric and yarn sourcing increases costs, reduces product quality and harms the competitiveness of apparel producers in AGOA member countries (Flatters, 2007). As a result, the YFR decreases the benefits of AGOA to African nations.

Another rule called the third-country fabric rule (TCFR), applicable in less developed beneficiary countries (LDBCs), allows AGOA member countries to incorporate yarn and fabric from any country in the world—for example, India or China. That is, under the TCFR, the USA can still import apparel duty-free from LDBCs even if the yarns and fabrics used in the production of the apparel are imported from non-AGOA member countries (Williams, 2014). The AGOA member countries that fall under the LDBC category are defined as having a per capita gross national product (GNP) of under US$1,500 as measured by the World Bank (Thompson & Jack, 2013). To benefit from the TCFR, the countries must have an effective visa system and the verification procedure to prevent illegal transshipments and counterfeit documentation. Inconveniently, the TCFR is subject to renewal every two or three years, resulting in uncertainties and causing loss of orders and employment. Costly investments in machines and training of employees may be risky in such circumstances, because investors may be inclined to manufacture only basic products and not engage in long-term plans such as improving and sustaining competitiveness of their apparel production. The AGOA needs to revisit the rules.

5 The trading blocs

Currently, there are ten trading blocs in Africa and almost every African nation is a member of at least one trading bloc (Geda & Kebret, 2008). Yet, there is weak evidence of trade and economic cooperation among them. Not surprisingly, some regional economic integration schemes have failed precisely because existing policies, barriers and tariffs still protect national industries (Hinkle & Newfarmer, 2005). For example, the Common Market for Eastern and Southern Africa (COMESA) is yet to achieve free trade among its members, movement of people across its borders, and integration of cross-border financial markets (Moyo & Page, 2010). Establishing trading blocs alone may not produce economic development; the AGOA needs to streamline its activities in trading blocs such as COMESA for the export of African products to the USA (Schaefer et al., 2014). Clearly, the AGOA could utilize the significant trade potential of COMESA.

The AGOA also needs to emphasize regional integration and trade capacity enhancement in order to foster growth in multilateral trade (Ngwenya, 2014). Regional integration is an important strategy as many African nations are small and landlocked, creating barriers for local firms to grow. It has already suggested that growth could be enhanced if the African Union establishes a continental free trade area by 2017 and integrates other regional economic communities into a single customs union by 2028 (Schaefer et al., 2014). Further, eliminating the need for business travelers to be cleared on both sides of the border would greatly reduce waiting time and enhance the flow of goods and people. A one-stop border has already proven to boost trade significantly between Zambia and Zimbabwe (Kieck, 2010). It is imperative that regional integration, customs and transportation regulations be streamlined for African nations to get the most value from the AGOA.

6 International relations (USA)

The AGOA member countries need to meet economic, social and political criteria. These countries are subject to ongoing monitoring that can result in countries being added or removed on an annual basis (Naumann, 2010). Meanwhile, the AGOA criteria—nontrade or investment related—allow the USA to intervene in member countries through political instigation or international sanctions. The USA frequently uses its hegemony to diminish the sovereignty of member countries. For example, Madagascar apparel exports to the USA plummeted as a result of its removal from AGOA membership due to the lack of democracy in this country (Ploch & Cook, 2012). The USA revoked Madagascar's duty-free access in 2010 when a collision between the president and the former mayor of the capital city caused a series of riots that resulted in the president being replaced following the incursion of the army into the presidential palace. This sanction had a disastrous impact on Madagascar's apparel export industry. Factory-level data demonstrate that the

AGOA suspension increased the probability of closure by 58% for the factories supplying exclusively to the USA market and eliminated 6,500 low-skilled jobs, which accounted for about 28% of the total job losses during the post-turmoil period (Fukunishi, 2013).

In another example, when the Ugandan government passed an Anti-Homosexuality Bill into law, the USA imposed global sanctions on the country. The legislation imposes the death penalty for certain homosexual activities and requires citizens to report homosexual activities to the police or face jail time. World leaders condemned the law and some Western governments threatened to withhold financial aid (Ewins, 2011). One of the eligibility requirements of the AGOA is that a member country must not engage in gross violation of internationally recognized human rights. As a result, the World Bank put a $90 million loan on hold even though these loans were originally scheduled for a healthcare program in Uganda and had nothing to do with the law. Although it is quite unusual for the World Bank to interfere in politics, it could do so because the USA is the largest shareholder of the World Bank. Several European countries also followed suit and suspended donations. Given that Uganda is an independent sovereign nation with its own legislature, the USA's interference through economic sanctions significantly reduced Uganda's political autonomy. Currently, 40 nations in SSA are eligible member countries under the AGOA agreement and 12 of these nations (not including Uganda) criminalize an adult consensual homosexual act. Thus, nearly half of the current member countries are already ineligible for assistance under the AGOA. Indeed, some argue that AGOA should be renamed the *American* Growth and Opportunity Act (Mushita, 2001) because AGOA is based on muddled perceptions of the USA's national interests (Davies, 2011).

7 International relations (China)

Chinese international relations policies are different from the policies of the USA in that China places sovereignty above human rights. Thus, the American nontrade terms can be contrasted with the Chinese noninterference trade policy. Noninterference in state sovereignty and freedom from hegemony have been themes of Chinese foreign policy since the Five Principles of Peaceful Co-existence formulated in the 1950s as the basis for Beijing's foreign relations (Lee et al., 2007). China's strong sentiment for sovereignty has helped it acquire natural resources and contracts from many governments. Besides the political support for state sovereignty, trade and investment activities, China has developed strong relations with the African nations through a debt relief policy. In 2000, China cancelled the bilateral debts, totaling $1.27 billion, of 31 African countries (Lammers, 2007). As a result, China significantly increased its involvement in Africa over the past decade (Tull, 2006).

Nonetheless, Chinese engagement in Africa has its own controversies, such as a poor record in human rights, governance, and environment (Yin &

Vaschetto, 2011). China has been criticized for a lack of transparency and disregard for human rights, which have led to the maintenance of dictators in power, avoiding true development (Lemos & Ribeiro, 2007). Ironically, Western countries ridicule China's relations with African nations, but African nations, in fact, view very positively China's contribution to improving economic conditions in Africa through trade, investment, and infrastructure. It is not surprising that in Zimbabwe and Sudan, where the USA and the European Union have imposed sanctions and bans on FDI, China has found niche markets with little or no competition from other countries. It appears that when the USA removes problematic countries from the list of member countries due to violation of the AGOA, China seems to get the opportunity to work with those authoritarian governments (Davies, 2011). The two distinct but conflicting foreign policies of the USA and China may mean that prospects for development in Africa could be bumpy.

8 Conclusion

It is certain that Africa's poverty is due to a lack of economic growth and declining economic development leading to their inability to remain competitive in international markets. The purpose of the chapter was to examine the effectiveness of the AGOA's trade agreement and highlight and propose strategies in the five areas—financial liberalization, export diversification, rules of origin, trading bloc, international relations (USA vs. China)—where the AGOA's performance is debatable. Based on our research, AGOA's next renewal needs to take into account the following recommendations: (i) financial liberalization is needed in SSA to make foreign capital available for firms—particularly for SMEs—to reduce the costs of financing in order to attract FDI; (ii) SSA nations need to diversify into new export categories such as agricultural products and avoid dependence on oil and apparel; (iii) the rules of origin should be relaxed so local firms could take advantage of inexpensive source of input and become flexible and competitive; (iv) the trading blocs need to remove barriers and tariffs that still protect national industries and contribute very little to trade development of the blocs; and finally (v) the terms of AGOA should be based on trade or investment rather than on international relations and politics. These recommendations are expected to contribute to African economic development through the policies of trade preferences of the AGOA.

References

Ackah, C. and Morrissey, O. (2005) Trade policy and performance in sub-Saharan Africa since the 1980s. University of Nottingham. hdl.handle.net/10419/80322 (accessed on October 4, 2015).

Bekaerta, G. (1995) Market integration and investment barriers in emerging and equity markets. *The World Bank Economic Review* 9(1): 75–107.

Coon, C. (2013) Embracing Africa's economic potential. U.S. Senator Christopher Coon of Delaware. www.coons.senate.gov/embracing-africas-economic-potential (accessed on January 2, 2016).

CSF (2014) Building a strategy for workers' rights and inclusive growth—A new vision for AGOA. Civil Society Forum (CSF). agoa.info/downloads/research.html (accessed on October 5, 2015).

Davies, J.E. (2011) Washington's growth and opportunity act or Beijing's 'overarching brilliance': Will African governments choose neither? *Third World Quarterly* 32(6): 1147–1163.

Evbuomwan, G.O. (2007) Africa regional integration and challenges of globalisation: A review of the New Partnership for African Development (NEPAD). *Farm Management Association of Nigeria Journal* 9(1): 40–48.

Ewins, L.H. (2011) Gross violation: Why Uganda's Anti-Homosexuality Act threatens its trade benefits with the United States. *Boston College International & Comparative Law Review* 34(1): 147.

Flatters, F. (2007) *Rules of Origin, Commercial Availability and Trade Preferences: Denim and AGOA*. USAID-funded report prepared for the Southern Africa Global Competitiveness Hub, Gaborone, Botswana.

Fukunishi, T. (2013) Political crisis and suspension of duty-free access in Madagascar: Assessment of impacts on the garment industry. *Institute of Developing Economies (JETRO)* 422: 7.

Geda, A. and Kebret, H. (2008) Regional economic integration in Africa: A review of problems and prospects with a case study of COMESA. *Journal of African Economies* 17(3): 357–394.

Hinkle, L.E. and Newfarmer, S.R. (2005) Risks and rewards of regional trading arrangements in Africa: Economic partnership agreements (EPAs) between the EU and SSA. *World Economy*, 1–40.

Jones, V.C. and Williams, B.R. (2012) US trade and investment relations with sub-Saharan Africa and the African Growth and Opportunity Act. *Congressional Research Service Report* RL31772(7–5700): 1–44.

Karingi, S.N., Kimenyi, M.S., Paulos, M. and Páez, L. (2010) AGOA at 10: Consolidating gains from Africa-U.S. trade: Post-AGOA options beyond 2015. *African Growth Initiative at Brookings*, 1–22.

Kieck, E. (2010) Co-ordinated border management: Unlocking trade opportunities through one stop border posts. *World Customs Journal* 4(1): 3–13.

Kira, A.R. (2013) Determinants of financing constraints in East African countries' SMEs. *International Journal of Business and Management* 8(8): 63–64.

Klein, M.W. and Olivei, G.P. (2008) Capital account liberalization, financial depth, and economic growth. *Journal of International Money and Finance* 27(6): 861–875.

Lall, S. and Narula, R. (2004) Foreign direct investment and its role in economic development: Do we need a new agenda? *The European Journal of Development Research* 16(3): 447–464.

Lammers, E. (2007) How will the Beijing consensus benefit Africa? *The Broker* 1: 16–18.

Lee, M.C., Melber, H.N. and Taylor, I. (2007) *China in Africa*. Uppsala: Nordiska Afrikainstitutet Publisher.

Lemos, A. and Ribeiro, D. (2007) *Taking Ownership or Just Changing Owners. African Perspectives on China in Africa*. Nairobi: Pambazuka Publisher.

Loewendahl, H. (2001) A framework for FDI promotion. *Transnational Corporations* 10(1): 1–42.

Moyo, N. and Page, J. (2010) AGOA at 10: AGOA and regional integration in Africa: A missed opportunity. *African Growth Initiative at Brookings*, 1–22.
Mushita, T.A. (2001) An African response to AGOA. *The Southern African Economist* 6: 17–19.
Naumann, E. (2010) AGOA at nine: Some reflections on the Act's impact on Africa-US trade. *Inside Southern African Trade.* agoa.info/downloads/research.html (accessed on October 4, 2015).
Ngwenya, S. (2014) The ideal trade and investment partnership between the U.S. and Africa. *The Habari Network*, 1–53.
Ploch, L. and Cook, N. (2012) Madagascar's political crisis. *Congressional Research Service* R40448(7–5700): 1–22.
Sanchez, D. (2014) DHL boss: AGOA creates virtuous circle of success in Africa. *AFK Insider.* afkinsider.com/69199/agoa-good-german-logistics-co-dhl (accessed on February 15, 2016).
Schaefer, B.D., Florance, C.M. and Kim, A.B. (2014) Congress should upgrade the African Growth and Opportunity Act. *The Heritage Foundation* 4255: 1–3.
Shapouri, S. and Trueblood, M. (2003) *The African Growth and Opportunity Act (AGOA): Does it Really Present Opportunities?* In International Agricultural Trade Research Consortium (IATRC) Conference, Capri, Italy.
Stiglitz, J. (2000) Capital market liberalization, economic growth, and instability. *World Development* 28(6): 1075–1086.
Thompson, D.M. and Jack, K.I. (2013) Strengthening the African Growth and Opportunity Act: Delivering on Africa's promise through NEPAD and the African diaspora to reinvigorate the commercial relationship between the United States and sub-Saharan African countries. *New York City Bar Association*, 1–28.
Tull, D.M. (2006) China's engagement in Africa: Scope, significance and consequences. *The Journal of Modern African Studies* 44(3): 459–479.
USITC (2005) Export opportunities and barriers in African Growth and Opportunity Act-eligible countries. US International Trade Commission, 1–588.
Williams, B.R. (2014) *African Growth and Opportunity Act (AGOA): Background and Reauthorization.* Congressional Research Service, May 27, 1–22.
World Bank (2010) An analysis of issues shaping Africa's economic future. *Africa's Pulse*, 9.
Yin, J.Z. and Vaschetto, S. (2011) China's business engagement in Africa. *The Chinese Economy* 44(2): 43–57.
Zappile, T.M. (2011) Non-reciprocal trade agreement and trade: Does the African Growth and Opportunity Act (AGOA) increase trade? *Auburn University: International Studies Perspectives* 12(1): 46–67.

26 Geoeconomic strategies and economic intelligence

Gyula Csurgai

1 Introduction

Classical economic theories on international exchanges and the main contemporary approaches to study economics do not reflect all aspects of international economic relations. For instance, conflicts have considerably increased in spite of the growing interdependence and interconnectedness that characterises the current globalisation process. Economic decisions of states and businesses are often fashioned along the tactics and strategies advocated by Sun Tzu and Machiavelli, and these decisions often depend on 'non-market' factors. Some of these non-market factors that increasingly influence contemporary international economic relations are: information strategies, lobbying and various other strategies of influence, state support to private business by different means, hostile acquisition of companies of strategic importance, hidden protectionist measures and currency manipulation, among others (Rickards, 2012).

Living standards, jobs, and prosperity of states in general depend more and more on external factors as globalisation has diminished the frontiers between domestic and international economies. Consequently, losing in globalised geoeconomic competition means a diminution of economic security for a given state resulting in possible economic decline, combined with growing domestic socioeconomic and political problems (Luttwak, 1998). For instance, the competition between the USA and European aviation industries has direct consequences for the prosperity of the respective states as these industries represent a strategic segment of the economies on the two sides of the Atlantic.

Since the end of the Cold War, economic competition has increased considerably as a result of the augmentation of industrialised powers (or countries that go through an intensive industrialisation process) mastering advanced technologies and production and therefore able to compete in world markets. An example is the rapid development of the *high speed train* industry in China. This process of multiplication of economic actors that export high added-value products combined with the general trend of reducing trade barriers and opening up of markets has increased the conflictive nature of international economic relations in the context of a global power shift. This shift has been manifesting in the gradual transition of the gravity of the world economy from the Euro-Atlantic zone to the Asia-Pacific zone, which is becoming the dominant pole of the world economy in the 21st century. Another factor that augments the potential of economic conflict is the fierce competition to obtain access to, and control of, energy resources (in particular, oil and gas) and strategic raw materials. This is a result of a variety of factors such as the demographic increase of the world population and the increased needs of states in the Global South. These locations are going through fast economic development, as the Chinese and Indian examples illustrate.

French scholar Pascal Lorot, director of the French review *Géoéconomie*, highlights the importance of state support to economic actors to achieve geoeconomic objectives, when he defines geoeconomics:

> as the analysis of economic strategies—notably commercial—decided upon by states in a political setting aiming to protect their own economies or certain well-identified sectors of it, to help their national enterprises acquire technology or to capture certain segments of the world market relative to production or commercialization of a product. The possession or control of such a share confers to the entity—state or national enterprise—an element of power and international influence and helps to reinforce its economic and social potential.
>
> (Lorot, 1999, p. 62)

States can play an important strategic role in developing geoeconomic strategies and implementing a coordinated framework to support their corporations by different means. One of the most important aspects of this public–private collaboration between state agencies and various economic sectors is the strategic management of information. As a matter of fact, information has always represented a power factor in the diplomatic, political, military and economic spheres. The rapid development of information and communications technology in recent decades has led to the production and dissemination of a huge quantity of information. Moreover, it is important for businesses and states to adapt constantly to the external environment. This environment is characterised by fluidity and complexity as a result of exchange rate fluctuations, financial crises, geopolitical risks, energy price fluctuations, hostile information operations, activities of transnational terrorist and organised crime networks, and technological changes, among others. It is increasingly important to master information as primary strategic support of geoeconomic strategies. The capacity to collect, produce, disseminate and analyse information, and control or influence networks of communication, became a primary source of power in contemporary economic rivalries. Information power also includes the capacity of waging *cognitive warfare* operations seeking to influence the thinking and reasoning processes and the mental representations and schemes of different target groups in order to exercise influence (Harbulot & Lucas, 2004). These above-mentioned factors highlight the importance of economic intelligence, which is the strategic management of information, and its strategic use seeking to maintain or increase the economic power position of a given state, its economic sectors and businesses in a globalised and highly competitive environment.

2 Strategic state and its geoeconomic disposition

Although states may be losing some ability to regulate internal and external affairs because of globalisation, they can still strongly impact their own geoeconomic disposition. There is no diminution of the importance of the state but a transformation of its role in order to adapt to a new power reality of the 21st century in which commercial, financial, technological and cultural factors play an increasing role (Gaiser, 2015). The nation-state still has an important role to play in the creation of a successful geoeconomic framework that can enhance public–private partnership (Delbeque, 2008). This refers to the notion of the '*strategic state*'. It does not, however, mean a return to a collectivist economic model that failed in the former communist countries.

The so-called *neoliberal* ideology advocates a high degree of deregulation, rapidly opening up the domestic economy to international exchanges and investments, privatisation of most sectors of the economy, and limitation of the public sector. This scenario minimises the role of the state in the economy. At the same time, this ideology over-emphasises the functionality of the market. The *neoliberal* model has failed in several countries. One could mention the Argentine economic depression taking place between 1998 and 2002, or the devastating consequences of the Russian '*shock therapy*' in the 1990s. Unfortunately, these are not isolated examples. The *strategic state* concept questions the neoliberal approach and argues for an important role for the state in the economy.

Contrary to the rapid liberalisation and deregulation of the economy, the East Asian states opted for a gradual opening of their economies combined with a long-term economic development approach in which the state played a strategic role. This economic development strategy has been influenced by cultural factors (Confucianism). It has been characterised by strong coordination between private and public sectors to support export-oriented growth, development of economic intelligence capacities on both state and business levels in a coordinated strategic framework, stable macroeconomic management, maintaining the national currency exchange rate low vis-à-vis the main currencies, technology transfer, and an emphasis on education, research and innovation, among others. One of the most obvious examples of this approach—also called *state capitalism*—is the successful economic development of South Korea. One of the poorest states on the globe in the 1960s, it became a developed and prosperous state with competitive export-oriented economic sectors by the 1990s.

The strategic state helps to create the conditions for establishing a successful geoeconomic disposition which can create synergy between the private sector and government agencies. This process is influenced by cultural, historical and geopolitical factors, and by a shared perception by various actors of public and private sectors, on the role of geoeconomics to enhance the economic security of the state. In this context, it is important to note the existence of different national approaches to develop and implement geoeconomic strategies (Harbulot, 1992).

The tools used to group together in a national geoeconomic framework of cooperation between the public and private sectors include education and training, research and development, commercial strategy, economic diplomacy, audiovisual strategy and economic intelligence, among others. Grouping together these elements into a national geoeconomic disposition may determine the influence of the state in the international system in the 21st century.

The increasing practise of geoeconomics by states does not mean the end of armed conflicts and the cessation of use of hard power. However, military confrontations and direct control of a given geographic zone by armed forces tend to be perceived by states as not a preferable option to project power. The recent experiences of the USA in Iraq and Afghanistan are relevant examples. Moreover, the declining demographies of a considerable number of industrialised powers and public opinion pressures make them reluctant to engage in armed conflict. Consequently, states use more and more soft power and various types of indirect strategies to achieve their objectives in which economic interests play a very important role. Instead of direct control of a given territory by a military force, states support their corporations to conquer markets. They aim to achieve technological superiority and to develop information strategies. Moreover, states seek influence on the normative and legal structures impacting trade relations and intellectual property rights. They shape negotiations in both multilateral and regional organisations to enhance the conditions of their businesses and compete in different markets. In this latter process, economic diplomacy plays a crucial role (Bayne & Woolcock, 2010).

Soft power strategies rely on the ability to shape the preferences, values, norms and perceptions of others by attraction, seduction and persuasion (Nye, 2004). In geoeconomic rivalries, various strategies of influence can play a primary role. In this context, the control or the capacity to shape different networks becomes an increasingly important instrument to exercise power (Castells, 2011). The capacity to influence nongovernmental organisations' (NGO) activities is important. Various types of information operations can be waged against businesses by using NGOs. A corporation can be attacked on ethical principles. It can withdraw from a given market and lose its stock market value. An NGO, manipulated by a rival business or intelligence agencies of a given state, can be a useful tool in these kinds of destabilisation operations. In such cases, social media tools become powerful weapons of manipulation.

3 Economic intelligence

One of the most important components of a successful geoeconomic strategy is economic intelligence (EI). The term of EI integrates competitive intelligence, business intelligence, market intelligence and all forms of 'strategic watch'. It includes strategic foresight analysis as well. EI can be defined as the research, analysis and dissemination of information, useful to different actors of a given business entity or of a given state to support geoeconomic strategies of these entities. To have an efficient geoeconomic disposition, strategic networks of EI should be established between the state level and business. Different state entities collect, analyse and disseminate useful information and intelligence analysis to different actors in a private-public partnership structure to support businesses in geoeconomic competition.

The other level of EI is the business level. A considerable number of businesses have established their own EI units. These entities can receive support from state structures. For instance, state security agencies can provide advice, training and technical support to protect businesses from hostile information gathering by competitors.

EI is an interdisciplinary approach and applied in the so-called *intelligence cycle*, to provide necessary information and useful analysis to businesses and states to enhance decision-making processes and contribute to the implementation of strategies in a complex and globalised economic competition (Jean & Savona, 2011).

The *intelligence cycle* is constituted of the following processes:

- Defining needs: what kind of information is needed?
- Collecting information: where and how to obtain key information.
- Analysing: processing the collected information, examining its value and putting it into context.
- Producing information: transforming the analysis into finished forms before it is sent to decision makers (daily briefs, periodic estimates, monthly reports, etc.).
- Disseminating: giving the processed information to those who requested or need it in decision-making processes.
- Utilising intelligence: helping the decision makers come up with sound decisions.

The source of information in EI is predominantly open source information. However, different forms of espionage and illicit electronic surveillance carried out by state and private intelligence agencies may occur. For example, the ECHELON network and more recently PRISM, a clandestine surveillance program under which the US National Security Agency (NSA) collects internet communications. The open sources of information may originate from a wide variety of sources such as databases, specialised literature, official documents, personal networks and informal meetings, among others.

Economic intelligence is not limited to the research, analysis and dissemination of information. This intelligence is often applied in offensive and indirect strategies such as disinformation, perception management, lobbying and destabilisation of an adversary company. Business and state entities therefore should develop both defensive and offensive capacities of EI (Harbulot, 2015). Defensive strategies related to information protection are very important as an enterprise can become a potential target of information gathering by competitors to obtain information on a company's financial situation, market penetration strategies, clients, potential clients and innovation, among others.

One of the key aspects of EI is anticipation and permanent crisis management capacities in order to deal efficiently with the complexity of the external environment in which states act and businesses operate in different economic spaces. When striving to make good decisions, geoeconomic strategies have become increasingly complicated due to the influence of rapidly evolving geopolitical, technological, cultural, financial and commercial factors. Consequently, the use of strategic foresight by providing analysis on the possible future evolutions in different time frames of geopolitical, economic, technological, cultural and demographic factors that may potentially impact the environments in which businesses operate, plays an important role in EI.

Economic intelligence is applied mainly on a national level due to the fact that political and military allies can become economic competitors. This nature of 'ally–adversary' relations makes states reluctant to collaborate with other states in EI (Harbulot, 2015). European member states of the North Atlantic Treaty Organization (NATO) are in a military alliance with the USA; however, commercial rivalries are part of European Union (EU)–US relations, as the mutual accusations on subsidies given to Boeing and Airbus in the World Trade Organization (WTO) illustrate. In certain cases, competitive intelligence can be applied on bilateral or regional levels in case of shared geoeconomic interests between states related to strategic segments of an industry. For instance, some European nations can cooperate with each other in successful competitive intelligence strategies for market penetration of the European aviation industry. This has been evident in the successful conquest of exports markets by Airbus, which had important ramifications for the French and German industries. At the same time, German and French businesses in other industrial sectors may compete with each other and receive various types of support from their respective states in forms of economic diplomacy and intelligence analysis, among others.

As emphasised, one of the major objectives of EI is to contribute to strategic decision-making processes to enhance the capacity of the state and businesses to achieve geoeconomic objectives. In this context, the following main tasks of EI can be mentioned:

- Analysis of the geopolitical and geoeconomic environment on different geographic scales: local, regional, continental and global.

- Strategic foresight analysis to anticipate different risk factors, crisis situations and trends related to the geoeconomic interests of the state and businesses.
- Analysis of strategies of different actors that impact or may impact the competitive position of a given enterprise and the economic situation of the state.
- Definition of potentially new markets.
- Permanent observation/vigilance on the evolution of important industrial sectors and technological innovation.
- Permanent observation of the competition.
- Information protection.
- Enhance information circulation in the corporation and in public–private partnership frameworks between state agencies and businesses.
- Identification of different national '*partners*' (potential, active, public and private) that can be useful to achieve geoeconomic objectives, for instance to help the penetration of business into emerging markets.
- Legal intelligence: permanent surveillance of regional (EU, for instance) and global normative frameworks such as legislation, jurisdictions, evolution of norms and standards.
- Develop efficient information/communication strategies (for instance, to respond to hostile information operations).
- Create various strategies of influence.
- Provide processed information to decision makers on both business and state levels in order to assist decision-making processes and implement geoeconomic strategies.

4 Strategic frameworks of economic intelligence: some elements of the Japanese and US approaches

Due to the limited length and scope of this chapter, an exhaustive examination of different national approaches to the coordination of geoeconomic dispositions and EI cannot be carried out. In this section, a few elements of strategic frameworks of EI are briefly presented through examples from Japan and the USA.

In the case of Japan, cultural, historical and geopolitical factors have influenced this nation to develop its geoeconomic power. The relatively small size of Japanese territory, combined with high population density, a lack of natural resources, a consensus-based society in which authority, discipline and collectivism are important values, and the country's defeat in World War II, all influenced post-war Japanese strategic thinking. The objective was to create a strong national geoeconomic disposition including an efficient system of EI. The Ministry of Economy, Trade and Industry (METI) has played an important role in the strategic coordination between the public and private sectors. Training and other activities in fields related to the elaboration of geoeconomic strategy were organised and a network, called *Keiretsu*, between industrial groups was created to develop a culture and practice of competitive intelligence based on the systematic collection, analysis and dissemination of information to actors in the economy (Laïdi, 2010). Competition within the Japanese economy, between different corporations, was encouraged to develop the competitiveness of companies. However, to conquer new markets abroad, national interest has prevailed. Consequently, it has been more important to position one Japanese enterprise in a new market than to compete with Japanese enterprises. The METI played an important role in the successful market penetration of Japanese firms in the USA, in Europe and in Latin America from the 1960s.

In 1992, the Clinton Administration in the USA defined the promotion of American economic interests in the world as one of its top priorities. Some of the instruments of US soft power that have been associated with a geoeconomic perspective include influence in major multilateral organisations (WTO, the World Bank, the International Monetary Fund and the Organisation for Economic Co-operation and Development, among others); a strong lobbying culture; leadership in key technological sectors; English as the dominant international language; influence through worldwide media networks such as CNN; and attraction of universities and research centres that contribute to 'brain drain' (human capital flight), among others. In 1993, the National Economic Council was created, seeking the following objectives: elaboration of a national export strategy, maintaining American leadership in key technologies, and supporting an '*offensive economic diplomacy*'. The related coordination between state agencies and enterprises in strategic sectors takes place through a public–private mechanism: the Advocacy Center carries out the analysis of information obtained from the State Department and from the US Department of Commerce, and the Advocacy Network disseminates this processed information to US corporations to support their geoeconomic strategies (Denécé & Revel, 2005).

The ECHELON electronic surveillance system, managed by the USA in collaboration with other English-speaking Western countries, played an important role in collecting strategic information during the Cold War. After the end of the Cold War, the system was maintained and also used in geoeconomic rivalry. Information collected by ECHELON was analysed by the NSA, and information of geoeconomic relevance was disseminated to public and private actors in economic diplomacy as well as to US corporations. The existence of PRISM illustrates as well that useful information from espionage networks may be given to economic actors to promote the economic interests of the USA. For instance, trade-related information gathered by ECHELON and PRISM from confidential high-level EU meetings benefited various US economic actors.

The use of *legal intelligence* such as the strategic manipulation of extraterritorial jurisdiction in economic conflicts can be mentioned as another element of the US geoeconomic disposition. In 2014, the French Bank BNP

Paribas had to pay US$8.9 billion to resolve accusations that it had violated US sanctions against Sudan, Cuba and Iran. Although France did not follow the US sanction policy against these countries, BNP Paribas decided to pay this huge sum of money in order to keep its access to US markets.

5 Concluding remarks

Defending states' national interests requires a modified perception of their security needs as commercial, technological, financial and cultural factors of power have become increasingly important since the end of the Cold War. Moreover, economic conflicts have been intensified between states and between businesses in spite of the growing interdependence and economic exchanges among states. To face the complex and fluid contemporary geopolitical and economic environment, states have had to increase their geoeconomic capacities. The mastering of EI is a primary factor to develop strategies seeking to enhance the power position of states, the strategic segments of their industries and businesses in a globalised geoeconomic struggle in the 21st century. Strategically thinking about economics, trade and finance, integrating non-market elements and developing foresight analysis are indispensable for business leaders and government elites to promote the interests of states and corporations.

Bibliography

Bayne, N. and Woolcock, S. (2010) *The New Economic Diplomacy, Decision-Making and Negotiation in International Economic Relations*. Burlington, VA: Ashgate.

Castells, M. (2011) *Communication Power*. New York: Oxford University Press.

Delbeque, E. (2008) *Quel patriotism économique?* Paris: PUF.

Denécé, E. and Revel, C. (2005) *L'autre guerre des Etats-Unis*. Paris: Robert Lafont.

Didier, L. and Tiffreau, A. (2001) *Guerre économique et information: les stratégies de subversion*. Paris: Ellipses.

Gaiser, L. (2015) Intelligence Economica: una proposata per l'Italia, in Sicurezza, Terrorismo e Societa. *EDUCAT* 2(2/2015), Milano, 63–63.

Halby, E. (2003) *Intelligenza Economica § Techniche Sovversive: le armi della nuova economia*. Milan: Franco Angelli.

Harbulot, C. (1992) *La Machine de Guerre Economique, Etats-Unis, Japon, Europe*. Paris: Economica.

Harbulot, C. (2007) *La main invisible des puissances*. Paris: Ellipses.

Harbulot, C. (2015) *Manuel d'Intelligence Economique*. Paris: PUF.

Harbulot, C. and Lucas, D. (2004) *La guerre cognitive: L'arme de la connaissance*. Panazole: Lavauzelle.

Jean, C. and Savona, P. (2011) *Intelligence economica. Il ciclo dell'informazione nell'era della globalizzazione*. Soveria Manelli: Casa Editrice Rubbettino.

Klare, M.T. (2002) *Resource Wars. The New Landscape of Global Conflict*. New York: Metropolitan/Owl Books.

Laïdi, A. (2010) *Les Etats en guerre économique*. Paris: Seuil.

Lorot, P. (ed.) (1999) *Introduction à la géoéconomie.* Paris: Economica.
Luttwak, E. (1998) *Turbocapitalism: Winners and Losers in the Global Economy.* London: Weidenfeld & Nicolson.
Nye, J.S. (2004) *Soft Power. The Means to Success in World Politics.* New York: Public Affairs.
Rickards, J. (2012) *Currency Wars.* New York: Penguin.

27 Conclusion

J. Mark Munoz

1 Introduction

Globalization has set the stage for a new economic order and 'flattened the world' (Slaughter, 2002; Friedman, 2005). Amidst all these changes is a heightened drive for trade liberalization and strengthening of ties across nations.

Nation-states are creating new policies to respond to global changes. New institutional frameworks set the stage for greater global integration and led to tariff reductions and heightened market integration (Tilly & Welfens, 2000; Aulakh et al., 2000). Cultural commonalities, social agenda, and diverse strategic approaches cultivated internationalization (Oviatt & McDougall, 1997). Some countries revamped their domestic banking system to pursue economic growth (King & Levine, 1993). Others underwent financial liberalization as a path to economic growth and the improvement of the financial system (Tornell et al., 2003).

Multinational corporations and international organizations have joined the fray. Many have reaped the rewards of global inclusion. In fact, multinational enterprises tend to prefer global alliances (Garcia-Canal & Guillen, 2008).

The heightened integration of markets led to both winners and losers. Stock market development impacts economic growth (Atje & Jovanovic, 1993). There are cases of third-party geoeconomic winners—for instance, European countries after the US–Iran sanctions (Bhatia & Trenin, 2015).

The featured chapters in this book point to the vast implications of geoeconomics and the diversity of geoeconomic strategies implemented around the world. In some cases, protectionism has been emphasized and internal trade trends were preferred over external trade (McCallum, 1995). Other nations take a more drastic approach by pursuing a beggar-thy-neighbor policy (Kronberger, 2002), where its economic challenges are prioritized over those of other countries.

With an intensified geoeconomic environment, a country's choice of action often leads to a reaction from other nations. Baldwin (1993) introduced a 'domino theory' where economic integration leads to a series of government and business reactions, including competitive action from other nations. For instance, heightened domestic competition forces firms to disperse into new locations (Crozet & Soubeyran, 2004). Reduction in import barriers encourages firm investment as a response to foreign competition (Neary, 2002). These collective enterprise actions have a deep impact on the economic performance of nations both locally and internationally.

Global changes have defined both the political and economic paradigm of countries. Nations have to think broadly in the context of global investors and a multitude of stakeholders. Some countries have found solace in the quest for democracy (Mobarak, 2005). Others have learned from unstable political environments, and planned a new path to progress (Cuervo-Cazurra & Genc, 2008).

2 The challenging geoeconomic path

As highlighted in several chapters in this book, the contemporary geoeconomic terrain is fraught with challenges. Regional integration especially in developing nations can be volatile and unstable (Krapohl et al., 2014).

Closely knit economic networks also mean one country's troubles can contaminate others. Countries may experience a contagion, or significant correlation with other nations in times of financial crisis (Forbes & Rigobon, 2002). Crisis can spread through trade and financial linkages, as well as operational weaknesses and policies (Berkmen et al., 2012). A centrally situated country in a trade network would likely experience detrimental effects during a financial crisis (Kali & Reyes, 2005).

Geoeconomic alignment can have uneven benefits across countries. There are limitations in intra-regional gains (Burges, 2005). In Central Asia, current economic agreement did not promote economic growth among its member countries (Qoraboyev, 2010). Regional integration among industrialized nations tends to be more successful than among developing countries (Mattli, 1999). Trade liberalization can weaken agglomeration (Crozet & Soubeyran, 2004).

The geoeconomic policies of a country can cause adverse reactions from other countries. Krugman and Elizondo (1996) argued that economic integration leads to the dispersal of industries to lower-cost locations.

3 Geoeconomic strategies

While countless challenges exist in geoeconomic alignment, there are numerous benefits. For instance, economic integration can boost trade, enhance knowledge and technology flows, boost investment, heighten operational standards, and lead to political harmony. Economic integration has the potential to result in a convergence of income per capita among participating nations (Martin, 1998).

In order to achieve geoeconomic success, nations, international organizations, and corporations need to get their strategy right. Internationalization is integral to strategy (Spreitzer et al., 1997).

Organizations internationalize for diverse reasons. Some organizations look to foreign shores to build their image and credibility (Meyer & Rowan, 1977). In some cases, trade restrictions in the home country can encourage international expansion (Lall, 1983). The extent to which local conditions are favorable, such as law and order, infrastructure, tax, exchange rates and similar factors, encourages firm internationalization and investment (Kuemmerle, 2002). Foreign markets offer cost advantages, profit opportunities, and a path towards a competitive advantage (Knight & Cavusgil, 1996; Hardy, 1986; Porter, 1990).

Some organizations are risk averse and are not keen on internationalization. Firm perceptions and past activities could prohibit internationalization (Manlova et al., 2002). Moreover, lack of experienced managers hinders internationalization (Reuber & Fischer, 1997).

Gathering appropriate and timely information and embracing global perspectives can help mitigate geoeconomic risk. Economic intelligence, or the research, analysis and distribution of economic information, is an important element in any geoeconomic strategy (Csurgai, 1998). Organizations need to breed global thinking to succeed (Lee & Park, 2006).

In planning for effective geoeconomic strategies, it is helpful to draw upon internationalization research and theories in order to find anchors for success:

- *Strategic planning*: much is unknown when forming geoeconomic relationships; planning ahead makes a difference. Unplanned ventures into foreign locations lead to failure (Monti & Yip, 2000). An organization that is new and simultaneously entering a foreign market needs to create a dual solution, image, and build credibility in both domestic and foreign locations (Pakes & Ericson, 1998).
- *Market environment research*: gathering the right kind of information at the right time is imperative. Internationalization can result in misunderstanding of consumer preferences, government laws and policies, competitive activity and country infrastructure, which can lead to problems (Mitchell et al., 1992). Language may factor into how information is gathered, processed and exchanged (Marschan-Piekkari et al., 1999). Laws may not be clear cut, and institutional factors, bureaucracy and operational approaches need to be carefully examined (Khanna & Palepu, 1997; Wrigley & Currah, 2003; Datta et al., 1991). It is important to know where advantages lie. The theory of eclectic paradigm indicates that specific advantages accrued to an organization encourage internationalization as other markets appear more attractive from a business development perspective (Dunning, 1993). Organizations need information collection efficiencies as well as global strategic coordination to succeed (Sanders & Carpenter, 1998).
- *Knowledge utilization*: knowledge and learning factor into internationalization (Johanson & Vahlne, 1977). Gathered knowledge shapes internationalization and helps create a competitive edge (Denis &

Depelteau, 1985; Grant, 1996). Internationalizing organizations tend to demonstrate absorptive capacity, where they gain knowledge and share it in conjunction with other endeavors (Cohen & Levinthal, 1990). Subsequently, international learning leads to high performance (Goshal, 1987).

- *Value creation*: organizations need to have a unique advantage to leverage internationally with success (Chang, 1995). Operating in multiple countries, organizations can leverage competencies over a broader span (Kim et al., 1993). Organizations gain a competitive edge when they: (i) tap into niches in foreign markets, (ii) leverage resources to take advantage of scope and scale, and (iii) frame their products on a global scale (Hamel & Prahalad, 1985). Successful international expansion entails four steps: (i) expand where the organization can optimize known knowledge, (ii) transfer competitive advantage strategically whether through greenfield investment or acquisition, (iii) prepare to customize approaches to suit markets, and (iv) assimilate quickly then move to other opportunities (Vermeulen, 2001). According to Porter (1990), the competitive advantage of countries is anchored in key factors such as: factor conditions (infrastructure, skills, capital); demand (market size); related and supporting industries; and organization strategy, structure, and competition.
- *Social posture*: market awareness is driven by social ties (Ellis, 2000). Relationships and networks facilitate internationalization and partner selection (Woolcock & Narayan, 2000; Wong & Ellis, 2002). An organization's social capital can provide a unique competitive advantage (Hitt et al., 2002). With international alliances, the level of internationalization increases and can enhance technological vigor (Kogut & Singh, 1988; Bonaglia et al., 2007). Organizations need to continuously engage in social interaction (Chetty & Agndal, 2007).
- *Financial considerations*: there are costs associated with internationalization (Zaheer & Mosakowski, 1997). International expansion increases costs such as business transactions, information processes, and communication-related expenses (Hitt et al., 1994). Organizations will have to manage set-up costs, monitor, and modify to thrive in foreign markets (Hitt et al., 1994). A common reason for internationalization is to capture entrepreneurial gain (Vermeulen & Barkema, 2001). In fact, internationalization heightens chances of survival (Hitt et al., 1994). Porter (1985) pointed out that five factors enhance firm profitability in a new environment: rivalry, potential of entrants, possibility of product substitution, ability of suppliers to bargain, and ability of buyers to bargain.
- *Management competencies*: management capabilities need to be considered in the organization. Matthews (2006) observed that innovative organizational forms have been used in internationalization. Lack of experienced managers hinders internationalization (Reuber & Fischer, 1997). Firms need to cultivate global thinking in their organizations (Lee & Park, 2006). Oftentimes, an advantage lies in creative utilization of

resources and strategies across product and business dimensions (Prahalad & Hamel, 1990).

- *Risk management and control*: there are risks associated with internationalization (Johanson & Vahlne, 1977; Lee & Kwok, 1988). Organizations need to stay in control of the internationalization process (Vermeulen, 2001).
- *Change and flexibility*: internationalization is driven by external change propagators (Bilkey, 1978). Internationalizing organizations need to deal with the uncertainty often associated with foreign expansion (Hambrick & Mason, 1984). Expansion decisions are sometimes driven by psychological distance, the extent to which a target country is different from the home country in terms of culture, politics, education and other factors (Johanson & Vahlne, 1977). Organizations need flexibility in the course of internationalization and may have to diversify what they offer (Harrigan, 2001; Zhao & Luo, 2002). Organizations need flexibility in the course of internationalization (Harrigan, 2001).
- *Long-term perspective*: in the course of internationalization, organizations go through a leverage and building process at different levels (Tallman & Fladmoe-Lindquist, 2002). Organizations internationalize in small steps over time; at times perceptions and past activities could prohibit internationalization (Johanson & Wiedersheim-Paul, 1975; Manlova et al., 2002).
- *Timing of implementation*: the timeline in which an internationalization effort is executed factors into its failure or success. Timing of action has to be considered in response to social, economic, and technological changes taking place (Antoncic & Hisrich, 2000).

Academic literature suggests that organizations shape their international success by understanding their operating environment well, finding value-added mechanisms, building relationships, preparing for and executing changes at the right time, and thinking through long-term gains and sustainability.

A holistic perspective can be beneficial. For instance, the geoeconomic posture of a country should converge the needs of business and government and include initiatives such as education and training, research and development, strategy development, diplomacy and economic intelligence (Csurgai, 1998).

Resource utilization and stakeholder relationships are key. In financial management, one needs to allocate resources where it is most productive (Fisman & Love, 2004). Investor protection is important in financial development (La Porta et al., 1997). High social capital cultivates trust and cooperation, leading to growth (Putnam, 1993).

Understanding and working through operational diversity and infrastructure differences of agglomerating countries is key. International distance is impacted by factors such as technological homogenization, and coordination costs, as well as cross-cultural and political frameworks that impact economic decisions (Capanelli et al., 2010). Knowledge can be gained from foreign or non-local sources (Gertler & Levitte, 2005).

Ultimately, the selected geoeconomic standpoint and resulting policies shape the nation's course. Studies suggest that export composition can alleviate the adverse effect of a financial crisis (Berkmen et al., 2012), and financial openness has a positive impact on financial development (Bekaert et al., 2005).

A well-conceived geoeconomic plan of action is important. Munoz and Liberatore (2013) recommend a four-point strategy to succeed in a geopolitically challenging world: geopolitical awareness, organizational preparedness, proactive thinking, and organizational indigenization.

Leonard (2015) recommends a new approach for countries, including: (i) developing well-defined strategies for economic battles, (ii) selecting the appropriate economic path, (iii) thinking carefully through issues on positioning and alignment, (iv) engaging in new rules of the game, and (v) developing a regional and subglobal political mindset.

4 Geoeconomics steps forward

In a contemporary geoeconomic world, there are winners and there are losers. Not all nations and organizations are happy with globalization. Bhatia and Trenin (2015) cited the risk of 'de-globalization.'

The nature of geoeconomics continues to evolve, bringing forth new roles and responsibilities for all participants. Regional powers need to take a leadership role in cross-country fellowship (Schirm, 2010). Pedersen (2002) recommends the pursuit of cooperative hegemony where regional powers share a strategy of offering support to other countries. Nations and organizations need to put in an effort to achieve their optimal geoeconomic potential, maintain policy independence, and manage potential incompatibilities with set geoeconomic goals (Szabo, 2015; Beeson, 2015).

Ultimately, a nation's or organization's geoeconomic posture defines its future path. Primary motives and goals have to be carefully considered. Integration works better when it is market based rather than agreement based (Aminian et al., 2008). For many countries, geoeconomic success will continue to prove elusive due to intense competition, poor strategic planning, infrastructure deficiencies, stagnating policies, self-serving agenda, limiting political architecture and influences, and market and economic weakness. Furthermore, a lack of economic and governance data, such as in regions in Africa, poses challenges in assessing integration and geoeconomic success (Ott & Patino, 2009).

A broad-based, holistic and objective perspective can be helpful for nations and organizations. This perspective has to be integrated into planning efforts. Organizations lack the tools for geoeconomic risk assessment and do not integrate them into their plans (Blanke & Kaspersen, 2015). There are accrued advantages in considering political, economic, geographical, legal, technological, as well as business and competitive factors when attempting to navigate through geopolitical forces (Munoz & Pettus, 2013). Considering these factors would be helpful in geoeconomic assessment and preparedness. As nations aim to strengthen their geoeconomic posture, adaptation is necessary along with due consideration of development opportunities, stability, risk management, and the optimization of trade and investment (Lesser, 2013).

In the practice of organizational internationalization, operational efficiency sets a path towards progress. Governments can promote internationalization efforts by implementing measures such as: (i) simplification of administrative procedures; (ii) providing adequate information access; (iii) facilitating financial resource acquisition; (iv) instituting internationalization support

Table 27.1 Munoz model: geoeconomic strategic plan

Strategic plan consideration	*Key questions*
Mission and goals objectives	What are the primary missions and goals? Which ones are the priority? How will this shape the nation's or organization's future?
Environmental and market analysis	What are the current opportunities and threats in the operating environment? What information do you currently know? What do you need to know? How and when will you get the needed information? What are the associated costs?
Trade and economic implications	How would the geoeconomic alignment impact trade? In what way will it affect the economy?
Impact on key relationships and alliances	How will your geoeconomic action affect relationships politically and economically? What will competitive reactions be?
Risk and compliance assessment	What risks do you face? What compliance issues need to be considered?
Infrastructure preparedness	Does the country or organization have the existing infrastructure to execute the geoeconomic plans? If not, what needs to be done and when?
Management and organizational competencies	Are management competencies in line with geoeconomic goals? Which management areas are strong? Which areas are weak? Would new people have to be hired? By when? What would it cost? What would its impact be?
Financial and investment considerations	What are the key financial considerations of the selected geoeconomic plans? Can projected expenses be sustained over the long term? Has a cost-benefit analysis been carried out? Are there provisions for unexpected or hidden costs?
Implementation approach	What are the best strategies for implementation? Were inputs from key people sought? Have resource needs been carefully considered? Are timelines clear?
Assessment and review	How will review and assessment be conducted? By whom and when?

programs, especially in the financial realm; (v) encouraging cross-institutional collaboration; and (vi) providing technology, research support and training assistance, among others (Svetlicic et al., 2007).

Developing a geoeconomic strategic plan would offer profound advantages to governments, international organizations and corporations. This plan should cover the following: mission and goal objectives, environmental and market analysis, trade and economic implications, impact on key relationships and alliances, risk and compliance assessment, infrastructure preparedness, management and organizational competencies, financial and investment considerations, implementation approach, assessment and review.

The geoeconomic strategic plan highlights important ingredients for geoeconomic success. It would answer a set of key questions (see Table 27.1).

In creating a geoeconomic strategic plan, a more definite set of strategies will emerge and help shape and refine the geoeconomic agenda. Planning for internationalization heightens the chances of survival (Hitt et al., 1994).

Geoeconomics will continue to define the nature of relationships and economic foundations of nations and companies for years to come. Amidst conflicts and triumphs, the victor's economic arsenal would likely contain a well-developed strategic plan and a carefully conceived plan of action.

References

Aminian, N., Fung, K.C. and Ng, F. (2008) *Integration of Markets vs. Integration by Agreements*. Policy Research Working Paper no. 4546. World Bank, Washington, DC.

Antoncic, B. and Hisrich, R.D. (2000) An integrative conceptual model. *Journal of Euromarketing* 9: 17–35.

Atje, R. and Jovanovic, B. (1993) Stock markets and development. *European Economic Review* 37: 632–640.

Aulakh, S.P., Kotabe, M. and Teegen, H. (2000) Export strategies and performance of firms from emerging economies: Evidence from Brazil, Chile, and Mexico. *Academy of Management Journal* 433: 342–336.

Baldwin, R. (1993) *A Domino Theory of Regionalism*. Working Paper no. 4465. National Bureau of Economic Research, Cambridge, MA.

Beeson, M. (2015) Geopolitics versus geoeconomics: The new international order. *The Conversation*. Accessed July 28, 2015. Available at: theconversation.com/geopolitics-versus-geoeconomics-the-new-international-order-38824.

Bekaert, G., Harvey, C.R. and Lundblad, C. (2005) Does financial liberalization spur growth? *Journal of Financial Economics* 77: 3–55.

Berkmen, P.S., Gelos, G., Rennhack, R. and Walsh, J.P. (2012) The global financial crisis: Explaining cross-country differences in the output impact. *Journal of International Money and Finance* 31(1): 42–59.

Bhatia, K. and Trenin, D. (2015) Challenge one: Economic warfare. World Economic Forum Report. Accessed July 15, 2015. Available at: www3.weforum.org/docs/WEF_Geo-economics_7_Challenges_Globalization_2015_report.pdf.

Bilkey, W.J. (1978) An attempted integration of the literature on the export behavior of firms. *Journal of International Business Studies* 9(1): 33–46.

Blanke, J. and Kaspersen, A. (2015) Business, like government must master geo-economics. Brink News. Accessed July 28, 2015. Available at: www.brinknews.com/business-like-government-must-master-geo-economics/.

Bonaglia, F., Goldstein, A. and Mathews, J.A. (2007) Accelerated internationalization by emerging markets multinationals: The case of the white goods sector. *Journal of World Business* 42: 369–383.

Burges, S.W. (2005) Bounded by the reality of trade: Practical limits to a South American region. *Cambridge Review of International Affairs* 18: 437–454.

Capanelli, G., Lee, J.-W. and Petri, P.A. (2010) Economic interdependence in Asia: Developing indicators for regional integration and cooperation. *The Singapore Economic Review* 55(1): 125–161.

Chang, S.J. (1995) International expansion strategy of Japanese firms: Capability building through sequential entry. *Academy of Management Journal* 38: 383–407.

Chetty, S. and Agndal, H. (2007) Social capital and its influence on changes in internationalization mode among small and medium sized enterprises. *Journal of International Marketing* 15(1): 1–29.

Cohen, W.M. and Levinthal, D.A. (1990) Absorptive capacity: A new perspective on learning and innovation. *Administrative Science Quarterly* 35: 128–152.

Crozet, M. and Soubeyran, P.K. (2004) EU enlargement and the internal geography of countries. *Journal of Comparative Economics* 32(2): 265–279.

Csurgai, G. (1998) *Geopolitics, Geoeconomics and Economic Intelligence*. The Canadian Institute of Strategic Studies. Accessed July 20, 2015. Available at: opencanada.org/wp-content/uploads/2011/05/SD-69-Csurgai.pdf.

Cuervo-Cazurra, A. and Genc, M. (2008) Transforming disadvantages into advantages: Developing country MNE's in the least developed countries. *Journal of International Business Studies* 39: 957–979.

Datta, D.K., Rajagopalan, N. and Rasheed, M.A. (1991) Diversification and performance: Critical review and future directions. *Journal of Management Studies* 28: 529–548.

Denis, J.E. and Depelteau, D. (1985) Market knowledge, diversification, and export expansion. *Journal of International Business Studies* 16(3): 77–89.

Dunning, J.H. (1993) *Multinational Enterprises and the Global Economy*. Workingham: Addison-Wesley.

Ellis, P. (2000) Social ties and foreign market entry. *Journal of International Business Studies* 31(3): 443–470.

Fisman, R. and Love, I. (2004) Financial development and intersector allocation: A new approach. *Journal of Finance* 59: 2785–2807.

Forbes, K. and Rigobon, R. (2002) No contagion, only interdependence: Measuring stock market comovements. *Journal of Finance* 57(5): 2223–2261.

Friedman, T.L. (2005) *The World is Flat*. New York: Farrar, Straus & Giroux.

Garcia-Canal, E. and Guillen, M.F. (2008) Risk and strategy of foreign location choice in regulated industries. *Strategic Management Journal* 29: 1097–1115.

Gertler, M. and Levitte, Y.M. (2005) Local nodes in global networks: The geography of knowledge flows in biotechnology innovation. *Industry & Innovation* 12(4): 487–507.

Goshal, S. (1987) Global strategy: An organizing framework. *Strategic Management Journal* 8: 425–440.

Grant, R.M. (1996) Prospering in dynamically-competitive environments: Organizational capability as knowledge integration. *Organization Science* 7: 375–387.

Hambrick, D.C. and Mason, P.A. (1984) Upper echelons: The organization as a reflection of its top managers. *Academy of Management Review* 9: 193–206.

Hamel, G. and Prahalad, C.K. (1985) Do you really have a global strategy? *Harvard Business Review* (July–August), 139–148.

Hardy, K. (1986) Key success factors for small/medium sized Canadian manufacturers doing business in the United States. *Business Quarterly* (March), 67–73.

Harrigan, K.R. (2001) Strategic flexibility in the old and new economies. In M.A. Hitt, R.E. Freeman and J.S. Harrison (eds), *Handbook of Strategic Management* (pp. 97–123). Oxford: Blackwell.

Hitt, M., Hoskisson, R.E. and Ireland, R.D. (1994) A mid-range theory of the interactive effects of international and product diversification on innovation and performance. *Journal of Management* 20: 297–326.

Hitt, M.A., Lee, H. and Yucel, E. (2002) The importance of social capital to the management of multinational enterprises: Relational networks among Asian and Western firms. *Asia Pacific Journal of Management* 19: 353–372.

Johanson, J. and Vahlne, J.E. (1977) The internationalization process of the firm. *Journal of International Business Studies* 8: 23–32.

Johanson, J. and Vahlne, J.E. (1990) The mechanism of internationalization. *International Marketing Review* 7(4): 11–24.

Johanson, J. and Weidershiem-Paul, F. (1975) The internationalization of the firm: Four Swedish cases. *Journal of Management Studies* 12: 305–322.

Kali, R. and Reyes, J.A. (2005) *Financial Contagion on the International Trade Network*. Working Paper, Department of Economics. Fayetteville: University of Arkansas, Sam M. Walton College of Business.

Khanna, T. and Palepu, K. (1997) Why focused strategies may be wrong for emerging markets. *Harvard Business Review* (July–August), 41–51.

Kim, W.C., Hwang, P. and Burgers, W.P. (1993) Multinationals' diversification and the risk-return trade-off. *Strategic Management Journal* 14: 275–286.

King, R. and Levine, R. (1993) Finance and growth: Schumpeter might be right. *Quarterly Journal of Economics* 108: 717–738.

Knight, G. and Cavusgil, T. (1996) The born global firm: A challenge to traditional internationalization theory. *Advances in International Marketing* 8: 11–26.

Kogut, B. and Singh, H. (1988) The effect of national culture on the choice of entry mode. *Journal of International Business Studies* 19(3): 411–432.

Krapohl, S., Meissner, K.L. and Muntschick, J. (2014) Regional powers as leaders or Rambos? The ambivalent behavior of Brazil and South Africa in regional economic integration. *Journal of Common Market Studies* 52(4): 879–895.

Kronberger, R. (2002) A cost-benefit analysis of a monetary union for Mercosur with particular emphasis on the optimum currency area theory. *Integration and Trade* 6: 29–93.

Krugman, P. and Elizondo, R.L. (1996) Trade policy and the Third World metropolis. *Journal of Development Economics* 49: 137–150.

Kuemmerle, W. (2002) Home base and knowledge management in international ventures. *Journal of Business Venturing* 17(2): 99–122.

Lall, S. (1983) *The New Multinationals*. New York: Wiley.

La Porta, R., Lopez-de-Silanes, F., Shleifer, A. and Vishny, R.W. (1997) Legal determinants of external finance. *Journal of Finance* 52: 1131–1150.

Lee, H. and Park, J. (2006) Top team diversity, internationalization and mediating effect of international alliances. *British Journal of Management* 17(3): 195–213.

Lee, K. and Kwok, C.C.Y. (1988) Multinational corporations vs domestic corporations: International environmental factors and determinants of capital structure. *Journal of International Business Studies* 19: 195–217.
Leonard, M. (2015) Conclusion: Five lessons for the world of geo-economics. Accessed July 15, 2015. Available at: www3.weforum.org/docs/WEF_Geo-economics_7_Challenges_Globalization_2015_report.pdf.
Lesser, I. (2013) *Morocco's New Geo-economics: Implications for US-Moroccan Partnership.* The German Marshall Fund of the United States. Accessed on July 28, 2015. Available at: www.gmfus.org/publications/morocco's-new-geo-economics-implications-us-moroccan-partnership.
Manlova, T.S., Brush, C.G., Edelman, E. and Greene, P.G. (2002) Internationalization of small firms: Personal factors revisited. *International Small Business Journal* 20(1): 9–31.
Marschan-Piekkari, R., Welch, D. and Welch, L. (1999) In the shadow: The impact of language on structure, power and communication in the multinational. *International Business Review* 8(4): 421–440.
Martin, P.H. (1998) Can regional policies affect growth and geography in Europe? *World Economy* 21(6): 757–774.
Matthews, J.A. (2006) Dragon multinationals. *Asia Pacific Journal of Management* 23: 5–27.
Mattli, W. (1999) *The Logic of Regional Integration.* Cambridge: Cambridge University Press.
McCallum, J. (1995) National borders matter: Canada-U.S. regional trade patterns. *American Economic Review* 85: 615–623.
Meyer, J.W. and Rowan, B. (1977) Institutionalized organizations: Formal structure as myth and ceremony. *American Journal of Sociology* 83: 340–363.
Mitchell, A., Shaver, M. and Yeung, B. (1992) Getting there in a global industry: Impacts on performance of changing international presence. *Strategic Management Journal* 13: 410–432.
Mobarak, A.M. (2005) Democracy, volatility, and economic development. *The Review of Economics and Statistics* 87: 348–361.
Monti, J.A. and Yip, G.S. (2000) Taking the high road when going international. *Business Horizons* (July–August), 65–72.
Munoz, J.M. and Liberatore, A. (2013) Executive perspectives on geopolitics: Management implications for international corporations. In *Handbook on the Geopolitics of Business*, J.M. Munoz (ed.) Cheltenham: Edward Elgar Publishing.
Munoz, J.M. and Pettus, M. (2013) Geopolitical forces and strategic approaches for the contemporary corporation. In *Handbook on the Geopolitics of Business*, J.M. Munoz (ed.) Cheltenham: Edward Elgar Publishing.
Neary, J.P. (2002) Foreign competition and wage inequality. *Review of International Economics* 10: 680–693.
Ott, A.F. and Patino, O. (2009) Is economic integration the solution to African development? *International Advances in Economic Research* 15: 278–295.
Oviatt, B.M. and McDougall, P.P. (1997) Challenges for internationalization theory: The case of international new ventures. *Management International Review* 37(2): 85–99.
Pakes, A. and Ericson, R. (1998) Empirical implications of alternative models of firm dynamics. *Journal of Economic Theory* 79: 1–45.

Pedersen, T. (2002) Cooperative hegemony: Power, ideas and institutions in regional integration. *Review of International Studies* 28: 677–696.
Porter, M.E. (1985) *Competitive Advantage: Creating and Sustaining Superior Performance.* New York: Free Press.
Porter, M.E. (1990) *The Competitive Advantage of Nations.* New York: Free Press.
Prahalad, C.K. and Hamel, G. (1990) The core competence of the corporation. *Harvard Business Review* 68(3): 79–91.
Putnam, R.D. (1993) *Making Democracy Work: Civic Traditions in Modern Italy.* Princeton, NJ: Princeton University Press.
Reuber, A.R. and Fischer, E. (1997) The influence of management team's international experience on the international behaviors of SMEs. *Journal of International Business Studies* 28: 807–825.
Qoraboyev, I. (2010) From Central Asian regional integration to Eurasian integration space? The changing dynamics of post-Soviet regionalism. In *EDB Eurasian Integration Yearbook 2010*, Evgeny Vinokurov (Ed.) (pp. 206–232). Almaty, Kazakhstan: Eurasian Development Bank.
Sanders, W. and Carpenter, M.A. (1998) Internationalization and firm governance: The roles of CEO compensation, top team composition, and board structure. *Academy of Management Journal* 41: 158–178.
Schirm, S.A. (2010) Leaders in need of followers: Emerging powers in global governance. *European Journal of International Relations* 16: 197–221.
Slaughter, A. (2002) Breaking out: The proliferation of actors in the international system. In Y. Dezaly and B.G. Garth (eds), *Global Prescriptions: The Production, Exportation, and Importation of a New Legal Orthodoxy* (pp. 12–26). Ann Arbor: University of Michigan Press.
Spreitzer, G.M., McCall, M.W. and Mahoney, J.D. (1997) Early identification of international executive potential. *Journal of Applied Psychology* 82: 6–29.
Svetlicic, M., Jacklic, A. and Burger, A. (2007) Internationalization of small and medium enterprises from selected Central European economies. *Eastern European Economics* 45(4): 36–65.
Szabo, S.F. (2015) Germany = geoeconomics, US = geopolitics? *The Globalist.* Accessed July 28, 2015. Available at: www.theglobalist.com/germany-united-states-difference-geoeconomics-geopolitics/.
Tallman, S. and Fladmoe-Lindquist, K. (2002) Internationalization, globalization, and capability-based strategy. *California Management Review* 45(1): 116–135.
Tilly, R. and Welfens, P.P.J. (2000) *Economic Globalization, International Organizations, and Crisis Management.* New York: Springer.
Tornell, A., Westermann, F. and Martínez, L. (2003) Liberalization, growth, and financial crises: Lessons from Mexico and the developing world. *Brookings Papers on Economic Activity* 34(2): 1–113.
Vermeulen, F. (2001) Controlling international expansion. *Business Strategy Review* 12 (3): 29–36.
Vermeulen, F. and Barkema, H. (2001) Learning through acquisitions. *Academy of Management Journal* 44: 457–476.
Wong, P.L. and Ellis, P. (2002) Social ties and partner identification in Sino-Hong Kong international joint ventures. *Journal of International Business Studies* 33(2): 267–289.
Woolcock, M. and Narayan, D. (2000) Social capital: Implications for theory, research, and policy. *The World Bank Observer* 15(2): 225–249.

Wrigley, N. and Currah, A. (2003) The stresses of retail internationalization: Lessons from Royal Ahold's experience in Latin America. *International Review of Retail, Distribution & Consumer Research* 13(3): 221–243.

Zaheer, S. and Mosakowski, E. (1997) The dynamics of the liability of foreignness: A global study of survival in financial services. *Strategic Management Journal* 18(6): 439–465.

Zhao, H. and Luo, Y. (2002) Product diversification, ownership structure, and subsidiary performance in China's dynamic market. *Management International Review* 42(1): 27–49.

Index

Note: page numbers in italic type refer to Figures; those in bold type refer to Tables.

www.ingramcontent.com/pod-product-compliance
Ingram Content Group UK Ltd.
Pitfield, Milton Keynes, MK11 3LW, UK
UKHW021622240425
457818UK00018B/686